Contexts for Prehistoric Exchange

This is a volume in

Studies in Archaeology

A complete list of titles in this series appears at the end of this volume.

Contexts for Prehistoric Exchange

Edited by

Jonathon E. Ericson

Department of Anthropology
Harvard University
Cambridge, Massachusetts

Timothy K. Earle

Department of Anthropology
University of California, Los Angeles
Los Angeles, California

ACADEMIC PRESS

A Subsidiary of Harcourt Brace Jovanovich, Publishers
New York   London
Paris   San Diego   San Francisco   São Paulo   Sydney   Tokyo   Toronto

ACADEMIC PRESS, INC.
111 Fifth Avenue, New York, New York 10003

United Kingdom Edition published by
ACADEMIC PRESS, INC. (LONDON) LTD.
24/28 Oval Road, London NW1 7DX

ISBN 0–12–241580–9

PRINTED IN THE UNITED STATES OF AMERICA

82 83 84 85   9 8 7 6 5 4 3 2 1

TO OUR CHILDREN
Burke Evan Ericson
Caroline Cartland Earle
Hester Ludlow Earle

Contents

1 Prehistoric Economics and the Archaeology of Exchange
TIMOTHY K. EARLE

Sourcing of Exchanged Material

2 Chemical Characterization in Archaeology
GARMAN HARBOTTLE

Spatial Patterning and the Modeling of Exchange

3 Regional Modeling of Obsidian Procurement in the American Southwest

FRANK J. FINDLOW AND MARISA BOLOGNESE

4 Marketplace Exchange as Indirect Distribution: An Iranian Example

JOHN R. ALDEN

5 Aboriginal Exchange and Territoriality in Owens Valley, California

ROBERT L. BETTINGER

Production for Exchange

6 Production for Obsidian Exchange in California
JONATHON E. ERICSON

7 Reduction Sequences and the Exchange of Obsidian in Neolithic Calabria
ALBERT J. AMMERMAN AND WILLIAM ANDREFSKY, JR.

8 The Social Context of Production and Exchange
MICHAEL W. SPENCE

Consumption and Symbolic Contexts

9 Toward a Contextual Approach to Prehistoric Exchange
IAN HODDER

10 A Contextual Examination of Neolithic Axe Distribution in Britain
IAN HODDER AND PAUL LANE

11 The Relationship of Stylistic Similarity to Patterns of Material Exchange
JEFFERY L. HANTMAN AND STEPHEN PLOG

Additional Approaches to Exchange

12 Storage Facilities and State Finance in the Upper Mantaro Valley, Peru
TIMOTHY K. EARLE AND TERENCE N. D'ALTROY

13 The Inca as a Nonmarket Economy: Supply on Command versus Supply and Demand

DARRELL E. LA LONE

Contributors

Numbers in parentheses indicate the pages on which the authors' contributions begin.

JOHN R. ALDEN (83), 1215 Lutz Avenue, Ann Arbor, Michigan 48103

ALBERT J. AMMERMAN (149), Department of Anthropology, State University of New York, Binghampton, New York 13901

WILLIAM ANDREFSKY, JR. (149), Department of Anthropology, State University of New York, Binghampton, New York 13901

ROBERT L. BETTINGER (103), Department of Anthropology, University of California, Davis, Davis, California 95616

MARISA BOLOGNESE (53), Department of Anthropology, Columbia University, New York, New York 10027

TERENCE N. D'ALTROY (265), Department of Anthropology, Columbia University, New York, New York 10027.

TIMOTHY K. EARLE (1, 265), Department of Anthropology, University of California, Los Angeles, Los Angeles, California 90024

JONATHON E. ERICSON (129), Department of Anthropology, Harvard University, Cambridge, Massachusetts 02138

FRANK J. FINDLOW (53), Taos, New Mexico.

JEFFREY L. HANTMAN (237), Department of Anthropology, Arizona State University, Tempe, Arizona 85281

GARMAN HARBOTTLE (13), Department of Chemistry, Brookhaven National Laboratory, Upton, New York 11973

IAN HODDER (199, 213), Department of Archaeology, University of Cambridge, Downing Street, Cambridge CB2 3DZ, England

DARRELL E. LA LONE (291), Department of Sociology and Anthropology, De Pauw University, Greencastle, Indiana 46135

PAUL LANE (213), Department of Archaeology, University of Cambridge, Downing Street, Cambridge CB2 3DZ, England

STEPHEN PLOG (237), Department of Anthropology, University of Virginia, Charlottesville, Virginia 22903

MICHAEL W. SPENCE (173), Department of Anthropology, University of Western Ontario, London, Ontario N6A 5C2, Canada

Preface

Regional exchange has become one of the most active areas of archaeological research. The study of exchange has stimulated the adoption of new analytical techniques and growth in archaeological science by drawing the attention of many contributing scientists. Since our earlier volume, *Exchange Systems in Prehistory*, studies have advanced from simple chemical characterization and pattern recognition to a new understanding of the context and variables underlying the exchange processes. Archaeologists are beginning to understand the anthropological basis for observed patterns of prehistoric exchange, and this new interest is seen clearly in the present volume.

Contexts for Prehistoric Exchange offers the researcher theoretical and methodological approaches to understand the many parameters of regional exchange. The chapters have been arranged into five sections: sourcing of exchange material, spatial patterning and the modeling of exchange, production for exchange, consumption and symbolic contexts, and additional approaches to exchange.

The volume provides a broad cross-cultural base drawing on geographical regions from both the Old and New World. New World studies have been conducted in California, the American Southwest, Ontario, Central Mexico, and Peru; Old World studies, in Iran, Italy, and England. From the Californian hunters-and-gatherers to the Incan Empire, the volume covers a wide range of social complexity in order to understand the effects of social and political organization on exchange.

Preliminary versions of some of the chapters were presented at a symposium at the forty-fifth annual meeting of the Society for American Archaeology, in Philadelphia, in May 1980. The symposium entitled "Advances in Studying Regional Exchange Systems" was organized and chaired by the editors and examined many of the advances in the field of prehistoric exchange.

The chapters by John R. Alden, Albert J. Ammerman and William Andrefsky, Jr., Jeffrey L. Hantman and Stephen Plog, Garman Harbottle, and Darrell E. La Lone were added to treat additional aspects of prehistoric exchange not covered in the original symposium. The introductory chapter was written by Timothy K. Earle especially for this volume.

The editors would like to thank the participants, contributors, and members of the Society for American Archaeology for their cooperation and support.

1

Prehistoric Economics and the Archaeology of Exchange

Timothy K. Earle

INTRODUCTION

Despite the clarion call of the 1960s and 1970s for a theoretical approach to prehistory, remarkably little has been done to enunciate overarching theories in archaeology. Why? In part, a strong focus on regional specializations directed our concern away from developing general theory and toward understanding local sequences. More generally in anthropology, a decreased emphasis on regional specializations has permitted the delimitation of subfields—like economic anthropology and symbolic anthropology—that explicitly crosscut the regionalistic interests to emphasize shared methodological and theoretical orientations. The time has come in archaeology to develop these subfields, and I hope that this book with its focus on exchange will help to identify the subdiscipline of prehistoric economics.

A suggested subfield of prehistoric economics has broadly shared interests. The central issues revolve around explaining subsistence, production, and exchange, as well as the interaction of these economic components. The theoretical interests—whether formalistic, substantivistic, or Marxian—share a common need to explain economic formations and their articulation with broader sociocultural contexts. In this volume, we examine exchange in prehistoric societies, and we must develop a methodology (*a*) to describe from archaeological data the form and content of exchange; and (*b*) to explain the exchange as it is determined by individual choice and by cultural context.

CONTEXTS FOR PREHISTORIC EXCHANGE

TOWARD AN EXPLANATION OF EXCHANGE

As considered in this volume, *exchange* is the spatial distribution of materials from hand to hand and from social group to social group. Exchange is a transfer with strong individual and social aspects. Individuals are the hands in exchange, and they strive within the constraints of their society, ideology, and environment to survive and to prosper. And the commodities exchanged—whether food products or subsistence technology or wealth objects—are essential for their strivings. The social contexts of exchange are equally critical because they define the social needs beyond biology, and because they profoundly affect the form and possibility of individual exchange relations.

These two aspects to exchange—the individual and the social—are represented by the two camps of formalism and substantivism with which economic anthropologists identify, and these schools of thought are normally seen as theoretically distinct (cf. Le Clair and Schneider 1968; Hodder, Chapter 9). In this brief chapter, I cannot summarize or resolve the long debate between these camps. Rather, I wish to show in a simple way the appropriateness of each approach in a more general analysis of prehistoric economies.

Formalists seek to investigate the outcome of rational decision making with regard to the choices available to a population. The most common application of the formalist theories in prehistoric economics has dealt with choices of food resources and of settlement locations (cf. Jochim 1976; Earle and Chistenson 1980). With specific reference to exchange, formalist theory can be used to explain the evolution of exchange systems. Based on cost considerations, Alden (Chapter 4) shows how indirect (market) distribution minimizes costs when production is locally specialized. As specialization increases, markets will be likely to develop because of the added efficiency. Similarly, Bettinger (Chapter 5) argues that exchange in subsistence goods among local territorial groups may develop because of the cost efficiency inherent in exploiting unpredictably high-yielding resources.

A formalist approach has also been used extensively to understand the organization of prehistoric exchange. As described by Hodder (Chapter 9), the use of falloff models to discriminate among possible exchange systems relies on the assumption of cost minimization within institutional constraints. Essentially, the sociopolitical institutions establish constraints in terms of the distribution and value of items. Then, individuals, acting within these institutional constraints, procure and distribute material in a cost-conscious manner.

In contrast, *substantivists* seek to investigate the way economic behavior, including exchange, is embedded in broader social and political institutions. Despite its present unattractiveness to most ethnographers who are working increasingly with market-oriented populations, substantivism remains appealing to archaeologists because it offers a means to identify prehistoric social organization and ideological systems, and because it offers a systemic framework to explain social and economic change.

First, following the substantivist assumption that the economy is embedded in general sociopolitical institutions, archaeological studies of exchange are a means to investigate prehistoric social organization and cultural formations. In other words, patterning in exchanged materials should reflect broader patterns of cultural contexts (cf. Hodder, Chapter 9). For example, Bettinger (Chapter 5) wants to reconstruct the social organization of hunter–gatherer populations in the Owens Valley in California. He first establishes the distribution pattern of obsidian among the local settlement types, and then he argues on this basis for a self-contained territory of that social group.

Closely aligned to the established substantivist approach is a new interest in symbolism and its function in cultural process. Chapters in this volume indicate two directions in this work. On the one hand is Hodder's (Chapter 9) focus on symbolism that derives in part from the neo-Marxian interest in ideology. On the other hand is Hantman's and Plog's (Chapter 11) focus on information flow as it operates to integrate social units horizontally and vertically. In both approaches, the interest is in exchange as embedded in symbolic systems that are seen as central to the operation of a culture.

Second, derived from the substantivists concern with the interrelationships between society and economy, is the evolutionary interest in exchange and social change. In evolutionary studies, researchers characteristically attempt to identify the social, political, economic, and ecological variables that interrelate to form a system that changes in response either to exogenous factors or to the internal interaction among the variables. Many such processual studies have emphasized the importance of exchange in the evolution of complex societies (cf. Sanders 1956; Adams 1966; Rathje 1971), and this orientation continues in the contributions included in this book. Findlow and Bolognese (Chapter 3) feel that they can identify a close link between the development of more complex societal forms in the American Southwest and of more complex exchange systems. In a study attempting to identify these evolutionary relationships, Spence (Chapter 8) argues that increasing social statification results from the elite's control over exchange and production of highly valued commodities, and he illustrates this argument with changing economic patterns in Mesoamerica and the American Northeast.

No coherent body of theory exists to explain exchange and its linkage to broader sociocultural forms. However, a theoretical approach drawing from the formalist's notion of individual rationality and from the substantivist's notions of social context and systemic interaction seems both appropriate and feasible for an emerging field of prehistoric economics.

TOWARD AN ARCHAEOLOGICAL DESCRIPTION OF EXCHANGE

To describe exchange, the prehistorian has three interrelated jobs: (*a*) to source the commodities of exchange; (*b*) to describe the spatial patterning of the commodities; and (*c*) to reconstruct the organization of the prehistoric exchange. These jobs logically represent steps in research on prehistoric exchange. What I will do is to outline these research steps and indicate how they are performed by illustrating with examples drawn from this book. It is the reconstruction of the organization of exchange in its societal contexts that is of central concern here.

SOURCING OF EXCHANGED MATERIAL

The ability to identify the physical source of a raw material or the production center of an artifact is essential to establish the presence and extent of prehistoric exchange. In "sourcing," a researcher seeks to demonstrate the physical or cultural identity between the material exchanged and the proposed source for that material. The most common procedures include chemical, petrographic, and stylistic analyses.

During the past 20 or so years, chemical analysis has revolutionized archaeological studies of exchange by providing convincing evidence on the probable origins of exchanged materials. Materials analysis, paralleling in many ways the revolution in chronometric dating, has encouraged large-scale, quantitative studies of prehistoric exchange that were previously not feasible. Harbottle (Chapter 2) summarizes the broad range of analytical procedures that may now be applied to an expanding number of sourceable materials. With increasing accuracy and flexibility in the available analytical procedures, the ability to identify a material's source is greatly enhanced.

Although the analytical capability to source archaeological materials is evident, the high costs of analysis are a binding constraint on extensive exchange studies. The researcher is increasingly caught between a desire for increased sourcing accuracy and the need for large data sets of sourced material. Earlier studies often were satisfied to identify the presence of exchange and roughly to assess the falloff in materials away from a source. However, variation in the amount of exchanged goods among a region's settlements and within individual sites is now used to study in detail the organizational properties of exchange. This contextual approach, as advocated by the authors in this volume, requires a much larger number of sourced artifacts, with the result that chemical analysis alone is usually prohibitively expensive. Search for alternative and auxiliary methods for source identification is thus an important concern of several chapters included here.

A standard procedure for sourcing is petrographic analysis, which offers an effective and cost-efficient way to source large samples (see Harbottle, Chapter 2; Hantman and Plog, Chapter 11; Fry 1980). In some cases, the appearance of a material is sufficiently distinctive to permit source identification megascopically; however, such qualitative identification should be cautiously evaluated for accuracy by chemical analysis (Findlow and Bolognese, Chapter 3; Bettinger, Chapter 5).

Stylistic analysis of artifacts is another standard and inexpensive way to source artifacts. The basic assumption is that an artifact can be assigned to its production center based on a similarity in stylistic traits, and it is often also assumed that the production center is identified with the focus of maximum abundance. Alden's contribution (Chapter 4) illustrates a more solid use of a stylistic study of exchange. He first conclusively identifies the production center by manufacturing waste and tools, analyzes the stylistic characteristics of the production center's ceramics, and then studies regionally the distribution of its associated ceramic types. Hantman and Plog (Chapter 11), however, show that—although stylistic similarities between assemblages may be the outcome of exchange—other forms of cultural interaction can cause stylistic similarities. The importance of using an auxiliary sourcing method such as petrographic analysis is well illustrated by their work.

To summarize, technical advances in sourcing have liberated exchange studies in prehistory, and the future seems bright for new technological developments. Costs, however, remain high, especially when considering the large sample sizes now considered necessary for detailed studies of exchange. To balance considerations of cost and accuracy, many studies now incorporate multiple analytical techniques with the more precise and expensive ones used to verify the accuracy of the cheaper methods.

DESCRIPTION OF SPATIAL PATTERNING OF EXCHANGED MATERIALS

After the sources for artifactual materials have been identified, several approaches may be used to describe the spatial patterning in the materials and to suggest the possible exchange mechanisms operating prehistorically. The three most common descriptive approaches are regional point scatters, regression analysis, and trend-surface analysis (Hodder and Orton 1976; Earle and Ericson 1977).

The regional point scatter of artifact distribution is the simplest descriptive approach. These "dots-on-maps" show the locations of archaeological finds with respect to the source of the raw material (see Hodder and Lane, Chapter 10, Figures 10.1–10.6). This approach, although only a qualitative statement of the distribution of exchanged materials, is a good visual representation of the extent and approximate symmetry of an exchange system.

Regression analysis has become a standard technique to describe the spatial distribution of artifactual materials (Renfrew, Dixon, and Cann 1968; Renfrew 1975). In the present volume, regression analysis is used by Findlow and Bolognese (Chapter 3), Alden (Chapter 4), and Bettinger (Chapter 5). The procedures for regression analysis are straightforward. First, from a sample of sites from the study area, the frequency of a source-specific material is calculated to measure the interaction between the site and the source. Frequency can be measured as a percentage (percentage of ceramics from Source A at Site 1) or as a ratio (count or weight of a material from Source A to a standard such as excavated volume or domestic ceramics at Site 1, cf. Hodder and Orton 1976; Sidrys 1977). Second, as a measure of transport cost, the straight-line distance from site to the source is usually measured. Other cost measurements include various distance transformations, considering such factors as intermediate population (Ericson 1977) and topography (Findlow and Bolognese, Chapter 3). Third, on a graph in which frequency is represented on the *y* axis and distance on the *x* axis, all sites are plotted such that spatial variation has been collapsed to show distance as the primary determinant of interaction. Fourth, the relationship between distance (transport cost) and frequency (interaction) is established by the regression line that best predicts the point scatter (see Hodder and Orton 1976). The search for this curve involves an examination of different families of curves and the parameter values within a possible family.

Trend-surface analysis (Hodder and Orton 1976:155–174), or the specific computerized option of SYMAP (Ericson 1977), offers a third, visually dramatic way to represent spatial patterning in exchanged commodities. All sites representing a region are located in space, and the frequency of a source-specific material at the sites is indicated. Then, using one of several averaging procedures, the frequency of the material is calculated on a regional basis to create a contoured surface. The result is a three-dimensional map with two dimensions of the standard spatial coordinates and one dimension of frequency for the exchanged commodity. If distance were the sole determinant of frequency, the map created would consist of a series of concentric rings, since frequency decays regularly with distance. In most cases, however, trend-surface analysis emphasizes asymmetrical patterning that may be related to preferred routes of distribution, boundaries, or competing sources (Ericson 1977). The SYMAP analysis of obsidian distributions in the American Southwest illustrates the usefulness of the technique for showing broad patterning in the distribution systems and how they change through time (Findlow and Bolognese, Chapter 3).

RECONSTRUCTING THE ORGANIZATION OF PREHISTORIC EXCHANGE

Reconstructing the organization of prehistoric exchange is aimed at recognizing the institutional framework of exchange and, more broadly, the function of the exchange in the prehistoric society. An analysis of the spatial patterning of exchanged material is usually the first way used to get a basic understanding of how the exchange took place.

Regression analysis is the most common approach now used to describe and to interpret the spatial patterning (Hodder 1974; Hodder and Orton 1976;

Renfrew 1975, 1977; Ericson 1977). The goal of this work has been to identify different exchange mechanisms based on distinct forms for the regression line representing frequency falloff with distance. Generally, it has been assumed that frequency of a material declines with distance from its source (Renfrew 1977), and that the specific shape and gradient of this falloff is affected by factors of transportation, value, and organization. A general optimism has existed that a typology of falloff curves could be used to identify a typology of exchange mechanisms.

As an example, Findlow and Bolognese (Chapter 3) devise various models of falloff based on different mathematical functions and attempt to identify these with different exchange mechanisms—linear model to identify direct access, power-function model to identify direct access and down-the-line exchange, and so forth. In a similar vein, Alden (Chapter 4) identifies indirect distribution (market exchange) on the basis of falloff from a central site rather than from the known producing site. Such a detailed usage of regression analysis to evaluate patterned falloff within a region seems to be a particularly effective way to identify different exchange mechanisms.

In recent advances in exchange studies, attention is being drawn to the local variation in exchanged materials *within* a region, because it is now felt that the variability obscured by the regression analysis offers key information for recognizing different exchange mechanisms. As mentioned earlier, trend-surface analysis highlights asymmetrical patterns in exchange that can be used to study directionality, competition, social borders, and the like. However, by its averaging procedure, considerable information on site-specific variability is still obscured. Hodder and Orton (1976:115–119) recommend in addition the analysis of residuals to highlight deviation from the regression line. The goal is to identify the factors causing variation as additional evidence on the exchange. In their example, they show that high positive residuals for a Romano–British pottery style are associated with water routes, strongly suggesting a water-based transport system. Similarly, Sidrys (1977) finds higher densities of obsidian at Mayan central places, and he explains this pattern as a result of a centralized distribution system. In this volume, Bettinger (Chapter 5) argues that positive residuals in his linear regression analysis are found mainly within 15 km of the source and negative residuals beyond 15 km. He interprets this as indicating a territorial boundary that impeded direct access to the source.

In general, researchers now recognize that although there is certainly a relationship between different exchange mechanisms and different spatial patterns, at least on a general level different mechanisms can produce very similar falloff patterns (Hodder, Chapter 9). The initial optimism that different mechanisms can be identified by falloff patterns has been dampened (cf. Renfrew 1977), and the question now is how to proceed beyond simple regional patterning to obtain a more thorough understanding of prehistoric exchange.

This book seeks explicitly to move exchange studies toward a more detailed contextual analysis that considers the broader economic, social, political, and ideological forms in which the exchange is embedded. As I will discuss now, possible approaches include investigations of (*a*) production; (*b*) consumption and symbolic contexts; and (*c*) the facilities and historic documents that deal directly with exchange.

PRODUCTION AND THE ANALYSIS OF EXCHANGE

An economy integrates the subsystems of production, exchange, and consumption. On theoretical grounds, exchange is of particular interest, despite the fact that archaeological evidence of the actual transfer from hand to hand is extremely limited. To circumvent this obvious difficulty, attention may be directed toward studying production and consumption as these processes articulate with exchange.

Production is closely tied to exchange, and it can be argued that, although the relationship is a complex one, different forms of production should correspond to different forms of exchange. Many of the basic variables critical to understanding exchange are also basic to understanding differences in production. Some of these variables include the size of population served, the periodicity of exchange, the kinds of goods involved, and the status of persons involved. The relationships between production and exchange are shown clearly in the contributions by Ericson (Chapter 6), Ammerman and Andrefsky (Chapter 7), and Spence (Chapter 8).

One interesting conclusion from these chapters is that the scale of distribution strongly affects the form of production. Ammerman and Andrefsky (Chapter 7) are studying obsidian exchange in a Neolithic, stateless society, and we might expect exchange to be largely in a down-the-line system with approximately equal participation by all communities in a region. However, probably resulting from the high volumes involved, exchange and production were locally controlled and specialized. With the development of marketing systems and wider distributions, specialization became more elaborated and localized near marketplaces. Spence's (Chapter 8) analysis of obsidian specialization at Teotihuacan shows how this type of specialization that is related to market exchange looks archaeologically.

Specialists may also be attached to elites and involved in the manufacture of wealth items (valuables) used primarily by the elites in special social and political exchanges. While the production of primitive valuables in non-stratified societies is typically decentralized, as social statification develops and valuables are used increasingly in political ways (Earle, n.d.), production most likely becomes more narrowly controlled by specialists working for elite patrons. Spence's (Chapter 8) study of Middle Woodland silver production in Ontario suggests that manufacture was restricted to a few locations and was carried on by specialized craftsmen. In this case, the development of social elites, political exchanges of wealth items, and attached specialists appear closely tied.

CONSUMPTION, SYMBOLIC CONTEXTS, AND EXCHANGE

By the nature of archaeology, artifactual material is recovered in contexts indicating how it was used prehistorically. Although this point is obvious, it is still important to make, and then one must ask whether the patterns of use are associated with different patterns of exchange. This issue is addressed by evaluating the distribution of exchanged artifacts within a site and the specific form of the artifacts.

The distribution of exchanged material in different archaeological contexts provides basic information on the use and exchange of the material. Perhaps most important is being able to distinguish between primitive valuables, used primarily in social and ritual contexts, and utilitarian goods, used primarily in subsistence contexts (cf. Hodder, Chapter 9). Generally, it has been assumed that these two classes of commodities are exchanged differentially in "spheres of exchange" (cf. Bohannan 1955). In the past, primitive valuables have been identified by the gradual slopes of their falloff curves (Renfrew 1975:50–51). However, the gradual slope shows only that the good is highly valued (and/or that its transport costs are low), and not that the valuable is restricted primarily to a social or ritual context. Very generally, the archaeologist can differentiate ritual contexts—burials, caches, special architectural features—from domestic contexts—houses, fill, midden—and the restriction of a good to one or another context should indicate the commodity's dominant use.

Despite the obvious importance of this basic contextual data, archaeologists studying exchange rarely analyze in detail the contexts of their finds. Although working with admittedly limited information, Hodder and Lane (Chapter 10) argue for the special meaning of the Neolithic stone axes, because they are found in burials and at the ceremonial "henges." Similarly, in Spence's (Chapter 8) analysis of long-distance exchange, the burial context of the goods and the changing distribution in the burials through time provide excellent evidence that the artifacts were primitive valuables that were linked to the developing social elites.

Closely related to context is the more general problem of meaning of the exchanged goods. As argued persuasively by Hodder (Chapter 9), the symbolic meaning of a commodity is basic to understanding the material item, the exchange that it involves, and its general significance in a society. Both a good's value and how it is exchanged are related to the object's meaning, and this neglected aspect of exchange deserves systematic attention. As an example, Hodder and Lane (Chapter 10) suggest how to evaluate the utilitarian versus prestige value of stone axes and the exchange systems involved, based on the changing length and blade angle of the axes.

An important material correlate of meaning is style, and stylistic analysis within a region can help delimit the spatial and hierarchical organization of the society by evaluating exchange and symbolic relationships. Hantman and Plog (Chapter 11) discuss the theoretical importance of style as a symbolizing device, and they show how stylistic similarity may result from several mechanisms of exchange or of symbolic identification. The main point is that style as a representation of meaning should be considered as an important component in regional interaction generally, and in exchange more narrowly.

THE FACILITIES AND HISTORICAL DOCUMENTS OF EXCHANGE

As mentioned previously, the actual distribution process of exchange is only rarely represented archaeologically. However, two ways to study exchange directly deal (a) with the facilities of exchange; and (b) with documentary evidence of exchange.

In the first instance, physical facilities are often necessary to aid the transfer and the temporary holding of exchange goods. Ideally, it is hoped that different forms of exchange may be associated with distinctive facilities. To illustrate this approach, I will briefly consider the facilities that might be associated with Polanyi's standard exchange forms. For a reciprocal exchange system, goods tend to move through many exchange links that are largely independent and regionally dispersed. Because such exchange is not highly structured as an institution, few distinctive facilities would be associated. Often such exchanges take place at ceremonial occasions when individuals from different communities gather together, and the ceremonial facilities—like the New Guinean dance ground (Brown 1978:47, 50)—are typically, but not unambiguously, associated.

For a market exchange, many individual exchanges are typically synchronized and centralized at a marketplace. Although little consistent archaeological work has been done on markets, they should be associated with specific facilities, including centrally located open spaces with unrestricted access, stall areas with small-scale storage, and small craft workshops (cf. Millon 1964:351). For redistribution, transactions involve the mobilization of local goods to central locations for use in financing administrative and elite activities. As illustrated by Earle and D'Altroy (Chapter 12), the central storage facilities provide vivid evidence of the organizational form of redistribution. Finally, Sabloff and Freidel (1975) attempt to identify the administered trading center of Cozumel based on the warehousing needed in transshipment.

In the second instance, historical documents often record specific exchange transactions. One important type of document is the society's administrative records. Such documents as the clay tablets from Mycenean palaces or from Mesopotamia provide a full record of the central economy of these states. Earle and D'Altroy (Chapter 12), for example, discuss the *khipu* records that enumerate commodity payments during the early historic period of Peru. It is necessary, however, to remember that such administrative documents record only institutionalized exchanges such as state taxation and payment, and they do not describe other exchanges that would be associated with markets (Adams 1974).

Other sorts of documents, such as the descriptions by foreign visitors and traditional histories, may provide important information on the less-formalized exchange systems. In Chapter 13, La Lone evaluates the historical evidence for markets in the Inca empire at time of first Western contact. Drawing from various documentary sources, he deals with the problems of bias and interpretation that are so essential to historical analysis. This chapter helps emphasize how historical documents offer considerable information on the social and political organization in which exchange is embedded as well as provide a useful auxiliary source to archaeology.

CONCLUSIONS

This book seeks to develop a detailed approach to prehistoric exchange. To accomplish this, we require both a coherent theoretical understanding of exchange and a means to study it archaeologically. The previous work on exchange is a firm foundation on which this volume takes its form, but all contributors sense a dissatisfaction with the existing approaches and a need to change the direction in research.

What is understood is a knowledge of the complexity of prehistoric exchange and a commitment to investigating its multifaceted character. To do this, the researcher needs a contextual approach in which exchange is viewed as embedded in broader cultural formations. This substantivist perspective must, however, be seen only as the constraints within which individuals maneuver, for it is this formalist perspective that gives us the process by which exchange evolves to solve key political, social, and economic problems. The most satisfying approach looks at exchange from different perspectives to get a detailed and rounded understanding of its operation.

REFERENCES

Adams, R. McC.
1966   *The evolution of urban society.* Chicago: Aldine.
1974   Anthropological perspectives on ancient trade. *Current Anthropology* 15:239–258.
Bohannan, P.
1955   Some principles of exchange and investment among the Tiv. *American Anthropologist* 57:60–70.
Brown, P.
1978   *Highland peoples of New Guinea.* Cambridge: Cambridge University Press.
Earle, T. K.
n.d.   The ecology and politics of primitive valuables. In *Culture and ecology: eclectic perspectives,* edited by J. Kennedy and R. Edgerton. Washington, D.C.: American Anthropological Association (forthcoming).
Earle, T. K., and A. Christenson
1980   *Modeling change in prehistoric subsistence economies.* New York: Academic Press.

Earle, T. K., and J. E. Ericson
  1977   Exchange systems in archaeological perspective. In *Exchange systems in prehistory,* edited by T. Earle and J. Ericson, pp. 3–12. New York: Academic Press.
Ericson, J.
  1977   Egalitarian exchange systems in California: a preliminary view. In *Exchange systems in prehistory,* edited by T. Earle and J. Ericson, pp. 109–126. New York: Academic Press.
Fry, R. E.
  1980   Models and methods in regional exchange. *SAA Paper* **1.** Washington, D.C.: Society for American Archaeology.
Hodder, I.
  1974   A regression analysis of some trade and marketing patterns. *World Archaeology* 6:172–189.
Hodder, I., and C. Orton
  1976   *Spatial analysis in archaeology.* Cambridge: Cambridge University Press.
Jochim, M.
  1976   *Hunter–gatherer subsistence and settlement.* New York: Academic Press.
Le Clair, E., and H. Schneider
  1968   *Economic anthropology.* New York: Holt, Rinehart & Winston.
Millon, R.
  1964   The Teotihuacan mapping project. *American Antiquity* 29:345–352.
Rathje, W.
  1971   The origin and development of lowland Classic Maya civilization. *American Antiquity* 36:275–285.
Renfrew, C.
  1975   Trade as action at a distance. In *Ancient civilization and trade,* edited by J. Sabloff and C. C. Lamberg-Karlovsky, pp. 1–59. Albuquerque: University of New Mexico Press.
  1977   Alternative models for exchange and spatial distribution. In *Exchange systems in prehistory,* edited by T. Earle and J. Ericson, pp. 71–90. New York: Academic Press.
Renfrew, C., J. E. Dixon, and J. R. Cann
  1968   Further analysis of Near Eastern obsidians. *Proceedings of the Prehistoric Society* 34:319–331.
Sabloff, J. A., and D. A. Freidel
  1975   A model of a pre-Columbian trading center. In *Ancient civilization and trade,* edited by J. Sabloff and C. C. Lamberg-Karlovsky, pp. 369–408. Albuquerque: University of New Mexico Press.
Sanders, W. T.
  1956   The central Mexican symbiotic region. In *Prehistoric settlement patterns in the New World,* edited by G. Willey. New York: Wenner-Gren Foundation.
Sidrys, R.
  1977   Mass-distance measures for the Maya obsidian trade. In *Exchange systems in prehistory,* edited by T. K. Earle and J. E. Ericson, pp. 91–108. New York: Academic Press.

Sourcing of Exchanged Material

2

Chemical Characterization in Archaeology

Garman Harbottle

INTRODUCTION

In this age of infinitely fine-grained specialization in the arts and sciences, one can look back with wondering admiration at those times when you were, at bottom, a learned man or you were not. And if you were, you took all knowledge for your province. Then, you could experiment in physics or chemistry in your own laboratory one day, and go out to examine and ultimately publish your thoughts on the latest discovery of "antiquities" turned up by the plow of a local farmer the next. Although we have used the term *Renaissance man* to describe this person, it is misleading, because he actually existed well into the 1800s.

Thus it is that in the eighteenth and nineteenth centuries we find outstanding physical scientists deeply involved in archaeological work and speculation. We find Martin Klaproth, a distinguished chemist, not merely analyzing three tesserae of Roman glass from the villa of Tiberius at Capri—bright red, brilliant green, sapphire blue—to determine the causes of their colors, but even inventing the science of glass analysis to do so. Klaproth also was the first to analyze ancient coinage—copper, brass, bronze, and silver alloys of Greece and Rome. All this took place around 1800, or a little before (Caley 1949). Another example is Sir Humphry Davy (1815) and his examination of specimens of pigments he himself collected at Rome and Pompeii, and in a Roman house in Sussex. The famous chemists Berzelius and Fresenius both analyzed

CONTEXTS FOR PREHISTORIC EXCHANGE

ancient bronzes—the first, by the way, in addition to being one of a very small number of chemists who have had a revolutionary impact in the field, was also an M.D. These men were working in the 1830s and 1840s (Caley 1951). Michael Faraday is mentioned in 1867 (Diamond 1867) as having examined a sample of Roman pottery and glaze, and he discovered it to be lead based. Surely this was the first chemical indication as to the antiquity of that particular technology.

But some of the earliest workers who bridged the gap between the sciences and archaeology and who are therefore of interest to us here were not of the exalted class of Klaproth, Davy, Berzelius, and Faraday. Notwithstanding this, the research of Gobel, Helm, and Damour belongs—in the interdisciplinary sense—to a high plane (Caley 1951). Gobel, a professor of chemistry at the University of Dorpat in Estonia in the 1840s, gains our attention when he suggests for the first time that chemistry may be of service to archaeology and prehistory. He analyzed numerous brass objects excavated in the Russian Baltic provinces and, by comparing their chemical compositions with those of prehistoric European, Greek, and Roman copper-based alloy artifacts, concluded that they were probably of Roman origin—at least, that the makers had knowledge of Roman techniques of metal fabrication.

This work of Gobel, significantly, involved the analysis of a statistically substantial number of related objects—he may thus be said, as will be seen, to be a pioneer in the chemical characterization of archaeological materials. And he established a group chemical property, as opposed to the analytical data of a single specimen. He therefore comes close to the topic of this chapter.

But how much closer does Damour come! (Damour 1865, 1866; Caley 1951). Damour was a French mineralogist who was concerned as to the origin of the numerous beautifully finished hard-stone axes found "in the Celtic monuments and among the wild tribes [p. 313]." His paper of 1865 is well worth reading: The archaeologists who "penetrate to the bottoms of ancient tombs" must invoke the aid of geologists, zoologists, and paleontologists to give meaning to their discoveries. Mineralogy and chemistry must make known the characteristics and composition of the artifacts unearthed. In this way one could cast new light on the migratory movements of peoples of prehistoric times. When one finds an object in an excavation, an artifact whose material is of a distant provenience, one must infer that either the object itself, or at least the raw material of which it is made, has been transported from there to here.

Damour looked mineralogically and chemically at quartz, agate, jasper, and fibrolite axes: His first love was, however, jade. Jade axes are found in the soil of France, and Damour pleads with archaeologists to take careful field notes. He analyzes jadeite, nephrite, and chloromelanite from around the world—one axe found under a dolmen in northern France even has the same composition as a jade of New Zealand! But he carefully spells out his reservations: There is no recorded jade deposit in Europe or the Alps; but before he would say that the Celtic jade axes came from Asia or China, it would be necessary to analyze many more samples from there and from India and Tibet, to compare and of course to check that there are really no nearby sources in the countries of Europe (Damour 1865:362–364).

Damour also studied obsidian: Four different sources were analyzed chemically—a first—and six artifacts were examined, among them a Mesoamerican mask, a projectile point, and a "thin chip used as a razor [p. 318]." He references, as a prior student of obsidian sources and properties, the Italian scientist Spallanzani (d. 1799) whom opera lovers will recall as the coinventor of the dancing robot Olympia in the first act of *Tales of Hoffman*.

The kind of chemical and petrological reasoning Damour aimed at in his hard-stone analyses—the proof of the origin through similarity in the properties of a transported artifact and of a source material—found a rather more satisfying home in the work of Helm, our third example. Helm in 1885 (Caley 1967; Beck *et al.* 1971) carried out chemical tests on amber beads found at Mycenae by Schliemann, and he concluded that the amber was of Baltic origin. Caley (1967) considers this "one of the first indications by chemical means of the existence of traffic in a particular material over a great distance in prehistoric times [p. 122]."

Damour and Helm are creeping up on some concepts we should now discuss and clarify. Archaeologists love the term *sourcing,* with its upbeat, positive thrust—that you analyze or examine an artifact and, by comparison with material of known origin, "source" it. In point of fact, with a very few exceptions, you cannot unequivocally source anything. What you can do is characterize the object, or better, groups of similar objects found in a site or archaeological zone by mineralogical, thermoluminescent, density, hardness, chemical, and other tests, and also characterize the equivalent source materials, if they are available, and look for similarities to generate attributions. A careful job of chemical characterization, plus a little numerical taxonomy and some auxiliary archaeological and/or stylistic information, will often do something almost as useful: It will produce groupings of artifacts that make archaeological sense. This, rather than absolute proof of origin, will often necessarily be the goal.

So let us talk of characterization. In many cases with artifacts this is all you can ever have anyhow, since many sources were used up in antiquity—the more so because they produced exactly the kinds of obsidian, ceramic clay, gemstones, etc., that were desired by the prehistoric artisan. And in his conservatism, he and his descendants kept using the source until it was exhausted. This chapter will be concerned with the different laboratory techniques for analyzing archaeological materials, their efficiency, "cost," and range of applicability, and how the data produced can be treated mathematically to generate the kinds of knowledge the archaeologist seeks.

It would be helpful in discussion if there were definitions that could become agreed usage between archaeologists and archaeometrists. Perhaps the following paragraphs can open a dialogue leading to agreement: They are a brief digression from our main concern.

Source and Origin

I see the *source* as the ultimate starting point—the clay bed, obsidian flow, mine of flint or copper or marble quarry, which is the natural deposit of a material. It is where one goes to procure and thus initiate the chain of processing and/or distribution. I take *source* to be a little more specific than *origin,* which could also refer to a production center. For example, "the origin of San Martin Orange pottery is Teotihuacan; the source is the clay of the Rio San Juan." One must admit that the two terms are often used interchangeably. We shall see later that the *source* has a very definite operational meaning when used in archaeometric discussion.

Production Center

A *production center* is the workshop, which need not bear any geographic relation to the source. Sometimes a production center is taken to denote a larger area containing many small workshops or craft production sites. *Production center* can perfectly well be equated to *origin.*

Provenience (= provenance)

It *ought* to mean *only* where something is found. Thus with a raw material it could be identical with *source.* For artifacts, the point of excavation or discovery is the *provenience.* But among art historians it generally means *presumed origin.* ("The provenience of the cylinder jar excavated at Kaminaljuyu was the Central Peten.") Some archaeometry papers have also used the term to mean *source* or *origin* (Wilson 1978). One suspects that we are seeing here an Old World–New World bias, the art-historical usage being common among Old World archaeologists.

Local and Imported

Local is generally taken to mean "near or associated with the production center." *Imported* is usually everything else, at least operationally. If the analyst recognizes a *local ceramic type* chemically, then a few sherds of a distinguishable composition may be taken to be *imports,* even though they might have originated in the same village, but in a different, as yet unrecognized, clay source. Clearly, these are unsatisfactory definitions, much in need of refinement, based as they are solely on the output of a taxonomic exercise. Archaeologists often decide what is local on the basis of the "criterion of abundance."

What you have the most of is local. But this rule cannot be applied to rare resources, which must have been imported in most cases.

When I have finished the section on the mathematical treatment of the data sets, I will return to the question of what, operationally, constitutes a source, because the answer is the key to what can be done with chemical characterization in archaeology.

In closing this introduction, the physical scientist must warn the archaeologist that chemical characterization and indeed all other physical methods are not panaceas. They will not, in general, supply information that is very meaningful unless they are projected against an extensive analytical and archaeological background. As an adjunct, however, they can often supply decisive hard data for hypothesis testing in the form of probabilistic statements. Another thing that they can do is to suggest unexpected connections, and from this allow the archaeologist to generate new hypotheses.

One final note: Archaeometry is still learning its trade, devising and refining methods at the same time it is applying them to archaeological investigations. In the past 10 years such a rapid advance has taken place in chemical characterization studies that one can be optimistic that in the future it will become a standard tool in the investigation of ancient societies.

CHEMICAL METHODS

In the beginning, there was wet chemistry. This means that the sample is somehow (often by use of brutally corrosive reagents) gotten into solution, the elements separated from one another, and ultimately individually estimated. It is slow, labor intensive and not sensitive to trace elements: Nonetheless, it has been used to characterize an extraordinary number of archaeological bronze specimens (Caley 1964). One of the first analyses of archaeological ceramics, by Richards at Harvard (1895), was by way of wet chemistry: His published figures on Athenian pottery from the Boston Museum of Fine Arts agree with our recent neutron activation analyses (Fillieres n.d.) of the same wares. There are so many superior techniques today that its use is only of historical interest.

One needed, and still needs, methods that produce diverse analytical data rapidly, precisely, sensitively, and with minimum operator intervention. We should examine some of these requirements individually, and then discuss the extent to which different available laboratory techniques can do the job: My approach will begin by justifying—from the theory and goals of taxonomy—these assertions.

According to Clarke (1968), "The main work of an archaeologist hinges on his ability to compare numbers of artifacts or numbers of assemblages and to assess their relative degrees of similarity one with another.... when comparing one artifact with another the archaeologist is intuitively comparing their respective attribute assemblages [p. 140]. Attributes can be of present–absent (bivalued) or multistate types. For example, color, material, profile shape, and mouth opening (of a vessel) are multistate, and in fact, they are continuous variables—i.e., there are infinitely many colors or mouth openings that are possible. In the language of numerical taxonomy, the *attribute* is almost exactly identified with the *character* (Sneath and Sokal 1973). In chemical characterization, the attributes or characters are the different chemical (or mineralogical) elements: This accords well with Clarke's definitions (Clarke 1968:134–145), and it places them in the class of multistate variables with, in principle, infinitely many states. We shall see, however, that in practice these states of the attributes (concentrations of the different chemical or mineralogical species) only have values and are only continuous within two classes of limits: those imposed by nature and by the discriminating ability of laboratory instrumentation.

In chemical characterization of archaeological material, we are fundamentally interested in taxonomy, and the convenient, continuous nature of the chemical variables measured is almost perfectly suited as an input to numerical taxonomy procedures. Let us quote Sneath and Sokal's "fundamental position" (1973), because these two principles, out of their seven, will govern to a large extent the instrumental approach needed in chemical characterization in archaeology.

1. The greater the content of information in the taxa of a classification and the more characters on which it is based, the better a given classification will be.
2. A priori, every character is of equal weight in creating natural taxa [p. 5].

I will return to some additional principles of Sneath and Sokal when I discuss the mathematical treatment of the data sets, for they will be relevant in that section.

Since the characters are elements, it follows that multielement methods are needed, and the more elements the better. It is unfortunate that in some recent research, assignment of obsidian to sources, and the construction of elaborate trade networks as a result of these assignments, has been made on basis of only two elements (Pires-Ferreira 1976a). The characterization of obsidian is quite a complex question, and to be reliable, it demands an extraordinary degree of care in sample collection and analysis, as will be discussed later. One often hears in discussions at symposia the query of "which elements are best to analyze, to discriminate sources of some archaeological material from one another, and which elements need not concern us?" There is no a priori answer. To hope to do an adequate job, analyze for everything you can, at whatever level of precision you can conveniently reach, and let the computer decide which combinations of elements can effect the desired group discriminations. Make no a priori assumptions about useful elements.

I have raised the question of precision again without justifying the previous assertion that precise analyses are desired. That will be easier when the mathematical section is reached. But another assertion, on sensitivity, is directly relevant here. All natural materials—ceramic clays, obsidian, shells, stones of different kinds, ores, and consequently the metals derived from them—are impure. Clays, for example, are hydrated aluminum silicates, often substituted with varying quantities (in the percent range) of sodium, magnesium, potassium, and iron; and they are often mixed with substantial amounts of calcium carbonate. But, beside these major elements that can be thought of as integral to the clay structure, there is a whole suite of trace elements with concentrations ranging from fractions of a percent (Mn, Ba, Cr) down to parts per billion (Au, Ir). For these trace elements, very sensitive methods are needed, but in general, each of the different methods has concentration cutoff levels that are characteristic, are well explored, and can be lowered somewhat if one takes the effort. So sensitivity is directly linked to *how many* impurity elements *can* be measured, and hence to the probable quality of the taxonomy obtained.

The final point—operator intervention necessary to analyze a specimen—is crucial. Since it is an archaeometric axiom that "in any given archaeological study the number of samples to be analyzed tends to increase without limit," and since one needs to analyze a considerable number of specimens to establish the multivariate parameters of a "group" of artifacts or a "source" to be characterized, it follows that the manpower input per sample per element is of great importance. When the actual characterization methods are discussed later, the qualities of speed and ease will receive major attention.

Sneath and Sokal's second principle—the equal a priori weight of characters—underscores what has just been said about the need, first, to analyze for many elements and second, to make no a priori assumptions as to which are useful. When one realizes that in analysis for characterization one encounters elements naturally present at widely varying (percent to ppb) levels, then an input method must be chosen such that the gross elements do not simply outweigh the trace ones. These methods, familiar to numerical taxonomists, will be discussed in the next section.

It would be presumptous of me to discuss *sampling* with an audience of archaeologists. After all, articles on sampling are no strangers to the pages of *American Antiquity*. Sampling for chemical characterization follows much the usual rationale: The hope is to take a small sample for analysis that will be representative of the whole object or source deposit. But many problems intrude, depending on what is to be analyzed. Potsherds are almost never a problem: They are usually plentiful even though you may not have so many as Berlin reported (1956): "At Jonuta there are literally tons of Z Fine Orange [p. 119]." Metal artifacts, carved stones, fine ceramics, etc., are often essentially museum objects, and sampling must be delicately done, if at all. Because of this vast range of sample availability, several types of analysis ought to be considered.

1. *Nondestructive analysis.* Either the whole object becomes the sample in a procedure like neutron activation (NAA), or the object may be nondestructively scanned by an analyzing beam, as in X-ray fluorescence or the various microprobes. Nondestructive NAA tends to be time-consuming.

2. *Slightly destructive analysis.* The object is burred or drilled for a sample (potsherds, vessels, hard stones, metals) or a chip is cut out (marble, obsidian blades). A technique for the analysis of precious metal objects, for example, ancient silver vessels, involves abrasion of a minute streak of metal (100 micrograms [μg]) onto a quartz tube, which is then subjected to neutron activation (Gordus 1971; Meyers *et al.* 1974). One must worry about how well the slightly destructive sample represents the whole.

3. *Destructive analysis:* When an object is so inhomogeneous that only the removal of a significant fraction of the whole will yield a representative sample, then one must either do that destructive act or satisfy oneself with a lesser sample and pay the price of a larger statistical error.

In working with field archaeologists on a large number of characterization studies, I have observed that once an archaeologist has drawn something, he tends to lose interest in the preservation of it; there are plenty of potsherds, and they are generally expendible; and archaeologists (and museum curators) who will initially fiercely deny drilling forays on their objects, will, once the value of chemical characterization has been demonstrated, beat a path to your door. Having said that, it is however still true that those methods that require only small samples are generally to be preferred to those that do not. Most of the modern techniques discussed later are fortunately oriented toward small samples. Obviously, every characterization study will present somewhat unique sampling problems.

One has the samples to be characterized; how then to proceed? Often the decision on which technique to use is governed by what and who are available locally. Archaeologists are not, and should not be, shy in seeking the help of nearby analysts with their projects. However, they must be prepared to accept the analysts as coauthors in publications if a significant number of analyses have been performed. Most archaeological characterization problems are sufficiently complex that a certain amount of research on sampling, analytical procedures, and data processing must be performed before the actual artifact work is begun. There are almost never cut-and-dried projects, where the analysts can merely "turn the crank" to generate results the archaeologist desires. The discussion that follows will therefore treat methods in a vacuum as it were, with but slight reference to their overall availability, leaving it to the archaeologist to seek out the kind of analyst who is best able and willing to deal with his particular study.

There are many multielement instrumental procedures. One that is widely used is emission spectroscopy (ES): The unknown is placed between electrodes, an electric arc is struck, and the sample's highly excited atoms emit light of characteristic wavelengths. The emitted light is separated by diffraction and recorded by photographic film. A standard is treated in the same way, and the film-blackening compared, to obtain the concentrations in the unknown (Boyko *et al.* 1980). A recent improvement has been the elimination of the photographic film through the use of photomultipliers. Many archaeological characterization studies have been made using ES (Catling and Jones 1977; Goad and Noakes 1978) but it suffers, in its classic form, from lack of sensitivity and precision. This was clearly brought out in two studies of the same material: the black-glazed Greek fine paste of the Hellenistic period, exported to Italy, and imitated locally there. The first study by Prag *et al.* (1974) utilized ES along with petrography, and it was well designed experimentally. But the sought-for discrimination was not found, and it was concluded that the inherent 5–20% analytical precision of ES was responsible. Later Hatcher *et al.* (1980) examined the same problem using AA (atomic absorption): Large discrepancies with the ES results appeared, and the group separations based on the new data were far more satisfying archaeologically. A significant improvement is the inductively coupled plasma atomic emission spectroscopy (ICPAES): Much more power is pumped into the emitting volume, and the sensitivity is markedly increased (Floyd *et al.* 1980). Although solid-source introduction is being developed, at the present it is customary to use solutions, an additional labor and time-consuming step to prepare. However, with the introduction of computer-controlled scanning monochromators and the development of solid-source capability, ICPAES becomes a potentially very useful method in archaeological characterization.

As mentioned before, atomic absorption has been used in archaeological characterization (Hughes *et al.* 1976; Hatcher *et al.* 1980). This method depends upon the vaporization of the analyte, usually by spraying the solution containing the sample into a flame. A lamp containing the desired element, let us say sodium, emits light that is characteristic of that element, which passes through the flame and is measured. If sodium is also present in the flame, then a portion of the light is absorbed, and thus a quantitative determination made of the analyte (Price 1972). The sensitivity and precision of AA are more than adequate, but there is interference from other components present in the solution, and this must be compensated. Also, only one element is usually done at a time. The same time-consuming dissolution of sample is encountered. AA is often used to supplement another method, such as INAA (to be discussed later), to obtain additional elements that are thought to be important in characterization. Its great virtue is that it is available almost everywhere in the academic world.

X-ray emission methods are numerous and valuable. X-ray fluorescence (XRF) has been widely used in archaeological characterization, especially of obsidian, where many of the so-called diagnostic elements are measureable (Cobean *et al.* 1971; Nelson *et al.* 1978). It is quick, multielement, takes powdered or even whole solid samples, and has been markedly improved in sensitivity of late, particularly by the Berkeley group (Giauque *et al.* 1973). XRF depends on the absorption of X-rays that excite the inner shells of electrons surrounding the atomic nucleus. The atoms then reemit their own characteristic X-rays that may be identified and counted. Two methods of excitation are used: X-ray generator tubes, whose targets produce 'particular characteristic radiation (chromium, molybdenum) but also a "white" continuous spectrum, and radioisotope sources. Two methods of separation of the emitted X-rays are used: wavelength dispersion (gratings or prisms) and non-dispersive solid-state detectors, which are similar in use to the GeLi detectors used in INAA. Unfortunately, no single combination suffices to cover the whole range of elements, and in any case the conditions that are best for one group of elements, whose atomic numbers are close together (for example P, S, Cl, K, Ca), are not at all optimal for a different group (Ni, Cu, Zn) that are also close together. Thus, for best sensitivity the exciting radiation must be "tuned" to the elements desired. An XRF unit designed by Kevex and recently installed at the Detroit Institute of Art does just this, and it achieves very high sensitivity (Carriveau 1981). Applications of XRF have been covered in a number of books and excellent review articles (Macdonald 1980). Standard XRF has been used in multielement characterization of ancient pottery (Birgul *et al.* 1979) and also as a supplement to INAA, to analyze for elements otherwise inaccessible, such as Pb, Ti, Ni, and Ca.

X-rays may also be excited by high-speed electrons, which can be focused on a tiny area of the artifact (electron microprobe) but also used (defocused) over a broad area as a tool for quantitative analysis (de Atley *et al.* n.d.). The same can be done with protons, either focused or unfocused—the proton microprobe. The more common term is *PIXE*, proton-induced X-ray emission (Nelson *et al.* 1977; Duerden *et al.* 1979). This device almost invariably is coupled to nondispersive silicon or germanium detectors, and it has considerably better sensitivity than conventional XRF because of the far-lower background (see Macdonald 1980). There has not been extensive use of microprobes in characterization: They are not found very readily.

A word of caution. Both XRF and PIXE are most sensitive to the surface composition of an artifact sample: This may make no difference for a powdered, homogenized specimen, but for nondestructive analysis, for example of a coin, it is often found that the surface composition varies considerably from that of the body (Hall 1961). Also, because the incoming and emitted radiations are both absorbed by the sample and internal secondary fluorescence can occur, successful use of PIXE or XRF often depends on having a computer virtually "on line" with the detectors (Macdonald 1980). Several commercial XRF units are available with this hard-ware–soft-ware built in, and they could perform well in chemical characterization.

I have first discussed multielement methods that depend on the outer (optical) and then inner (X-ray) shells of electrons, and now I go still deeper—to those methods in which the atomic nucleus itself supplies the characteristic signature of the element to be analyzed. The first of these is neutron activation analysis (generally, NAA). If the whole procedure is instrumental, i.e., no chemical separations, then it is INAA. The sample is exposed to a source of neutrons, some of which are absorbed by the nuclei of the different atoms, according to the relationship

$$N = N_0 \sigma f t \tag{1}$$

in which N_0 is the number of target nuclei of neutron capture cross-section σ, f the flux (neutrons/cm^2 sec), and t the time. N is the number of radioisotope atoms formed, i.e., radioiron, radiocobalt, etc., from the N_0 target iron, cobalt, etc., atoms present. A relation similar to Equation 1, but with the same f and t, holds for each element species present. If the radioisotope formed decays by gamma-ray emission in a reasonable proportion of its decays (they do not all do so), then those gamma rays, which have energies characteristic of the particular element, can be detected, usually by a solid-state diode device of the Germanium type. The gamma rays measured by the detector are proportional in number to

$$A = (.693/t_{1/2})N \tag{2}$$

in which A is the net decay rate of the N radioisotopic atoms of a certain elementary kind, having a half-life $t_{1/2}$. I have short-cut a number of complications, such as saturation effects, geometry, branching ratios, detector efficiency, and isotopic abundance that are treated in the standard textbooks (DeSoete *et al.* 1972): What is relevant is that, in general, the longer the time t and higher the flux f, the more activity A will result—hence the better the signal. And finally, what you can see, given reasonable values of (ft) (called the "integrated flux") and half-life, i.e., the number of atoms N_0 that will just give a detectible signal, the sensitivity, is governed by the cross section. Whereas the X-ray fluorescence yields vary smoothly from element to element in the periodic table, values of σ jump wildly about. For example calcium, silicon, and magnesium—common mineral constitutents—all have small cross sections; hence they are difficult to detect by neutron activation. Also, they suffer from low isotopic abundance, few gamma rays, and too short a half-life for convenience, respectively. On the other hand, cobalt, scandium, and europium—all common trace elements—are exactly the opposite, and they are readily detected down to sub-ppm levels. In neutron activation you analyze not necessarily for what you would like, so much as for what you can.

There are several operational advantages to neutron activation that are important to the archaeological artifact analyst.

1. Because neutrons penetrate matter so readily, the results generally correspond to the composition of the whole sample and not merely its surface.
2. A small sample (N_0 in Equation 1) can be compensated by a longer bombardment time t or greater flux f, and vice versa.

3. Although it is more trouble, there is no reason why objects of interest to archaeologists, which curators will not allow to be sampled, cannot still be characterized by nondestructively exposing the whole object to neutron activation. Bishop (Lange *et al.* n.d.) has repeatedly done this with carved Mesoamerican jadeite artifacts.

What has been written in preceding paragraphs by implication refers to NAA with thermal neutrons, but activation may also be done with energetic (14 MeV) neutrons (Meyers 1969). Here the cross sections are smaller, and they do not vary so wildly. Activities are much smaller, and sensitivity generally less, but some few elements are accessible with energetic neutrons that are not with thermal ones. There has been relatively little characterization work done with 14 MeV neutron generators.

In a very few cases, other forms of nuclear activation have been used, for example, by photons (Reimers *et al.* 1977) and high-energy charged particles (protons). Here again, cross sections tend to be low, and consequently sensitivity is poor. Nonetheless, activation can be matrix insensitive and nondestructive, provided beam currents are not too high. When particle energies are very high, then multiple pathways for the nuclear reactions result, with attendant difficulty in identifying the target nucleus responsible. Protons have, however, been employed from time to time in archaeological characterization analyses (Meyers 1969; Bird *et al.* 1978).

A number of other, more exotic techniques have also been used, and they deserve to be briefly mentioned at this time. The Mossbauer effect enables one to determine the chemical state of the iron in a sample, and this can be used in certain cases of artifact-source characterization (Tominaga *et al.* 1978; Longworth and Warren 1979; Lazzarini *et al.* 1980a). The measurements are, however, limited to iron-containing specimens. They are slow, and they are made on highly specialized equipment, which is not generally available. It is my feeling that, in archaeological research, Mossbauer studies are far more useful in ceramic firing-temperature and kiln-technology research than in characterization (Bakas *et al.* 1980).

The phenomonon of thermoluminescence (TL), better known for ceramic age-determination, has also been employed to characterize materials (Huntley and Bailey 1978). It is unfortunately lacking in discriminating power, since only an integral signal is measured, and this is the sum of several simultaneously occurring effects in the crystalline specimen analyzed. A way around this, the "3D–TL" technique, requires highly specialized apparatus (Levy 1979), and it has not, to date, been applied to archaeological characterization.

Stable isotope ratios have been applied to the characterization, for provenience determination, of bronze and marble (Goucher *et al.* 1978; Coleman and Walker 1979) and galena (Hassan and Hassan 1981). Artifact materials containing lead in any form are more likely to be successfully separated by source because lead, of all the elements, shows the greatest natural variation in isotope ratios. This comes from the natural decay processes of the different uranium and thorium families, which generate leads of differing atomic weights. Given the specialized equipment, the method would appear to have real potential. However, if an archaeologist entertains serious thought of using it in characterizing his artifacts, he had better have a close personal relationship with a professional mass spectroscopist. Another form of multielement quantitative analysis also involves mass spectroscopy (MS) in a spark-source (SS) machine, following addition of an isotopic "spike" to determine yield. The sample must be put in solution for the "isotopic dilution" (ID) step to take place: Although "IDSSMS" is relatively new and requires exotic equipment, it would certainly operate effectively in archaeological characterization studies, and it deserves to be tried (Knab and Hintenberger 1980).

Although it is not, strictly, a method of chemical characterization, petrography has been so widely used, and it has such a distinguished history, especially in ceramic studies (Shepard 1957, 1968), that it must be included. In this I summarize Bishop *et al.* (n.d.*a*) who recognize three levels of examination of ceramics for paste characterization: binocular-microscope, thin-section, and point-count analyses. The labor per sherd increases sharply from the first to the third, as does the level of quantitative information obtained. Nonetheless, even binocular examination can be an effective adjunct to chemical characterization of ceramic paste and also, presumably, of other archaeological materials of the natural, stone variety: For example, petrographic microscopy has been used with archaeological marble from Greece (Lazzarini *et al.* 1980b). Sometimes compositionally overlapping ceramic classes are readily separable on the basis of their temper or other accessory mineral inclusions, but more often petrography is used to effect a preliminary logical separation of ceramic materials that are subsequently analyzed chemically. Bishop *et al.* (n.d.) should be consulted for references to the interplay of these taxonomic methods and the close relationship of petrographic content to the geological (Shepard 1968) and geochemical environments.

Another petrographic tool used in characterization is X-ray diffraction (XRD). The material studied is exposed in powder form to a finely collimated monochromatic X-ray source. The different crystalline components present scatter the X-rays at preferred angles: The angle and intensity are recorded, so that one may have a roughly quantitative record of the number and kinds of species present. XRD is not very sensitive, but it has been used to characterize pottery (Weymouth 1973) and steatite-chlorite (Kohl 1974; Kohl *et al.* 1979).

Some years ago MacNeish (1970) suggested the establishment of centers for technical studies of ceramics in archaeology; those desiring characterization analyses could ship off their sherds and have them analyzed by whichever of the above methods seemed appropriate. Although the idea has some attractive features (centralization, uniformity of standards and records, high technical expertise combined with archaeological understanding), I am now persuaded that the actual "hands-on" experience of a field archaeologist in laboratory analytical work is valuable in providing a new level of understanding of the materials he or she excavates and their relationships with one another and with their sources. To do a good analysis on something you have found, thereby to fit it into an archaeological pattern, is an almost mystical experience.

What I am saying is that ideally the archaeologist should—with a little training and supervision—carry out his own analyses: Given this, the choice of analytical method often boils down to what is available, not what is ideal. Even within these limitations, however, the archaeologist should choose a procedure that yields an absolute chemical concentration relative to recognized standard material, or on an absolute basis (Harbottle n.d.). There is nothing more frustrating than to discover that another research group has studied materials similar to yours, but reported their results in units that cannot be translated into simple concentrations.

At present, INAA is clearly the best all-around method. If it is not available, atomic absorption and XRF are viable alternatives. Binocular and thin-section studies provide (especially in ceramics) the most valuable preliminary screening and auxiliary information. When solid-source introduction is paired to ICPAES, it may well become the method of choice (Van Loon 1980). But these remarks apply only in general; for specific archaeological materials to be characterized, specific analytical methods will have to be sought out.

MATHEMATICAL TREATMENT OF THE DATA SETS

Before undertaking the analysis of a large set of possibly related archaeological specimens, for purposes of characterization and the testing of hypotheses of trade, origin, and the like, it is well that the archaeologist have at least a rough idea of how one proposes to attack the resultant data set—the table of analytical values after the lab work is done. Practically, we ought to recognize two extreme domains: the minimal project (small number of samples, one or two specific questions to be answered) and the full project (many samples, unsuspected relationships to be sought, hypotheses tested, groups to be developed, characterized, and discriminated). It cannot be overemphasized that until some full projects have been carried out with a particular archaeological resource in a certain geographic area, there is no hope of carrying out a minimal project that means much.

We shall see in this section how the full projects lead to the formation of reference groups that can be mathematically discriminated one from another, and against which the small number of samples in the minimal project can be projected. This process, which amounts to recognizing the nature of distributions of sample points in a multivariate (hypergeometric) space, cannot be generalized too much: The distribution laws and the extent of overlapping of groups will probably differ for each archaeological resource studied.

In setting up the multivariate space used in characterization studies, we have argued for the use of a Euclidean space whose N coordinates are the logarithms of concentrations of the N elements analyzed (Harbottle 1976; Sayre n.d.). Sayre's study sets forth the arguments: In any case some form of standardization must be employed to keep the elements present in large concentrations (percent) from outweighing those present in traces (parts per million or less). This is very much in the spirit of Sneath and Sokal's second fundamental principle quoted previously on a priori equal weight of characters. Another technique is to standardize the data element by element.

With analytical data in hand, the first step is usually some form of cluster analysis, operating in the log concentration space. There are a large number of clustering algorithms available, reflecting many different philosophical approaches (Sneath and Sokal 1973; Bieber, Jr., *et al.* 1976; Harbottle 1976; Everitt 1977; Wishart 1978; Olivier n.d.): The clustering of points that are hypergeometrically close is equivalent to linking samples of similar chemical profile, hence compositionally "like" one another, averaging over many elements.

To begin clustering, one could simply dump all the data into a computer and crunch them with the aid of one clustering algorithm or another—a blindfold, ab initio procedure. But many studies of actual field problems in our laboratory have shown that it is very important to incorporate both archaeological and nonanalytical, technical examination data at an early stage, along with the results of chemical analysis. In this plea to avoid "black-box" number crunching, I follow the recent paper by Bishop *et al.* (n.d.*a*). Although the steps they describe relate to ceramics, aside from changes in the levels of elements analyzed and their relative standard deviations, the procedures and arguments advanced could well apply to almost any material subjected to characterization analysis.

A first precomputer step then is the screening of all the samples into broad microscopic–macroscopic, or visibly separable, categories. For example, in ceramics, use binocular examination to categorize fine paste versus carbonate tempered versus volcanic ash tempered; in obsidian, separation by colors; in blue-green stones separation of the malachite, turquoise, azurite, etc., on the basis of X-ray diffraction, into their proper mineral class. Then through cluster analysis, one begins to identify groups of chemically similar samples, and proceeds to reference-group formation (Bishop's PCRUs) through additional consideration of stylistic and technological attributes, i.e., the "archaeological" similarity. The archaeological and chemical sorting thus go hand in hand.

To be a little clearer, let us consider two actual examples—one from ceramics and one from blue-green stones. At the site of Patarata, Veracruz, in the mangrove swamps of the lower Papaloapan, Stark (1977) established through type-variety stylistic analysis, a number of wares: Mojarra orange-gray, Prieto gray-black, Tlacotalpan orange, etc., having rather fine pastes of similar texture. She also established other wares with coarse-sand or fine-sand tempers, or different paste colors: Escolleras chalk, Tanare (fine) white, etc., running in some cases through several of the four phases—Camaron 1, 2, and 3, and Limon. About 20 of each type and phase are presently being analyzed: The first clustering and cluster-testing pass will examine whether the separate archaeological type-varieties are also compositional types (Stark and Harbottle n.d.). Then, does a given compositional type continue to agree with the stylistic type "vertically," i.e., through several temporal phases? And, do any compositional groups also extend "horizontally," i.e., to include more than one type-variety? These procedures generate what Bishop (Bishop *et al.* n.d. *b*) terms the "chemical paste compositional reference unit" or CPCRU (the chemically recognizable group) leading to the PCRU, which is the chemical unit additionally strengthened and tested by inclusion of color, decoration, and other stylistic attributes, and petrographic (binocular) aplastic examination. One can then turn to the "criterion of abundance"—whatever there is the most of was probably made locally, and the direct examination and analysis of known local (though contemporary today, not to the date of ancient pottery-making!) clay resources to make a plausible case for sourcing. A gold mine of information to the investigator of ancient ceramics is the discovery of a kiln and/or its wasters: These can usually be assumed to be local. Such reasoning leads to the formation of a "local" CPCRU, and one may then move to "regional" questions as a beginning to research on exchange pathways: What is the geographical extent of the "local" unit? Which PCRUs are "intrusive"? Do the intrusive type samples found far away belong to the same PCRU as those found in the local excavation? A chemically "nonlocal" sample often turns out, in the case of ceramic clays, to belong to a CPCRU that has its source nearby: There is no a priori reason to assume that *chemically dissimilar* necessarily means *geographically distant* or vice versa. For hundreds of miles along the Nile (Tobia and Sayre 1974) and the Usumacinta (Bishop *et al.* n.d. *b*), the ceramic clays have a pronounced chemical similarity, provided one keeps to the same geological stratigraphy.

What emerges from this section—focusing on ceramics—is that at each stage of data growth in a "full project" there must be active interaction of geological, archaeological, and perhaps ethnographic data with the interpretation of the chemical analyses.

Turning to the second example, blue-green stones, I have been concerned with both jade (Lange *et al.* n.d.) and turquoise (Weigand *et al.* 1977). I will discuss only the latter. As mentioned before, the first step is to sort out the turquoise from other blue-green minerals and then to make chemical analysis by INAA. We studied sources first, for we felt that if sources could not be chemically characterized and discriminated, there would be no point in proceeding. This was equivalent to seeing if the "provenience postulate" (Weigand *et al.* 1977) applied here. For turquoise, the logical, source-oriented reference unit—the CCRU (CC=chemical compositional)—would be the individual mine or mining district. Again, archaeological information is included: evidence of aboriginal mining activity, stratigraphy, site, and dating of artifacts and mines. But with that data in hand, the procedures of numerical taxonomy flow much as before.

I have made a rather long digression, from the previous statement in this section that one usually begins with some form of cluster analysis, to advocate the early incorporation of a variety of auxiliary data into the procedure of forming groups, or RUs. I ought now to return to the numerical procedures themselves. Rather than fill the pages with equations defining possible methods of linking points in a hyperspace, I prefer to try to give some feeling for the flow of the data processing toward its goal—the possible characterization of the RUs.

Although cluster-analysis packages are effective, one ought to remember that the algorithms will produce "groups" out of any data whatever. For this reason one must be very careful in interpreting the output of a cluster-analysis program, which is usually in the form of a dendrogram (Sneath and Sokal 1973:259). Since a dendrogram is a two-dimensional representation of a multidimensional relationship, it cannot possibly represent that relationship without distortion. Nonetheless, closely related (chemically very similar) specimens will generally appear as tightly linked points on a dendrogram. Connections at higher linkages do not, however, necessarily imply any meaningful association (Rohlf 1970).

Another point to consider is that unspecialized clustering algorithms operating on a Euclidean distance matrix often work well with nice hyperspherical, multidimensionally well-separated data groups, but that they fail miserably when highly correlated data are processed (see Harbottle [1976] and Sayre n.d. for an archaeological example). This is because the appropriate distance measure for such data is not the Euclidean but the Mahalanobis distance (Soloman 1971). Many archaeological materials studied—jade, turquoise, native copper—do not show a large number of high two-element correlations. But ceramics are often correlated, and in obsidian correlations can be extreme (Bowman et al. 1973; Neivens *et al.* n.d.).

Other problems arise from the sequential, hierarchical nature of some clustering procedures (Sneath and Sokal 1973, Chapter 5.5), producing misleading dendrogram patterns. Iterative methods, which can reassign misplaced samples, are helpful but require specialized computer programs (Sneath and Sokal 1973:209–214).

Despite its problems, which are in general well understood, clustering is a rapid and useful method of getting a rough, overall view of the compositionally based similarities in a set of samples. It is not, however, a good way to arrive at final assignments. The preliminary group formations emerging from simple cluster analysis, whether hierarchical or iterative, must be refined through different multivariate procedures before they can finally be accepted as chemical reference units, CCRUs—i.e., groups whose average analytical values and standard deviations from those values and whose multielement correlations are all reasonably well known. Unfortunately, to have the complete multivariate statistical properties of a group of analyses, one must be able to calculate the variance–covariance matrix of the data and its inverse, and this requires that one has at least one sample more than the number of elements analyzed (Sayre n.d.). This is a basic reason why "full" projects have to be done before minimal projects: Good CCRUs are needed, against which to compare single samples.

Once you have a well-established CCRU, however, you can resort to programs that will calculate probabilities that *any* other specimen belong—which at the level of a few percentage points gives you a helpful in-group, out-group dichotomy. We have such a program—ADCORR—in-house at Brookhaven (Sayre n.d.). For a group of samples it calculates the variance–covariance matrix and the centroid, the Mahalanobis distance from the centroid to each sample, and the probabilities that each individual could belong to the group and yet have that great a Mahalanobis distance from the centroid.

A natural consequence of any well-designed full project is, however, not one CCRU but several—sometimes many. Thus data banks arise that contain not merely arrays of *single* archaeological specimens but also of *groupings* or CCRUs. And one needs methods for the discrimination of one CCRU from another and the assignment of new samples to a particular CCRU. In a recent study of trade relations between Classic Teotihuacan and the Gulf Coast, ceramic sherds found at Teotihuacan were assigned to Gulf Coast CCRUs such as El Tajin, Rio Panuco, etc. with a high probability (Sayre and Harbottle n.d.). The key tool is discriminant analysis, where the computer considers a number of previously established CCRUs and calculates the equations of those planes in the hyperspace in which the CCRUs form discrete "clouds" that best separate the CCRUs from one another (Bishop *et al.* n.d. *b*).

To carry out this type of analysis, we use the subprogram DISCRIM in the SPSS package (Nie *et al.* 1975): It has a number of features that make it particularly desirable in this application. For example, for each sample one gets not only the probability that, given the available groups, the sample belongs to a particular (assigned) group. But one also gets the probability, given a multivariate normal distribution, that a member of that group would have *that sample's* distance from the centroid, or one greater.

In a previous section, it was stated that precise analyses are desired. It ought to be clear why—by now. In cluster and discriminant analysis, analytical imprecision constitutes a kind of "noise" that obscures the characterizing "signal." This noise, measured by the additional variance introduced by the analytical method, ought to be kept as small or smaller than the natural variance present in the source (Harbottle 1976), thereby sharpening the discrimination.

We may close this section by returning to the question, "What is a source?" To the archaeologist the answer is simple—a particular obsidian flow or a clay bed or mine shaft. For characterization, the "provenience postulate" implies that the source is mathematically recognizable and differentiable: The tools for doing this are the variance–covariance matrix and the falloff of probability of group membership with increasing Mahalanobis distance (Ward 1974). It is only within the resolving power of these mathematically defined sources that the archaeologist will be able to phrase questions of origin and exchange: One must never assume that the physical and mathematical sources have to coincide.

MATERIALS THAT HAVE BEEN CHARACTERIZED

This section, which is little more than a bibliographic tabulation of recent contributions dealing with particular characterization problems, is not exhaustive, but for the archaeologist who encounters a particular field problem, it may provide at least a starting point. It is divided somewhat arbitrarily into five categories: stones and minerals; ceramics and clays; natural products; metals; and glass. Within each subdivision I have tried to reference some of the key, though certainly not all, publications.

Stones and Minerals

Sandstone was characterized by Heizer and associates (1973). An interesting study was able to locate the quarry of the original stone of the Colossi of Memnon at Thebes (Egypt) and also of the stone used in repairs made by Emperor Septimius Severus.

Marble, especially that used by the classic Greek sculptors, has been characterized petrographically (Renfrew and Peacy 1968; Lazzarini *et al.* 1980b), but a more promising technique is the measurement of isotopic ratios (Craig and Craig 1972; Manfra *et al.* 1975; Herz and Wenner 1978; Coleman and Walker 1979; Germann *et al.* 1980). There is also hope, however, that chemical analysis is applicable to the discrimination of marble quarries from one another, and the sourcing of statues, temple materials, and inscriptions (Rybach and Nissen 1964; Conforto *et al.* 1975; Lazzarini *et al.* 1980b). In the end, it might prove necessary to utilize a combination of techniques.

Limestone has been characterized through trace element profiles (INAA) by Meyers and van Zelst (1977) in a pilot study.

Alabaster, or natural gypsum, is briefly mentioned by Warren (1979) in connection with characterization by AA, XRF, and INAA.

Sanukite is a black andesitic rock, with conchoidal fracture, used in Japan from approximately the first century B.C. to the first century A.D. for toolmaking. Higashimura and Warashina (1975) (Warashina *et al.* 1978) showed that by XRF one could confirm the "provenience postulate"—that intrasource variation was smaller than intersource variation, for eight sources.

Chert and *flint* have, because of their importance in primitive toolmaking and, in Europe, Neolithic exchange processes, been the object of considerable characterization effort. Sieveking and colleagues (1972:151) go so far as to say that "artefacts made from flint are the commonest and indeed almost the only surviving relics in Western Europe for by far the greater part of Man's existence" in an article in which they use AA analysis (Hughes *et al.* 1976). DeBruin *et al.* (1972) and Aspinall and Feather (1972) both used INAA: The former utilized "pattern recognition" in the numerical taxonomy and discrimination. The recent paper of Shotton and Hendry (1979) contains an excellent review and bibliography on the use of optical petrology in the characterization of archaeological stone of several kinds, including flint, vis-à-vis the trace element determination method. For chert studies, one should consult Luedtke (1978, 1979).

Obsidian was used throughout much of the ancient world for the production of blades, scrapers, and projectile points. Its importance in trade, as the sources are strictly limited, cannot be overemphasized. To quote Millon (1973:45): "We have found more than five hundred workshop areas . . . the vast majority are obsidian workshops.. . . Did the growth potential represented by the expansion of the craft of obsidian working play a significant role in the rise of Teotihuacan as a city?" Cann *et al.* (1968, 1969) have discussed the obsidian trade in Europe and Asia in the Neolithic, and they give numerous references.

The fact that obsidian sources are often quite uniform internally, at least over the ancient production areas, while the source-to-source variations are substantial, has given the archaeologist an opportunity for rather precise sourcing, leading to hard data useful in testing trade models (Renfrew *et al.* 1966, 1968; Sidrys 1977). Many methods have been used for the analysis of obsidian: emission spectroscopy (Cann *et al.* 1969); X-ray fluorescence (Stross *et al.* 1971; Cobean *et al.* 1971; Stevenson *et al.* 1971; Nelson *et al.* 1975; Nelson *et al.* 1978); nuclear activation (Gordus *et al.* 1971; Coote *et al* 1972; Bowman *et al.* 1973; Carlton *et al.* 1978); isotopic analysis (Gale 1981); thermoluminescence (Huntley and Bailey 1978); and Mossbauer spectroscopy (Longworth and Warren 1979). This last study contains a useful bibliography of other methods of characterization of obsidian. In any case, the questions of ease, precision, and cost of data production per sample for available analytical tools must be faced in each particular project.

It must be noted that obsidian can show extreme elemental correlation (Bowman *et al.* 1973). Neivens and associates (n.d.) have noted several other examples similar to those presented by Bowman and his colleagues. Such correlation dictates the use of Mahalanobis distance in taxonomy of obsidian by chemical analysis.

Soapstone, including both *steatite* and *chlorite*, has been characterized in several ways: The stone derives interest in archaeology from its millennia-long trade patterns. At Brookhaven, we characterized steatite (chlorite) from Tepe Yahya, a third-millennium B.C. site in southeastern Iran, by the relative intensities of X-ray diffraction basal-plane reflections (Kohl 1974; Kohl *et al.*

1979). Allen *et al.* (1975) used INAA to analyze American soapstone sources and artifacts in a novel way. Although the *amounts* of trace elements scattered badly even within a given quarry, the *pattern* of the rare earth elements was stable and could be used for characterization (Allen *et al.* 1978; Allen and Pennell 1978). Although the method works well in the areas tested, in other parts of the world preliminary analyses ought to be made to assess the degree of intersource variation.

Hematite, ilmenite and magnetite. These minerals are of special archaeological interest in Olmec Mesoamerica (Bernal 1969:78), where they were used for small, highly polished mirrors of possible ritual significance (Coe and Diehl 1980:244) and perhaps even as lodestone compasses (Carlson 1975). Pires-Ferreira (1976b) has characterized iron-ore mirror material in Formative period trade networks in Oaxaca, Mexico, by measuring the Mossbauer spectra. Gordus and associates (1971:233) mention in passing preliminary studies with NAA. Obviously, several methods need to be investigated with a wider range of specimens.

Galena has been reported in Egypt in pre-Dynastic sites, often in association with burials (see Hassan and Hassan 1981). It is thought to have been used cosmetically (the eyeliner Kohl) and medicinally. Hassan and Hassan characterized galena by isotopic ratios, which would seem to be the method of choice if for no other reason than the possibility of correlation with very extensive lead and lead-ore isotopic-ratio data banks. On the other hand, Walthall *et al.* (1980) characterized galena from Middle Woodland Copena burial mounds by the Ag, Sb, and Cu contents, with some success. They used AA for this analysis. It ought to be a good candidate for NAA, inasmuch as the lead does not produce, with neutrons, any interfering radioisotope (see lead).

Turquoise has been used in many civilizations as an ornament or a charm (Pogue 1915, reprinted 1975) and can be characterized by trace element analysis (Sigleo 1975; Weigand *et al.* 1977). There is currently a large turquoise characterization project under way at Stony Brook and Brookhaven, continuing the work reported by Weigand and his colleagues.

Jade, either of the two very different minerals *jadeite* and *nephrite,* is also currently under investigation at Brookhaven in a collaborative program with the Boston Museum of Fine Arts (Lange *et al.* n.d.), and has been characterized by Hammond *et al.* (1977) in an earlier contribution. It will be recalled that Damour first analyzed archaeological jade in the nineteenth century.

Bitumen, a black sticky tar associated with petroleum, seeps to the surface at many places in the Middle East, where it was mixed with fine sand by early civilizations to form *asphalt.* The use of this material as an adhesive and sealant, and as a mortar, may be traced back to the eighth millennium B.C. (Marschner and Wright 1978). These authors characterized asphalt, a difficult task technically, through classic petroleum-industry procedures—liquid chromatography and vanadium–nickel ratios.

Ceramics and Clays

In my 1976 article, I reviewed a large number of studies involving characterization of archaeological ceramics (Harbottle 1976). In fact, the great majority of all characterization studies have been of this material. Many studies will be found in the papers of *Archaeometry,* the bulletin of the Research Laboratory for Archaeology and the History of Art at Oxford, and in other journals (Wilson 1978). In the present section I will reference only a selection of the papers appearing in the last three or four years.

Work on ceramic characterization tends to be done in a few centers: One of the more recent arrivals is McGill University, where Attas and coworkers have analyzed Bronze Age pottery from Greece (Attas *et al.* 1977) and Turkey (Birgul *et al.* 1977, 1979) using INAA and XRF. Ancient Greek and Hellenistic ceramics have also been studied by Stern and Descoeudres (1977); by Catling and Jones (1977) in a continuation of the long-standing Oxford interest (see also Jones and Rutter [1977]); by Hatcher *et al.* (1980) (see earlier work of Prag *et al.* [1974]); and by Fillieres at Brookhaven (1978). An imaginative recent paper by Lambert and colleagues (1978), also on Greek (Mycenaean) pottery, introduces the new analytical technique of X-ray photoelectron spectroscopy (XPS). It is still too soon to know if this will become a competitive characterization technique.

Another recent group is that of Mejdahl and coworkers in Denmark (Hansen *et al.* 1979). In France there are a number of projects that have been based on the GANOS (Groupe d'Archeologie Nucleaire d'Orsay-Saclay) organization (Fontes *et al.* 1979; Widemann *et al.* 1975, 1979). Also concerned with characterization of Gallo–Roman figurines, but by XRF, is the Louvre laboratory (Lahanier and Rouvier-Jeanlin 1977) in Paris. Roman coarse wares from North Africa have been analyzed by Krywonos and associates (1980) at Manchester. De Atley, Blackman, and Olin at the Smithsonian Institution have been active (de Atley *et al.* n.d.), while in Germany several groups based in Berlin have analyzed ceramics. An article by Schneider and colleagues (1979) is interesting in not merely reporting analytical data but also in discussing the philosophy of reference-group formation. Of the senior laboratories— Brookhaven, Berkeley, and Oxford—Berkeley has of late concentrated more on obsidian studies and less on ceramics (see, however, Branstetter 1979). At Jerusalem Yellin and Perlman have collaborated with Asaro and his Berkeley coworkers (Yellin *et al.* 1978) on a two-laboratory intercomparison of analyses—an important first step toward the ultimate goal of data intercomparison (see also Schneider *et al.* 1979:Table 5, and Harbottle 1981).

I have already mentioned the work of Fillieres (1978) at Brookhaven on Greek-style amphoras from Marseilles: A recent unpublished study is concerned with material excavated at the Athenian Agora. Also from the Mediterranean area is Kaplan's work on Tell el Yahudiyeh ware (Kaplan 1978; Kaplan *et al.* n.d. *a,* n.d. *b*). In these studies, clustering on stylistic parameters paralleled the chemical results. The largest fraction of our effort has, however, been on ancient Mesoamerican ceramics, from Teotihuacan (trade objects) (Sayre and Harbottle n.d.); the Gulf Coast (Stark and Harbottle n.d.; Stark 1977); Oaxaca (Abascal M. *et al.* 1974); and especially the Maya world. Beginning with some ad hoc studies of Mayan Fine Orange ceramics in conjunction with the Peabody Museum (Sayre *et al.* 1971), we were led to a continuing study of ceramics from the Classic Mayan site of Palenque (Bishop 1975; Rands *et al.* 1975, 1979; Rands and Bishop 1980; Bishop *et al.* n.d. *b*, n.d. *c*, n.d. *d*) and, by extension, to the whole Maya zone. Much has been learned in this series of studies of area-wide ceramic-pattern similarities and variations and the relationships between geochemical and petrological variables.

Natural Products

Amber has the distinction, as mentioned before, of being one of the earliest archaeological materials on which an attempt was made to source through characterization (by succinic acid content) (see references in Beck *et al.* 1971, 1978). Currently, the best method is through measurement of IR spectra. One study has been made of NAA of amber. This ought to be pursued for it could, conceivably, lead to a narrower sourcing than the Baltic–non-Baltic dichotomy (Das 1969).

Seashells have been extensively traded in Mesoamerica and early southwestern United States (Brand 1938; Miller n.d.). At Brookhaven a pilot study has recently been carried out in collaboration with Harvard on the chemical characterization of *Mercenaria mercenaria,* the northern quahog clamshell used by the aboriginal North American Indians (Miller n.d.) as "wampum." The results are definitely encouraging, and the work ought to be extended.

Ivory and bone are interesting because one expects them to show chemical characterization profiles that are, on the one hand, species specific, but on the other, dependent upon local environment and nutritional trace element contents. An encouraging beginning has been made by Wessen and coworkers (1978), who determined alkaline earths in elk, bison, deer, and seal bones; but it is clear that much more work must be done with both bone and ivory before this method can be reduced to archaeometric utility. A recurring problem (investigated by Wessen *et al.* 1978) is the alteration with time of the chemical content of buried bone (see also Meyers 1968).

Metals

Caley (1964) has reported extensively on the chemical analysis of archaeological metals. Often, however, such analyses have been more oriented toward the aims of historical metallurgy than toward origin-dependent characterization (Caley 1949; Braidwood *et al.* 1951; Northover 1979). An important contribution, which should serve as a starting point for archaeologists concerned with native copper, silver, and gold, is by Patterson (1971). Trace elements in these metals might be expected to show regional patterns, which could survive in some way the trip from ore deposit to finished artifact. But all metals, including precious ones, can be deliberately alloyed, or remelted as scrap to form new starting materials for artifacts. It is clear that in these cases characterization by means of chemical analysis cannot be expected to work in the same way as with a material like obsidian, which must be used in its unaltered form. However, the deliberate alteration of a basic metal like copper—with tin, arsenic, lead, and zinc to form bronze or brass alloys—often followed a recipe that was itself characteristic of a particular temporal period or cultural region. Thus, the end result of chemical characterization often will refer as much to cultures or temporal periods as to geographic sources. This tendency is found in a number of the contributions referred to later in this section.

Copper has been investigated in some detail. Veakis (1979) and Goad and Noakes (1978) have worked on the trace element characterization of *native* copper by NAA and ES. The Argonne group, in several papers (Fields *et al.* 1971; Friedman *et al.* 1966, 1972; Bowman *et al.* 1975), have examined the types of compositional profiles found in various kinds of ores and their relationship to the final compositions of the metallic copper. A beautiful example of what can be done to locate the sources of the copper employed in making ancient artifacts is reported by Berthoud (1979) (Berthoud *et al.* 1979). The sources are in Iran. Along the same lines, Ottaway (1979) shows us how multivariate (cluster) analysis can be of value in the interpretation of analytical data of Neolithic European copper artifacts. There have been many studies of copper-based coins in which the analytical profile has been related to a particular historical period or minting place (see, for example, Carter 1978).

Brass and Bronze. Although they are alloys, hence compositionally affected by remelting and culturally dependent technology, they have nonetheless been usefully characterized analytically (Ottaway 1974; Schwabe and Slusallek 1981). An interesting example is the work of Goucher and associates (1978) who measured isotope ratios in the lead portion of Nigerian "bronzes" to suggest sources. They also included a useful bibliography of earlier chemical analyses. In the same volume, Chase and Ziebold (1978) reported on the affiliations of Chinese bronzes evidenced by analysis. A dramatic example is the study of the famous (or notorious) "Plate of Brass" found in California, which was thought to be related to Sir Francis Drake. The work of Hedges (1979) and Michel and Asaro (1979) demonstrates rather conclusively that it is a fraud.

Silver and Gold (see Patterson 1971). Much of the work on analytical characterization of precious metal objects has involved coins (Harbottle 1976:66–68; Reimers *et al.* 1977; Barrandon *et al.* 1977; Muller and Gentner 1979; Gale 1979). A special case is the long-term extensive examination of objects of Sasanian (A.D. 224–651) origin by Meyers at the Metropolitan Museum (Harper and Meyers 1981).

Lead. Roman lead was analyzed by NAA by Wyttenbach and Schubiger (1973). The authors felt that because of remelting, mixing, etc., it might prove difficult to assign lead artifacts to sources. This method deserves more study. However, it has also emerged that isotopic-ratio measurements in lead can be highly characteristic of sources (Brill and Wampler 1967; Goucher *et al.* 1978; Hassan and Hassan 1981), not merely of lead itself, but also of the lead present as an impurity in silver and gold (Gale 1979; Stos-Fertner and Gale 1979).

Other metals. To close this section I can mention two interesting studies in which iron and pewter were characterized analytically. British Iron Age iron "currency" bars were described through the chemical profiles of the mineral inclusions (Hedges and Salter 1979), which were thought to be related to the respective iron-ore sources. The pewter objects were actually wine measures from seventeenth- to nineteenth-century England and Scotland: Distinct temporal and geographic characteristics were observed (Carlson 1977) in a large sample.

Glass and Faience

As with metals, the proper starting point is again the comprehensive work of Caley (1962), which ought to be consulted. In 1961, Sayre and Smith (1961) found that compositions of glass, at least in the elements Mg, K, Mn, Sb, and Pb, were strongly culturally dependent, i.e., Roman, Islamic, etc., glass tended to show the same composition over great areas and long temporal spans. This is, of course, the opposite of what one wants for source assignment, but when trace elements were analyzed in stained-glass windows, a somewhat different picture emerged (Olin and Sayre 1974; Olin *et al.* 1976). The one large-scale attempt to trace the movement of glass (African trade beads) in an exchange network was that of Davison (1972). All in all it would seem that the characterization of ancient glass by means of trace element taxonomy deserves more research than is presently appearing (Christie *et al.* 1979; Velde and Gendron 1980; Henderson and Warren 1981). A useful up-to-date bibliography will be found in Kaplan (1979). Again, as with metals, isotopic measurements can be used to characterize the lead portion of glass compositions (Brill 1969, 1970; Brill *et al.* 1973).

Faience, a kind of sintered glass made by coating a core of powdered quartz with a vitreous alkaline glaze (Aspinall *et al.* 1972), has an enormous time depth in the Middle East, from pre-Dynastic Egypt to modern times (Petrie 1920). There have been a number of studies, in some cases involving reinterpretation of earlier data, on the origin of faience beads found in Britain (Stone and Thomas 1956; Newton and Renfrew 1970; Aspinall *et al.* 1972; Aspinall and Warren 1976; McKerrell 1976). These studies amply illustrate the changes in archaeological perspective that can occur in a given field of study—British faience—as the technical means of laboratory examination and data handling grow ever more sophisticated. And that is a good text upon which to end this section.

CONCLUSION

It might be useful to review briefly the requisites for a successful chemical characterization study of an archaeological problem. First, the subject matter. If one wishes to characterize materials that are already highly studied, he or she may have every expectation of results helpful to his or her project on trade or sources. These would include obsidian, ceramics, flint, and perhaps one or two other materials like marble and metals that contain lead. With many other materials, there have been a few studies, but nothing more than experimentation as yet. In these cases the archaeologist–analyst team will have to do some initial research themselves, with no certainty as to the successful outcome. Finally, there are archaeological materials much used in antiquity, for example cinnabar in Mesoamerica, that have never been examined, and where it might provide exchange data of great interest if they were. Here one may blaze a new trail.

Second, there is the problem of access to analytical service. There are very few first-class analytical chemists or petrographers who will spend months in the laboratory analyzing an archaeologist's samples out of sheer goodwill; therefore archaeologists must do one of three things: (*a*) have them done commercially; (*b*) do them themselves; or (*c*) find an analyst willing to collaborate in the analyses and interpretation of the data. The first method is, because of expense, rarely used: NAA commercially runs about $500 per sample. The second and third routes are sometimes combined, i.e., the analyst trains the archaeologist who then does the work. I personally think that is the best way: The archaeologist who has carried out the analyses and data processing alone gains a new respect for the statistical and taxonomic limitations of chemical data, and will collect the next set of field samples with these limitations in mind. At Brookhaven, we have participated in a large number of these combined exercises, and we find that they work out well. But the third route alone is also much used. Here I must be blunt. If an analyst collaborates with an archaeologist, there should be coauthorship of at least the technical articles covering the work, and it is imperative that publication arrangements be agreed upon in advance.

In all of these cases, access to analytical equipment and funds to cover costs of use are decisive factors. There is no point in comparing effectiveness and costs of various characterization methods if the archaeologist concerned has, in fact, little or no choice. Also, costs in an academic setting are usually artificial or subsidized: The equipment is usually on hand already, and labor costs are the decisive element. Graduate students can be coerced or made interested in performing analyses after training. I have tried to suggest in the second section of this chapter some of the parameters of effectiveness of chemical or physical (instrumental) techniques; but when in doubt, remember the first principle of Sneath and Sokal (1973:5): You get the best classifications out of the most information, and therefore the best analytical technique a priori is the one that yields reliable data on the largest number of elements.

During the period when each full project in archaeological characterization stood alone as an event involving one team of archaeologists and one laboratory doing analyses, the problem of intercomparison of results was unimportant. But now, at least in the work with ancient ceramics and obsidian, many different groups are involved, and the intercomparability of data becomes an urgent necessity. As an example, the Brookhaven data bank now contains some 10,000–15,000 analyses of archaeological ceramics, while the Berkeley group, with its extension in Jerusalem (Yellin *et al.* 1978), probably has as many more. In Europe, laboratories in several countries are busily engaged in the analysis of Greek, Roman, and other indigenous ceramics. Every laboratory tends to use its own standards, and when comparisons are carried out, it is found that the different analysts agree well on some elements—like iron, sodium, and cobalt—but disagree on others—some of the rare earths, chromium, barium, and zinc. Obviously there would be a great benefit to the archaeological community to bring all this data under one roof, so to speak, as when it was decided to use the Munsell color chart to describe paste and slip colors in ceramic pots, instead of using terms like *apricot* and *tawny-vinaceous*. There is considerable interest in the resolution of these problems of intercomparison (Harbottle n.d.), but for the time being, archaeologists should realize that the solution may lie a few years in the future. Obsidian analyses are especially susceptible to this difficulty.

In closing, let it be said that chemical characterization ought to have a bright future in archaeological field studies, especially where problems of origin or exchange are involved. The development of new, faster, broader, more sensitive and precise analytical techniques, and the reduction of new and existing analytical data to agreed bases of standardization will have the greatest overall impact. These advances, coupled to presently existing computational and numerical taxonomic–multivariate statistical procedures, will supply the archaeologist with the hard data needed to test exchange hypotheses.

REFERENCES

Abascal M, R., G. Harbottle, and E. V. Sayre
 1974 Correlation between terra cotta figurines and pottery from the Valley of Mexico and source clays by activation analysis. In *Archaeological chemistry*, edited by C. W. Beck, pp. 81–99. Washington, D. C.: American Chemical Society.

Allen, R. O., and S. E. Pennell
   1978   Rare earth element distribution patterns to characterize soapstone artifacts. In *Archaeological chemistry* II, edited by G. F. Carter, pp. 230–257. Washington, D. C.: American Chemical Society.

Allen, R. O., A. H. Luckenbach, and C. G. Holland
   1975   The application of instrumental neutron activation analysis to a study of prehistoric steatite artifacts and source materials. *Archaeometry* 17:69–83. (See also *Science* 1975 187:57.)

Allen, R. O., K. K. Allen, C. G. Holland, and W. W. Fitzhugh
   1978   Utilisation of soapstone in Labrador by Indians, Eskimos and Norse. *Nature* 271:237–238.

Aspinall, A., and S. W. Feather
   1972   Neutron activation analysis of prehistoric flint mine products. *Archaeometry* 14:41–53.

Aspinall, A., and S. E. Warren
   1976   The provenance of British faience beads: a study using neutron activation analysis. In *Accademia Nazionale dei Lincei, applicazione dei metodi nucleari nel campo delle opere d'arte,* edited by R. Cesareo, pp. 145–152. Rome: Accademia Nazionale dei Lincei.

Aspinall, A., S. E. Warren, J. G. Crummett, and R. G. Newton
   1972   Neutron activation analysis of faience beads. *Archaeometry* 14:27–40.

Attas, M., L. Yaffe, and J. M. Fossey
   1977   Neutron activation analysis of early Bronze Age pottery from Lake Vouliagmeni, Perakhora, central Greece. *Archaeometry* 19:33–43.

Bakas, Th., N.-H. Gangas, I. Sigalas, and M. J. Aitken
   1980   Mossbauer study of Glozel tablet 19861. *Archaeometry* 22:9–80.

Banks, M., and E. T. Hall
   1963   X-Ray fluorescent analysis in archaeology: the milliprobe. *Archaeometry* 6:31–36.

Barrandon, J. N., J. P. Callu, and C. Brenot
   1977   The analysis of Constantinian coins (A.D. 313–340) by nondestructive Californium 252 activation analysis. *Archaeometry* 19:173–186.

Beck, C. W., A. B. Adams, G. C. Southard, and C. Fellows
   1971   Determination of the origin of Greek amber artifacts by computer classification of infrared spectra. In *Science and archaeology,* edited by R. H. Brill, pp. 235–240. Cambridge: MIT Press.

Beck, C. W., J. Greenlie, M. P. Diamond, A. M. Macchiarulo, A. A. Hannenberg, and M. S. Hauck
   1978   The chemical identification of Baltic amber at the Celtic oppidum Stare Hradisko in Moravia. *Journal of Archaeological Science* 5:343–354.

Berlin, H.
   1956   Late pottery horizons of Tabasco, Mexico. *Carnegie Institute of Washington, Publication* 606, *Contributions* 59.

Bernal, I.
   1969   *The Olmec world.* Berkeley and Los Angeles: University of California Press.

Berthoud, T.
   1979   Étude par l'analyse de traces et la modelisation de la filiation entre minerai de cuivre et objets archeologiques du moyen-orient. Unpublished dissertation, Université Pierre et Marie Curie, Docteur es Science Physiques, Paris.

Berthoud, T., R. Besenval, F. Cesbron, S. Cleuziou, M. Pechoux, J. Francaix, and J. Liszak-hours
   1979   The early Iranian metallurgy analytical study of copper ores from Iran. *Archaeophysika* 10:68–74.

Bieber, Jr., A. M., D. W. Brooks, G. Harbottle, and E. V. Sayre
   1976   Application of multivariate techniques to analytical data on Aegean ceramics. *Archaeometry* 18:59–74.

Bird, J. R., L. H. Russell, M. D. Scott, and W. R. Ambrose
    1978   Obsidian characterization with elemental analysis by proton induced γ-ray emission. *Analytical Chemistry* **50**:2082–2084.
Birgul, O., M. Diksic, and L. Yaffe
    1977   Activation analysis of Turkish and Canadian clays and Turkish pottery. *Radioanalytical Chemistry* **39**:45–62.
    1979   X-Ray fluorescence analysis of Turkish clays and pottery. *Archaeometry* **21**:203–218.
Bishop, R. L.
    1975   Western lowland Maya ceramic trade: an archaeological application of nuclear chemistry and geological data analysis. Unpublished Ph.D. dissertation, Department of Anthropology, Southern Illinois University, Carbondale.
Bishop, R. L., R. L. Rands and G. R. Holley
    n.d.*a*   Ceramic compositional analysis in archaeological perspective. In *Advances in archaeological theory and method* 5, edited by M. B. Schiffer, pp. 275–330. New York: Academic Press.
Bishop, R. L., G. Harbottle, R. L. Rands, J. A. Sabloff, and E. V. Sayre
    n.d.*b*   Analyses of fine paste ceramics. In *Excavations at Seibal,* edited by J. A. Sabloff. Cambridge: Harvard University Press (forthcoming).
Bishop, R. L., G. Harbottle, E. V. Sayre, and L. van Zelst
    n.d.*c*   A paste compositional investigation of Classic Maya polychrome art. In *Quarto Mesa Redonda de Palenque,* edited by B. E. Benson. Austin: University of Texas Press (forthcoming).
Bishop, R. L., M. P. Beaudry, R. M. Leventhal and R. J. Sharer
    n.d.*d*   Compositional analysis of Classic period painted ceramics in the southeast Maya area. *Yax Kin* Tegucigalpa, Honduras: Instituto Hondureño de Antropologia, e Historia (forthcoming).
Bowman, H. R., F. Asaro, and I. Perlman
    1973   Composition variations in obsidian sources and the archaeological implications. *Archaeometry* **15**:123–127.
Bowman, R., A. M. Friedman, J. Lerner, and J. Milsted
    1975   A statistical study of the impurity occurrences in copper ores and their relationship to ore types. *Archaeometry* **17**:157–163.
Boyko, W. J., P. N. Keliher, and J. M. Malloy
    1980   Emission spectrometry. *Analytical Chemistry* **52**:53R–69R.
Braidwood, R. J., J. E. Burke, and N. Nachtrieb
    1951   Ancient Syrian coppers and bronzes. *Journal of Chemical Education* **28**:87–97.
Brand, D. D.
    1938   Aboriginal trade routes for sea shells. In *The classic Southwest,* edited by B. Hedrick, J. C. Kelley, and C. Riley, pp. 92–101. Carbondale: Southern Illinois University Press.
Branstetter, B.
    1979   Ceramics of Cerro Portesuelo, Mexico: an industry in transition. Unpublished Ph.D. dissertation, Department of Anthropology, University of California, Los Angeles.
Brill, R. H.
    1969   Lead isotopes in ancient glass. In *Annales du 4ᵉ Congrès des Journées Internationales du Verre* 255–261.
    1970   Lead and oxygen isotopes in ancient objects. *Philosophical Transactions of the Royal Society, London* **A269**: 143–164.
Brill, R. H., and J. M. Wampler
    1967   Isotope studies in ancient objects. *American Journal of Archaeology* **71**:63–77.
Brill, R. H., W. R. Shields, and J. M. Wampler
    1973   New directions in lead isotope research. In *Application of science in examination of works of art,* edited by W. J. Young, pp. 73–83. Boston: Boston Museum of Fine arts.

Caley, E. R.
   1949   Klaproth as a pioneer in the chemical investigation of antiquities. *Journal of Chemical Education* **26**:242–247.
   1951   Early history and literature of archaeological chemistry. *Journal of Chemical Education* **28**:64–68.
   1962   *Analysis of ancient glasses 1790–1957.* Corning: The Corning Museum of Glass.
   1964   *Analysis of ancient metals.* Oxford: Pergamon Press.
   1967   The early history of chemistry in the service of archaeology. *Journal of Chemical Education* **44**:120–123.
Cann, J. R., J. E. Dixon, and C. Renfrew
   1968   Obsidian and the origins of trade. *Scientific American* **218**:38–46.
   1969   Obsidian analysis and the obsidian trade. In *Science in archaeology,* edited by D. Brothwell and E. Higgs, pp. 578–591. London: Thames and Hudson.
Carlson, J.
   1975   Lodestone compass: Chinese or Olmec primacy? *Science* **189**:753–760.
Carlson, J. H.
   1977   X-ray fluorescence analysis of pewter: English and Scottish measures. *Archaeometry* **19**:147–155.
Carriveau, G.
   1981   Private communication.
Carter, G. F.
   1978   Chemical composition of copper-based Roman coins. Augustan Quadrantes, ca. 9–4 B.C. In *Archaeological chemistry* II, edited by G. F. Carter, pp. 347–377. Washington, D.C.: American Chemical Society.
Catling, H. W., and R. E. Jones
   1977   A reinvestigation of the provenance of the inscribed stirrup jars found at Thebes. *Archaeometry* **19**:137–146.
Charlton, T. H., D. C. Grove, and P. K. Hopke
   1978   The Paredon, Mexico, obsidian source and Early Formative exchange. *Science* **201**:807–809.
Chase, W. T., and T. O. Ziebold
   1978   Ternary representations of ancient Chinese bronze compositions. In *Archaeological chemistry* II, edited by G. F. Carter, pp. 293–334. Washington, D.C.: American Chemical Society.
Christie, D. H. J., J. A. Brenna, and E. Straume
   1979   Multivariate classification of Roman glasses found in Norway. *Archaeometry* **21**:233–241.
Clarke, D. L.
   1968   *Analytical archaeology,* London: Methuen.
Cobean, R. H., M. D. Coe, E. A. Perry, Jr., K. K. Turekian, and D. P. Kharkar
   1971   Obsidian trade at San Lorenzo Tenochtitlan, Mexico. *Science* **174**:666–671.
Coe, M. D., and R. A. Diehl
   1980   *In the land of the Olmec.* Austin: University of Texas Press.
Coleman, M., and S. Walker
   1979   Stable isotope identification of Greek and Turkish marbles. *Archaeometry* **21**:107–112.
Conforto, L., M. Felici, D. Monna, L. Serva, and A. Taddeucci
   1975   A preliminary evaluation of chemical data (trace element) from classical marble quarries in the Mediterranean. *Archaeometry* **17**:201–213.
Coote, G. E., N. E. Whitehead, and G. J. McCallum
   1972   Rapid method of obsidian characterization by inelastic scattering of protons. *Journal of Radioanalytical Chemistry* **12**:491–496.

Craig, H., and V. Craig
1972   Greek marbles: determination of provenance by isotopic analysis. *Science* 176:401–403.
Damour, M. A.
1865   Sur la composition des haches en pierre trouvées dans les monuments celtiques et chez les tribus sauvages. *Comptes Rendus* 61:313–321, 357–368.
1866   Sur la composition des haches en pierre trouvées dans les monuments celtiques et chez les tribus sauvages. *Comptes Rendus* 63:1038–1050.
Das, H. A.
1969   Examination of amber samples by nondestructive activation analysis. *Radiochemical Radioanalytical Letters* 1:289–294.
Davison, C. C.
1972   Glass beads in African archaeology: results of neutron activation analysis, supplemented by results of X-ray fluorescence analysis. Unpublished Ph.D. dissertation, Department of Anthropology, University of California. (September 1972 published as Lawrence Berkeley Laboratory Report No. 1240 [Microfiche] 371 pp.)
Davy, H.
1815   On the colours used in painting by the ancients. *Philosophical Transactions of the Royal Society London* 105:97.
de Atley, S., M. J. Blackman, and J. Olin
n.d.   Comparison of neutron activation and electron microprobe analyses of ceramics. In *Archaeological ceramics*, edited by A. D. Franklin and J. Olin. Washington, D.C.: Smithsonian Institution Press (forthcoming).
DeBruin, M., P. J. M. Korthoven, C. C. Bakels, and F. C. A. Groen
1972   The use of non-destructive activation analysis and pattern recognition in the study of flint artifacts. *Archaeometry* 14:55–63.
DeSoete, D., R. Gijbels, and J. Hoste
1972   *Neutron activation analysis.* New York: Wiley.
Diamond, H.
1867   Accounts of wells or pits, containing Roman remains, discovered at Ewell in Surrey. *Archaeologia* 32:451.
Duerden, P., D. D. Cohen, E. Clayton, J. R. Bird, W. R. Ambrose, and B. F. Leach
1979   Elemental analysis of thick obsidian samples by proton induced X-ray emission spectrometry. *Analytical Chemistry* 51:2350–2354.
Everitt, B.
1977   *Cluster analysis.* London: Heinemann Educational Books.
Fields, P. R., J. Milsted, E. Henrickson, and R. Ramette
1971   Trace impurity patterns in copper ores and artifacts. In *Science and archaeology*, edited by R. H. Brill, pp. 131–143. Cambridge: MIT Press.
Fillieres, D.
1978   Contribution à l'étude de la production et de l'exportation des amphores dites Marseillaises. Unpublished dissertation, University of Paris I, Panthéon-Sorbonne, Doctorat 3e cycle, Paris.
n.d.   Private communication.
Floyd, M. A., V. A. Fassel, R. K. Winge, J. M. Katzenberger, and A. P. D'Silva
1980   Inductively couple plasma-atomic emission spectroscopy: a computer controlled scanning monochrometer system for the rapid determination of the elements. *Analytical Chemistry* 52:431–438.
Fontes, P., M. Attas, H. Vertet, F. Widemann, K. Gruel, F. Laubenheimer, J. Leblanc, and J. Lleres
1979   Analytical study of three Gallo–Roman white figurine workshops. *Archaeophysika* 10:101–112.

Friedman, A., E. Olsen, and J. B. Bird
  1972   Moche copper analyses: early New World metal technology. *American Antiquity* 37:254–258.
Friedman, A. M., M. Conway, M. Kastner, J. Milsted, D. Metta, P. R. Fields, and E. Olsen
  1966   Copper objects: relation to the source of the copper ore. *Science* 152:1504–1506.
Gale, N. H.
  1979   Lead isotopes and archaic Greek silver coins. *Archaeophysika* 10:194–208.
  1981   Mediterranean obsidian source characterization by strontium isotope analysis. *Archaeometry* 23:41–51.
Germann, K., G. Holzmann, and F. J. Winkler
  1980   Determination of marble provenance: limits of isotopic analysis. *Archaeometry* 22:99–106.
Giauque, R. D., F. S. Goulding, J. M. Jaklevic, and R. H. Pehl
  1973   Trace element determination with semiconductor detector, X-ray spectrometers. *Analytical Chemistry* 45:671–681.
Goad, S. I., and J. Noakes
  1978   Prehistoric copper artifacts in the eastern United States. In *Archaeological chemistry* II, edited by G. F. Carter, pp. 335–346. Washington, D.C.: American Chemical Society.
Gordus, A. A.
  1971   Rapid nondestructive activation analysis of silver in coins. In *Science and archaeology,* edited by R. H. Brill, pp. 145–155. Cambridge: MIT Press.
Gordus, A. A., J. B. Griffin, and G. A. Wright
  1971   Activation analysis identification of the geologic origins of prehistoric obsidian artifacts. In *Science and archaeology,* edited by R. H. Brill, pp. 222–234. Cambridge: MIT Press.
Goucher, C. L., J. H. Teilhat, K. R. Wilson, and T. J. Chow
  1978   Lead isotope analyses and possible metal sources for Nigerian "bronzes." In *Archaeological Chemistry* II, edited by G. F. Carter, pp. 278–292. Washington, D.C.: American Chemical Society.
Hall, E. T.
  1961   Surface enrichment of buried metals. *Archaeometry* 4:62–66.
Hammond, N., A. Aspinall, S. Feather, J. Hazelden, T. Gazard, and S. Agrell
  1977   Maya jade: source location and analysis. In *Exchange systems in prehistory,* edited by T. K. Earle and J. E. Ericson, pp. 35–67. New York: Academic Press.
Hansen, B. A., M. A. Sorenson, K. Heydorn, V. Mejdahl, and K. Conradsen
  1979   Provenance study of medieval, decorated floor-tiles carried out by means of neutron activation analysis. *Archaeophysika* 10:119–140.
Harbottle, G.
  1976   Activation analysis in archaeology. In *Radiochemistry* 3, edited by G. W. A. Newton, pp. 33–72. London: The Chemical Society.
  n.d.   Provenance studies using neutron activation analysis: the role of standardization. In *Archaeological ceramics,* edited by A. D. Franklin and J. Olin. Washington, D.C.: Smithsonian Institution Press (forthcoming).
Harper, P. O., and P. Meyers
  1981   *Silver vessels of the Sasanian period. Vol. I. Royal imagery* New York: The Metropolitan Museum of Art.
Hassan, A. A., and F. A. Hassan
  1981   Source of galena in predynastic Egypt at Nagada. *Archaeometry* 23:77–82.
Hatcher, H., R. E. M. Hedges, A. M. Pollard, and P. M. Kenrick
  1980   Analysis of Hellenistic and Roman fine pottery from Benghazi. *Archaeometry* 22:133–151.

Hedges, R. E. M.
  1979 Analysis of the "Drake Plate": comparison with the composition of Elizabethan brass. *Archaeometry* **21**:21–26.
Hedges, R. E. M., and C. J. Salter
  1979 Source determination of iron currency bars through analysis of the slag inclusions. *Archaeometry* **21**:161–175.
Heizer, R. F., F. Stross, T. R. Hester, A. Albee, I. Perlman, F. Asaro, and H. Bowman
  1973 The Colossi of Memnon revisited. *Science* **182**:1219–1225.
Henderson, J., and S. E. Warren
  1981 X-ray fluorescence analyses of Iron Age glass: beads from Meare and Glastonbury Lake villages. *Archaeometry* **23**:83–94.
Herz, N., and D. B. Wenner
  1978 Assembly of Greek marble inscriptions by isotopic methods. *Science* **199**:1070–1072.
Higashimura, T., and T. Warashina
  1975 Sourcing of Sanukite stone implements by X-ray fluorescence analysis. *Journal of Archaeological Science* **2**:169–178.
Hughes, M. J., M. R. Cowell, and P. T. Craddock
  1976 Atomic absorption techniques in archaeology. *Archaeometry* **18**:19–37.
Huntley, D. J., and D. C. Bailey
  1978 Obsidian source identification by thermoluminescence. *Archaeometry* **20**:159–170.
Jones, R. E., and J. B. Rutter
  1977 Resident Minoan potters on the Greek mainland? Pottery composition analyses from Ayois Stephanos. *Archaeometry* **19**:211–219.
Kaplan, M. F.
  1978 The origin and distribution of Tell el Yahudiyeh ware. Unpublished Ph.D. dissertation, Department of Anthropology, Brandeis University.
  1979 Ancient materials data as a basis for waste form integrity projections. Report TR–1749–1 prepared for U.S. Department of Energy, Division of Nuclear Waste Management by The Analytical Science Corporation, Reading, Mass., 20 December 1979.
Kaplan, M. F., G. Harbottle, and E. V. Sayre
  n.d.*a* Multidisciplinary analysis of Tell el Yahudiyeh ware. *Archaeometry* (in press).
  n.d.*b* Tell el Yahudiyeh ware: a re-evaluation. BNL Report No. 29258. Upton, New York: Brookhaven National Laboratory.
Knab, H.-J., and H. Hintenberger
  1980 Simultaneous determination of 20 trace elements in geologic samples by the isotope dilution method combined with spark source mass spectrography. *Analytical Chemistry* **52**:390–394.
Kohl, P. L.
  1974 Seeds of upheaval: the production of chlorite at Tepe Yahya and an analysis of commodity production and trade in southwestern Asia in the mid-third millennium. Unpublished Ph.D. dissertation, Department of Anthropology, Harvard University, Cambridge, Massachusetts.
Kohl, P. L., G. Harbottle, and E. V. Sayre
  1979 Physical and chemical analyses of softstone vessels from Southwest Asia. *Archaeometry* **21**:131–159.
Krywonos, W., G. W. A. Newton, V. J. Robinson, and J. A. Riley
  1980 Neutron activation analysis of Roman coarse ware from Cyrenaica. *Archaeometry* **22**:189–196.
Lahanier, C., and M. Rouvier-Jeanlin
  1977 Analyse de 120 figurines gallo–romaines en terre cuite blanche. *PACT* **1**:110–130.

Lambert, J. B., C. D. McLaughlin, and A. Leonard, Jr.
  1978   X-ray photoelectron spectroscopic analysis of the Mycenaean pottery from Megiddo. *Archaeometry* 20:107–122.
Lange, F. W., R. L. Bishop, and L. van Zelst
  n.d.   Perspectives on Costa Rican jade: compositional analyses and cultural implications. In *Between continents/between seas/art in ancient Costa Rica,* edited by E. P. Benson. Detroit: Detroit Institute of Art (forthcoming).
Lazzarini, L., S. Calogero, N. Burriesci, and M. Petrera
  1980a   Chemical, mineralogical and Mossbauer studies of Venetian and Paduan Renaissance Sgraffito ceramics. *Archaeometry* 22:57–68.
Lazzarini, L., G. Moschini, and B. M. Stievano
  1980b   A contribution to the identification of Italian, Greek and Anatolian marbles through a petrological study and the evaluation of Ca/Sr ratios. *Archaeometry* 22:173–183.
Levy, P. W.
  1979   Thermoluminescence studies having applications to geology and archaeometry. *PACT* 3:466.
Longworth G., and S. E. Warren
  1979   The application of Mossbauer spectroscopy to the characterization of western Mediterranean obsidian. *Journal of Archaeological Science* 6:179–193.
Luedtke, B. E.
  1978   Chert sources and trace element analysis. *American Antiquity* 43:413–423.
  1979   The identification of sources of chert artifacts. *American Antiquity* 44:744–757.
Macdonald, G. L.
  1980   X-ray spectrometry. *Analytical Chemistry* 52:100R–106R.
MacNeish, R. S. (ed.)
  1970   Preface, *Ceramics,* by R. S. MacNeish, F. A. Peterson, and K. V. Flannery, Vol. 3. In *The prehistory of the Tehuacan Valley.* Austin: University of Texas Press.
Manfra, L., U. Masi, and B. Turi
  1975   Carbon and oxygen isotope ratios of marbles from some ancient quarries of western Anatolia and their archaeological significance. *Archaeometry* 17:215–221.
Marschner, R. F., and H. T. Wright
  1978   Asphalts from Middle Eastern archaeological sites. In *Archaeological chemistry* II, edited by G. F. Carter, pp. 150–171. Washington, D.C.: American Chemical Society.
McKerrell, H.
  1976   Prehistoric trade in blue glazed faience. In *Accademia Nazionale dei Lincei, applicazione dei metodi nucleari nel campo delle opere d'arte,* edited by R. Cesaro, pp. 297–316. Rome: Accademia Nazionale dei Lincei.
Meyers, P.
  1968   Some applications of non-destructive activation analysis. Unpublished Ph.D. dissertation, Department of Chemistry, University of Amsterdam.
  1969   Non-destructive activation analysis of ancient coins using charged particles and fast neutrons. *Archaeometry* 11:67–83.
Meyers, P., and L. van Zelst
  1977   Neutron activation analysis of limestone objects: a pilot study. *Radiochimica Acta* 24:197–204.
Meyers, P., L. van Zelst, and E. V. Sayre
  1974   Major and trace elements in Sasanian silver. In *Archaeological chemistry,* edited by Curt W. Beck, pp. 22–23. Washington, D.C.: American Chemical Society.
Michel, H. V., and F. Asaro
  1979   Chemical study of the Plate of Brass. *Archaeometry* 21:3–19.

Miller, K. S.
  n.d.   Chemical characterization of archaeological shell: initial experiments. Senior honors thesis dated March 2, 1980, Department of Anthropology, Harvard University, Cambridge, Massachusetts.

Millon, R.
  1973   *Urbanization at Teotihuacan, Mexico,* Vol. 1, edited by R. Millon. Austin: University of Texas Press.

Muller, O., and W. Gentner
  1979   On the composition and silver sources of Aeginetan coins from the Asyut hoard. *Archaeophysika* **10**:176–193.

Neivens, M., G. Harbottle, and J. Kimberlin
  n.d.   Some geochemical characteristics of the Pachuca obsidian region: a strategy for interpreting artifact groups. In *Proceedings simposio la obsidiana en Mesoamerica,* edited by R. Abascal. Pachuca, Mexico: INAH (forthcoming).

Nelson, D. E., J. M. D'Auria, and R. B. Bennett
  1975   Characterization of Pacific Northwest obsidian by X-ray fluorescence analysis. *Archaeometry* **17**:85–97.

Nelson, F. W., K. K. Nielsen, N. F. Mangelson, M. W. Hill, and R. T. Matheny
  1977   Preliminary studies of the trace element composition of obsidian artifacts from northern Campeche, Mexico. *American Antiquity* **42**:209–225.

Nelson, F. W., R. V. Sidrys, and R. D. Holmes
  1978   Trace element analysis by X-ray fluorescence of obsidian artifacts from Guatemala and Belize. In *Excavations at Seibal,* edited by G. R. Willey, pp. 153–161. Cambridge: Harvard University Press.

Newton, R. G., and C. Renfrew
  1970   British faience beads reconsidered. *Antiquity* **44**:199–206.

Nie, N. H., C. H. Hull, J. G. Jenkins, K. Steinbrenner, and D. H. Bent
  1975   *SPSS statistical package for the social sciences.* New York: McGraw-Hill.

Northover, J. P.
  1979   The application of metallurgical studies to Late Bronze Age material. *Archaeophysika* **10**:244–247.

Olin, J. S., and E. V. Sayre
  1974   Neutron activation analytical survey of some intact medieval glass panels and related specimens. In *Archaeological chemistry.* edited by C. W. Beck, pp. 100–123. Washington, D.C.: American Chemical Society.

Olin, J. S., M. E. Salmon and E. V. Sayre
  1976   Neutron activation and electron beam microprobe study of a XIV century Austrian stained glass panel. In *Accademia Nazionale die Lincei, applicazione dei metodi nucleairi nel campo delle opere d'arte,* edited by R. Cesareo, pp. 99–110. Rome: Accademia, Nazionale dei Lincei.

Olivier, D. C.
  n.d.   *AGCLUS, an aggregative, hierarchical clustering program.* Department of Psychology and Social Relations, Harvard University.

Ottaway, B. S.
  1974   Cluster analysis of impurity patterns in Armorico—British daggers. *Archaeometry* **16**:221–231.

Ottaway, B. S.
  1979   Interpretation of prehistoric metal artifacts with the aid of cluster analysis. *Archaeophysika* **10**:597–606.

Patterson, C. C.
  1971 Native copper, silver and gold accessible to early metallurgists. *American Antiquity* 36:286–321.

Petrie, W. M. F.
  1920 *Prehistoric Egypt.* London: University College.

Pires-Ferreira, J. W.
  1976a Obsidian exchange in Formative Mesoamerica. In *The early Mesoamerican village,* edited by K. V. Flannery, pp. 292–306. New York: Academic Press.
  1976b Shell and iron-ore mirror exchange in Formative Mesoamerica, with comments on other commodities. In *The early Mesoamerican village,* edited by K. V. Flannery, pp. 311–328. New York: Academic Press.

Pogue, J. E.
  1915 Turquois. *Memoirs of the National Academy of Sciences* 12(2). (Reprinted by Rio Grande Press, Glorieta, N. M. in 1975.)

Prag, A. J. N. W., F. Schweizer, J. Ll, W. Williams, and P. A. Schubiger
  1974 Hellenistic glazed wares from Athens and southern Italy: analytical techniques and implications. *Archaeometry* 16:153–187.

Price, W. J.
  1972 *Analytical atomic absorption spectroscopy.* London: Heyden.

Rands, R. L., and R. Bishop
  1980 Resource procurement zones and patterns of ceramic exchange in the Palenque region, Mexico. In *Models and methods in regional exchange,* edited by R. E. Fry, pp. 19–46. Washington, D.C.: Society for American Archaeology.

Rands, R. L., R. L. Bishop, and G. Harbottle
  1979 Thematic and compositional variation in Palenque region incensarios. In *Tercera Mesa Redonda de Palenque,* edited by M. R. Robertson, pp. 19–30. Austin: University of Texas Press.

Rands, R. L., P. H. Benson, P.-Y. Chen, G. Harbottle, B. C. Rands, and E. V. Sayre
  1975 Western Maya fine paste pottery: chemical and petrographic correlations. In *Actas del XLI Congreso Internacional de Americanistas* 1:534–541.

Reimers, P., G. J. Lutz, and C. Segebade
  1977 The non-destructive determination of gold, silver and copper by photon activation analysis of coins and art objects. *Archaeometry,* 19:167–172.

Renfrew, C., and J. S. Peacy
  1968 Aegean marbles: a petrological study. *Journal of the British School of Archaeology at Athens,* 63:45.

Renfrew, C., J. E. Dixon, and J. R. Cann
  1966 Obsidian and early culture contact in the Near East. *Proceedings of the Prehistoric Society* 32:30–72.
  1968 Further analysis of Near Eastern obsidians. *Proceedings of the Prehistoric Society* 34:319–331.

Richards, T. W.
  1895 The composition of Athenian pottery. *Journal of the American Chemical Society* 17:152–154.

Rohlf, F. J.
  1970 Adaptive hierarchical clustering schemes. *Systematic Zoology* 19:58–82.

Rybach, L., and H. U. Nissen
  1964 Neutron activation of Mn and Na traces in marbles worked by the ancient Greeks. In *Proceedings of radiochemical methods of analysis,* edited by C. N. Welsh, pp. 105–117. Vienna: International Atomic Energy Agency.

Sayre, E. V.
   n.d.   Brookhaven procedures for statistical analysis of multivariate archaeometric data. In *Proceedings of the conference on the application of physical sciences to medieval ceramics,* edited by J. D. Frierman and F. Asaro. Berkeley: Lawrence Berkeley Laboratory (forthcoming).
Sayre, E. V., and R. W. Smith
   1961   Compositional categories of ancient glass. *Science* 133:1824–1826.
Sayre, E. V., and G. Harbottle
   n.d.   The analysis by neutron activation of archaeological ceramics related to Teotihuacan: local wares and trade sherds. In *Urbanization at Teotihuacan,* Vol. 4, edited by R. Millon. Austin: University of Texas Press (forthcoming).
Sayre, E. V., L.-H. Chan, and J. A. Sabloff
   1971   High-resolution gamma ray spectroscopic analyses of Mayan Fine Orange pottery. In *Science and archaeology,* edited by R. H. Brill, pp. 165–181. Cambridge: MIT Press.
Schneider, G., B. Hoffmann, and E. Wirz
   1979   Significance and dependability of reference groups for chemical determinations of provenance of ceramic artifacts. *Archaeophysika* 10:269–283.
Schwabe, R., and K. Slusallek
   1981   Applications of the cluster analysis on element concentrations of archaeological bronzes, ceramics and glass. *Revue d'Archeometrie* 5:109–117.
Shepard, A. O.
   1957   Ceramics for the archaeologist. *Carnegie Institute of Washington, Publication* 609.
   1968   Preliminary notes on the paste composition of Monte Alban pottery. In *La cerámica de Monte Albán,* by A. Caso, I. Bernal, and J. R. Acosta, pp. 477–484. Mexico: INAH.
Shotton, F. W., and G. L. Hendry
   1979   The developing field of petrology in archaeology. *Journal of Archaeological Science* 6:75–84.
Sidrys, R.
   1977   Mass-distance measures for the Maya obsidian trade. In *Exchange systems in prehistory,* edited by T. K. Earle and J. E. Ericson, pp. 91–108. New York: Academic Press.
Sieveking, G. de G., P. Bush, F. Ferguson, P. R. Craddock, M. J. Hughes, and M. R. Crowell
   1972   Prehistoric flint mines and their identification as sources of raw material. *Archaeometry* 14:151–176.
Sigleo, A. C.
   1975   Turquoise mine and artifact correlation for Snaketown site, Arizona. *Science* 189:459–460.
Sneath, P. H. A., and R. R. Sokal
   1973   *Numerical taxonomy.* San Francisco: W. H. Freeman
Soloman, H.
   1971   Cluster analysis. In *Mathematics in the archaeological and historical sciences,* edited by F. R. Hodson, D. G. Kendall, and P. Tautu, pp. 62–81. Edinburgh: University Press.
Stark, B. L.
   1977   Prehistoric ecology at Patarata 52, Veracruz, Mexico: adaptation to the mangrove swamp. *Vanderbilt University Publications in Anthropology,* **18.**
Stark, B. L., and G. Harbottle
   n.d.   Analytical study of the ceramics from Patarata, Veracruz. Unpublished research.
Stern, W. B., and J.-P. Descoeudres
   1977   X-ray fluorescence analysis of archaic Greek pottery. *Archaeometry* 19:73–86.
Stevenson, D. P., F. H. Stross, and R. F. Heizer
   1971   An evolution of X-ray fluorescence analysis as a method for correlating obsidian artifacts with source location. *Archaeometry* 13:17–25.

Stone, J. F. S., and L. C. Thomas
  1956   The use and distribution of faience in the ancient East and prehistoric Europe. *Proceedings of the Prehistoric Society* 22:37–84.
Stos-Fertner, Z., and Gale, N. H.
  1979   Chemical and lead isotope analysis of ancient Egyptian gold, silver and lead. *Archaeophysika* 10:299–314.
Stross, F. H., D. P. Stevenson, J. R. Weaver, and G. Wyld
  1971   Analysis of American obsidians by X-ray fluorescence and neutron activation analysis. In *Science and archaeology,* edited by R. H. Brill, pp. 210–221. Cambridge: MIT Press.
    Tobia, S. K., and E. V. Sayre
  1974   An analytical comparison of various Egyptian soils, clays, shales and some ancient pottery by neutron activation. In *Recent advances in science and technology of materials* 3, edited by A. Bishay, pp. 47–70. New York: Plenum Press.
Tominaga, T., M. Takeda, H. Mabuchi, and Y. Emoto
  1978   Characterization of ancient Japanese roofing tiles by ^{57}Fe Mossbauer spectroscopy. *Archaeometry* 20:135–146.
Van Loon, J. C.
  1980   Direct trace elemental analysis of solids by atomic (absorption, fluorescence, and emission) spectroscopy. *Analytical Chemistry* 52:955A–963A.
Veakis, E.
  1979   Archaeometric study of native copper in prehistoric North America. Unpublished Ph.D. dissertation, Department of Anthropology, State University of New York at Stony Brook.
Velde, B., and C. Gendron
  1980   Chemical composition of some Gallo–Roman glass fragments from central western France. *Archaeometry* 22:183–187.
Walthall, J. A., S. H. Stow, and M. J. Karson
  1980   Copena galena: source identification and analysis. *American Antiquity* 45:21–42.
Warashina, T., Y. Kamaki, and T. Higashimura
  1978   Sourcing of sanukite implements by X-ray fluorescence analysis II. *Journal of Archaeological Science* 5:283–291.
Ward, G. K.
  1974   A systematic approach to the definition of sources of raw material. *Archaeometry* 16:41–53.
Warren, S. E.
  1979   Analytical problems in the sourcing of English medieval alabasters. *Archaeophysika* 10:316.
Weigand, P. C., G. Harbottle, and E. V. Sayre
  1977   Turquoise sources and source analysis. In *Exchange systems in prehistory,* edited by T. K. Earle and J. E. Ericson, pp. 15–34. New York: Academic Press.
Wessen, G., F. H. Ruddy, C. E. Gustafson, and H. Irwin
  1978   Trace element analysis in the characterization of archaeological bone. In *Archaeological chemistry* II, edited by G. F. Carter, pp. 99–116. Washington, D.C.: American Chemical Society.
Weymouth, J. W.
  1973   X-ray diffraction analysis of prehistoric pottery. *American Antiquity* 38:339–344.
Widemann, F., M. Picon, F. Asaro, H. V. Michel, and I. Perlman
  1975   A Lyon branch of the pottery-making firm of Ateius of Arezzo. *Archaeometry* 17:45–59.
Widemann, F., F. Laubenheimer, M. Attas, P. Fontes, K. Gruel, J. Leblanc, and J. Lleres
  1979   Analytical and typological study of Gallo–Roman workshops producing amphorae in the area of Narbonne. *Archaeophysika* 10:317–341.

Wilson, A. L.
    1978   Elemental analysis of pottery in the study of its provenance: a review. *Journal of Archaeological Science* 5:219–236.
Wishart, D.
    1978   *Cluster user manual. Version 1C, release 2.* Edinburgh: University Press.
Wyttenbach, A., and P. A. Schubiger
    1973   Trace element content of Roman lead by neutron activation analysis. *Archaeometry* 15:199–207.
Yellin, J., I. Perlman, F. Asaro, H. V. Michel, and D. F. Foster
    1978   Comparison of neutron activation analysis from the Lawrence Berkeley Laboratory and the Hebrew University. *Archaeometry* 20:95–100.

Spatial Patterning and the Modeling of Exchange

3

Regional Modeling of Obsidian Procurement in the American Southwest

Frank J. Findlow and Marisa Bolognese

INTRODUCTION

Although New Mexico has a long history of archaeological research, quantitative analyses of prehistoric obsidian procurement have not been common. In large part, this is due to the overall complexity of statewide geology and the limited availability of quantified data in published accounts. Recently, however, several large research-oriented survey projects and greater interest in the cultural processes underlying the operation of prehistoric exchange systems have resulted in more quantitative studies (cf. Plog 1977; Erwin-Williams 1977; Findlow and Bolognese 1980, n.d.). This, together with increased availability of site inventories from CRM work in New Mexico, has made it possible to analyze prehistoric obsidian use across the entire state within all time periods from the terminal Archaic through the Early Historic period.

This chapter has three primary objectives: (*a*) to describe prehistoric and historic obsidian use throughout New Mexico; (*b*) to isolate mathematical representations of the procurement strategies associated with different obsidian source areas and different time periods; and (*c*) to integrate these analyses with the available body of theory on raw-material procurement and exchange. The data used were obtained from published and unpublished accounts on prehistoric and historic sites from throughout New Mexico.

NEW MEXICO OBSIDIAN SOURCES

The six major obsidian–perlite sources in New Mexico are distributed un-evenly along a rough arc extending northeast–southwest from the midpoint of the state's northern border down through the extreme southwestern corner of the state (see Figure 3.1). Each of the major sources along this arc resulted from relatively recent Tertiary and Quaternary volcanic activity. Although these sources vary considerably in their geomorphic setting, they form a rela-tively homogeneous group insofar as the culturally relevant characteristics of their available obsidian. For each source, the available volcanic glass exhibits characteristics that are ideal for the manufacture of chipped-stone tools. All of the volcanic glass has a phenocryst-free matrix and a highly developed concoi-dal fracture, and it occurs in nodules or blocks large enough for the manufac-ture of almost all chipped-stone tools used prehistorically in the Southwest. For most sources, the obsidian occurs as nodules 5–20 cm in diameter that have been water-washed and redeposited in recent alluvium or streambed gravels. In general, the color varies widely within each source, ranging from colorless to opaque black.

As a result of the megascopic similarity between New Mexico obsidians, it is likely that variation in the pattern of prehistoric exchange around each source locality was a product of cultural rather than geologic factors. The only physi-cal property that could have played a role in the prehistoric use of these obsidians was the intrasource variation in the size range of the available raw-material nodules. However—even for this factor—most of the major source areas overlap, and it is unlikely that it played a critical part in the prehistoric procurements and exchange of obsidian.

Mount San Antonio

The Mount San Antonio obsidian source is located in Rio Arriba county in the Mount San Antonio quadrangle. Several exposures of this obsidian are known both in association with Mount San Antonio and in streambed deposits around it. The obsidian from this source is associated with Quaternary flows of andesite and basaltic andesite (QTb) (Dane and Bochman 1965).

Jemez Mountains

The Jemez obsidian source consists of several dozen geologically related minor source areas, all of which are located in the Jemez Moun-tains–Polvadara Peak area of Sandoval and Rio Arriba counties. Known ex-posures occur within the Polvadara Peak, Valle Toledo, Bland, Redondo Peak, Jemez Springs, Valle San Antonio, and Seven Springs quadrangles. In addition to these source localities, others probably exist within adjacent quadrangles. Obsidian from these source areas all derive from Tertiary extrusives (Tv, Tb)

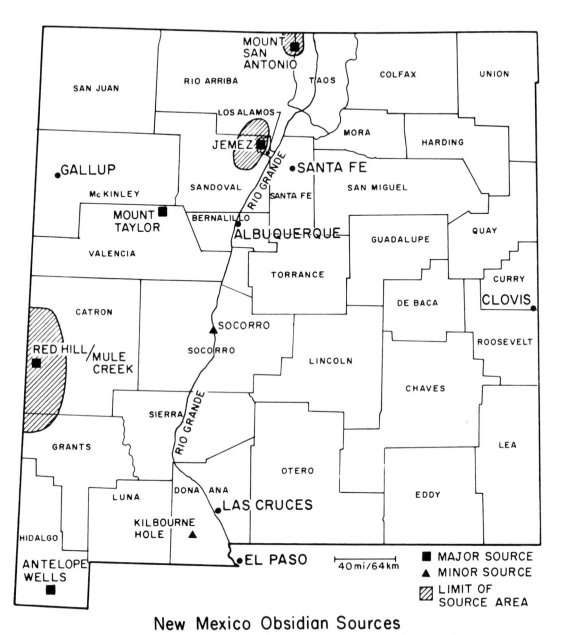

New Mexico Obsidian Sources

Figure 3.1. The location of obsidian sources within New Mexico. Hatched areas represent regions in which erosional or redeposited obsidian is available.

and Quaternary volcanics like the Bandelier Tuff (Qr). Obsidian from the various localities within the Jemez Mountains area occurs both in the form of nodules and block obsidian directly associated with *in situ* flows. As a consequence, the Jemez Mountains sources offered prehistoric populations larger pieces of obsidian than were available at other source areas. The physical appearance of Jemez obsidians varies greatly, with colors ranging from colorless through black (Dane and Bachman 1965; Findlow *et al.* 1975).

Mount Taylor

The isolated Mount Taylor obsidian source is just north of San Fidel, Valencia County, in the Mount Taylor and Cerro Pelon quadrangles. All of the obsidian from this source is derived from Tertiary extrusives (Tv). Exposures of obsidian from this source occur both on Mount Taylor itself and on several of the foothill ridges surrounding it. Mount Taylor obsidian occurs both as blowout fragments and as redeposited nodules. Mount Taylor obsidian varies in color, but it most often occurs as a black obsidian with numerous inclusions in its matrix.

Red Hill

The Red Hill source area is best known from a series of exposures near the hamlet of Red Hill in Catron County, New Mexico. In general, this obsidian occurs as nodules 5–25 cm in diameter in layers of Quaternary basalt and tuff (Qb). The Red Hill source is a true "source area" in that formations from which the obsidian derives extend over much of Catron County. Red Hill obsidian also varies in color, but occurs most often in a colorless form that resembles window glass. The totally inclusion-free matrix and the perfectly developed concoidal fracture make Red Hill obsidian among the best in the Southwest for the manufacture of chipped-stone tools. (Dane and Bachman 1965; Findlow and Bolognese n.d.).

Mule Creek

The Mule Creek source, like the Red Hill source immediately to the north, is a source area rather than a point source. Centered on Mule Creek, in the Mule Creek quadrangle, Grants County, the source extends over much of northwestern Grants County and southwestern Catron County, New Mexico, as well as adjacent Greenlee County, Arizona. The obsidian from this source derives primarily from formations of Quaternary basalts and tuffs (Qtb). Most obsidian from the Mule Creek source ranges in color from colorless through smoky gray. Frequently, this obsidian occurs as pieces with a colorless matrix and smoky-gray bands running through it.

There is some question whether or not the Red Hill and Mule Creek sources should be treated as one or two sources. Both obsidians occur over large adjacent areas and derive from closely related geologic formations; consequently, in this study both are treated as a single regional source. We feel that this allows for a much more realistic approximation of prehistoric obsidian use since prehistoric populations could not distinguish the compositional factors that separate these two otherwise similar obsidians.

Antelope Wells

The Antelope Wells obsidian source is located in portions of three Tertiary formations in southern Hidalgo County, New Mexico, and extreme northwestern Chihuahua, Mexico—the Gillespie Tuff (Tg), the Felsite formation (Tf), and the Park Tuff (Tp) (Alper 1957; De Atley and Findlow 1979; Findlow and Bolognese n.d.). Unlike the Red Hill or Mule Creek sources, the Antelope Wells source is a point source, with exposures confined primarily to the Deer Creek drainage in the Antelope Wells quadrangle and the Clanton Draw drainage in the Peloncillo Mountains (Animas Peak quadrangle). Obsidian from this source occurs exclusively as small nodules, 5–15 cm in diameter. Color varies from greenish black through greenish brown. Except for size constraints, this material is a perfect medium for use in the manufacture of chipped-stone tools (Dane and Bachman 1965; De Atley and Findlow 1979).

Minor Source Areas

In addition to the six major source areas, obsidian occurs at three other places in and around New Mexico: within Rio Grande gravels near Socorro, at Kilbourne Hole in Otero County (Noria quadrangle), and just over the Texas boundary near El Paso. For various reasons, none of these sources were of economic importance prehistorically. In the case of the Rio Grande gravels, the deposits consist primarily of occasional pieces of obsidian derived from all of the northern New Mexico sources. The very low density of the material in the Rio Grande gravels eliminated the possibility of major exchange in these materials. The Kilbourne Hole and El Paso obsidians both are derived from Quaternary basalt and tuff deposits (Qb). In each case, the obsidian occurs as quite small nodules, usually less than 5 cm in diameter that are generally unsuitable for the manufacture of chipped-stone tools. Consequently, while obsidian from these two sources shows up in local prehistoric assemblages, neither was involved in patterned exchange.

DATA ON THE PREHISTORIC AND HISTORIC USE OF OBSIDIAN IN NEW MEXICO

This study has two primary data requirements: accurate quantitative information on the frequency of obsidian use within a particular site's assemblage,

TABLE 3.1
Chronological Divisions. Temporal dimension for grouping the data on New Mexico obsidian use. Divisions follow the Anasazi sequence in common use throughout much of northwestern New Mexico.

Period	Date range
1. Archaic	Prior to A.D. 1
2. Basketmaker II	A.D. 1 to A.D. 500
3. Basketmaker III	A.D. 500 to A.D. 700
4. Pueblo I	A.D. 700 to A.D. 900
5. Pueblo II	A.D. 900 to A.D. 1100
6. Pueblo III	A.D. 1100 to A.D. 1300
7. Pueblo IV	A.D. 1300 to A.D. 1600
8. Historic	A.D. 1600 to A.D. 1880

and reliable dating of a site's occupation. Frequency was measured as the percentage of obsidian used within a lithic assemblage. Dating was determined by one or more absolute or relative dates, and the sites were grouped into eight temporal periods that correspond to the Anasazi Basketmaket–Pueblo sequence commonly used in the northwestern quarter of the state (see Table 3.1).

The actual data used in this chapter derive from three primary sources: published reports, unpublished CRM reports, and published and unpublished survey data collected by Findlow in southwestern New Mexico. In all, data from over 20,000 sites are included in the analyses. Of the 20,000 sites used, just over 2,000 provided positive evidence of obsidian use, with the remainder providing information on where obsidian was *not* used prehistorically. The fact that only 10% of the sites have evidence of obsidian use is not unreasonable, as more than half of the state's counties are 200 km or more from the nearest source.

To insure an even statewide coverage, an attempt was made to obtain data—either positive or negative—from each of the state's 31 counties over the eight

TABLE 3.2
Geographical Separation of Sources.[a] A matrix of the distances separating the five major obsidian sources in New Mexico.

Source	Mt. San Antonio	Jemez	Mt. Taylor	Red Hill–Mule Creek	Antelope Wells
Mt. San Antonio	0				
Jemez	175	0			
Mt. Taylor	260	140	0		
Red Hill–Mule Creek	525	350	262	0	
Antelope Wells	725	550	462	262	0

[a]All distances in kilometers.

time periods considered. Unfortunately, the lack of archaeological research in some counties, coupled with poor chronological control in many reports, made it impossible to achieve this objective completely. Usable data were obtained from only 25 of the state's counties. However, the 6 counties for which reliable data were absent were all confined to the extreme eastern portion of the state where obsidian use was low or nonexistent.

For the regression analyses, only the five major source areas were used. Because of the distances separating source areas (see Table 3.2), spatial patterning of source-specific distributions could be obtained with minimal chemi-

TABLE 3.3
New Mexico Obsidian Use by County.[a] Breakdown of New Mexico obsidian use by county and time period. County boundaries are shown in Figure 3.1. Time periods are the same as those shown in Table 3.1.

County	Archaic	BM II	BM III	P I	P II	P III	P IV	Historic
Bernalillo	0.00(5)	0.00(1)	10.66(1)	16.00(3)	12.50(4)	9.00(8)	8.00(6)	0.00(3)
Catron	0.00(104)	0.00(1)	10.00(9)	10.00(20)	11.23(154)	12.46(57)	0.00(10)	0.00(2)
Chavez	0.00(5)	0.00(1)	0.00(1)	0.00(1)	0.00(1)	0.01(2)	0.00(5)	0.00(8)
Colfax	—	—	—	—	—	—	—	—
Curry	—	—	—	—	—	—	—	—
De Baca	0.00(1)	0.00(1)	0.00(1)	0.00(1)	0.00(1)	0.00(1)	0.00(1)	0.00(1)
Dona Ana	0.41(3)	0.23(5)	0.23(5)	0.23(1)	0.67(1)	1.49(1)	0.00(17)	0.00(17)
Eddy	0.00(11)	1.60(1)	1.60(1)	1.60(1)	1.30(14)	1.00(14)	0.14(79)	0.00(1)
Grants	0.00(1)	0.00(1)	0.00(1)	0.17(3)	0.12(1)	0.13(14)	0.00(145)	0.00(1)
Guadalupe	0.26(3)	0.03(3)	0.03(3)	0.44(1)	0.44(1)	0.44(1)	0.44(1)	0.00(1)
Harding	—	—	—	—	—	—	—	—
Hidalgo	3.76(3)	3.45(83)	3.45(86)	3.15(86)	3.18(18)	7.99(18)	7.91(18)	0.00(2)
Lea	0.00(1)	0.00(1)	0.00(1)	0.00(1)	0.00(7)	0.00(7)	0.03(7)	0.06(1)
Lincoln	0.00(5)	0.00(1)	0.00(1)	0.00(4)	0.00(4)	0.00(4)	0.00(2)	0.00(1)
Luna	0.00(3)	0.00(1)	0.00(1)	0.00(1)	0.00(51)	0.00(51)	0.00(51)	—
McKinley	0.00(26)	5.55(15)	3.70(50)	1.23(140)	0.66(704)	1.69(298)	0.00(7)	0.00(92)
Mora	—	—	—	—	—	—	—	—
Otero	0.02(15)	0.01(2)	0.01(2)	0.01(1)	0.01(1)	0.46(2)	0.00(3)	0.00(48)
Quay	0.01(1)	0.00(1)	0.00(1)	0.00(1)	0.00(1)	0.00(1)	0.00(1)	0.00(1)
Rio Arriba	—	6.63(25)	2.94(65)	2.65(107)	0.00(32)	0.00(30)	0.00(49)	0.00(39)
Roosevelt	—	—	—	—	—	—	—	—
Sandoval	0.56(15)	6.91(4)	6.91(1)	13.25(16)	10.60(29)	4.80(48)	5.00(52)	0.01(2)
San Juan	0.04(315)	0.00(18)	0.03(187)	1.00(289)	0.81(651)	1.14(547)	0.00(8)	0.00(21)
San Miguel	0.01(2)	2.50(4)	2.50(4)	2.50(6)	2.50(6)	5.01(4)	0.00(2)	0.00(1)
Santa Fe	—	—	—	—	9.00(13)	13.40(53)	11.10(39)	6.00(4)
Sierra	0.00(1)	0.00(1)	0.00(1)	0.00(1)	0.00(1)	0.00(2)	0.00(2)	0.00(2)
Socorro	0.00(11)	0.00(1)	0.00(8)	0.00(15)	0.00(48)	0.00(47)	0.00(24)	0.00(8)
Taos	—	—	—	—	12.65(1)	13.54(3)	18.00(1)	18.00(1)
Torrance	—	—	—	—	—	—	—	—
Union	—	—	—	—	—	0.10(1)	0.10(1)	0.10(1)
Valencia	10.13(44)	7.07(3)	7.08(15)	4.00(59)	2.18(138)	1.09(97)	0.00(13)	0.00(5)

[a]All values represent percentage of lithic assemblages, dashes represent absence of data, numbers in parentheses represent the number of sites used in the SYMAP analyses.

cal characterization. Source determination was based on a limited X-ray flourescence analysis of geological and artifactual samples (see Harbottle, Chapter 2). For each geological source area, 20 or more samples were analyzed to determine the characteristic chemical composition of the source. Then roughly .5% sample of the available obsidian artifacts from throughout the state (approximately 2000 artifacts) was similarly analyzed and assigned to source, using discriminant analysis. This study permitted us to determine the directionality and spatial limits of the distribution from each source.

It is unfeasible to illustrate the entire data base used in this study, but a summary for the 25 counties during the eight time periods is presented in Table 3.3. While these data do not illustrate local patterning within the data, they do provide an accurate representation of the general pattern of prehistoric obsidian use throughout the state.

TREND-SURFACE ANALYSIS OF NEW MEXICO OBSIDIAN

Using all available data, statewide trend-surface SYMAP (Lankford 1974; Hodder and Orton 1976) displays were produced for the time periods listed in Table 3.1. Although the maps generated do not allow either local or regional obsidian exchange systems to be described with the same precision found in the regression analysis, they do provide important information on the territorial nature and directionality of New Mexico obsidian procurement.

Archaic (5000 B.C.–A.D. 1)

Obsidian exchange during the Archaic period is restricted (see Figure 3.2). Throughout the 5000 years in question, recognizable obsidian distributions are confined to a relatively small part of the state. The most extensive distributions surrounded the Mount San Antonio and Mount Taylor sources. In each case the pattern of distribution is quite simple, and is confined to the immediate environs of each source. For the Mount San Antonio source, the distribution appears to center on the Rio Grande Valley. A simple obsidian-use gradient can also be seen in the area around the Antelope Wells source, where overall obsidian use was quite low and no directionality is apparent.

Basketmaker II (A.D. 1–A.D. 500)

The period A.D. 1–A.D. 500 is marked by important changes in obsidian distribution throughout New Mexico (see Figure 3.3). The territory using obsidian increased greatly, and exchange systems probably developed locally. This is most evident in the northwestern quarter of the state. During this period, the Mount San Antonio source appears to have remained the most important source area, and Rio Grande Valley was still a focus for obsidian

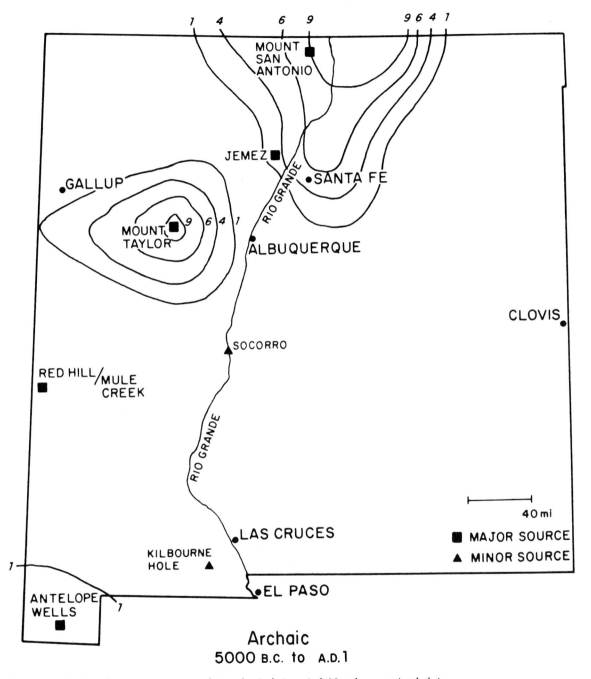

Figure 3.2. Obsidian procurement systems during the Archaic period. Note how restricted obsidian use was throughout this period. Contour and intervals in percentages of lithic assemblages.

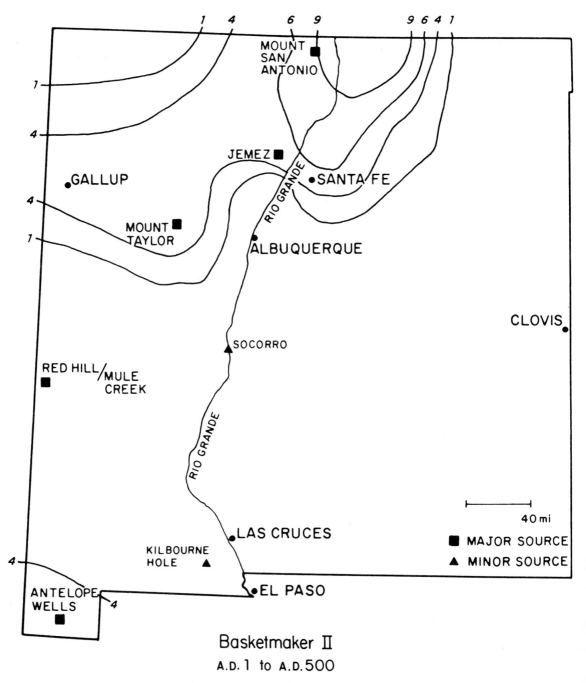

Basketmaker II
A.D. 1 to A.D. 500

Figure 3.3. Obsidian procurement systems during the Basketmaker II period. Note the great expansion of obsidian use throughout the northwest quarter of the state. Contour and intervals in percentages of lithic assemblages.

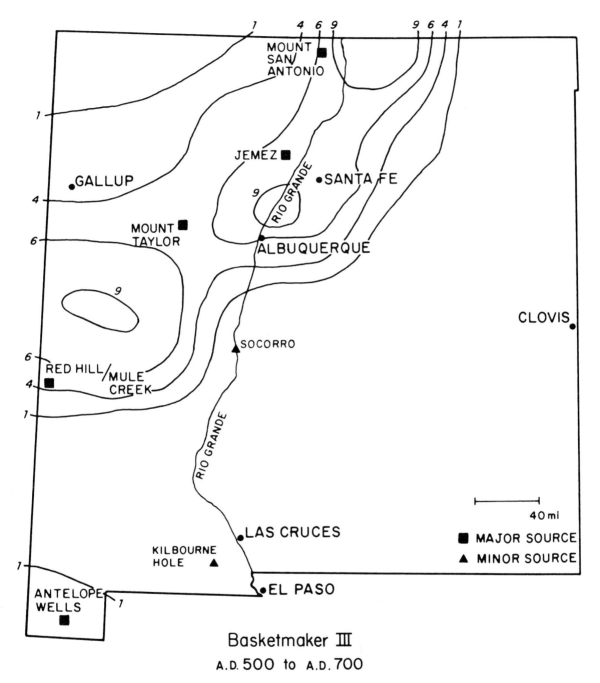

Basketmaker Ⅲ
A.D. 500 to A.D. 700

Figure 3.4. Obsidian procurement systems during the Basketmaker III period. The major event during this period is the large-scale development of the Red Hill–Mule Creek source as the focal point of obsidian exchange throughout the Mogollon Rim area. Contour and intervals in percentages of lithic assemblages.

distribution. At the same time, obsidian from this source was also moving to the west in considerable amounts. Also, the use of the Mount Taylor source expanded, especially in the region northwest of Mount Taylor. Despite the increase in area over which Mount Taylor obsidian was used, the use of this commodity declined in the region immediately surrounding the source. The Antelope Wells source maintained a weakly developed use gradient.

Basketmaker III (A.D. 500–A.D. 700)

The expansion of obsidian distribution that began at the end of the Archaic continues through Basketmaker III times (see Figure 3.4). The regions to the north of the Red Hill–Mule Creek source areas and near the Jemez ones emerge as centers of major obsidian exchange. For the first time, there is evidence that the Mount San Antonio source is being displaced by obsidian exchanged from Jemez exposures. Together, the three source areas of Jemez, Mount San Antonio, and Red Hill–Mule Creek supplied obsidian for over one third of New Mexico. Similar patterns characterized all three source areas. Each shows a gradual falloff in obsidian use in the area northwest of a line linking the three sources and a relatively steep falloff southeast of that line—a situation that suggests that two distinct forms of procurement systems may have been used around the sources. During this period, Mount Taylor continues to decline as an important source and its obsidian is little used except in the area immediately around that source. In fact, it appears that populations within 25 km of Mount Taylor preferred to obtain obsidian from the more remote Jemez and Red Hill–Mule Creek source areas. As in the preceding period, the Antelope Wells source remained the focus of a clearly recognizable, although limited, distribution system.

Pueblo I (A.D. 700–A.D. 900)

In the northwestern quarter of New Mexico, the trends that started during the A.D. 500–A.D. 700 period continue (see Figure 3.5). The decline in the Mount San Antonio source is even more marked, and obsidian exchanged outward from the Jemez sources dominates north-central and northwestern New Mexico. The great increase in the intensity of procurement from Jemez can be seen in the extent of the high-use zone immediately surrounding the source. Clearly, Jemez is the most important source in the state during this period. During this time, the Red Hill–Mule Creek distribution system expands to cover almost the entire Mogollon Rim area, a reflection of the increased population within that mountainous area. Nevertheless, the clearly developed falloff pattern around this source illustrates the continued importance of Red Hill–Mule Creek obsidian in the lower regions adjacent to the Mogollon uplands. Also of interest in this period is the apparent collapse of the exchange system centered on the Antelope Wells source.

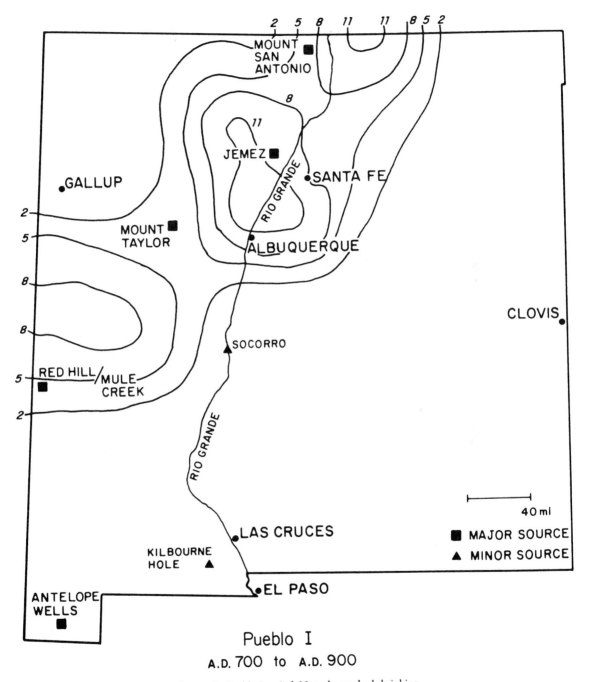

Figure 3.5. Obsidian procurement systems during the Pueblo I period. Note the gradual shrinking of the obsidian distribution system in the northwest quarter of the state. Contour and intervals in percentages of lithic assemblages.

Pueblo II (A.D. 900–A.D. 1100)

During this period, extensive procurement systems associated with Mount San Antonio and Antelope Wells reappeared, and a pattern similar to that in the Basketmaker III period is reasserted (see Figure 3.6). In the northwestern portions of the state, this results in the Mount San Antonio, Jemez, and Red Hill–Mule Creek source areas forming three roughly equivalent procurement systems. Important differences from the Basketmaker III period are the intense use of obsidian around each source area and the symmetry in falloff northwest and southeast of the line joining the three source areas. In the case of the reemergence of the Antelope Wells exchange system, the pattern is almost identical to that in the period A.D. 500 to A.D. 700.

Pueblo III (A.D. 1100–A.D. 1300)

Insofar as the northwestern quarter of the state is concerned, the pattern is only slightly different from the preceding period (see Figure 3.7). High obsidian use links the entire area from Mount San Antonio to the Mogollon Rim. During this period, Mount Taylor obsidian is apparently avoided. Throughout the 200 years in question, the area around Mount Taylor is characterized by low obsidian usage. An important change is the rapid expansion of the Antelope Wells exchange system. The total area involved roughly doubles, and a relatively flat falloff gradient develops.

Pueblo IV (A.D. 1300–A.D. 1600)

The end of the prehistoric period in New Mexico is marked by the collapse of most obsidian distribution systems throughout the state. Much of the reduction in obsidian distribution can be attributed to the abandonment of large areas by agricultural populations, the extremely low population density of the seminomadic groups that replaced them, and finally the impact of European goods. Only the areas most heavily occupied by agricultural populations—namely the upper Rio Grande and portions of the Casas Grandes culture area in the extreme southwest—maintain obsidian procurement systems. In the upper Rio Grande Valley, the exchange pattern resembles the one found in the A.D. 1–A.D. 500 period. In this area, the Mount San Antonio source, supplemented by obsidian from Jemez, supplies communities located primarily within the confines of the Rio Grande Valley. Around Antelope Wells, the first part of this period (1300–1400) witnesses both the maximum development of the Casas Grandes culture in southern New Mexico, and the maximum development of the Antelope Wells obsidian exchange system.

Historic Period (A.D. 1600–A.D. 1880)

During the Historic period, all organized obsidian exchange gradually ends. The SYMAP for this period indicates a gradual shrinkage of obsidian procurement.

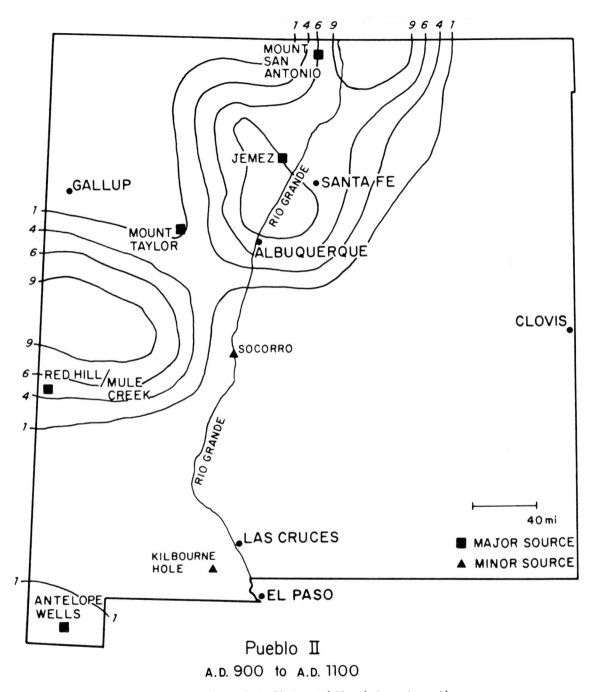

Pueblo II
A.D. 900 to A.D. 1100

Figure 3.6. Obsidian procurement systems during the Pueblo II period. Note the increasing avoidance of Mount Taylor as the source of obsidian. Contour and intervals in percentages of lithic assemblages.

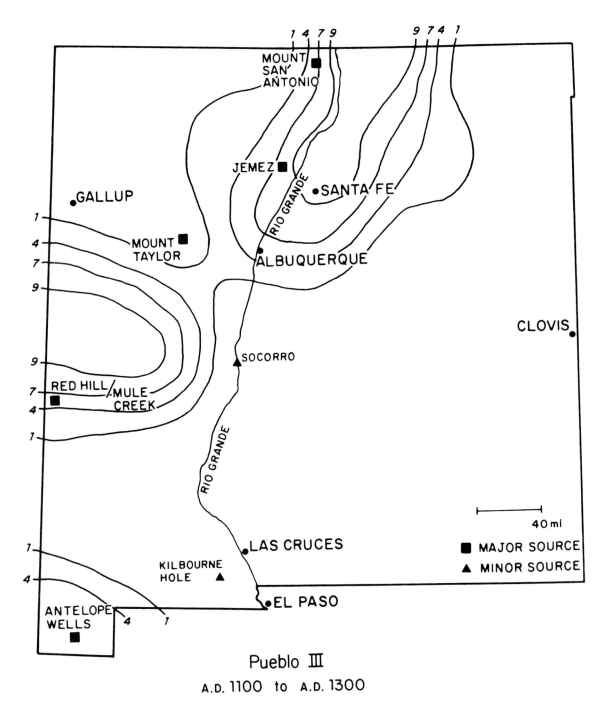

Pueblo III
A.D. 1100 to A.D. 1300

Figure 3.7. Obsidian procurement systems during the Pueblo III period. Note the increasing separation of the Jemez–Mount San Antonio procurement area from the Red Hill–Mule Creek system. Note also the increased volume of obsidian moving outward from the Antelope Wells source. Contour and intervals in percentages of lithic assemblages.

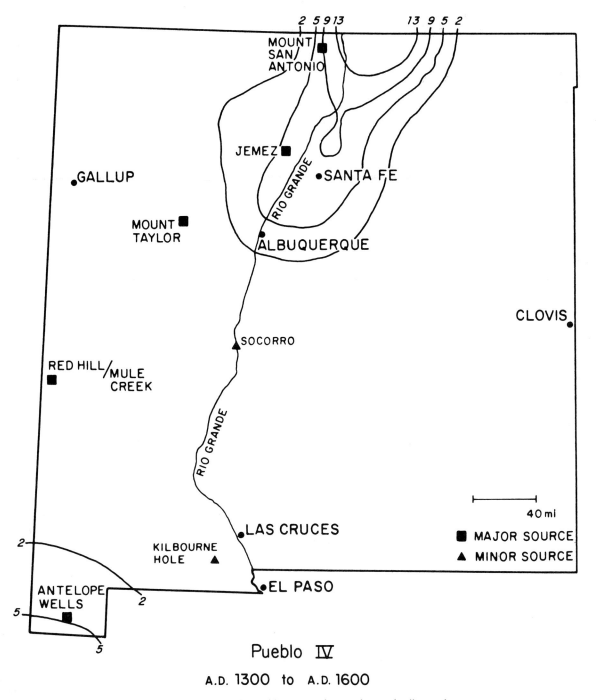

2 5 9 13   13 9 5 2

MOUNT
SAN/
ANTONIO

JEMEZ

GALLUP

SANTA FE

MOUNT
TAYLOR

ALBUQUERQUE

RIO GRANDE

CLOVIS

SOCORRO

RED HILL/MULE
CREEK

RIO GRANDE

LAS CRUCES

40 mi

KILBOURNE
HOLE

■ MAJOR SOURCE
▲ MINOR SOURCE

2

EL PASO

ANTELOPE
WELLS

2

5

5

Pueblo IV

A.D. 1300 to A.D. 1600

Figure 3.8. Obsidian procurement systems during the Pueblo IV period. Note the rapid collapse of the Red Hill–Mule Creek procurement system. Contour and intervals in percentages of lithic assemblages.

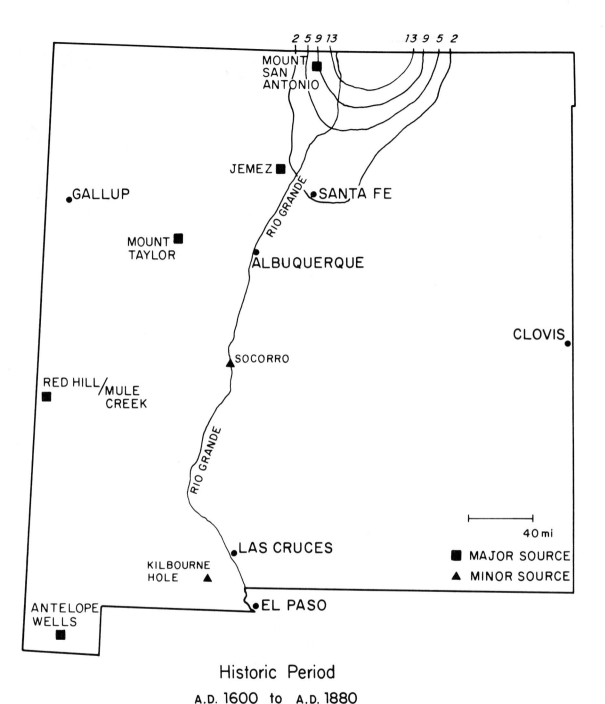

Historic Period
A.D. 1600 to A.D. 1880

Figure 3.9. Obsidian procurement system during the Historic period. During this period obsidian procurement is rapidly dying out, and the observed pattern probably reflects the earlier patterns of the period. By 1880 all organized procurement of obsidian has ended. Contour and intervals in percentages of lithic assemblages.

REGRESSION ANALYSIS OF OBSIDIAN USE IN NEW MEXICO

In this section we describe the regression analyses (Hodder and Orton 1976) of obsidian use around New Mexico's five major source areas. The methodology is identical to that used in two previous studies (Findlow and Bolognese 1980, n.d.); however, in this analysis we consider a much larger sample of sites and develop more reliable measures of distance-related cost. As the nature of the falloff pattern around a source allows different forms of exchange systems to be recognized, improvements in the measurement of cost factors, like those used here, should improve our ability to isolate evolutionary trends in the development of local and regional obsidian exchange networks.

Linear Distance as a Measure of Transport Costs

Although archaeologists have had some success in using regression analysis as a means of isolating patterns of prehistoric exchange, few have considered the adequacy of linear distance to estimate transport costs (cf. Wright 1970; Hodder 1974; Sidrys 1977; Findlow and Bolognese n.d.). One assumption underlying such usage is that movement and transport costs promoted by topographic relief are essentially random with respect to the nature of prehistoric exchange systems. Under ideal conditions, i.e., a region totally lacking relief, such an assumption is justified, and linear distance could be used as a reliable estimate of most of the movement-related costs involved in exchange. Unfortunately, this is not often the case and most prehistoric exchange systems involved areas of both high and low relief. An example of this would be the movement of a lithic raw material from a source in a mountainous region into a low-relief plain, such as the prehistoric movement of Anatolian obsidian southward onto the Syrian steppe and beyond (Wright 1970). Obviously, in such a case the spatial pattern of the exchanged material would reflect both the relief involved and the form of the exchange system.

Standardizing the Effects of Topographic Relief

In an earlier study (Findlow and Bolognese 1980), we reduced the effects of topographic relief on movement costs by using a measure that minimized distance and relief in traversing a path from an obsidian quarry to a particular site (cf. Ericson and Goldstein 1980). This measure, however, was not entirely satisfactory, for it was concerned only with a single path to and from a source and did not allow for all of the subtle effects of topography within a particular region.

In this analysis, we use factor analysis to estimate the movement costs involved in transporting obsidian from the New Mexico sources. This is accomplished by first obtaining a multivariate estimate of the topographic relief around each obsidian source using the methods described by Mather (1972:305–322) and the variables listed in Table 3.4. Subsequently, the impact of topographic relief on transport costs is measured by isolating the underlying dimensionality within the topographic data through the use of factor analysis. Representing, as they do, aspects of topographic relief, the isolated factors represent a series of potential measures of transport costs. The actual values assumed by the individual factors for specific data points around each obsidian source are produced in the form of factor scores. The relative efficiency of the different factors-as-measures can be determined through standard curve-fitting procedures (Findlow and Bolognese 1980). In such an examination the factor scores for each factor would be compared with the occurrence of obsidian at each data point. The relative goodness-of-fit obtained for each of these factors would in turn determine their utility as cost–distance estimators.

Test Models

The regression analyses test the fit of alternative functions that can be seen as modeling different exchange mechanisms. While these analyses are based on the work of Hodder (1974:172–189; Hodder and Orton 1976), they differ from that work in terms of the models tested. Table 3.5 shows the models used in these analyses. These models allow six distinct forms of exchange to be isolated. Specifically, this group of models can be divided as follows according to their properties.

LINEAR MODELS

Linear models with the form $Y = A + (BX)$, where A and B are constants, can be used to isolate prehistoric exchange systems in which all access to the source area is direct and in which the frequency of visits to the source decreases in a linear fashion with increasing distance. Renfrew, Dixon, and Cann (1968:327) suggest that these models offer a good approximation of "supply-zone" usage. Hudson (1978) used this form to examine long-distance exchange of raw materials throughout the prehistoric Southwest.

POWER FUNCTION MODELS

Power function models with the form $Y = AX^B$ can be used to model prehistoric exchange systems in which an area of direct-access, supply-zone

TABLE 3.4
Geomorphic Variables.[a] Geomorphic variables used to characterize landscapes around the five major New Mexico obsidian sources.

Maximum elevation
Minimum elevation
Number of drainages
Number of contours
Number of closed contours
Number of drainage heads

[a]After Mather (1972).

TABLE 3.5
Test Models. The test models used in the curve-fitting analyses. Individual models are used to characterize different forms of exchange systems.

Model	Form	Source
$Y = A + (BX)$	Linear	Ericson 1977; Hudson 1978
$Y = AX^B$	Power function	Wright 1970
$Y = Ae^{(BX)}$	Exponential	Hodder 1974; Hogg 1971
$Y = X/(A + [BX])$	Hyperbolic	De Atley and Findlow 1979

procurement is joined to areas with down-the-line, directional exchange by a steep falloff zone (Renfrew 1977:74). In this type of exchange, the direct-access area most closely resembles a simple linear direct-access system, while the down-the-line area resembles an exponential distance decay pattern (Renfrew 1977:74). Wright (1970) used this sort of model in his examination of Near Eastern obsidian exchange.

EXPONENTIAL MODELS

Using a general exponential model with the form $Y = Ae^{(BX)}$, it is possible to recognize three distinct forms of exchange systems, depending on the beta value that best fits the observed data.

Gaussian Random Walk Systems When beta has a value near to or higher than 2, the distribution of obsidian approximates a Guassian random walk distribution (Renfrew 1977:74–75). Such systems suggest the presence of an exchange system or systems with a number of exchange mechanisms operating simultaneously such that their combined movement resembles a random pattern, leaving only a simple decrease in obsidian use with increasing distance away from the source. Hogg (1971) used this form of model to analyze the distribution of Iron Age coins in southern Britain.

Exponential Distance Decay Systems When beta is near to 1, directional, down-the-line procurement is indicated. In such a system, the absolute frequency of obsidian at any point results from the up-the-line trading partner's available surplus and the overall distance from the source. This also would occur if, with a hierarchical arrangement of settlements, the obsidian available to lower-tier settlements is a function of the amount available in settlements higher in the system (Sidrys 1977). Renfrew, Dixon, and Cann (1968) found that this model best described the directional exchange of obsidian during the Near Eastern Neolithic.

Supply Zone Exponential Systems When beta approaches 0, a form of direct-access, supply-zone procurement is indicated (Renfrew 1977:84). In most cases, a simple linear model will fit this sort of situation; however, in those instances where it does not, this sort of model may indicate an exponential distance-decay pattern in which the supply-zone area is abnormally large.

Hyperbolic Models   The hyperbolic model used in this study has the form $Y = X/(A + [BX])$. This falloff function models an exchange system that is intermediate between a simple linear system and an exponential distance-decay system. Like the exponential distance-decay model, this model contrasts a "supply zone" with an area of down-the-line exchange; however, unlike the exponential model, the hyperbolic model indicates a much gentler zone of falloff between the two areas. While little empirical data fit this model (Findlow and Bolognese 1980), it may represent an intermediate stage in the development of more complex directional exchange systems.

Throughout this study the relative goodness-of-fit of these models are assessed using the Pearson's *r*; however, unlike more normal useage, this statistic is used here only as a relative measure that will allow morphological changes in obsidian exchange systems to be recognized. The nature of the available data makes it impossible to use Pearson's *r* in a true statistical sense.

Data and Measurement

Following the methodological procedures just outlined, the regression analysis of obsidian use in New Mexico was carried out in the four following steps:

1. Topographic relief was measured using the six variables in Table 3.4. Using these variables, topographic relief was measured for all portions of New Mexico from which obsidian data were available.
2. The topographic data were reduced to a more manageable form by factor analysis. A principal components factoring with varimax rotation was used to

TABLE 3.6
Factor Analysis of Geomorphic Variables. Varimax factor loadings of the geomorphic variables on each of the two significant factors. Normally loadings greater than .30 or smaller than −.30 are considered significant.

Variable	Factor 1	Factor 2
Maximum elevation	.97	.07
Minimum elevation	.87	−.12
Number of drainages	−.02	−.11
Number of contours	.39	.81
Number of closed contours	−.28	.46
Number of drainage heads	−.31	.81

TABLE 3.7
Best Model for Each of the Major Source Areas, All Time Periods Combined.[a] Empirical regression models isolated for each of the eight time periods when all of the obsidian data irrespective of source were treated as a single group.

Mount Taylor	$Y = 2.292 + 2.6845\ E^X$	.86	.74	Exponential
Jemez	$Y = 7.483 + 1.699\ (X)$	.36	.13	Linear
San Antonio	$Y = 8.971 + 1.254\ (X)$	.75	.57	Linear
Antelope Wells	$Y = 13.337 + 1/7.553\ (X)$	.52	.27	Hyperbolic
Red Hill–Mule Creek	$Y = 18.211 + (-6.161\ E^X)$	.84	.71	Exponential

[a]Where Y = percentage of obsidian used and X = Factor 1.

insure that all factors extracted were independent. Table 3.6 shows the two significant factors extracted.

3. The loadings of the original variables on the significant factors were examined to determine what aspects of topographic variation were represented by each factor. The two factors can best be labeled *elevation* and *roughness*. Factor 1 represents the elevational dimension, with maximum and minimum elevation providing the highest significant loadings. Factor 2 exhibits high loadings for three variables: the number of contours, the number of closed contours, and the number of drainage heads—all indicators of the relative unevenness or "roughness" of the landscape.

4. Finally, the relative efficiency of each of the two factors as a measure of movement costs was assessed by calculating the partial correlation of each factor with the percentage of obsidian in the sites in the New Mexico's data. For comparison, linear distance's partial correlation with the percentage of obsidian was also calculated. The results of these correlation analyses show that Factor 1 had a partial correlation of .70; linear distance a partial correla-

TABLE 3.8
Best Fit Model for Each Time Period, All Sources Combined.[a] Empirical regression models isolated for each of New Mexico's five major source areas when the obsidian data for all eight time periods were treated as a single group.

Period	Model	R	R^2	Form
Archaic	$Y = 6.261 + 2.513\ (X)$	.65	.43	Linear
BM II	$Y = 6.148 + 2.421\ (X)$	.61	.37	Linear
BM III	$Y = 7.769 + 2.282\ (X)$	.72	.52	Linear
P I	$Y = 7.917 + 2.854\ (X)$	.60	.36	Linear
P II	$Y = 7.757 + 3.153\ (X)$	.68	.47	Linear
P III	$Y = 8.838 + 2.649\ (X)$	.73	.53	Linear
P IV	$Y = 7.33 + 1.225\ E^X$	.75	.57	Exponential
Historic	$Y = 4.723 + 3.462\ (X^2)$	.60	.36	Power

[a]Where Y = percentage of obsidian used and X = Factor 1.

TABLE 3.9
Best Fit Model for Each Source During Each of the Eight Time Periods.[a] Empirical regression models isolated for the major source areas with enough obsidian data to allow individual time periods to be treated separately. The data for the Mount Taylor source were so scattered temporally that it was impossible to obtain enough data points to undertake a regression analysis without collapsing several time periods together.

Source	Period	Model	R	R^2	Form
Jemez	Archaic	$Y = 4.61 + 1.477\ (X)$	.83	.70	Linear
Jemez	BM II	$Y = 5.982 + 1.258\ (X)$	.85	.73	Linear
Jemez	BM III	$Y = 8.6 + 1.589\ (X)$	.90	.82	Linear
Jemez	P I	$Y = 10.625 + 1.927\ (X)$	.73	.54	Linear
Jemez	P II	$Y = 9.288 + 1.887\ (X)$	.85	.72	Linear
Jemez	P III	$Y = 9.138 + 2.178\ (X)$	.90	.81	Linear
Jemez	P IV	$Y = 8.464 + 2.415\ (X)$	.95	.91	Linear
Jemez	Historic	$Y = 3.152 + .924\ (X)$	.97	.94	Linear
San Antonio	Archaic	$Y = 9.096 + .767\ (X)$	.98	.97	Linear
San Antonio	BM II	$Y = 9.28 + .953\ (X)$	.93	.87	Linear
San Antonio	BM III	$Y = 8.594 + .832\ (X)$	.97	.93	Linear
San Antonio	P I	$Y = 8.109 + 1.124\ (X)$	.99	.98	Linear
San Antonio	P II	$Y = 7.811 + 1.422\ (X)$	.97	.92	Linear
San Antonio	P III	$Y = 8.979 + 1.387\ (X)$	.98	.97	Linear
San Antonio	P IV	$Y = 10.211 + 1.354\ (X)$	.93	.86	Linear
San Antonio	Historic	$Y = 9.692 + 2.197\ (X)$	.94	.88	Linear
Antelope Wells	Archaic	$Y = -7.721 + (-13.12\ (X)$	.73	.53	Linear
Antelope Wells	BM II	$Y = 15.756 + (-28.771E^x)$	.72	.53	Exponential
Antelope Wells	BM III	$Y = 14.597 + (-25.216E^x)$	.77	.60	Exponential
Antelope Wells	P I	$Y = 15.478 + (-27.585E^x)$	.84	.71	Exponential
Antelope Wells	P II	$Y = 15.756 + (-28.771E^x)$	.73	.53	Exponential
Antelope Wells	P III	$Y = 12.095 + 1/(7.005\ (X))$	.93	.86	Hyperbolic
Antelope Wells	P IV	$Y = 12.732 + (-8.48E\ 1/(7.656\ (X))$	.84	.71	Hyperbolic
Red Hill–Mule Creek	P I	$Y = 20.5 + (-8.48E^x)$	.98	.97	Exponential
Red Hill–Mule Creek	P II	$Y = 19.24 + (-6.749E^x)$	.98	.97	Exponential
Red Hill–Mule Creek	P III	$Y = 19.20 + (-5.9E^x)$	.97	.96	Exponential

[a]Where Y = percentage of obsidian used and X = Factor 1.

tion of −.44; and for Factor 2, a partial correlation of .13. Additional partial correlations were calculated for linear distance and Factor 2 with the percentage of obsidian, while controlling for the effects of Factor 1. The results of this analysis were a partial correlation of −.21 for linear distance and .26 for Factor 2. Based on these results, it was determined that Factor 1 should be used alone as the best measure of procurement costs. Specifically, Factor 1 was felt to be the most efficient measure of procurement costs since it was able to explain a larger proportion of the total variance in the available data than the other variables. We felt it was best to use Factor 1 alone rather than in combination with Factor 2 since the addition of the second factor would have contributed little in the way of additional information (R^2 .06) and would have increased the problem of interpretation.

Using the factor scores for Factor 1 along the most direct line from a particular site to the source from which its obsidian was obtained as a measure of procurement costs, each of the alternate test models was fitted using standard regression-analysis procedures (cf. Findlow and Bolognese 1980). Separate analyses were undertaken for each of the eight temporal periods and for each of the five major source areas. Additional analyses were carried out simultaneously for each time period and source (Tables 3.7, 3.8, and 3.9).

THE EVOLUTION OF LOCAL AND REGIONAL OBSIDIAN PROCUREMENT SYSTEMS

Based on the regression analyses, a number of specific and general conclusions can be drawn concerning obsidian use in New Mexico from 5000 B.C. to A.D. 1880. The analyses provide specific information about the nature of the exchange systems that operated around each source during the eight temporal periods and general conclusions concerning lithic exchange.

Source-specific Exchange Systems

The most obvious aspect of the particular models isolated for each source area is the difference in the relative goodness-of-fit obtained (see Table 3.7). Consequently, there are good fits with the models representing exchange around some areas, i.e., Mount Taylor ($r = .86$), and poor representations around other sources, i.e., Antelope Wells ($r = .27$) and Jemez ($r = .36$). The inability to isolate essentially temporally free representations of spatial patterning reflects the change that occurred in a particular obsidian procurement system over time. While it seems safe to conclude that Mount Taylor, Antelope Wells, and Red Hill–Mule Creek source areas were always involved in some form of complex down-the-line exchange pattern, relatively little can be said about the other source areas, except that major variations in their exchange systems must have occurred.

Time-specific Exchange Systems

It is evident from the general pattern seen in the r values listed in Table 3.8 that for the entire state of New Mexico "direct access" was succeeded by more complex down-the-line systems; however, the relatively low r value suggests that considerable regional variation existed. Nevertheless, the characterization of "direct access" for most temporal periods is probably accurate, and is confirmed by the trend-surface analyses that showed complex patterning to be confined to small portions of the state.

Source-specific Models of Exchange for Each Temporal Period

The simultaneous partitioning of the data by time period and source area (see Table 3.9) provides additional support for the hypothesis that complex down-the-line exchange systems were relatively rare in New Mexico's history. These results show that complex down-the-line exchange patterns for obsidian were confined to the later prehistoric periods around two sources—Red Hill-Mule Creek and Antelope Wells. Indeed, the frequent and marked shifts in the exchange systems associated with the latter sources explain much of the variability within the data. In all other cases, the best-fit model is the linear model, representing direct-access procurement. It is apparent then, that the trend seen in Table 3.8 is actually a reflection of the relatively late date of the down-the-line exchange system associated with the Antelope Wells source, as well as the decline in obsidian use in the Historic period. The stability of simple direct access procurement systems, both temporally and spatially, indicates that the changes isolated in the trend-surface analyses were produced by changes in the directionality and magnitude of obsidian exchange rather than by changes in the form of the exchange systems themselves.

CONCLUSIONS

The most important implications of this analysis relate to the economics of lithic raw-material procurement and exchange. Specifically, these analyses provide support for the following hypotheses:

1. Changes in the directionality (Plog 1977) of exchange systems are independent of changes in their form (Renfrew 1977).
2. Changes in the magnitude of exchange systems are independent of their form.
3. Movements away from direct-access procurement systems to down-the-line exchange systems are promoted primarily by changes in the sociopolitical complexity of the societies involved and the relative geographic separation between a source locality and the point of consumption. The greater the separation, the more likely that some form of complex exchange system will evolve.

Evidence for the first two of these hypotheses comes from the results of both the trend-surface and regression analyses. In the trend-surface analyses, marked change can be seen in the overall scope and directionality of exchange as one progresses temporally. At the same time, the regression analyses also indicate a relative stability in the form of exchange. For example, around the northern New Mexico sources of Mount San Antonio and Jemez, significant shifts occur in the spatial characteristics of exchange from the Archaic to the Historic periods, but they continue to be associated with a direct-access procurement system. The same sort of independence of exchange form and directionality–magnitude can be seen around the Antelope Wells source. In this case, however, directionality, or rather the lack thereof, remains roughly constant while the form of exchange system changes.

The most important implication for the study of prehistoric exchange is the third point listed before, namely that complex down-the-line exchange systems are probably a product of sociopolitical factors rather than a consequence of the size of the region involved in the exchange network (Findlow and Bolognese 1980). Further evidence for this hypothesis is provided by the Antelope Wells data. Unlike any of the other source areas in the state, the Antelope Wells source was sequentially incorporated into cultural systems of increasing complexity. The areas around the source were first occupied by Archaic hunter–gatherers, then by small independent farming communities (San Luis phase), and later by communities that were a part of the larger cultural system focused on Casas Grandes in Chihuahua (Animas phase) (Findlow and Bolognese 1980). Directly correlated with these temporal changes were changes in local obsidian procurement—from direct access during the Archaic to an exponential system at the end of the San Luis phase and to a hyperbolic, down-the-line system during the Animas phase (Findlow and Bolognese 1980).

A related hypothesis suggests that complex down-the-line obsidian exchange systems can be promoted in egalitarian societies when great distances separate the quarry area from the point of initial redistribution. The data from the Red Hill–Mule Creek source provide support for this hypothesis. In this case, whenever the source was utilized, i.e., from the Pueblo I through Pueblo III periods, down-the-line exchange apparently resulted. While these data are not conclusive, it does appear that obsidian exchange was focused on large communities outside the mountainous source area, either on the plateau to the north or the desert area to the south. This separation seems to be responsible for producing a down-the-line exchange system in which redistribution begins—not at the source area but at communities removed from the source.

In conclusion, the set of analyses discussed in this chapter are relevant on two distinct levels: first, for the insights they provide concerning the nature of prehistoric and historic obsidian procurement in New Mexico; and second, for the more general information they provide concerning the evolution of raw-material exchange systems.

In the first of these areas, the analyses illustrate the conservatism and general simplicity of New Mexico obsidian procurement. Overwhelmingly simple, direct access was the rule. Only for the Red Hill–Mule Creek and Antelope Wells sources were direct-access systems ever replaced by more complex forms of exchange. Consequently, if obsidian procurement in New Mexico were to be described in general terms, the best characterization would be that acquisition and utilization processes were carried out by the same individuals. In such a procurement system, obsidian would be obtained as needed, directly from the closest source, and the relative value of the material would have been determined only by the costs associated with movement to and from the source and the volume of obsidian needed.

The most important general conclusions of this chapter concern the factors that promote movements away from direct-access procurement toward complex down-the-line exchange. Movement, either up or down the scale of sociopolitical complexity, would seem to promote concomitant movement either toward or away from direct access. Unfortunately, these analyses neither provide data relevant to the discovery of the exact cultural factors involved in such evolution, nor do they establish that similar evolutionary changes would occur when other raw materials besides obsidian were involved. The fact that certain geographic factors, such as the need to transport obsidian over long distances (i.e., as in the case of the Red Hill–Mule Creek exchange system), are also capable of promoting complex exchange systems further complicates any attempt at isolating the cultural mechanisms underlying the evolution of complex raw-material exchange systems.

ACKNOWLEDGMENTS

We would like to thank the following people and institutions for their help in making this chapter possible: Suzanne De Atley, Timothy Earle, Jonathon Ericson, Andrew Lo, Mary Jane Berman, Curtis Schaafsma, Marsha Jackson, Stewart Peckham, Nancy Fox, Laura Holt, Rosemary Talley, George Pendleton, Laboratory of Anthropology–Museum of New Mexico, Phelps-Dodge Corporation, Victorio Land and Cattle Company, and Columbia University's Council for Research in the Social Sciences. We would also like to extend our special thanks to Barbara E. Cohen whose sound advice and judgement were a constant help during all stages of this chapter, from the formulation of the research design through the editing of the final manuscript.

REFERENCES

Alper, A.
  1957   Geology of Walnut Wells quadrangle, Hidalgo County, New Mexico. Unpublished
         Ph.D. dissertation, Columbia University, New York.
Dane, C. H., and G. O. Bachman
  1965   Geologic map of New Mexico. Washington, D.C.: United States Geological Survey.
De Atley, S. P., and F. J. Findlow
  1979   Community integration along the Casas Grandes frontier. Manuscript on file, Department of Anthropology, M.I.T.
Ericson, J. E.
  1977   Egalitarian exchange systems in California: a preliminary view. In *Exchange systems in prehistory*, edited by T. K. Earle and J. E. Ericson, pp. 109–126. New York: Academic Press.

Ericson, J. E., and R. Goldstein
  1980 Work space: a new approach to the analysis of energy expenditure within site catch-
        ments. In *Catchment analysis: essays on prehistoric resource space,* edited by F. J.
        Findlow and J. E. Ericson, pp. 21–30. Los Angeles: Department of Anthropology,
        University of California.
Erwin-Williams, C.
  1977 A network model for the analysis of prehistoric trade. In *Exchange systems in prehisto-
        ry,* edited by T. K. Earle and J. E. Ericson, pp. 141–151. New York: Academic Press.
Findlow, F. J., V. C. Bennett, J. E. Ericson, and S. P. De Atley
  1975 A new obsidian hydration rate for certain obsidians in the American Southwest. *Ameri-
        can Antiquity* **40**:344–348.
Findlow, F. J., and M. Bolognese
  1980 An initial examination of prehistoric obsidian exchange in Hidalgo County, New Mex-
        ico. *Kiva* **45**(3):227–251.
  n.d. A preliminary analysis of prehistoric obsidian use within the Mogollon area. In *The
        Proceedings of the Mogollon Conference,* edited by P. Beckett (forthcoming).
Hodder, I.
  1974 Regression analysis of some trade and marketing patterns. *World Archaeology*
        6:172–180.
Hodder, I., and C. Orton
  1976 *Spatial analysis in archaeology.* Cambridge: Cambridge University Press.
Hogg, A. H. A.
  1971 Some applications of surface fieldwork. In *The Iron Age and its hillforts,* edited by M.
        Jesson and D. Hill, pp. 105–125. Southampton: University of Southampton Press.
Hudson, L.
  1978 *A quantitative analysis of prehistoric exchange in the southwest United States.* Ann
        Arbor: University Microfilms.
Lankford, P.
  1974 A guide to SUPERMAP. Classnotes, Department of Geography, University of California,
        Los Angeles.
Mather, P. M.
  1972 Area classification in geomorphology. In *Spatial analysis in geomorphology,* edited by R.
        J. Chorley, pp. 305–322. New York: Harper and Row.
Plog, F. T.
  1977 Modeling economic exchange. In *Exchange systems in prehistory,* edited by T. K. Earle
        and J. E. Ericson, pp. 127–140. New York: Academic Press.
Renfrew, C.
  1977 Alternate models for exchange and spatial distribution. In *Exchange systems in prehisto-
        ry,* edited by T. K. Earle and J. E. Ericson, pp. 71–90. New York: Academic Press.
Renfrew, C., J. E. Dixon, and J. R. Cann
  1968 Further analysis of Near Eastern obsidians. *Proceedings of the Prehistoric Society*
        34:319–331.
Sidrys, R.
  1977 Mass-distance measures for the Maya obsidian trade. In *Exchange systems in prehistory,*
        edited by T. K. Earle and J. E. Ericson, pp. 91–108. New York: Academic Press.
Wright, G. A.
  1970 On trade and culture process in prehistory. *Current Anthropology* **11**:171–173.

4

Marketplace Exchange as Indirect Distribution: An Iranian Example

John R. Alden

INTRODUCTION

Archaeological studies of complex economic systems usually assume one of two forms. More traditional studies are concerned with defining spheres of distribution for particular distinctive products. The results of such studies can be fascinating in their details, but they add little of a general nature to either anthropology or prehistory. The more recent fashion has been to take some theory of regional settlement organization (primate and central-place patterns are current favorites) and to deduce various sorts of societal behavior for situations where the particular settlement pattern is present. This sort of study displays a concern with more general issues, but the conclusions are frequently little more than vague generalizations. A more helpful approach is to use the results of detailed studies to clarify particular aspects of general theoretical issues. This chapter represents my attempt to do this.

If general issues are to be treated in a short chapter, they must be narrowly defined. This contribution considers the broad issue of development of complex economic exchange systems but focuses on the appearance of indirect distribution. The defining characteristic of indirect distribution is that consumers do not acquire goods from the places where the goods are manufactured. Instead, items are moved to some other spot, to be exchanged or reallocated from there. I argue that indirect distribution defines complex exchange systems and that it will be evidenced by a certain pattern of product frequency in the

CONTEXTS FOR PREHISTORIC EXCHANGE

archaeological record. Indirect distribution merits investigation because it is considerably more efficient than direct distribution. Savings in distribution costs generated by indirect systems can go into increased accumulation or status differentiation, and thus they may lead to increased sociopolitical complexity. Before proceeding, however, definitions of the terms and concepts to be used in this chapter are in order.

Economic refers to all aspects of a sociocultural system relating to the production, distribution, consumption, and disposal of material goods and services (cf. Earle, Chapter 1). I examine production and distribution in this chapter. The term *complex* is used to mean hierarchically organized, with one person or institution managing some kind of activity through their authority over a number of subordinates. Finally, *exchanges* are transfers of goods or services between individuals. In common parlance, the term exchange encompasses nonmaterial transfers, transfers with a high or a low symbolic content, and cases where the quid pro quo is immediate and direct or where it is much less explicit. As such, exchange is too broad a concept to be useful.

First, this chapter will consider only exchanges of material goods or services. Second, I will separate two independent dimensions of exchange: the symbolic or signifying content of an exchange and the nature of the quid pro quo. Tribute and ritual offerings have a high symbolic content, while sharing or market-type exchanges rank much lower in that dimension. In market exchanges and tribute, the understanding of what is being given and what is returned is explicit and the exchange is generally immediate; for sharing or ritual offerings, the quid pro quo is usually implicit and frequently delayed. Table 4.1 shows these types of exchange and the two dimensions that distinguish them. Here, I will only examine exchanges having a low symbolic content and clearly defined reciprocation.

TABLE 4.1

Types of Material Exchanges. These types are distinguished by their characteristics in two dimensions: symbolic content of the exchange, high or low, and the participant's understanding of what is being exchanged, the quid pro quo.

		Symbolic–signifying content	
		Low	High
Quid pro quo	Immediate and explicit	Market-type exchange	Tribute
	Delayed and implicit	Sharing	Ritual offerings

THE DEVELOPMENT OF COMPLEX ECONOMIES

From the definition of *complex,* it follows that specialization in production is a necessary feature for the development of hierarchical economic organization. When production is specialized, the minimal economic unit[1] is not independent; it does not control the production or extraction of all that it consumes. This can be true whether the specialization is *serial,* divorcing extractive from finishing operations, or *discrete,* where one craft is separated from another. For example, ore may be mined and smelted at one site and the metal worked into objects elsewhere (*serial specialization*). Alternatively, the inhabitants of a site might collect wood, make charcoal, mine and smelt ore, refine the metal, cast it into tools, and control the distribution of these tools to other sites (*discrete specialization*). With either kind of specialization, the different sites in the regional system use products produced at other locations. Settlements are not independent, but require regular contact and exchange with the other sites in the system.

This, however, is not a sufficient condition for the appearance of complex economies. There are numerous ethnographic examples of such specialization in economies that are not hierarchically organized (Harding 1967:27–60; Chagnon 1968:21, 100–101). In complex economies production is specialized, and in addition, most exchange is channeled through special locations. Thus, the second necessary condition for hierarchical economic organization is the presence of nodes of exchange within the regional system; in other words, locations where the distributive functions of the economy are concentrated.

Nodes of distribution and exchange are the defining characteristic of *indirect distribution systems.* When distribution systems are *direct,* members of each minimal economic unit travel to other locations to acquire what they need. In most cases such systems of distribution do not utilize specialists, although in some instances they may. For example, an individual might regularly travel to the location where certain goods are produced and return with enough for a number of consumers in his or her village. Here distribution would be through a specialist, but that person would function in a direct distribution system where there were no nodes of exchange external to the minimal economic unit. In another variation of direct distribution, itinerant craftsmen might travel from site to site hawking their wares. Again distribution would be direct, involving specialized production but taking place through face-to-face contact between producer and consumer rather than through nodes of exchange. In general, it would be at best inconvenient to administer a direct distribution system.

[1]In this discussion, the *settlement* will be treated as the minimal economic unit, because I am concerned with organization of a regional economy and not organization within villages or households. I do not intend to belittle the importance of variability within a settlement, but it is not of interest here.

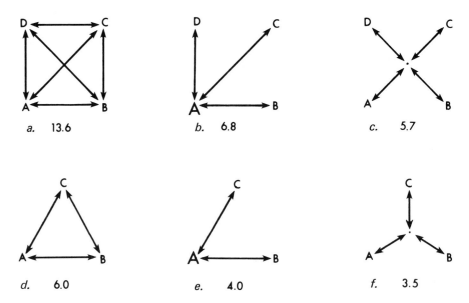

Figure 4.1. Efficiency of alternative distribution systems in terms of total distance traveled, for systems with four (*a–c*) and three (*d–f*) settlements. In (*a*) and (*d*) each settlement is in direct contact with every other settlement. In (*b*) and (*e*) one of the existing settlements serves as an exchange point, while in (*c*) and (*f*) a geographically central location is made the node of exchange.

In an *indirect* distribution system, goods and services from outside the minimal economic unit are acquired from some central location where exchanges take place. Consumers do not have to travel to a number of places to get what they want; in indirect systems, produce and products move to nodes of exchange from where they go to consumers by way of trade or allocation. Unlike direct distribution systems, indirect systems lend themselves to direction by a higher-level authority. In summary, two features necessary for complex economies are locationally specialized production and indirect distribution systems.

Indirect distribution systems are inherently more efficient than direct systems. Consider four settlements with equal populations located in the corners of a square with sides one unit long. If each village provides all its own needs there will be no distribution costs for the system as a whole.[2] If the communities are specialized, with each producing something required by the others, there are three alternate systems through which all can acquire what they need.

[2]In this case, each site will have its own procurement costs, but that is another problem. Essentially, when the sum of procurement costs for independent sites in a regional system is greater than the sum of procurement *and* distribution costs for the same sites in an economy with local specialization, there will be some incentive toward specialized craft production. Such a savings would probably have to be considerable, however, before it would precipitate the change to a specialized economy.

Figure 4.1*a* shows the most expensive of these, where the residents of each site travel to the others to distribute their products. Assuming that the people of Site A carry their product to Site B and return with B's product, the cost of distribution for the system will be 13.6 units of travel, divided equally among all four communities. If one of the sites functions as a distribution center—either an allocation or a market location—for the system, as in Figure 4.1*b*, the cost of distribution is 6.8 travel units, divided unequally among three of the four communities. Still, even the most distant settlement expends less effort than in the first case, so this system is better than the first for each settlement individually. In the second case, the site serving as the distribution center does not share the costs of distribution. The situation shown in Figure 4.1*c* minimizes distribution costs for the system (5.7 units) and for three of the four settlements involved. Figure 4.1*d–f* repeats these situations for a three-settlement system. Data for all cases are summarized in Table 4.2.

In general, the more settlements involved in specialized production within the regional system the greater the savings in distribution costs achieved through indirect distribution. Because each settlement achieves considerable savings in time and effort from such an economic system, self-interest would encourage the adoption of indirect distribution systems in any regional economy with local specialization in more than two crafts.

The type of distribution—direct versus indirect—should affect patterns of consumption of goods and services within the regional economy. This is because indirect distribution systems decrease the importance of distance. Suppose the "cost" of an item equals the cost of production plus the cost of distribution. With direct distribution, a village far from production locations would minimize costs by minimizing demand for externally produced goods. This would be particularly true for goods produced at more distant sites. With indirect distribution, where goods are distributed through nodes or centers of

TABLE 4.2

Efficiency of Distribution Using Various Alternatives. Efficiencies of the alternative distribution systems shown in Figure 4.1. Direct distribution systems are the least efficient in terms of distance traveled, and indirect centralized systems are the most efficient.

Figure 1	Type of distribution	Total distance traveled	% above minimum
A	Direct, noncentral	13.6	140
B	Indirect, noncentral	6.8	20
C	Indirect, central	5.7	0
D	Direct, noncentral	6.0	74
E	Indirect, noncentral	4.0	16
F	Indirect, central	3.5	0

exchange, acquisition costs for all participating settlements are proportional to distance from the point of distribution rather than distance from the point of production. This feature is most easily illustrated by considering a centrally located place of exchange, as in Figure 4.1c. Since Sites B and C both travel the same distance to get the products of Site A, the cost of that product will be the same for both sites, even though C is farther from A than B is. Consequently, we would expect no reduction in the use of the product produced by Site A among the sites (B, C, and D) serviced by an indirect distribution system. All sites equidistant from the central point would be expected to consume approximately equal per capita amounts, even though some sites are farther from the point of production than others. With direct distribution, there should be a reduction in the use of products of more distant settlements, and that reduction should be proportional to the travel time between the sites.

Any real situation is of course more complex than that shown in Figure 4.1a–f. First, distance should have little or no effect on the intensity of ceremonial exchanges. In fact, in certain stratified or state-level societies the intensity of ceremonial exchange might increase with distance rather than decrease. The densities of objects with symbolic significance would reflect social, political, or ritual behaviors and systems rather than geographical relationships. Second, the intensity of market-type exchanges should be inversely proportional to distance from consumer to the node or center of exchange, but relatively unaffected by varying distance from the production location to the center of exchange.

Settlement patterns should also reflect the type of distribution system that is in operation. Direct distribution systems would encourage a tighter clustering of settlements than indirect systems, because the potential savings through reduced travel costs are greater in the direct system, and it is likely that such clusters of settlements would occur around the production centers. Thus, it would be predicted that, with all other conditions held constant, a change from direct to indirect distribution would result in a more dispersed settlement pattern. The difficulty with such a test, of course, lies in showing that all other factors affecting settlement patterns remained unchanged.

In summary, direct distribution systems (a) will tend to be associated with more agglomerated settlement patterns; and (b) will show an inverse relationship between the amount of a product consumed and the distance to its source. Indirect distribution systems (a) will tend to be marked by more dispersed settlement patterns; and (b) will show an inverse relationship between the amount of a product consumed and the distance to the center of distribution.

The distinction between types of distribution systems made here is significant because the appearance of indirect systems marks the watershed between simple and complex economies. Specialization in production is the first step away from simple economic organization, but an economy does not become truly complex until indirect distribution occurs. The change from independent to interdependent regional economic systems is an important concomitant to political evolution, for manipulation and control of economic factors is one of the easier ways for ambitious personages of higher status to solidify their positions in the social order. Thus, the identification of indirect distribution systems is a problem deserving serious attention.

A CASE STUDY—HIGHLAND IRAN CIRCA 3200 B.C.

Settlement patterns can help to reveal the existence of indirect distribution, but an unambiguous demonstration demands an examination of material objects. To identify types of prehistoric distribution systems, we need data from a set of contemporaneous archaeological sites, including information on both specialized local production and the density of these locally produced objects at all other sites in the regional system. The sample of sites need not be complete, but the materials being studied must be assignable to particular site sources. Here I examine the distribution of utilitarian ceramics during the Banesh period (3400–2600 B.C.) in the Kur River basin in highland Iran.

This region was chosen because it appeared to be an example of early state development. The boundaries of the region were clear; prehistoric developments in the area had been outlined; and it seemed potentially interesting to compare highland developments with what is known of contemporaneous events in the lowlands (Adams and Nissen 1972; Johnson 1973).

The Kur River basin is a high (1600 m) closed drainage in Fars Province, Iran. The central valley is quite large (2600 km²), and while dry by American standards (350 mm of annual precipitation), it is relatively well watered for Iran. This rainfall is generally sufficient to support crops of winter wheat or barley, and numerous springs issuing from the edges of the valley alluvium allow localized irrigation of small gardens and orchards. It snows in the winter and is hot and rainless in the summer—a climate similar in many ways to that of the higher regions in the American Southwest.

The Banesh period is the era during which state-level polities first appear in highland Iran. It is defined by a series of locally distinctive ceramic types, but these have good parallels to Late Uruk, Jemdet Nasr, and Early Dynastic I materials in Mesopotamia (see Porada 1965; Lloyd 1978 for details of the Mesopotamian chronological sequence). Banesh-style ceramics appear to be introduced into the Kur River basin around 3400 B.C., and by the Early phase of the Banesh period (3300–3200 B.C.) the population of the valley was stable, neither growing nor in decline. During the Late Middle phase (3050–2900 B.C.), the Banesh population of the region more than tripled, presumably through immigration, and Site 8F8 grew to a size of at least 40 ha. This city—historic Anshan—dominated much of the Middle East for a century or two and then declined in both size and political importance during the Late Banesh phase (2900–2600 B.C.).

A general survey of the Kur basin (Sumner 1972) had discovered 26 Banesh

John R. Alden

period sites. Nothing was known, however, about chronological subdivisions of the Banesh, and nothing was known about regional settlement organization. These two issues became a major part of my dissertation research, which was carried out in 1976 and 1977 with the aid of a dissertation improvement grant (#BNS–76–81955) from the National Science Foundation. During this study a dozen new Banesh sites were located, and the period was divided into five subphases. Data on each site were gathered through systematic surface collecting, and phase-by-phase patterns of population size and distribution were examined (Alden 1979). In addition, considerable attention was devoted to reconstructing patterns of ceramic production and distribution in the region. The remaining portion of this chapter is drawn from that phase of my study.

Data were collected using a two-stage program of survey. All known sites in the region with Banesh period occupations were visited, and purposive collections of 10 to 40 distinctive Banesh sherds were made at each site. A 5% stratified random sample of surface material was collected from sites without extensive overburden from later occupations. Each site to be systematically collected was mapped with alidade and plane table and divided into 10m × 10m squares oriented along a N–S axis. The area of occupation was divided into units of 25 squares, and one square was randomly chosen from each unit of 25. Then one additional square was drawn from each unit of 100 squares, giving a total of five 10m × 10m squares from every 100, or 5%. Then all material on the surface of each selected square was gathered and bagged.[3]

The collections were then taken to a laboratory where they were washed, sorted, counted, and weighed. All rims, bases, and decorated body sherds were separated from the undecorated body sherds and then numbered. After all collecting was completed, these diagnostic sherds were sorted into types and their frequencies tabulated. For selected types a series of formal attributes was measured; drawings were made of a sample of each ceramic type. These counts, weights, drawings, and measurements constituted the basic data from which I intended to reconstruct patterns of ceramic production and distribution.[4]

During the survey, five Banesh sites were identified where grit-tempered ceramics had been produced. They were distinguished by the presence of slag from ceramic kilns, by a specialized ceramic working tool called a ring scraper, and by a peculiar ceramic vessel form, the pierced bowl. Each grit-tempered ceramic production site had at least two of these three features, while no other site had any (Alden 1979:87–91).

---

[3]Generally, collecting the purposive sample of sherds and mapping a site took one day. Eight to 10 of the 10m × 10m squares could be collected in a day, so on the average, surveying each site took two to three days. In total, this phase of the survey required a little over a month to complete, with the assistance of three locally employed workmen.

[4]About two tons of sherds were collected, weighed, and counted. Ten types (about 800 examples) were measured and over 500 sherds were drawn. Weighing and counting took about three weeks, measuring attributes took another three weeks, and drawing took about a month. Most of this material is published in Alden (1979).

Four of the five production centers could be assigned to one of the five phases within the Banesh period. This proved possible because each site was only utilized for a short time, presumably because ceramic production shifted when the locally available fuel supply was exhausted. Hence, if it is possible to identify the production location of chronologically distinctive ceramic types, it will also be possible to examine the distribution processes operating during the relatively short spans of time that each site served as a production center.

To do so, appropriate ceramic types must be identified. Ceramics useful for analyses of distribution patterns should have several characteristics. First, they must be functional vessels, to avoid distributional patterns determined more by social or political factors than by economic ones. Second, each must be clearly distinguishable as a type. Categories that encompass too much variability are not useful. Third, they should be types that would be frequently utilized and frequently broken, to ensure that they would distinguish distribution during the phase in question. It would be misleading if the pottery types studied became heirlooms, passing from parent to child and moving from site to site. This criterion also eliminates vessels acquired through trade with distant regions and particularly fine or elaborate pieces. Fourth, they should be common enough to be found on the surface of most of the sites where they were used. Finally, their production should have been limited to a single phase, and the site or sites where they were made should be known.

There is one Banesh grit-tempered ceramic type fitting all these requirements—the pinched-rim bowl. It was common (109 examples), utilitarian, clearly distinguishable, limited to a single chronological phase, and at least one site where these bowls were produced has been identified. Four other Banesh types are potential indicators of distribution patterns: large storage jars, band-rim jars, expanded-rim jars, and deep bowls with exterior grooves and impressed rims. At present, however, there are not enough examples of any of these types to make a useful statistical population. Consequently, the analysis of distribution patterns will have to be limited to the Early phase production and distribution of pinched-rim bowls. Figure 4.2 shows the Early phase (3300–3200 B.C.) occupations in the Kur River basin, with sites mentioned in this chapter identified by number.

Pinched-rim bowls (Figure 4.3) have several characteristics that are easily measurable and that show some stylistic variability: pinch length, pinch thickness, outside diameter, and body thickness (see Figure 4.4). There were no categorical characteristics, such as lip type or decorative motifs, that appeared useful to record, although these kinds of characteristics can also be considered when doing stylistic analyses. The choices of what to measure were based on experience with the body of pottery being considered and on intuition, because there has been almost no other work done with Banesh pottery that would indicate useful details to record and examine.

The first question to be answered is Were all pinched-rim bowls made at Site 7F1, the Early Banesh ceramic production site, or could some have been manufactured at some undiscovered location? Let us assume that measurements

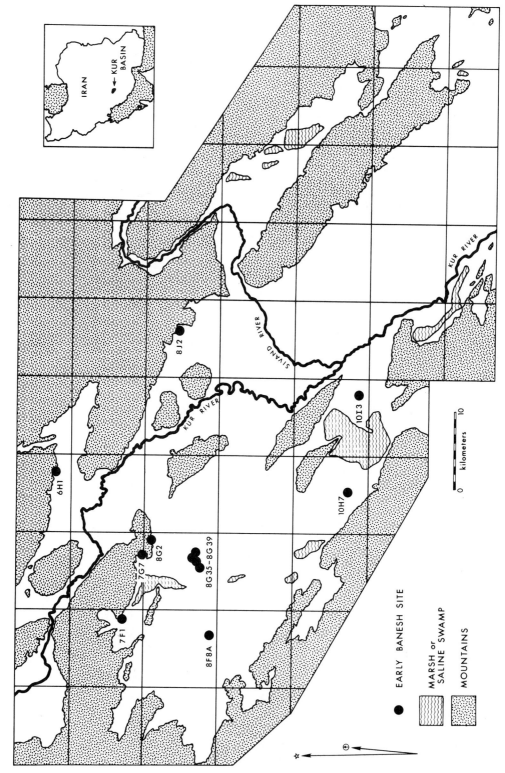

Figure 4.2. Early Banesh sites in the Kur River basin. Only sites with definite occupations and where systematic surface collections were made are shown.

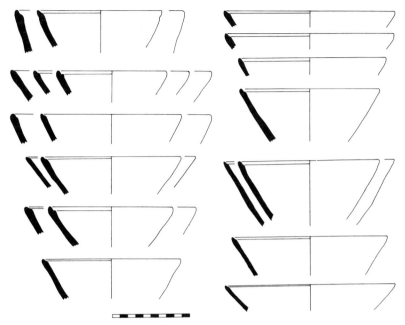

Figure 4.3. Drawings of 20 pinched-rim bowl sherd profiles. The scale is in centimeters.

made on vessels from a single production source and made by a single group of potters will show normal distributions. Examination of histograms allowed sherds with highly abnormal dimensions to be removed from the sample of sherds to be studied.[5] These histograms also revealed cases where distributions were distinctly skewed or potentially multimodal. All distributions not obviously nonnormal were tested for normality using the Lilliefors statistic; the hypothesis of normality was rejected only if the chance was less than 5% that the distribution was a sample from a normally distributed population. These and all other statistical tests were done using the MIDAS statistical analysis program of the Michigan Terminal System. Details of the Lilliefors test are given in Lilliefors (1967). In general, for samples with $N > 30$, the assumption of normality can be rejected at a .05 level of confidence if the Lilliefors statistic is greater than .886/sqrt (N). As shown in Table 4.3, neither the distribution of pinch length nor of pinch thickness was different from normal at the .05 level of confidence. These results support the proposition that all pinched-rim bowls were made by a single group of potters at a single production location, Site 7F1.

There are several more questions that should be asked at this point. Are the

[5]Two sherds had unusually thick bodies and five showed abnormally high pinch thickness. These cases were eliminated from the sample for analysis, reducing it to 102 cases with all data except outside diameter and 61 cases with all data. These constitute the tested sample of pinched-rim bowls. Measurements for individual sherds have been published in Alden (1979:Table 28).

John R. Alden

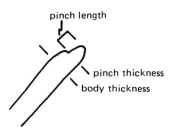

Figure 4.4. Locations of the measured attributes on pinched-rim bowl rims.

measurements of the bowls from Site 7F1 (the known production site) normally distributed? Are the measurements of the bowls from all other sites normally distributed? And finally, do these two subgroups of pinched-rim bowls have statistically different means or variances?

As Table 4.4 shows, pinch length, pinch thickness, and body thickness from both of the bowl populations have distributions not significantly different from normal, and they have similar variances. However, the means of all three measurements are slightly but significantly different between bowls from the manufacturing site (7F1) and bowls from all other sites. The 7F1 examples have shorter (by 1 mm) and thinner (by .5 mm) pinched rims and bodies that average .3 mm thicker than the sherds from all other sites. I conclude that the 7F1 pieces represent a different population from the sherds found on other sites.

This result, however, does not necessarily contradict the hypothesis that all pinched-rim bowls were made at Site 7F1. Instead, it seems to show that bowls for export were not selected randomly from the products of 7F1. Someone—producer, distributor, or consumer—was systematically choosing the bowls with longer and thicker pinches and slightly thicker bodies for exportation. This might seem to indicate that the larger vessels were being exported. Yet as Table 4.4 shows, the exported bowls had a slightly smaller mean rim diameter

TABLE 4.3

Pinched-rim Bowl Statistics (Selected Sample). Descriptive statistics for four measured attributes of pinched-rim bowls. The Lilliefors statistic is a measure of the deviation of observed data from a normal distribution, and is the criterion by which the hypothesis of normality is tested for each measured attribute.

	N	Min	Max	Mean	Standard deviation	Lilliefors statistic	Reject normal?
Pinch length	102	.18	.63	.40	.10	0.077	No
Pinch thickness	102	.32	.68	.51	.08	0.055	No
Body thickness	102	.52	1.00	.74	.10	0.080	Yes
O.D.	61	12	26	19.7	2.7	0.156	Yes

TABLE 4.4
Comparison between Sites of Pinched-rim Bowls. Comparisons of the measured attributes of sherds from the production site, 7F1, with sherds from all other Early Banesh sites in the region. The exported examples have thicker bodies and thicker, longer pinches. T and F tests are inappropriate for the diameter measurements because those data show nonnormal distributions.

Sample	N	Mean	Var.	Lilliefors statistic	Reject normal?	T^a	F^b
Pinch length							
Production site	58	.36	.008	.095	No		
Other sites	44	.45	.011	.110	No	-4.6	1.4
Pinch thickness							
Production site	58	.49	.007	.101	No		
Other sites	44	.54	.006	.075	No	-3.4	1.1
Body thickness							
Production site	58	.73	.009	.086	No		
Other sites	44	.76	.009	.087	No	-2.0	1.1
Rim diameter							
Production site	38	20.1	7.99	.222	Yes		
Other sites	23	19.0	5.04	.277	Yes	—	—

[a]T (difference of means).
[b]F (difference of variance).
Statistics are underlined if they are significant at the .05 level.

than the bowls found on the production site. This means that the exported vessels were not thicker because of a correlation between size and thickness. Instead, I would suggest that the thicker vessels were exported because they were less likely to break during transport. Since exporters would want both minimum weight and maximum durability, they would tend to choose the smaller and thicker bowls from the products of Site 7F1. They would be limited, however, by two factors. Consumers desire vessels large enough to serve a variety of purposes, and potters wish to make thinner vessels that can be fired more quickly and with less breakage. The observed pattern of minimal differences between bowls left at the production site and bowls exported to the rest of the valley would result from the operation of these conflicting interests.

It would appear that the same kind of bowl was being chosen for export to all sites in the valley. This implies that the choice was being made by a small set of people other than the producers, and it is good, albeit circumstantial, evidence against a direct mode of distribution. Because individuals from a number of different sites would not be likely to select bowls by the same criteria, these patterns support the hypothesis that pinched-rim bowls were distributed through an indirect system. Let us now test this hypothesis more formally.

John R. Alden

In the introductory section of this chapter, it was predicted that in a direct distribution system there would be a regular falloff in product frequency with distance from the production site. Alternatively, if the producers brought their products to a central distribution point from where they were passed on through market-type exchange, product frequencies should decrease with increasing distance from the market center. In an allocation system controlled by a central authority (rather than reflecting principles of economic maximization and supply and demand), the importance of distribution costs should be minimal, and there should be little or no relationship between distance to the distribution or production center and product frequency. For products of a functional nature, such as ceramics, I would expect that allocation in a controlled, nonmaximizing system would be more or less equitable. Thus, there should be little difference in product frequency within such a regional system. Table 4.5 presents the data necessary to differentiate between these three situations by examining frequencies of pinched-rim bowl rims from the systematically surveyed sites. Figure 4.5 shows the predicted and observed patterns graphically.

The number of pinched-rim bowls per diagnostic sherd varies considerably from site to site, indicating that a system of controlled redistribution of grit-tempered pottery—the third possibility—is unlikely. That is, ceramic distribution is not under the control of a central agency that collects the products of manufacturing sites and allocates them equitably to the population under its

TABLE 4.5
Pinched-rim Bowl Frequencies at Systematically Surveyed Sites. The frequency data include only pinched rims from the random surface collections, with total counts for both random and purposive collections shown in parentheses.

Site	No. of bowl rims	% Early phase occupation[a]	No. of grit-tempered RBD[b]	Early phase RBD	Pinched-rim bowls per Early phase RBD	Distance (in km) from 7F1	Distance (in km) from 8G38
6H1	0	0.4/0.8 = 50%	53	26.5	.000	24.9	22.8
7F1	13(58)	2.6/10.6 = 24.5%	777	190.4	.068	0.0	14.5
7G7	20(20)	2.9/14.5 = 20%	791	158.2	.126	9.0	7.0
8F8A	1(1)	3.1/12.4 = 25%	184	46.0	.022	11.5	14.5
8G2	8(10)	1.3/6.5 = 20%	231	46.2	.174	12.0	5.5
8G35	0(5)	0.7/1.4 = 50%	30	15.0			
8G37	3(4)	0.1/0.2 = 50%	16	8.0	.041	14.5	
8G38	0(2)	2.7/10.8 = 25%	198	49.5	(8G35–8G39		
8G39	0(2)	0.3/0.6 = 50%	0	0	combined)		
8J2	0	1.2/4.8 = 25%	266	66.5	.000	38.4	29.4
10H7	0	0.3/0.6 = 50%	11	6.5	.000	34.8	21.2
10I3	0	0.9/3.6 = 25%	31	7.75	.000	43.6	29.9

[a]Early phase area/sum of areas from all phases of occupation.
[b]RBD = rim, base, and decorated body sherds.

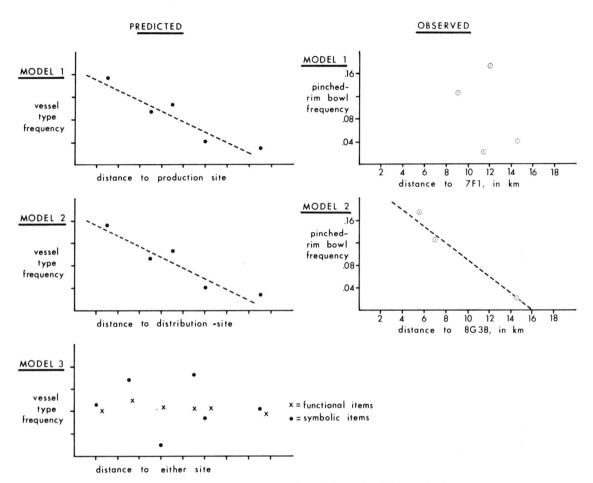

Figure 4.5. Predicted (left) and observed (right) patterns of pinched-rim bowl frequencies in random surface collections. Model 1 is of direct distribution; Model 2 shows indirect distribution; and Model 3 indicates two possible patterns for a controlled allocation system. The observed data fit the indirect distribution model.

domain. The ratio of bowls per diagnostic sherd does not covary with distance from the production site, indicating that we are not dealing with a direct distribution system. Instead, with the production location excluded from consideration, pinched-rim bowl frequency varies with distance from the 8G35–8G39 site cluster. Sites closest to this cluster have higher frequencies of pinched-rim bowls, and more distant sites have lower frequencies. This pattern implies that a market-type distribution system existed, with bowls being selected at and transported in bulk from the production site to the distribution center. There they were exchanged for the products of other sites on an individual basis, resulting in nearby sites (whose residents came to the market more frequently) having more bowls and distant sites having fewer. This market would appear to have been created and controlled by some central authority, otherwise, direct and indirect exchange would be expected to coexist, and the bowl frequencies at Sites 8F8A and 8G2 do not indicate that they did.

The regression line for the observed data in Figure 4.5 crosses the *x* axis at about 16 km, indicating that the radius of the area served by the 8G38 market was between 14 and 18 km. This is about the maximum distance that a person on foot could go and return in a day if they carried a reasonably sized burden. People from sites more than 16 km or so from 8G38 would not use it as a market center. In support of this speculation, no site more than 20 km from 8G38 had any pinched-rim bowls in either the systematic or purposive sample collections.

Most readers will have at least two additional questions. First, why did Site 8G38 become the center of the indirect distribution system? Second, the demand for pottery should be relatively inelastic. If only one site was producing grit-tempered ceramics and each settlement used and broke bowls at a similar per capita rate, why didn't each site acquire pinched-rim bowls in the same proportions, even though it would be a bit more expensive for the more distant locations? Both questions need to be answered before the arguments presented previously will be convincing.

There is an excellent reason why Site 8G38 would have been chosen as a center for indirect distribution: It is close both to the mean center of settlements and to the mean center of Early Banesh population in the Kur River basin. The mean center of settlements is defined as the average of the coordinates of every site occupied during a particular time (King 1969:93–96). The mean center of population is calculated by summing the products of the population and geographical coordinates of each site and dividing the sum by the total population of all sites. In formal terms, for N sites with populations p and locations (x,y), the mean center of settlements has the coordinates

$$(\Sigma x_i/N, \ \Sigma y_i/N),$$

and the mean center of population has coordinates

$$(\Sigma x_i p_i/\Sigma p_i, \ \Sigma y_i p_i/\Sigma p_i).$$

Applying these formulae, Site 8G38 is 3.3 km south of the center of Early Banesh settlements and 4.9 km southeast of the center of population. It is thus a central place geographically, as well as a central place in the distribution system.

I do not believe, however, that 8G38 was founded to serve as a center for indirect distribution. It is in an ideal location for the production of chaff-tempered pottery—a low area of the valley with both rushes and clay nearby and with soil suitable for growing either wheat or barley. Chaff-tempered pottery is a distinguishing characteristic of the Banesh period. It was made by mixing clay, chaff, and water to make a coarse, ill-knit paste from which crude vessels were formed. After being sun dried, these vessels were fired in heaps of straw or dry rushes. The chaff-tempered pottery could not replace the grit-tempered ware, for it has neither the strength nor the resistance to thermal shock offered by grit-tempered pottery. Yet the frequency of chaff-tempered pottery demonstrates that these vessels served important functions.

It is not necessary to speculate that chaff-tempered pottery may have been made near Site 8G38, for two of the sites in the 8G35–8G38 cluster were dumps for chaff-tempered vessels that had broken during firing. One of the dumps is small, but the other covers some 7000 m² and contains an estimated 600,000 kg of debris. It appears that enough chaff-tempered pottery was made at this one site to supply the entire Banesh population of the Kur basin for at least 200 years (Alden 1979:102–114). I would propose that the 8G35–8G38 settlements were founded in the most central location where the resources to manufacture chaff-tempered pottery were available, and that this locale later became the nexus of a regional distribution system for Early Banesh society. Chaff-tempered pottery was distributed directly, because it moved straight from its production site to the consumer, but the distribution of grit-tempered wares was indirect.[6]

The second question is potentially more important, because it indicates a basic contradiction in the assumptions made earlier in this chapter. If consumption is invariant, then each family at each site in the valley will use and break an equivalent number of bowls. Such inelastic demand should make meaningless the portion of vessel cost that is due to travel requirements, and pinched-rim bowls should be equally frequent in all parts of the valley. The explanation for this apparent inconsistency is straightforward. Demand *was* inelastic, and Site 7E1 *was* the only specialized production site for grit-tempered ceramics, but nothing prevented the residents of other sites from making their own grit-tempered pottery. The techniques were certainly generally known, and the necessary materials were generally available. The proportion of locally manufactured pottery would depend on some balance between the relative desirability, convenience, quality, and cost of ceramics made by specialists and ceramics made by the users.

If ceramics were occasionally produced at settlements other than the specialized production site, then why is production debris not found at all sites? First, two of the three types of evidence used to define ceramic production locations are specialized tools. Neither pierced bowls nor ceramic ring scrapers would be useful for anything but ceramic manufacture in quantity. The time and effort they would save a part-time potter would not repay the effort required to make and fire the tools. Second, large kilns are expensive to build

---

[6]Grit-tempered pottery could not be manufactured at the more central 8G35 settlement because the clays from the center of the valley contain too much calcium carbonate to allow firing at high temperatures (Blackman n.d.). In addition, the wood necessary to fuel ceramic kilns was probably only available in quantity at the valley margins (Alden 1979:92).

and tricky to use. Consumer-produced ceramics were probably fired in ad hoc kilns or in the open air rather than in the large, two-chambered kilns that were apparently used by the specialists. In fact, a nonspecialist would not even make enough pottery to fill such a kiln. Ceramic slag is an unavoidable by-product of the large kilns, but it would not result from the kind of direct firing that small-scale producers would employ. With neither ceramic slag nor specialized production tools, there would be no surface evidence of ceramic manufacture at such sites.

CONCLUSIONS

The availability of systematically collected, chronologically controlled data allows us to reach a number of conclusions. The normal distribution (lack of multimodality) of pinch length and pinch thickness indicates that the pinched-rim bowls were made at a single site by a single school of potters. The difference in means between exported bowls and those found on the production sites implies that the bowls were selected for export on stylistic and functional criteria by a small group of distributors. The frequency of bowls in the 100% surface collection units implies that consumers acquired their bowls from the cluster of sites around 8G38. Covariation of surface frequency with distance from this group of sites indicates that the distance component of distribution cost was significant, and it hints at a market rather than a managed allocation system for the distribution of grit-tempered ceramics. Although ceramics were certainly manufactured on a small scale at many of the Early Banesh sites in the region, the indirect distribution system clearly filled an important portion of most sites' demand for pottery.

Data on the density of a particular ceramic type from a series of stratified random surface collections have been used to demonstrate the operation of an indirect distribution system in highland Iran as early as 3200 B.C. This is intrinsically interesting, but in and of itself, it may not seem particularly important. However, it has significant implications. It demonstrates, by definition, the presence of a complex economic organization, which generates significant savings in transportation costs by centralizing exchange. These savings, however, are made at the cost of local independence, for all sites involved in such systems cede a degree of control to whoever controls the nexus of exchange. The savings from a more efficient system can go into increasing status differentiation rather than being returned to the populace, and the potential for manipulating access to necessary goods or services is an important means through which an emerging elite can enforce its authority. Thus the development of complex economies is at least one mechanism of societal evolution.

I hope to have demonstrated that it is possible to reconstruct forms of economic organization directly from archaeological evidence. We need not be limited to inferring such patterns from settlement sizes and locations, and we do not have to depend on physical procedures like neutron activation, which may be incapable of distinguishing sources within a single geological province. Economic organization can be recovered directly from the archaeological record, and we should regularly attempt to do so.

REFERENCES

Adams, R. McC., and H. J. Nissen
   1972   *The Uruk countryside: the natural setting of urban societies*. Chicago: University of Chicago Press.
Alden, J. R.
   1979   *Regional economic organization in Banesh period Iran*. Ph.D. dissertation, Department of Anthropology, Ann Arbor: University of Michigan.
Blackman, M. J.
   n.d.   The mineralogical and chemical analysis of Banesh period ceramics from Tal-e Malyan, Iran. London: *Proceedings of the 1979 Archaeometry and Archaeological Symposium* (forthcoming).
Chagnon, N. A.
   1968   *Yanomamö—the fierce people*. New York: Holt, Rinehart & Winston.
Harding, T. G.
   1967   *Voyagers of the Vitiaz strait*. Seattle: University of Washington Press.
Johnson, G. A.
   1973   *Local exchange and early state development in southwestern Iran*. University of Michigan Museum of Anthropology *Anthropological Papers*. No. 51.
King, L. J.
   1969   *Statistical analysis in geography*. Englewood Cliffs, N. J.: Prentice-Hall.
Lilliefors, H. W.
   1967   On the Kolmogorov–Smirnov test for normality with mean and variance unknown. *Journal of the American Statistical Association* 62:399–402.
Lloyd, S.
   1978   *The archaeology of Mesopotamia*. London: Thames and Hudson.
Porada, E.
   1965   The relative chronology of Mesopotamia. Part I—seals and trade (6000–1600 B.C.). In *Chronologies in old world archaeology*, edited by R. Ehrich, pp. 133–200. Chicago: University of Chicago Press.
Sumner, W. M.
   1972   *Cultural development in the Kur River basin: an archaeological analysis of settlement patterns*. Ph.D. dissertation, Department of Anthropology, University of Pennsylvania.

5

Aboriginal Exchange and Territoriality in Owens Valley, California

Robert L. Bettinger

It is widely held that throughout the Great Basin of the United States successful adaptation by hunter–gatherers required social fragmentation into economically independent and highly mobile family units whose movements were unencumbered by social or territorial barriers. It is argued here, however, that many of the same problems solved by this fragmentation were in some localities resolved by the formation of more complex suprafamilial organizations in which the exchange of resources and the ownership of territories figured prominently. The first part of this chapter examines the differences between these contrasting adaptive strategies. The second part proposes a method for distinguishing them archaeologically by the use of lithic source analysis. The approach is illustrated with an example from Owens Valley in California.

OBSIDIAN IN CALIFORNIA

Of all the raw materials used by native Californians, none has drawn so much scientific attention as has obsidian. This is understandable, of course, because few areas of the world are as rich in this natural glass as California, with 14 or more individual sources concentrated principally in the central and northern parts of the state (see Ericson, Hagan, and Chesterman 1976). That aboriginal groups took full advantage of these glasses is clearly attested to by their abundant representation in both the precontact and postcontact as-

103

semblages of California—a feature that has evoked comment virtually from the inception of anthropological interest in the area.

Early studies dealing with the procurement, exchange, and circulation of this material—both in raw form and as finished products—lacked adequate data on quarry locations and trustworthy methods for sourcing glass, and were necessarily confined to ethnographic accounts and tentative archaeological speculation (e.g., Steward 1933; Meighan 1955; Lanning 1963). This greatly restricted the scope of inferences that could be made, and precluded the undertaking of specialized research on the topic. More recently, however, with the development of reliable physical techniques capable of distinguishing material from different sources (e.g., X-ray fluorescence, neutron activation, thermoluminescence, etc.), there is renewed interest in obsidian distributions and their prehistoric procurement systems.

The signal work in this recent cycle of obsidian studies is Jack's (1976) X-ray fluorescence source analysis of some 1500 obsidian artifacts recovered from major ethnolinguistic areas within California. Although this study was essentially descriptive, Ericson (1977, 1981) subsequently reanalyzed Jack's data using multivariate techniques to elicit regional patterns of aboriginal obsidian exchange in California. From this, he constructed a model to predict for any geographical point the frequency of material from a given obsidian source based on the local population of that point, the distance to the obsidian source, and the distance to the nearest competing obsidian source. This yielded satisfactory results for most sources.

The resurgence of interest in obsidian brought by newer analytical techniques has produced other studies less broad in scope, dealing with artifacts from single sites. Although many of these studies lack explicit problem orientation and are concerned merely with documenting the origins of glass used in tool production, in some cases specific research questions have been formulated and tested. An example is Hughes's (1978) study of obsidian *beigaben,* or burial furniture, from a prehistoric Wiyot site in northwestern California, in which X-ray fluorescence source analysis demonstrated source differences between the glass used for utilitarian reasons and that used for socioceremonial reasons.

Despite the obvious differences in scale between Ericson's study, which is concerned with regional patterns for the whole state of California, and Hughes's study, which is concerned with patterns pertaining to a single village, both investigations are similar. Their concern lies not so much with obsidian sourcing and distributions, as it does with the underlying acquisition systems—both those of direct procurement and those of exchange—by which obsidian, and presumably other goods, were obtained, and with the relationship of these acquisition systems to other aspects of sociopolitical organization.

Based on his findings Ericson proposes, for instance, that obsidian distributions throughout California are most easily explained as resulting from chains of individual exchanges—the material passing through many hands before reaching its final destination. He argues moreover that this acquisition system is compatible with what he believes to be a prevailing pattern of egalitarian social organization in precontact aborginal California.

Hughes, by contrast, suggests that the use of separate networks to obtain obsidian for utilitarian and socioceremonial purposes implies a developed system of social ranking that was supported at least in part by the regular acquisition and subsequent conspicuous display of exotic wealth items.

Clearly, obsidian source analysis perhaps holds its greatest promise for the information it can shed on the acquisition systems and sociopolitical organization of aboriginal California. What is needed is a research design that incorporates source analysis and theories of acquisition as they are embedded in the larger sociopolitical context. That is, in contrast to the present primary focus on acquisition itself, it may be more profitable to begin by considering the nature of a society's organization units themselves and the ways in which they operated internally and externally through exchange. For example, it is reasonably well established that at least some aboriginal groups in California were organized in nonegalitarian units, but that the nature of these varied substantially, ranging from the quasi anarchy of northwestern California to the structured patrilineages in the southern part of the state (Bean 1978). One would expect, therefore, that these organizational differences would correspond to basic differences in patterns of resource acquisition, shaping and being shaped by them. In short, this analytical framework shifts attention away from exchange and procurement per se, and draws it to the broader social and political context in which the exchange takes place (see Earle, Chapter 1; Hodder, Chapter 9).

THE PROBLEM OF OWENS VALLEY SOCIOPOLITICAL ORGANIZATION

Over the past four decades, Great Basin anthropologists have explored the problem of man–land relationships. The basic analytical framework for this research is patterned closely after Julian Steward's 1938 analysis of Great Basin society in which he proposed that aboriginal organization in the Great Basin was ultimately grounded in technical capability and environmental setting. Additionally, because this area is generally agreed to have been broadly uniform with respect to technology, variability in adaptation has come to be accepted as reflecting differences of environment. The prevailing environmental conditions were marginal for human occupation, and based on this, Steward held that the need to rely on scarce and unpredictable resources, combined with a simple technology, required frequent movements in small, widely scattered groups. This precluded the ownership of territories and prevented the formation of stable organizations that were more complex than the family band. Only a few obvious exceptions to this pattern existed, of which the Owens Valley Paiute was perhaps the most notable.

Owens Valley is a long trough flanked by high mountain ranges—the Sierra Nevada to the west and the Inyo–White Mountains to the east—and is situated in central-eastern California (Figure 5.1). In ethnographic times, Owens Valley was occupied by Mono-speakers numbering between 1000 and 3000 individuals or about .4 to 1.2 persons per mi.^{2}. Although the subsistence resources and the tools and techniques for their procurement within Owens Valley were typical of the Great Basin as a whole, settlement patterns and sociopolitical organization were anomalous. In particular, rather than moving at frequent intervals in small groups, the Owens Valley Paiute occupied relatively large, permanent villages on the floor of the valley. These villages were inhabited virtually year round, except for trips to collect resources some distance from the village and for the fall pinyon harvest in the Inyo–White Mountains, which—if the crop were large—might occasion fall or winter occupation of upland pinyon camps in the vicinity of pine-nut caches, although this was apparently infrequent. Although the family was an important sociopolitical unit among the Owens Valley Paiute in contrast to other localities, the family's role was restricted by district-level organization, consisting of an autonomous village or several politically allied villages. Districts owned and defended subsistence territories that included seed plots, irrigated gathering lands, fishing and hunting grounds, and salt sources. Within the district, political power was concentrated in hereditary chiefs who organized, or delegated the authority to organize, communal undertakings including the construction and maintenance of irrigation systems and sweat houses, fish poisoning and animal drives, and mourning ceremonies and annual fiestas to which other neighboring districts were invited.

Steward (1938, 1955, 1970) attributed the unusual residential stability and relatively complex sociopolitical organization of the Owens Valley Paiute to the productivity of their local environment. This productivity resulted from exceptional vertical relief that brought a variety of important resources into close juxaposition and from abundant water resources. This environmental explanation of sociopolitical complexity is not altogether satisfying. Granted that Owens Valley is more hospitable than some parts of the Great Basin, there remain nevertheless many other areas where subsistence resources approach or exceed in abundance those in Owens Valley but which are ethnographically associated with adaptive patterns not perceptibly different from the typical transhumant family-band pattern. Steward's technoenvironmental determinist model thus does not explain why stable villages and districts developed in Owens Valley and did not develop in other equally productive environments.

Several possible explanations exist for this inadequacy. Conceivably, the ethnographic accounts are in error. Perhaps the Owens Valley Paiute pattern was less well developed than the ethnographic sources suggest, or other, equal-

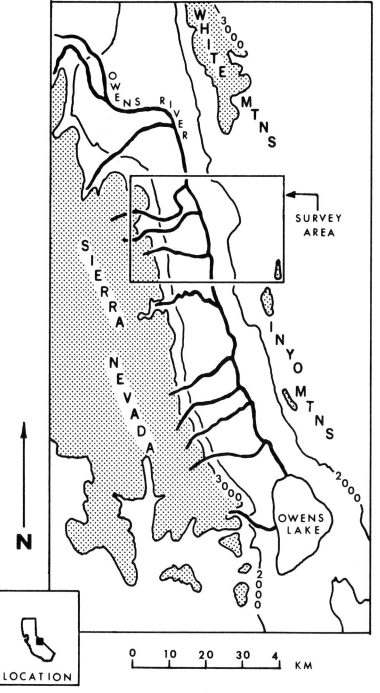

Figure 5.1. Map of Owens Valley showing location of archaeological survey area. Contour intervals are in meters.

ly complex systems went unrecorded (e.g., Thomas 1979). On the other hand, our current understanding of native environments may be so imperfect that we will ultimately be able to explain the peculiarities of Owens Valley Paiute adaptive strategies on these grounds alone. Although neither of these explanations can be discounted, neither is particularly telling. It seems unlikely that the ethnographic accounts are grossly in error—notwithstanding some distortion deriving from informant error and interpretive bias, as a consequence of their having been obtained long after European contact. Similarly, while future research may disclose heretofore unsuspected aspects of past environment or of man–land interaction, there is at present no clue as to what these might be or how they would help explain the adaptive contrast between Owens Valley and other areas.

There remains yet a third alternative. It can be argued that the aboriginal adaptive repertoire was not restricted to "hard" technology alone, but included a variety of viable organizational responses. For instance, it would seem reasonable that having a specific hard technology—i.e., the ability to produce certain tools and facilities—and a given environment, it would be possible to develop a variety of workable adaptations, each characterized by differences in subsistence emphases and consequent differences in settlement patterns and sociopolitical organization (e.g., Bettinger 1980). Organizational responses might also include those of "soft" technology; that is, the development of more complex or formalized institutions capable of undertakings beyond the capacities of smaller or more loosely organized groups.

Accepting the validity of this premise requires that we consider the organizational alternatives available to the typical Great Basin family-band system. Reduced to its essentials, Steward's family-band model turns on the premise that because desert resources are sparse and unreliable, aboriginal groups are forced to move almost constantly in small family units in order to find plants and animals in quantities worth harvesting. From this, the failure to develop territories and/or cohesive sociopolitical groups logically follows. In essence, then, Steward's model is one in which the resources stay put and the people move—a system Lee (1972) argues is typical of hunter–gatherers.

The clearest alternative to this transhumant system is one in which the resources move and the people stay put; that is, one in which resources are distributed within a region by exchange. Such a system would consist of several discrete and locationally stable sociopolitical units. Each of these would be linked to the others by social, ritual, and economic ties, as a consequence of which resource surpluses experienced by one group would be transferred to others having resource shortfalls. In return for this, the resource donor would obtain from the recipients a proportionate quantity of currency, thus assuring future access to resources that would be equivalent in quantity to those transferred.

The advantage of such a system is not, as is commonly thought, that it permits survival, i.e., prevents starvation, although this occasionally might be the case. Rather, the benefits of this exchange can be measured in purely economic terms: It is less costly to exploit abundant resources than scarce ones, because with the former, the travel, search, and processing times associated with subsistence procurement are lower than with the latter (MacArthur and Pianka 1966; Schoener 1971; Pyke, Pulliam, and Charnov 1977; see Earle and Christenson 1980). Accordingly, a system that makes maximal use of resource surpluses, such as the exchange system previously described, will tend to be more efficient than a system in which surpluses are underused.

Presumably, the area covered by this exchange would have to be sufficiently diverse so that resource discrepancies would occur regularly, and yet not be so severe as to make wholesale resettlement more attractive than the use of exchange to make up for resource scarcity. In addition, within this larger area, it would be necessary that individual groups exploit resources within a restricted area, thereby keeping travel costs to a minimum and insuring optimal efficiency of the system. In turn, for each of these groups the ability to transform surplus subsistence resources into some form of currency—especially if it were one applicable to other transactions, such as bride wealth and political exchanges—would likely encourage the harvesting of these resources beyond the group's own needs. It would also follow that broad use of such currency would bring a concomitant increase in the value of resource surpluses and in the competition over them. Ultimately, one would expect this to lead to the development of more or less rigidly defined territories, each owned and defended by one group. Finally, the territories themselves would bring certain adaptive advantages, among them the ability to develop resource-management strategies and to make maximal use of permanent facilities connected with subsistence procurement, e.g., fish wiers, game corrals, etc.

Based on the ethnographic accounts from eastern California, Bettinger and King (1971) proposed that such an exchange system existed prehistorically in the Owens Valley. They argue that the Owens Valley Paiute districts acted as centers of resource accumulation and that between districts exchange was transacted with shell currency. Apparently exchange occurred in the context of annual fiestas, in which resource surpluses were distributed among the various districts in return for shell currency that could be saved against future resource shortfalls, or applied to defray costs incurred in other activities such as bridewealth.

Bettinger and King (1971) held that in the absence of this formal interdistrict exchange, subsistence–settlement patterns and sociopolitical organization in Owens Valley would have closely resembled those of the transhumant family system found elsewhere in the Great Basin. To test this proposition archaeologically required that the character of prehistoric subsistence–settlement patterns be documented through time, and the beginnings of the ethnographic pattern of stable villages dated. According to the hypothesis, the inception of this pattern should coincide with the appearance of districts and interdistrict exchange.

PREHISTORIC SUBSISTENCE AND SETTLEMENT IN OWENS VALLEY

In 1972 and 1973, probabilistic surface surveys were undertaken in a sample transect centering on the modern town of Big Pine in the central Owens Valley (Bettinger 1975, 1977). Random quadrats were intensively surveyed in six sampling strata representing the dominant biotic communities of the valley. This resulted in the location of 107 sites. At each site, features and ground-stone artifacts were noted by number and kind, and all ceramics, projectile points, drills, and bifaces were collected. The balance of the chipped-stone assemblage was sampled by 4- or 5-m-wide transects at the larger sites and completely collected at the smaller ones. Based on their archaeological assemblage, size, and location, these sites were subsequently divided into three major settlement categories: occupation sites, pinyon camps, and temporary camps.

To describe them briefly, *occupation sites* are large settlements (average .67 ha) situated in either riparian or desert-scrub communities on the valley floor. Their archaeological assemblages display the full range of features and artifacts known for the region—including dwellings, ceramics, ground-stone implements, and a variety of chipped-stone artifacts, notably projectile points, drills, bifaces, roughouts, unifaces, cores, and debitage. It is thought that these sites were occupied essentially year round by groups of between 50 and 200 individuals.

Pinyon camps are small-sized to medium-sized sites (average .28 ha) located in the pinyon–juniper woodlands of the Inyo–White Mountains east of the valley floor. They are characterized by archaeological assemblages both sparser and less diverse than those of occupation sites. Most commonly represented at these settlements are the tools and facilities associated with fall pinyon procurement and related activities, such as hunting and occasional winter occupation. These sites include storage facilities, dwellings, milling stones, projectile points, and unifaces. Pinyon camps were probably used by one to three nuclear families during the few weeks of the fall pinyon harvest, although the occupation may have lasted into spring when the stored nut crop was sufficiently large.

Temporary camps occur in all biotic communities and range in size from small to very large (average .27 ha). Although there is considerable variation in the density of cultural materials at these sites, their assemblages are typically restricted to items directly linked to resource procurement and tool repair, especially projectile points, point blanks, and debitage. It is suggested that temporary camps were occupied for no more than a few days at a time between early spring and late fall by family-sized parties for seed collecting, by small hunting parties, or by large groups engaged in communal fishing or animal drives.

Time-sensitive projectile points were used to date the sites, and this evidence—along with knowledge of the function and seasonality of the site types—was used to construct simple subsistence–settlement models for four archaeological phases spanning the interval from 3500 B.C. to historic times, about A.D. 1860 (Bettinger 1977). These data suggested that subsistence and settlement patterns in all phases were broadly similar to those of the late precontact–early historic period. That is, over the last 5500 years, the aboriginal inhabitants of Owens Valley occupied large villages on the valley floor and subsisted primarily on lowland plant resources. Lowland temporary seed-collecting camps and both lowland and upland hunting camps were also used when conditions demanded.

There were only two notable exceptions to this long-term stability. One was a change in the relative importance of wetland and dryland plants which affected the location of villages and the distances over which large game animals were pursued. The other was the relatively late inception of pinyon procurement at A.D. 600, at which time the intermittent fall–winter pattern of temporary residence began in the Inyo–White Mountains where this resource was located. None of these adaptive shifts, however, substantially disrupted the basic pattern noted before. Given this, if Bettinger and King are correct in their argument that settlement stability in Owens Valley is attributable to the presence of exchange systems rather than abundant resources, it would follow that these exchange systems would have to have been present by 3500 B.C. The remainder of this discussion is devoted to an archaeological test of this proposition.

IDENTIFYING EXCHANGE

Given the available archaeological data, no convincing way exists to document directly an exchange system of the kind already discussed. The subsistence resources moving between groups are of species generally available throughout the valley, and even in the absence of regular exchange these would have been accumulated and stored in large quantities to offset seasonal fluctuations in abundance. Thus, neither particular resources nor storage facilities would provide clear evidence of exchange. The same is true of the shell and stone currency used in exchange. This material could have served various purposes, in addition to its use in the kind of exchange proposed here.

Short of demonstrating interdistrict exchange directly, several associated organizational features should be identifiable archaeologically, and their presence would make such a system more probable. Territoriality is particularly attractive in this regard because, according to the model previously outlined, territories are inextricably linked to district exchange—both in the sense that by minimizing travel and harvest time, territorial systems offer an efficient means for the procurement of surplus resources ultimately intended for exchange, and in the sense that the possibility of such exchange increases the value of resource surpluses and leads to their protection through territories. Further, without exchange, resource fluctuations would preclude development of the preemptive land-use rights associated with territorial systems.

Although one might demonstrate territoriality in several ways, e.g., by the presence of stylistic boundaries, etc., its characteristic effect on the distribution of critical raw materials is especially susceptible to archaeological study. Put in simple terms, territorial and nonterritorial systems contrast in the degree to which specific resources are accessible for use. In a nonterritorial system, preemptive-use rights are lacking, and materials are generally obtained from their sources by *direct access*. Because the cost of procurement for a specific resource under these circumstances is primarily a function of travel distance to its source, its frequency declines gradually and without obvious changes in rate as distance from the source increases. As Findlow and Bolognese (Chapter 3) discuss, this would be modeled as a linear falloff. In a territorial system, on the other hand, resources are owned by specific groups, for whom they are available by direct access, and therefore they are relatively low in cost. But they can also be obtained by outside groups through the more costly process of trade. This dichotomy of acquisition is archaeologically reflected by a *supply zone*, where the resource was obtained by direct access and occurs in high frequencies, and a *falloff zone*, where the resource was obtained by exchange and occurs in substantially lower frequencies (Ericson 1981). A linear regression would in this case be inadequate, as within the territory it would occur in greater than expected frequency, and outside the territory in less than expected frequency.

ARCHAEOLOGICAL IDENTIFICATION OF PREHISTORIC TERRITORIES IN OWENS VALLEY

The present study examines the problem of prehistoric territoriality in Owens Valley by analyzing the distribution of obsidian from Fish Springs, a source located within the Big Pine survey transect for which well-controlled archaeological data are available.

The Fish Springs outcrop consists of a small perlite dome about 11 km south of the modern town of Big Pine. Within the quarry area, glass suitable for tool production occurs over an area of about .4 km^2. Generally the glass is found as small nodules and tabular slabs; most of them are less than 15 cm long.

The presumption underlying this analysis is that if Owens Valley groups were territorial, the distribution of Fish Springs obsidian would show (*a*) high frequencies within the territory where the source was located and where procurement would have been by direct access; (*b*) low frequencies in adjacent territories where it would have been obtained by trade; and (*c*) a sharp truncation of frequency, marking the boundary between these areas. To be convincing, it would have to be shown also that the territory associated with Fish Springs encompassed all settlement categories and biotic communities characterizing a complete subsistence–settlement system, i.e., occupation sites, pinyon camps, and temporary camps, as well as both lowland and upland zones in the Sierra Nevada and the Inyo–White Mountains. In the absence of territories, it would be expected that obsidian distributions would conform to Ericson's (1977, 1981) general model: Assuming that population densities were roughly equivalent within the valley, Fish Springs obsidian frequency would gradually decrease with distance from the source, with the rate of decrease in any direction being dependent upon proximity to other sources.

Comparison of obsidian frequencies between settlement categories can also shed light on the question of territoriality. In a nonterritorial system, representation of different stone sources tends to vary within the category of short-term sites and between short-term and long-term sites, while in a territorial system such variation is minor. This proposition rests on the assumption that—with or without territories—the use of different stone sources at a given site is strongly dependent on its length of occupation within a year. On the one hand, it is reasonable to assume that the longer the occupation, the greater the use of material from the nearest source, so as to minimize costs. With shorter occupation, on the other hand, other elements come into play. In general, it would seem to be the case that the shorter the occupation, the greater the use of materials from the source nearest the long-term base of operations rather than the source nearest the short-term site itself. This derives from the observation that such brief occupations are largely devoted to subsistence procurement, which would preclude time-consuming trips to obtain raw materials such as stone. This is true, especially since in such cases implement attrition is not severe, and replacement tools would likely be made from blanks routinely carried for that purpose.

In brief, for the most part short-term sites have little to do with direct lithic procurement, and their chipped-stone assemblages are a product of acquisition patterns prevailing at the base camps to which they are linked. Because of this, where territories are absent and resource areas may be exploited by several diverse groups working out of widely separated base camps, the representation of different stone sources will vary between different short-term sites. Moreover, for the same reason, the stone sources represented at a particular short-term site may be quite different from those found at base camps nearby. In a territorial system, however, all the temporary camps in a given area will be linked to the same base camp, and consequently, both temporary and base camps will tend to exhibit similar frequencies of lithic material from specific sources.

A similar contrast between territorial and nonterritorial systems applies also when a single source is considered. Here it can be proposed that when no territories intervene, differences in the archaeological representation of a specific obsidian will tend to increase gradually between settlement categories, as distance from its source increases. This is because, as the obsidian becomes more costly to procure by trade or travel, it will tend to be used in the manufacture of an ever-smaller set of artifact types (e.g., for projectile points but not knives or scrapers). This leads to increasing differentiation in the use of the obsidian between settlement categories that, by definition, are characterized by distinct sets of tool types. In the presence of territories, on the other hand, the frequency of the obsidian will show little variation between settlement categories for sites lying within the territory where the obsidian occurs and is acquired by direct access. And, at the same time, outside this territory—where this material must be acquired by trade—there will be sharp differentiation between settlement categories.

In short, given a territorial system, Fish Springs obsidian frequencies ought to be relatively uniform for sites within the aboriginal territory containing the Fish Springs source. Further, the frequency of this glass would not vary with the function of these sites or with the length of time they were occupied. Substantial variation in these respects would reduce the probability that territories existed.

Two circumstances might conceivably affect the relationships between obsidian distribution and territoriality previously noted. First, the sharpness of territory definition as marked by obsidian frequency depends on the degree to which territories were recognized and defended, and the antiquity of those territories within the span of human occupation. If territories were recent or weakly developed, discrete archaeological-boundaries would be unlikely. Because it is proposed here that territoriality was an important practice of long standing in Owens Valley, it is expected that territory boundaries should be well defined.

Second, Fish Springs obsidian frequencies might be poor indicators of prehistoric boundaries if—within Owens Valley—obsidian was rare, and consequently was widely traded between groups, thus blurring potential boundaries. This might present a problem. Although there are no fewer than six other glass sources within 160 km of Fish Springs, the distance to the nearest—Coso, 140 km to the south, and Mono Glass Mountain, 85 km to the north—raises the possibility that Fish Springs obsidian could have been the source of extensive exchange. Nevertheless, if the Fish Springs source were owned as part of an aboriginal territory, one would expect this to be perceivable. Most likely it would be perceivable in the form of a boundary dividing the territory in which it was found, and in which it was freely accessible to the inhabitants, and adjacent territories where it could be obtained only in exchange for some commodity—thereby raising its cost of procurement beyond that merely associated with travel and making other sources or other materials potentially more attractive.

THE ANALYSIS OF OBSIDIAN ARTIFACTS

The archaeological distribution of Fish Springs obsidian was established by calculating its frequency by weight in obsidian samples from archaeological sites located by the probabilistic quadrat surveys in the Big Pine transect. All sites containing this material were sampled. Other artifacts and raw materials were excluded from consideration on the grounds that differences in their weight, function, or curation might unduly distort their representation in different settlement categories. The actual separation of Fish Springs and non-Fish Springs obsidian was done by a combination of megascopic and microscopic analysis—a controversial technique that requires some discussion.

As indicated before, the recent growth of interest in obsidian is primarily due to the development of precise chemical and physical techniques capable of producing accurate source identifications (see Harbottle, Chapter 2). The reliability of these techniques is beyond question, and their use is preferred whenever it is feasible. Even so, the cost of analysis, although modest for individual specimens (roughly $15 per sample) becomes prohibitive for large-scale analyses that can involve thousands of specimens. For instance, at current rates, Jack's (1976) original study of California obsidian distributions would run close to $23,000, even though the coverage it provides is far too thinly spread to be of use in identifying the kind of boundaries sought here. The present study is based on nearly 4000 samples and provides a sample saturation—i.e., samples per unit of area—more than 1000 times more dense than that in Jack's study. Although barely adequate for its purpose, chemical characterization of these samples would have cost about $60,000 at current prices.

To minimize analytical costs, sourcing was based on megascopic and microscopic examination of the obsidian. This method usually has been considered unreliable because glass from diverse sources often shares generic similarities in color, texture, and inclusions; and because especially large outcrops tend to display substantial internal variability (cf. Hughes 1978:54, 63). The impression here, however, is that errors in identification have often occurred because investigators were either unfamiliar with regional variability within sources or because they made no conscious attempt at rigorous analysis. Many investigators, however, are increasingly convinced that reliable megascopic source identifications are possible if the source in question is relatively small and internally homogeneous, or if it produces glass that is in some way distinctive (F. Findlow, personal communication; D. H. Thomas, personal communication; G. Russell, personal communication).

Obsidian from the Fish Springs source would appear to be suitable for megascopic analysis based on these criteria. It is spatially restricted and displays several properties not known to occur consistently in material from other east–central Californian sources (Ericson 1981:Tables 3–4). In general Fish Springs obsidian shows sharply separated bands of clear to smoky brown and apple to olive green. These alternate with much finer, feather-like bands of reddish brown that, when struck by low-angle light, reflect a play of blue iridescence. The pattern of flow-banding is usually contorted, but it may occasionally appear as straight, parallel bands. Overall, the material is moderately translucent—the clear to smoky-brown bands more so than the green bands—

TABLE 5.1

Composition of debitage samples from sites within the Big Pine survey transect. Site numbers are given by biotic community, tract number, and site number within the tract. The letter preceding the slash (/) in the number refers to the community: A, riverine; B, desert scrub; C, pinyon woodland; E, upper sagebrush; F, Sierran meadowland. The number preceding the slash refers to the tract number; the number following the slash, the site number within the tract. Site type is given by category: O, occupation site; PC, pinyon camp; T, temporary camp.

Site number	Site type	Sample size	Fraction obsidian	Obsidian fraction Fish Springs
A1/1	T	14	100%	20%
A1/2	O	38	61%	28%
A2/1	O	113	98%	77%
A3/1	T	53	100%	56%
A3/2	T	66	99%	86%
A3/3	O	42	99%	82%
A3/4	T	33	100%	69%
A3/5	T	54	100%	74%
A5/1	T	36	100%	83%
A5/2	T	15	100%	89%
A6/1	T	41	100%	2%
A6/2	T	69	100%	81%
A6/3	T	61	99%	44%
A8/1	O	29	97%	71%
A8/2	T	16	100%	79%
A9/1	O	51	100%	71%
A9/2	T	40	100%	69%
A10/2	O	42	98%	82%
A10/3	T	9	100%	98%
B1/1	T	85	93%	33%
B25/1	T	6	100%	0%
B25/2	O	50	97%	65%
B25/3	O	8	100%	30%
B29/1	T	6	100%	63%
B29/2	T	40	98%	35%
B29/3	T	55	100%	42%
B48/1	T	59	89%	73%
B48/2	T	80	98%	53%
B48/3	T	9	100%	50%
B48/4	T	9	100%	30%
B53/1	O	72	79%	94%
B53/3	O	63	85%	62%
B56/1	O	10	100%	96%
B56/3	T	11	100%	90%
B56/4	T	54	100%	66%
B57/1	T	85	100%	78%
B68/1	T	79	100%	79%
B68/2	O	90	98%	70%
B70/1	T	62	99%	78%
B70/2	T	8	100%	78%
B70/3	T	54	100%	77%
B73/2	T	44	98%	60%
B83/1	T	142	99%	86%

(*continued*)

TABLE 5.1—*Continued*

Site number	Site type	Sample size	Fraction obsidian	Obsidian fraction Fish Springs
B86/1	T	58	100%	68%
B86/4	O	12	60%	68%
B92/1	T	36	100%	92%
B92/2	T	8	89%	96%
B92/3	T	27	100%	96%
B92/4	T	6	86%	92%
B92/5	T	23	96%	94%
B92/6	T	8	100%	91%
B95/1	T	16	100%	77%
B95/2	T	19	100%	93%
B111/1	T	—	0%	—
B116/1	T	59	100%	64%
B116/2	T	50	100%	66%
C1/1	PC	55	67%	57%
C9/1	PC	56	95%	63%
C9/2	PC	48	72%	65%
C10/1	PC	132	89%	65%
C11/1	PC	25	37%	66%
C11/2	PC	58	89%	68%
C25/2	PC	18	58%	19%
C25/4	T	19	95%	1%
C25/5	T	10	100%	3%
C25/6	T	84	96%	6%
C27/1	T	54	98%	13%
C29/1	T	5	100%	89%
C29/2	PC	3	23%	0%
C29/3	T	4	100%	0%
C35/3	T	13	100%	0%
C45/5	T	158	100%	56%
C56/2	PC	34	94%	10%
C56/5	PC	8	100%	51%
C56/7	PC	61	97%	11%
C83/2	PC	26	100%	77%
C90/1	T	14	100%	27%
C95/1	T	4	100%	0%
C95/2	PC	68	99%	16%
C102/1	T	31	100%	0%
C105/1	PC	6	100%	22%
C105/4	T	80	94%	12%
E1/1	T	3	60%	0%
E1/3	T	28	100%	9%
E3/1	T	6	100%	0%
E6/1	T	13	93%	0%
E8/1	T	58	100%	45%
E9/1	T	76	97%	21%
E10/2	T	3	100%	93%
E13/1	T	72	92%	8%
F1/1	T	2	67%	14%
F1/2	T	45	96%	6%
F1/3	T	17	100%	35%

in contrast to glass from the Casa Diablo source to the north, much of which is virtually opaque, and the glass from the Queen source, also to the north, much of which is highly translucent. Black and white phenocrysts of varying size are abundant in the Fish Springs obsidian, giving it a characteristically "dirty" appearance under magnification.

For this analysis, any piece of nonopaque obsidian debitage that could be described as either green in color or as displaying sheet-like blue iridescence was classified as Fish Springs. These particular characteristics were chosen because they were found to be present in 95% of a large and varied sample of modern debitage flakes removed from Fish Springs nodules, and because at the same time they could not be found in our collections from other quarries.

During the identification, pieces were first candled to determine the translucency and color. Specimens equivocal on these grounds were then examined under a binocular dissecting microscope set at 15X. The entire process takes from one to three minutes per piece. All specimens were independently identified by two workers, and any dubious pieces—usually fewer than 10%—were routinely classified as non-Fish Springs.

To test the accuracy of this technique, visual source identification following the above procedures was performed on a sample of 39 projectile points and 15 pieces of debitage that was subsequently shown by X-ray flourescence analysis to compose 25 examples of Fish Springs obsidian and 29 examples of non-Fish Springs obsidian. The visual identifications were correct for all 25 Fish Springs specimens and for 27 of the 29 non-Fish Springs specimens—the remaining 2 non-Fish Springs specimens being incorrectly identified as Fish Springs (cf. Bettinger, Jackson, and Hughes n.d.). That visual sourcing of Fish Springs obsidian in this case so closely agrees with chemical sourcing provides ample justification for its use in the present study.

In all, 3878 pieces of debitage from 94 sites were examined. Exceptionally large debitage collections from individual sites were sampled in order to facilitate analysis. In such cases, an attempt was made to draw a random sample consisting of at least 40 pieces. The material classifiable as Fish Springs was then weighed, and its fraction was calculated in terms of the total sample weight. These data are presented in Table 5.1, which indicates for each site the site category (occupation site, pinyon camp, temporary camp), the number of pieces actually examined, the obsidian fraction contained in the entire debitage sample from the site, and the fraction of material classified as Fish Springs in the sample examined. Table 5.2 provides summary source data for individual survey quadrats in which the sites were located. In this case, the frequency of material classified as Fish Springs was calculated for the quadrat by taking the mean value for all sites within the quadrat weighted by the total debitage count for each site. Because total debitage counts furnish a rough estimate of occupational intensity, the effect is to give greater weight to sites more intensively occupied.

TABLE 5.2
Distribution of Fish Springs obsidian within sample tracts in the Big Pine transect. Asterisks (*) indicate values based on samples consisting of less than 10 pieces of obsidian debitage.

Tract number	Number of sites	Combined sample size	Weighted mean	Range	Distance from source (km)
A1	2	52	27%	20 –28%	18.0
A2	1	113	77%	—	8.3
A3	5	248	80%	56 –86%	9.5
A5	2	51	84%	83 –89%	7.2
A6	3	234	45%	2 –81%	15.4
A8	2	46	75%	71 –79%	8.2
A10	3	107	77%	62 –98%*	10.4
B1	1	85	33%	—	20.9
B25	3	64	65%	0*–65%	18.0
B29	3	101	42%	35 –63%*	15.3
B48	4	157	66%	30*–70%	11.7
B53	2	135	80%	62 –94%	9.5
B56	3	75	91%	66 –96%	9.1
B57	1	85	78%	—	9.7
B68	2	169	71%	70 –79%	7.4
B70	3	124	78%	77 –78%	8.5
B73	1	44	60%	—	8.6
B83	1	142	86%	—	6.8
B86	2	70	68%	—	4.1
B92	6	108	94%	91*–96%	9.3
B95	2	35	86%	77 –93%	2.0
B116	2	109	64%	64 –66%	8.0
C1	1	55	57%	—	24.7
C9	2	104	65%	63 –65%	22.4
C10	1	132	65%	—	24.8
C11	2	83	67%	66 –68%	24.1
C25	4	131	9%	1 –19%	28.9
C27	1	54	13%	—	24.7
C29	3	12	19%	0 –89%*	27.7
C35	1	13	0%	—	24.3
C45	1	158	56%	—	14.0
C56	3	103	11%	10 –51%*	25.5
C83	1	26	77%	—	18.3
C90	1	14	27%	—	18.8
C95	2	72	16%	0*–16%	23.9
C102	1	31	0%	—	19.6
C105	2	86	13%	12 –22%*	16.9
E1	3	67	16%	0*–23%	26.6
E3	1	6	0%*	—	26.7
E6	1	13	0%	—	22.4
E8	1	58	45%	—	19.4
E9	1	76	21%	—	23.7
E10	1	3	93%*	—	16.8
E13	1	72	8%	—	17.5
F1	3	64	13%	6 –35%	23.3

THE RESULTS OF OBSIDIAN ANALYSIS

The frequency of glass identified as being from the Fish Springs source varied substantially in obsidian samples from the Big Pine transect. For the 94 individual sites, the percentage of Fish Springs obsidian ranged from 0% to 100%, with a mean of 51.7%; for the 46 quadrats that contained at least one site with obsidian debitage, it ranged from 0% to 94%, with a mean of 49.8%. These data were analyzed in a variety of ways, and in each instance the results were consistent with the notion that a territorial system was present prehistorically in the Owens Valley.

In Figure 5.2 the quadrat frequency of blue-iridescent–green obsidian is plotted against quadrat distance from Fish Springs, its probable source. Figure 5.2 shows the falloff as a linear regression of frequency with distance ($r = -.74, p \leq .001$). It is apparent, however, that the rate of decrease in frequency is not uniform, but rather it varies with distance from the source. Thus, with respect to a simple least squares regression line for frequency on distance, quadrats within 15 km of the source tend to show higher-than-expected frequencies, and those beyond 15 km tend to show lower-than-expected frequencies. This approximates the patterns originally described by Renfrew, Dixon, and Cann (1968:328–329), in which a specific resource shows a supply area in which it predominates and a falloff zone where it comes in contact with the supply zones of other resources used for the same purposes. In this case, however, owing to the substantial distances to the nearest alternative obsidian sources, the proximity of the Fish Springs falloff zone to the Fish Springs source would appear explicable only if the Fish Springs supply zone were defined by territorial boundaries restricting direct access to the source. To this it might be added that the substantial variability in the frequencies observed among quadrats lying between 15 km and 25 km from Fish Springs could best be accounted for by arguing either that the Fish Springs source was not centrally located within its territorial supply zone or that the zone itself was irregular—rather than being perfectly circular, its edges varying between 15 km and 25 km from this source.

The preceding relationships are made clearer when the quadrat frequencies are actually mapped on the Big Pine transect (Figure 5.3). This reveals a supply area characterized by quadrats with high frequencies of between 57% and 94% and an outlying area with substantially lower quadrat frequencies of between 0% and 45%. The transition between the two was marked by a fairly abrupt decrease in frequency. The northern, eastern, and southeastern boundaries of this supply area are relatively clearly shown by shifts in obsidian frequencies. A southwestern boundary is not evident from the scanty quadrat data available, but the single value for that vicinity is comparable to those near boundaries elsewhere in this supply area, suggesting that its southern edge lies not far south of the Pig Pine transect. To the west, high frequencies of blue-iridescent–green glass extend to the area immediately adjacent to an inhospita-

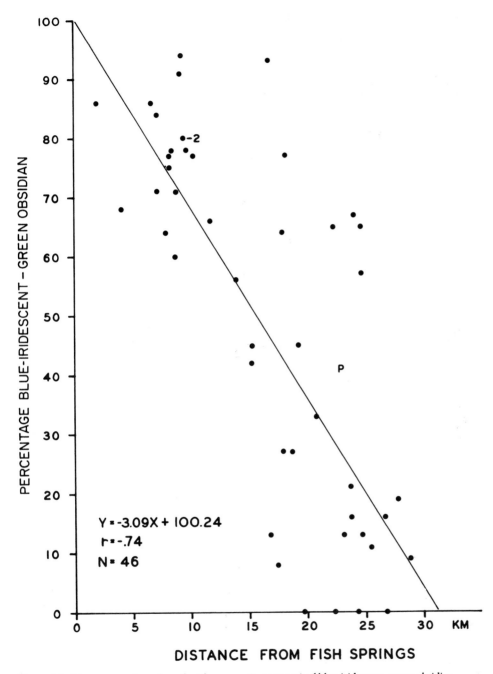

$$Y = -3.09X + 100.24$$
$$r = -.74$$
$$N = 46$$

Figure 5.2. Linear regression of quadrat frequency (percentage) of blue-iridescent–green obsidian on quadrat distance from Fish Springs source. The numeral 2 denotes two quadrats with identical distance and frequency values; the letter p the distance and frequency values for the Pinyon House site mentioned in the text.

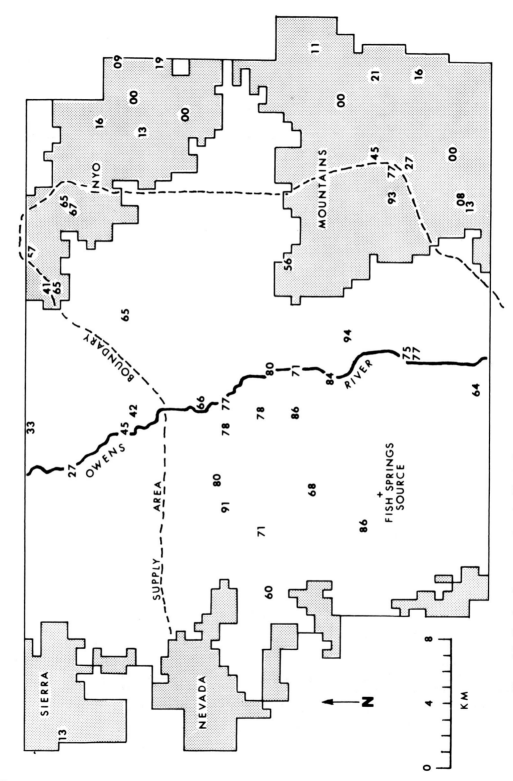

Figure 5.3. Quadrat frequency values for blue-iridescent–green obsidian plotted by location within archaeological survey area.

ble and aboriginally unoccupied stretch of the Sierra Nevada. Here the boundary is delimited by geographical features rather than by obsidian-frequency shifts. Thus defined, this supply area comprises a section of land that extends across central Owens Valley, running from high in the Sierra Nevada to the crest of the Inyo Mountains. Roughly 750 km² (290 mi.²), this territory encompasses large portions of all the major biotic communities present in the valley; thus it would be well suited to serve as the subsistence territory for an aboriginal group. Indeed, the supply area as traced by these frequencies is virtually conterminous with the combined territories of the ethnographic Big Pine and Fish Springs districts as mapped by Steward (1933:Map 2; 1938:Figure 7). In keeping with the earlier suggestion based on obsidian frequencies, the southern district boundary of Steward lies south of the Big Pine transect.

Finally, the notion that the supply area was a recognized aboriginal territory is supported by the lack of variation in frequencies between sites of different settlement categories in the same quadrats (see Tables 5.1 and 5.2). As explained earlier, this would indicate that the supply area was used almost exclusively by groups with easy access to the blue-iridescent–green glass available at Fish Springs and avoided by groups with access to other glasses that—under other circumstances—might have found it desirable to exploit the pinyon crops, game herds, and other resources found there. Only one quadrat, A6, shows substantial internal variation that cannot be attributed to sampling error. This unit, however, lies quite close to the northern supply-area boundary, and it is possible the variation is attributable to minor boundary shifts through time. Two other quadrats, B29 and E8, that show similar variability values and lie near boundaries, may also reflect such shifts.

It might also be noted that within certain quadrats—most notably A9, B70, B86, B92, B116, and C11—there is a puzzling lack of variation in frequencies between sites. Part of this, of course, is probably attributable to chance variation, particularly for the quadrats that contain only two sites—A9, B86, B116, and C11. With regard to B92, where a total of six sites showed blue-iridescent–green glass frequencies ranging only between 91% and 96%, it would seem most likely the obsidian samples examined consisted entirely of Fish Springs material, and what little variation is observed reflects only a consistent inability to recognize a certain fraction of this obsidian based on the identification criteria employed.

To summarize the preceding, the distribution of blue-iridescent–green glass shows sharply differentiated zones of supply and falloff, and based on the following, it can be argued that the zone of supply corresponds to an aboriginal territory.

First, in the absence of any competing glass sources close by, the proximity of the zone of falloff to the presumed source—Fish Springs—seems best explained as resulting from sociopolitical boundaries. It is notable in this regard that Ericson (1977, 1981) was unable to explain the distribution of Fish Springs obsidian by his population–distance model; therefore, his findings furnish additional support for the inferences drawn here. Indeed, it is clear from the present study, as well as those of Jack (1976) and Ericson (1981), that the procurement and distribution of Fish Springs obsidian followed a pattern quite different from that observed for other obsidian sources in central-eastern California. In particular, it would appear that its use was almost entirely confined to those groups having direct access to it, because there is no evidence of the regular occurrence of Fish Springs glass outside the immediate vicinity of the source. Ericson (1977) indicates that of the California sources he analyzed, Fish Springs had the most restricted distribution and, in keeping with this, only a few pieces have been found west of the Sierra Nevada crest. This is in marked contrast to the neighboring Coso and Casa Diablo sources, the distributions of which are quite large. This suggests use both by groups having direct access to them and by groups obtaining these glasses by trade.

Second, given its biotic diversity, the supply zone is fully capable of serving as the subsistence territory of an aboriginal group, as is shown by its use as such in early historic times. Third, the lack of obvious variation in glass frequencies for sites of different categories within the same quadrat or neighboring quadrats is consistent with the notion of preemptory land use by a single, highly localized group rather than shared use by groups originating in different localities.

In keeping with the argument made earlier, the sharpness of definition between the supply and falloff zones would seem to indicate that the Fish Springs-Big Pine territory may have been recognized virtually from the first intensive occupation of central Owens Valley. Or at least, it would seem to indicate that the territory was present during the period after 2000 B.P. when the occupation appears the heaviest and the archaeological record is the most complete.

To explore this problem further, a sample of 147 time-sensitive projectile points from the Big Pine transect were examined megascopically and microscopically to document the use of blue-iridescent–green glass in the manufacture of these items for three archaeological phases dating from 1200 B.C. to historic times. The sample from a fourth phase, dating between 3500 B.C. and 1200 B.C., is too small to be useful and was not examined. The collection consisted of all pieces recovered from the transect, both inside and outside sample tracts, so it is a nonprobabilistic sample.

The analysis (Table 5.3) shows that the frequency of points made of this distinctive glass was consistently lower than those made from silicates and other glass. This pattern, however, shows little variability through time, and thus it is consistent with the long-term stability in land-use patterns suggested by the debitage analysis. At the same time, however, a shift is noted when the points from the supply zone are compared to those from the falloff zone. Here it was found that between 1200 B.C. and A.D. 1300 the frequency of points made of blue-iridescent–green glass is higher in the supply zone than in the falloff zone, which is to be expected. After A.D. 1300 the reverse is true, and this is not expected. Despite the lack of sampling control and the rather small

TABLE 5.3
Frequency of blue-iridescent–green projectile points by time period. Frequency of blue-iridescent–green glass points was computed against all materials including silicates. There were three silicate specimens for the period between A.D. 600 and A.D. 1300 and two for the period from A.D. 1300 to historic times. Projectile points in the sample included pieces collected within sample tracts and those outside sample tracts but from within the Big Pine transect.

Time period	Transect total	Supply zone	Falloff zone
1200 B.C.–A.D. 600	39	19	20
Blue-iridescent–green	14 (36%)	8 (42%)	6 (30%)
A.D. 600–A.D. 1300	50	24	26
Blue-iridescent–green	17 (34%)	10 (42%)	7 (27%)
A.D. 1300–Historic period	58	34	24
Blue-iridescent–green	22 (38%)	11 (32%)	11 (46%)

shift in frequencies, it is worth considering some explanations for this situation.

For one thing, the shift cannot be attributed to the appearance or disappearance of territories or to shifts in territory boundaries. Were these circumstances acting alone, the frequency of blue-iridescent–green points would always be at least as high, and probably higher, near the probable source as it would at greater distances. This does not appear to be the case after A.D. 1300. There are at least two other possibilities. One is that at A.D. 1300 an increase took place in the trade of point blanks, points, or arrows between aboriginal groups. This would explain the decrease of blue-iridescent–green points within the supply zone and their increase in the falloff zone.

A change in postmarital residence patterns offers a second explanation. If it is assumed that males were responsible for point manufacture and that for this purpose they would have tended to use materials with which they were familiar or, more likely, signified for them a spiritual or sociopolitical affiliation—for example, a material from the territory in which they were born (cf. Gould 1978)—then the decrease in these points in the Fish Springs supply zone and their concomitant increase in the falloff zone might reflect the replacement of a system in which males stayed put after marriage by a system in which they moved. Thus, in this limited context, the use of Fish Springs obsidian would be a function of its value as an act of social or religious symbolism rather than a function of its utilitarian value.

CONCLUSION

Having concluded that prehistoric Owens Valley groups developed a territorial district system based on resource exchange rather than the more common band system based on transhumance, it may also be concluded that this development was in part a response to geographical location. To the south and east of Owens Valley were a series of valleys extremely marginal for human occupation, e.g., Death Valley, that probably experienced substantial population fluctuations as a consequence of climatic change. Groups in Owens Valley periodically would have had to compete for resources with groups moving away from these areas during intervals of climatic deterioration. An advantage of the district system would have been its ability to resist such encroachment since it differs from the family band system chiefly in its greater concentration of a stable population at given points over longer periods of time. At the same time, to the west, across the Sierra Nevada, Owens Valley was flanked by densely settled areas where, based in part on extensive trade in shell currency, non-egalitarian sociopolitical systems not unlike those in Owens Valley seem to have developed at least as early as 2500 B.P. The particular form of the Owens Valley district system may be an emulation of the systems of these central California groups, with whom the people of Owens Valley traded extensively.

REFERENCES

Bean, L. J.
    1978   Social organization. In *Handbook of North American Indians,* Vol. 8, *California,* Washington, D.C.: Smithsonian Institution.
Bettinger, R. L.
    1975   The surface archaeology of Owens Valley, eastern California: prehistoric man–land relationships in the Great Basin. Unpublished Ph.D. dissertation, Department of Anthropology, University of California, Riverside.
    1977   Aboriginal human ecology in Owens Valley, eastern California: prehistoric change in the Great Basin. *American Antiquity* **42**:3–17.
    1980   Explanatory/predictive models of hunter–gatherer adaptation. In *Advances in archaeological theory and method,* edited by M. B. Schiffer, pp. 189–255. New York: Academic Press.
Bettinger, R. L., and T. F. King
    1971   Interaction and political organization: a theoretical framework for archaeology in Owens Valley, California. *University of California Archaeological Survey Annual Report* **13**:187–195.
Bettinger, R. L., R. Jackson, and R. Hughes
    n.d.   The visual sourcing of obsidians in California (in preparation).
Earle, T. K., and A. L. Christenson (eds.)
    1980   *Modeling change in prehistoric subsistence economies.* New York: Academic Press.
Ericson, J. E.
    1977   Egalitarian exchange systems in California: a preliminary view. In *Exchange systems in prehistory,* edited by T. K. Earle and J. E. Ericson, pp. 109–126. New York: Academic Press.
    1981   *Exchange and production systems in Californian prehistory.* Oxford: British Archaeological Reports.
Ericson, J. E., T. A. Hagan, and C. W. Chesterman
    1976   Prehistoric obsidian sources in California, II: geological and geographical aspects, edited by R. E. Taylor, pp. 218–239. Park Ridge, N. J.: Noyes Press.

Gould, R. A.
  1978 Beyond analogy in ethnoarchaeology. In *Explorations in ethnoarchaeology*, edited by R. A. Gould, pp. 249–293. Albuquerque: University of New Mexico Press.
Hughes, R. E.
  1978 Aspects of prehistoric Wiyot exchange and social ranking. *Journal of California Anthropology* 5:53–66.
Jack, R. N.
  1976 Prehistoric obsidian in California I: geochemical aspects. In *Advances in obsidian glass studies*, edited by R. E. Taylor, pp. 183–217. Park Ridge, N. J.: Noyes Press.
Lanning, E. P.
  1963 Archaeology of the Rose Spring site, Iny–372. *University of California Publications in American Archaeology and Ethnology* 49:237–336.
Lee, R. B.
  1972 !Kung spatial organization: an ecological and historical perspective. *Human Ecology* 1:125–147.
MacArthur, R. H., and E. R. Pianka
  1966 On optimal use of a patchy environment. *American Naturalist* 100:603–609.
Meighan, C. W.
  1955 Notes on the archaeology of Mono County, California. *University of California Archaeological Survey Reports* 28:6–28.
Pyke, G. H., H. R. Pulliam, and E. L. Charnov
  1977 Optimal foraging: a selective review of theory and tests. *Quarterly Review of Biology* 52:137–154.
Renfrew, C. J., J. E. Dixon, and J. R. Cann
  1968 Further analysis of Near Eastern obsidians. *Proceedings of the Prehistoric Society* 34:319–331.
Schoener, T. W.
  1971 Theory of feeding strategies. *Annual Review of Ecology and Systematics* 2:369–404.
Steward, J. H.
  1933 Ethnography of the Owens Valley Paiute. *University of California Publications in American Archaeology and Ethnology* 33:233–350.
  1938 Basin-Plateau aboriginal sociopolitical groups. *Bureau of American Ethnology Bulletin* 120.
  1955 *Theory of culture change.* Urbana: University of Illinois Press.
  1970 Foundations of Basin-Plateau Shoshonean society. In *Languages and cultures of western North America: essays in honor of Sven Liljeblad*, edited by E. H. Swanson, Jr., pp. 113–151. Pocatello: Idaho State Museum.
Thomas, D. H.
  1979 Bias in the Basin? Paper presented at the Annual Meeting of the American Ethnological Society, Vancouver, B. C.

Production for Exchange

6

Production for Obsidian
Exchange in California

Jonathon E. Ericson

INTRODUCTION

Production in the context of prehistoric exchange is a new and interesting area for investigation. We would like to describe production system in terms of the modes of production (what and how), the rates of production, the organizational features of the centers of production and cost (value) criteria involved in production, transportation, and exchange. Also, we would like to know more about the factors controlling the primary input of resources and products into prehistoric exchange networks. This chapter will examine first the nature of production in the context of exchange and will present a case study of production for exchange among the prehistoric hunters and gatherers of California.

Production in the context of exchange will be a fruitful area of research. There are a number of basic questions which deserve consideration:

(a) Why and under what conditions are raw materials modified into products for exchange?

(b) What are the characteristic differences between production for exchange of luxury and utilitarian items?

(c) How does the mode of transportation influence the structure of a lithic production system?

(d) How responsive is a production system to other regional conditions and changes?

(e) Are there significant cross-cultural differences in the organization of production at different levels of social organization?

It is important to address these questions in a preliminary fashion in order to set the stage for studying production and how it reflects changes in exchange patterns and other cultural variables. In the next section, I will suggest some of the characeristics and responses of production systems under particular conditions.

SOME EXPECTATIONS

For purposes of study, we may define a lithic production system as the total of the locations and activities involved in the production of a single source of lithic material for exchange. The production system may be restricted to the immediate source area, the local region, or throughout the entire region. The products may involve any stage of reduction that take place at different locations. It is the nature and organization of these processes of production that are important to understand in the context of exchange. For these reasons, the lithic production system is introduced here as an analytical entity for further study in the dimensions of time, space, and behavior. Now let us consider some of the basic questions involving the characteristics and responses of the lithic production systems to particular conditions.

Why are Raw Materials Modified into Products for Exchange?

Although there are a variety of reasons that can explain this behavior, we can consider the act of production as an act that sets value, reduces transport costs, or does both. Production may be as general as selecting a rock and striking a flake to test for internal flaws, or as detailed as producing a finished item for exchange. In the former case, the untransformed material will be transported to the site of production. In the latter case, the production of finished items, as well as reducing transport of waste, fixes form and, most likely, value. Our understanding of the mechanisms of why production occurs in primitive societies remains to be determined. We should focus on the balances maintained between function, value, production, and transport costs.

Are There Characteristic Difference between Production for Exchange of Luxury Items and Utilitarian Items?

Luxury items are inherently valuable as products and objects, whereas, utilitarian items of the same material are valuable as a functional material having particular physical properties. This argument has been advanced by several authors (Tourtellot and Sabloff 1972; Wright 1974). The diversity of luxury products most likely is small, being produced by relatively few producers at relatively few centers of production. On the other hand, the characteristics of production of utilitarian exchange are expected to be nearly reverse. The production system may be extensive in area with different stages of production will be carried out in different areas. Most likely the products will have a generalized form that is easily transported and distributed at many junctures. Primary producers may tend to reduce the amount of modification of the natural material in consideration of the diversity of consumer technologies. The degree of modification of the original stone places morphological constraints on the use of the material. However, there can be instances where tool function is universal for a region, in which case, finished items may be produced by the primary producers. The Teotihuacan blade industry (Spence, Chapter 8) appears to illustrate this latter case. It will be interesting to discover the degree of distinctiveness between different production systems and why certain characteristics are shared.

Does the Mode of Transportation Influence the Structure of a Lithic Production System?

It is expected that there is a balance struck between production and transport costs, although it is not clear how the balance is achieved. As transport costs are reduced, raw materials or products tend to be transported to further distances. We consistently find the reduction of raw materials into blades, flakes, bifaces, or preforms at or near their sources. Ammerman and Andrefsky (Chapter 7) observe the affects of water transport on the production of obsidian in Calabria. They observe that obsidian is further reduced once it arrives on the coast which is the juncture of two different transport modes. In a sense, we can consider production for exchange as a waste reduction process to reduce transport cost in many cases. However, we must sort out other variables related to these processes.

Direct access and regional exchanges are different modes of procurement of resources. There are major differences between the transport costs involved in direct access and regional exchange (Ericson 1981). Regional exchange appears to be far more cost effective than direct access. These differences are greatly amplified as the demand for different types of non-local goods increases. As a consequence it is expected that there will be major differences in the organization of the production systems reflecting the mode of procurement. Under direct access, the production system may be quite inhomogeneous, showing variations in reduction technology, debitage, and products at the centers of production. This variation will make it very difficult to predict the type of production occurring at any point. A production system linked to regional exchange is expected to have more regularity of structure in terms of the just mentioned criteria. Nevertheless, transport costs can be decreased by reducing the amount of waste, it expected that there will be a greater proportion of debitage at the source of direct access procurement. It will be interesting to understand the interdependency of transport efficiency and production.

Is the Production System Responsive to Other Regional Conditions and Changes?

It is expected that the presence of alternate sources of lithic materials will decrease the use of material from each source, other things being equal. The size and shape of the lithic production system will reflect the location and importance of other sources. If different materials have very dissimilar physical properties, different sources will be used for different tool categories (e.g., in California obsidian was used preferentially for projectile points and knives, whereas, basalt and chert were used for scrapers.)

It is expected that changes in the value of items, their functions within different societies, increased population, increased demand, and changes in the reduction technology will be reflected in the modes of production and the production rates. If regional utilization patterns switch, we would expect major changes in the production system to accomodate changes in supply and demand. For example, there may have been a change in the use of a material serving sociotechnic functions to solely technological functions (Binford 1965). Production systems may be extremely sensitive to changes in the region as a whole. In this case, the study of production in the context of regional exchange may provide critical data to monitor other regional systems and register specific prehistoric events.

Are There Significant Cross-Cultural Differences in the Organization of Production at Different Levels of Social Organization?

There are most likely major differences directly linked to degree of administration and specialization (see Spence, Chapter 8). In complex societies, the form and degree of regional administration will greatly influence lithic production systems. Access to sources will be defined by regional political and economic conditions. In a centrally administered system, the primary producers can receive support from other members of their society. In that case, we would expect to see a tremendous increase in the rate of production. Such a transitional phase might be interesting to observe. In an administered system, the transport costs can be reduced, or are of little concern to primary producers. As a result, raw materials may travel to centers of production over greater distances (see Spence, Chapter 8). Even within the political domains of a centralized administration, it is possible that the production systems involving secondary sources of similar material are not affected. It will be interesting to know more about the affects of administration on production systems and if there exists a cross-cultural developmental sequence related to levels of social organization.

RECONSTRUCTION OF PRODUCTION SYSTEMS

The first priority in reconstructing a lithic production system is to determine the sequence of prehistoric events and activities at the source. Generally speaking, quarry workshops have been badly neglected in terms of archaeological research. This neglect is, in part, due to a lack of problem orientation and overcoming the methodological problems presented in sampling, analyzing, and dating these specialized sites. Generally, the artifacts are redundant rather than diagnostic, and the workshops contain massive amounts of fragmentary material which must be dealt with to describe both reduction technology and production rates. Since the source is the point of input of a resource into an exchange network, a careful analysis will reveal critical details about production (see Ericson and Purdy n.d.) in the context of exchange.

Workshops can vary greatly from a sparse surface scatter to a deep stratified midden packed with debitage. The activities of production can also vary greatly, from nodule testing which produces one of more primary decortication flakes, to core preparation, whereby primary, secondary, and even tertiary decortication flakes are removed, to preform preparation, whereby, thinning flakes are also removed, or finished tool production which leaves a nearly complete record of the whole reduction process. At the workshops the reconstruction of the reduction technology will indicate the product that is being formed at the site. It will be possible to extrapolate a production rate by reconstructing the amount of products produced per unit of time. If there are a number of different workshops at a source, the data must be merged to form a composite picture of the production.

It is also important to determine the processes of extraction, selection, and rejection of materials to gain a clearer picture of production-related activities at the site. The natural form of material, and the nature of the deposit will have an influence on behavior. If the desired stone lies in hardrock, specialized techniques for prospection and extraction will be required to remove the material. Stopes, ventilation shafts, hammers, picks, bars, and evidence for fire-spalling may be observed. These observations will provide a clearer picture of the activities of the primary producers and production.

The study of a source area is probably best approached by using several phases of research. A strategy can be employed that includes an initial survey of the source area in order to sample and map the individual workshops. The counting of surface debitage along sample transects has been useful. The location and boundaries of workshops can be determined. In conjunction with this, obsidian hydration dating has been used to establish a chronological framework of the different workshops. In addition, limited excavation of workshops with a 100% recovery of sample units is extremely useful in working out reduction sequences. Also, the three dimensional location of each artifact being excavated can be helpful in obtaining greater detail of the reduction process. A prototype study of an extensive quarry area is presented for the Bodie Hills obsidian source in California (Singer and Ericson 1977). In addition, a number of new, innovative, and useful techniques have been developed for quarry site analysis (Ericson and Purdy n.d.).

Although the source is a good starting point for reconstructing a production system, it cannot be the exclusive point of observation. It is important to describe the modes of production in the surrounding region to ascertain spatial patterns of the materials upon their arrival and departure from different locales. Here, the recovery and analysis of debitage, particularly that with the original cortex, plays a key role. A production index may be used like an exchange index to reconstruct the lithic production system in space (see for example, Ammerman and Andrefsky, Chapter 7).

(a) *The Exchange Index:* The ratio of a source material to total material used in the chipped stone tool category expressed as a percent is commonly used to reconstruct spatial patterns of prehistoric exchange (Renfrew, Dixon, and Cann 1968).

(b) *The Debitage Index:* The amount of debitage, excluding retouch/sharpening flakes to the sum of tools and debitage expressed as a percent. Here, size criteria can be used to exclude retouch/sharpening flakes. This is a key index which reflects the amount of production at any location. At a biface workshop, we would expect that the index would be nearly 100%, and much lower throughout the region.

(c) *The Cortex Index:* The ratio of the primary and secondary decortication flakes to total debitage excluding retouch expressed as a percent is a key index which indicates the import of raw materials to a site. If raw materials "as found" at the source area are being transported away, the Cortex index will indicate these activities. This index will be very useful in evaluating transport cost versus production cost. This index also reflects the number and location of primary producers actually handling the raw material who are being supplied by other individuals or allowed direct access to the source.

If there are manpower shortages among the primary producing groups, raw materials will begin to travel further away from its source. The index can be used to study adjustments in supply and demand. In summary, this index is extremely important and versatile for reconstruction of the production system.

(d) *The Core Index:* The ratio of source-specific cores to the sum of tools and cores is expressed as a percent is another production index. The Core index will be important if cores are the medium of exchange. There are numerous references to the exchange of prepared cores in the literature. This index can be quite useful in studying this form of exchange.

(e) The Industry Indexes: The ratios of preforms or blades or bifaces to the total debitage expressed as a percent can be used to describe the industry of the production system and stages of the reduction technology.

Since the nodules, cores, preforms, blades, flakes, and finished tools probably have somewhat different trajectories with an exchange system, these Industry Indexes will describe the spatial patterns involved in production and exchange.

The above indexes are not original ideas. They have been designed and used by many researchers. What is different here is the use of these indexes to reconstruct lithic production systems.

Discovering how production is linked to exchange at many junctures is well worth the effort. The reconstruction of lithic production system will be a monumental task combining test excavations at many sites, analysis of museum collections, chemical characterization of debitage, spatial analysis, lithic analysis, and gaining chronological control over the data. The study of production within a region is crucial to our understanding of an interplay of context, value, specialization, technology, and exchange. In the next section, preliminary work on production for exchange, illustrates some of the potentials of this research.

PRODUCTION FOR OBSIDIAN EXCHANGE IN CENTRAL CALIFORNIA

What happens to lithic production systems under conditions of continual population increase on a regional scale (Heizer 1964; Moratto 1972), major technological changes in subsistence tools, and a shifting away from luxury to utilitarian use of specific resources? California prehistory provides the laboratory and experiments to examine the affect of these changes on regional systems.

In this section, the production systems of three obsidian sources in Central California are preliminarily examined. These sources appear to have supplied most of the obsidian for the densely populated San Joaquin Valley and the western foothills of the Sierra Nevada over the past 4000–7000 years. The obsidian exchange systems which existed in the Late Horizon at the time of European contact has been described elsewhere (Ericson 1977). The analysis of the three sources under consideration provides a diachronic picture of responses of the lithic production systems relative to specific changes. Although the production systems remain to be reconstructed, there are a number of observations which can be made which have general archaeological significance.

The three sources under study form an inverted triangle. Each of the source specific systems have been synthesized by synagraphic mapping of data obtained by chemical characterization of obsidian artifacts through neutron activation and x-ray fluorescence analysis (Ericson 1981). The St. Helena source is located in western Central California, northeast of San Francisco. The Bodie Hills source is located in a remote section of high desert on the eastern flank of Sierra Nevadas, approximately 285 km east of the St. Helena source. The Casa Diablo source is also located in the high desert east of the Sierras, approximately 130 km south southeast of the Bodie Hill source.

During the Late Horizon, the St. Helena system was the largest of all the obsidian exchange systems in California (Figure 6.1) which supplied, in part, an estimated 400,000 people. It was an asymmetrical system with its greatest extension to the southeast and northeast. The Wappo Indians are reported to have occupied the area surrounding the source and were surrounded, in turn, by the Lake Miwok, Coast Miwok, Wintun, and Pomo ethnic units (Kroeber 1925). Since the ethnographic data are sparse, it is not known if other groups had access to the source, but the Wappo reportedly received a variety of items including bows, beads, shells, mats, fish, headbands, and clams in exchange for obsidian. (Davis 1961). Obsidian also moved south toward the San Francisco Bay area and east toward the Sacramento Delta region. Although the rate of production has not yet been fully established for the St. Helena system, some data can be used to present a preliminary picture. Within a 4 km radius of the town of Alamo, three sites provide a nearly continuous record of the utilization of St. Helena obsidian and lithic materials for the last four millenia (Frederickson 1969). From these data it would appear that the use of obsidian increased *continuously* during the Late Horizon until interrupted by European contact as shown in Figure 6.2. The gradual, but steady increase in the utilization of obsidian is an important finding.

The examination of debitage in this area indicates that the expansion of the production system parallels expansion of the St. Helena exchange system. Frederickson (1969:120) recovered very little obsidian debitage in the earlier periods, which suggest that the obsidian was arriving as completed tools. However, in the Late Horizon, the production system expanded to include the Alamo sites, since there was a definite increase in debitage, indicating the on-site production of obsidian tools.

In the final analysis, these data are only suggestive of the types of changes in the production exchange of St. Helena obsidian. It is vital that the quarry workshops be studied at the source. Since this is the largest exchange system in California, it is important that we learn as much as possible about its prehistory. Currently, the source and quarry workshops are being developed for homes under a master plan to protect many of the site features (K. Flynn, personal communication).

During the Late Horizon, the Bodie Hills system was the third largest of all the obsidian exchange systems in California (Figure 6.3). It supplied an estimated 100,000 people and was an asymmetrical system with its greatest extension to the west–southwest. The Washo appear to have visited the source, but

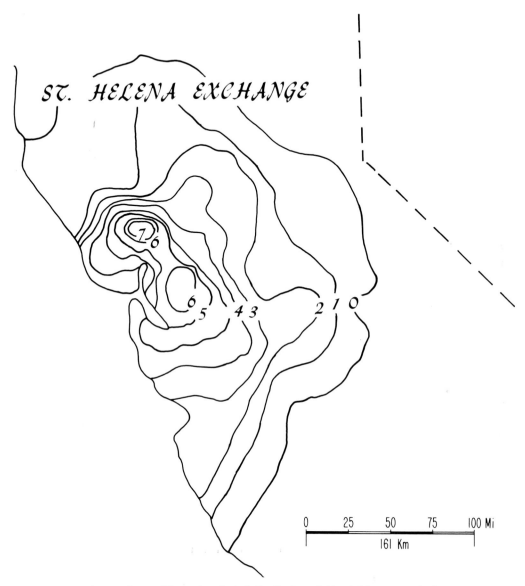

Figure 6.1. St. Helena exchange. The archaeological distribution of this obsidian source is the result of the synagraphic mapping of data provided by Jack (1976). Each contour represents a 10% interval of the total chipped-stone tool industry.

it is not clear from ethnographic sources whether other groups obtained access to it. In exchange for obsidian, the Washo reportedly received acorns, shells, baskets, bulbs, kutsavi, beads, and berries among other items (Davis 1961).

The curve of the production rates at the Bodie Hills source, shown in Figure

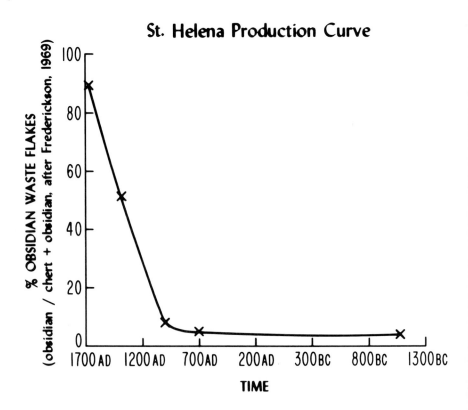

Figure 6.2. St. Helena exchange system obsidian product rate curve. This diachronic production curve was drawn from combining the data information derived from the obsidian- and chert-utilization indexes presented by Frederickson (1969) and associated radiocarbon dates from three Contra Costa archaeological sites.

6.4, is based on obsidian hydration dates (Singer and Ericson 1977). These data show that production began before 5000 B.P. This is further substantiated by Windmiller Culture artifacts, found to the west, which were made of Bodie Hills obsidian (Heizer 1974). Production was relatively constant until about 4000 B.P. when it began to increase for 1000 years. This gradual rate of increase and subsequent decrease is noteworthy. Production appears to terminate during the Late Horizon–Middle Horizon transition period. Unfortunately, this termination is inconsistent with the observed exchange system which existed during the Late Horizon. How can this discrepancy be explained?

Two different modes of lithic production are represented at Bodie Hills, and shown in Figure 6.5. There seems to have been an early, intensive biface production technology observed at the quarry workshops, followed by a less intensive blade/flake production technology. Early biface production is linked to "luxury" exchange. These artifacts often appear in burial contexts in the San Joaquin Valley and elsewhere (Ragir 1972). The later blade/flake technology appears to be linked to utilitarian use of obsidian in the Late Horizon (Singer and Ericson 1977). Although the lithic production system of Bodie Hills remains to be reconstructed, the decrease in the production rate and few workshops suggest that production shifted away from the quarry workshops

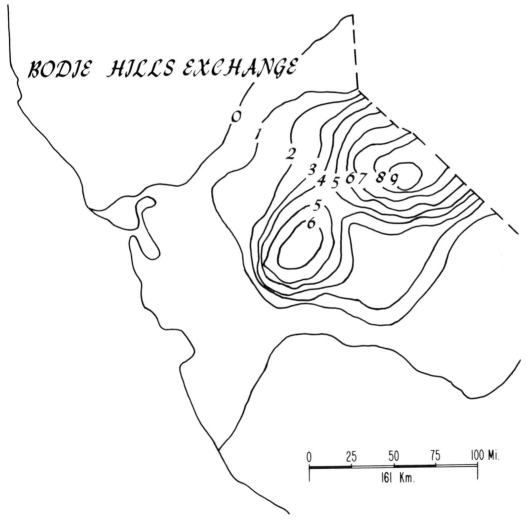

Figure 6.3. Bodie Hills exchange. The archaeological distribution of this obsidian source is the result of the synagraphic mapping of data provided by Jack (1976). The contour interval is 10%.

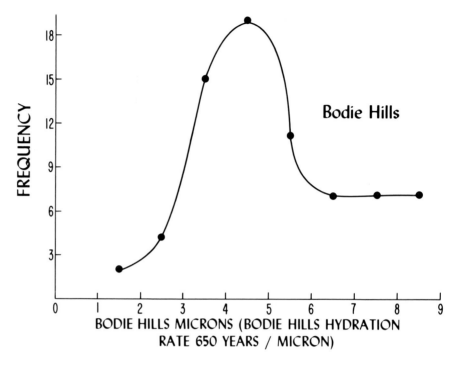

Figure 6.4. Bodie Hills obsidian production-rate curve. The curve was drawn using data presented by Singer and Ericson (1977).

during the Late Horizon. During this period production was carried out elsewhere in the Sierras. This change in the production system suggests that it was more efficient to transport the material to nearby sites of production than to move the producers to the quarry workshops. A similar pattern is observed for the St. Helena system, that is, early quarry production of finished tools followed by the growth of a regional production system during the Late Horizon (Frederickson 1969:120). It is noteworthy that Jackson (1974) also commented on the absence of any obsidian debitage from the earlier sites in the lower Sacramento and upper San Joaquin valleys. Yet at the same time, the Windmiller people of the Middle Horizon were receiving finished obsidian artifacts (Jackson 1974; Heizer 1974).

> The large exotic blades and points of the Delta Valley area which exhibit the fine 'ripple' or 'ribbon' flaking are generally made of obsidian from the Bodie Hills (especially the ceremonial side-notched points with elongated blade elements) or Casa Diablo sources (especially the larger and heavier blades for ceremonial use).

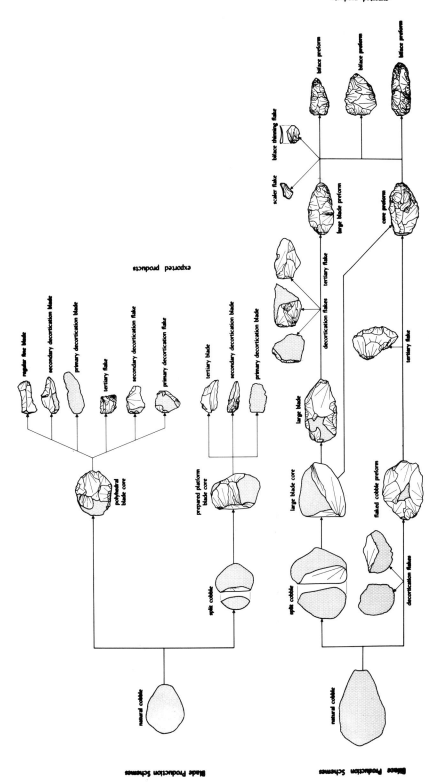

Figure 6.5. Bodie Hills lithic production modes, discussed by Singer and Ericson (1977). The biface production scheme indicates the forms and amounts of debitage in producing a single biface preform. On the other hand, the blade production scheme indicates the forms and amounts of flakes and blades produced by this lithic industry. A comparison of the two schemes indicates the approximate differences in morphological characteristics and number of exportable products. Actual artifacts were used as models in drawing these schemes.

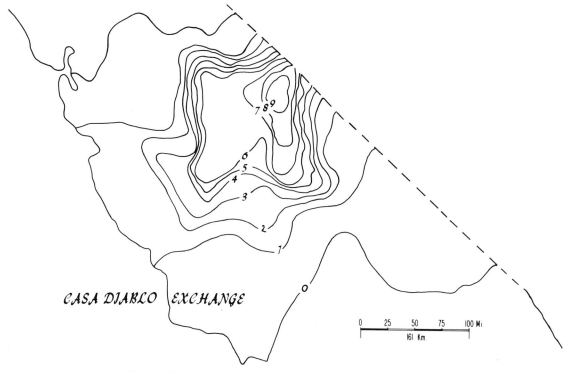

Figure 6.6. Casa Diablo exchange. The archaeological distribution of this obsidian source is the result of the synagraphic mapping of data provided by Jack (1976). The contour interval is 10%.

Although there are large blades and points manufactured from Napa Glass Mountain material, these do not demonstrate the fine precision of flaking (Jackson 1974:80).

This pattern changes in the later period to the import of raw materials indicated by the presence of debitage at most sites in this area.

During the Late Horizon, Casa Diablo was the second largest exchange system in California, supplying as many as 350,000 persons (Fig. 6.6). Obsidian moved over the Sierra Nevada into the San Joaquin Valley, as well as south through the Owens Valley (Bettinger, Chapter 5). The system was asymmetrical with its greatest extent to the south. The Mono Lake Paiute (or Eastern Paiute) surrounded the source. They were in turn surrounded by the Washo, Western Mono, Koso, and Owens Valley Paiute. It is not known whether other groups had direct access to the source. It is interesting to note the diversity of exchanged goods, presented by Davis (1961) and, also, that many of the imported items were subsequently exported. Here, the source served a focal point where a great diversity of materials moved along different branches of the exchange network. The primary producers at the source were certainly aware of regional resource patterns, and knew precisely which trade partner had exchangeable resources. In this way, producers may have redirected specific resources along specific branches of the exchange system.

The Mammoth Junction site is adjacent to the Casa Diablo source. This site provides a continuous record of the products and reduction technology for the last 7000 years (Michels 1965). Obsidian hydration dates were used to draw the curve of the production rates for the site as shown in Figure 6.7. Michels (1965) presents details of production technology based on excavated data. Heavy bifaces ("knives") were produced beginning 7000 B.P. From 5500–3700 B.P., their frequency and variety increased steadily. Scrapers also exhibit a steady increase during this time. Then, from 3600 to 2180 B.P., there was a peak in the production of bifaces, which coincides with an abrupt reduction in the frequency and type of projectile points. Following this peak, the frequency and diversity of products diminish. From 170 B.C.–A.D. 300, the site was abandoned, but it was later to be reoccupied by people with a "very simple hunting technology" (Michels 1965).

For a moment let us examine all three production rate curves, presented in Figure 6.8. The Bodie Hills and Casa Diablo system have almost identical forms. Although it is clear that these production systems are well separated in

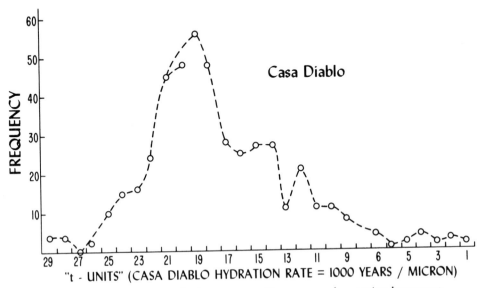

Figure 6.7. Casa Diablo obsidian production-rate curve. The curve was drawn using data presented by Michels (1965).

Diachronic Obsidian Production of 3 Obsidian Sources in California

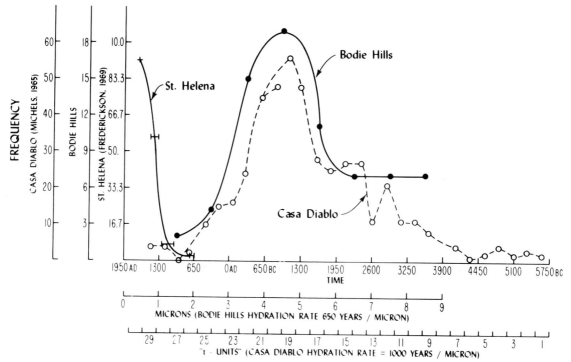

Figure 6.8. Production rates of the three exchange systems in this study. The obsidian production rate curves are grouped in order to understand their interaction. It does appear that there is similarity in the diachronic production rates of the Bodie Hills and Casa Diablo obsidian sources. After the apparent decline in these production rates, the St. Helena production rates begin to increase.

space and affiliation, the coincidence of these two curves indicates the similarities of supply and demand registered in the production systems. Both systems responded to similar conditions in similar ways. Maximum production of bifaces occurs at the same time. The quarry production at each "collapses" at about the same time of the Late Horizon–Middle Horizon transition. What was going on that caused such a fundamental change in production at both of these sources, as well as the simultaneous expansion of the St. Helena system to the west? What I suspect is that we are observing the impact of bow and arrow technology on all obsidian sources (i.e., a major change from luxury to utilitarian function of the obsidians).

At this point of transition, it appears that production becomes dispersed away from quarry workshops and is being carried out at many sites at greater distances from the source. There are vast quantities of Late Horizon debitage located throughout the Sierras, noted by most archaeologists who have surveyed the area. Likewise, as already noted, debitage occurs at greater distances from the St. Helena source in the Central Valley (Frederickson 1969; Jackson 1974). An analysis of the debitage throughout the Sierras and Central Valley will resolve exactly what happened during the Late Horizon. Nevertheless, it is clear that there was a dispersion in production systems. Why does production disperse throughout these three systems? It is hypothesized that the primary producers, who originally produced bifaces, simply could not meet new demands. In the following estimate, a 2500–fold to 125,000–fold increase in production for arrow points relative to bifaces can be demonstrated.

Let us consider the change in demand for a sequence of products from large bifaces to medium projectile points (ataltl) to small arrow points. Perhaps 1–5 large bifaces were required by each hunter per lifetime. If these were used as burial items upon death, the demand for bifaces would be 1–5 per hunter. For ataltl projectile points, perhaps a hunter would require 5–20 per year for 25 years of hunting, or 125–500 per lifetime per hunter. Perhaps a hunter would require 50–100 arrow points per year for 25 years of hunting, or 1250–2500 per lifetime per hunter considering point loss and breakage. The demand schedule for obsidian thus changed from 1–5 to 125–500 to 1250–2500 per lifetime per hunter. This estimated 250–fold to 2500–fold increase in the demand per hunter would have had a direct impact on producers at all lithic sources.

Yet these estimates do not consider population expansion. Actually, the total demand was even greater. All evidence points to the fact that in 7000–year period, the population in Central California expanded tremendously (Heizer 1964). Let us suppose there was a 10–fold to 50–fold increase in population. The total demand for finished tools over this 7000 year period was perhaps 2500 to 125,000–fold. It would not have been surprising to see that the primary producers at the sources could not meet the increasing demands for finished items from central California. To meet this increasing demand it appears that the primary producers later changed their technology from biface production to blade–flake production, to outright export of raw materials. The sequence of events we have observed at the quarry workshops are understandable if we consider simultaneous changes in lithic technology and population expansion that are equated into rising demand for obsidian. The labor cost of producing one finished biface is greater than reducing all the material to blades and flakes, useable for arrow point production. The producers could increase production perhaps 50–fold to 100–fold by producing only blades and flakes, a case where debitage becomes product. However, this increase does not begin to match the estimated 2500–fold to 125,000–fold increase in demand. The demand could only have been met by the active participation of 25–2500 additional groups engaged in production. Most likely, the dispersion of the production systems away from the sources is a direct response to the limited manpower available for production under such conditions.

The most important result of this study is the recognition of the marked, gradual response of the lithic production and exchange systems to changing conditions. These changes are witnessed by the similarities between the Bodie Hills and Casa Diablo production rate curves. We also see the growth of the St. Helena system during the Late Horizon–Middle Horizon transition. All of these systems appear to have been quite stable for long periods of time, a fact quite consistent with the findings of other researchers (Ammerman and Andrefsky, Chapter 7; Spence, Chapter 8). Long-term stability seems to be a characteristic of production systems involved in the exchange of lithic materials. In contrast, it is worthwhile to note the rapid changes in patterns of procurement when obsidian was obtained by direct access in the American Southwest (Findlow and Bolognese, Chapter 3).

The issue of stability of lithic production systems in the context of exchange is an interesting question. Wright and Zeder (1977) propose a model of linear exchange based on Rappaport's ethnographic work in New Guinea (Rappaport, 1968). Here, producers are extremely sensitive to changes in demands and adjust their yearly output to compensate for changes from previous years. Although the California data are not refined enough, it is expected that short-term dramatic responses might be reflected as perturbations in the production rates. These variations are not observed, rather the data indicates an overall pattern of long-term stability and gradual change.

SUMMARY AND CONCLUSIONS

The central California data suggest a very interesting picture of production in the context of exchange. Over several millenia, three slightly overlapping exchange systems supplied obsidian to this area. Two sources that were centers of biface production show similarities in their production rates through time until the Middle Horizon–Late Horizon transition. At this point production of bifaces decreases abruptly, and there is a major change in reduction technology to produce prismatic blades and flakes. Also, the center of production appears to disperse away from the quarry workshops, which is considered a response to increased demand and limited workforce of primary producers. The impacts of increasing population in the Central Valley and Sierra foothills and a gradual shift from atlatl to bow and arrow technology appear to be responsible for the observed changes.

There were a number of basic questions which were addressed in Section 2. The California data suggest that it does appear that production for exchange is very sensitive to other regional changes, particularly under conditions of population change, change in lithic technology and a change in the functional use of the material within different societies. The changes in the production rates and reduction technologies are coincident with these major changes. There appear to be differences in the production systems engaged in producing luxury and utilitarian items. Luxury biface production appears to have been restricted mainly to the quarry workshops, and limited to a few forms; whereas, the production of utilitarian items appears to have been dispersed away from the source, and provided a wide diversity of generalized items. Although it is difficult to evaluate the influence of transportation, here, there was a concern for reducing waste.

Perhaps the most important finding of this study is that all these systems demonstrate long-term stability with rather harmonious, gradual responses to external stimuli. It is not clear why these systems appear to be so stable, or what mechanisms operated to insure their stability. Future study of production for exchange in central California will shed light on these questions.

ACKNOWLEDGMENTS

I am grateful for the editorial assistance and useful comments of Clay Singer, T. K. Earle, and Peter S. Wells on an earlier version of this chapter. This chapter is available at Harvard Center for Archaeological Research and Development, Reprint Number 8.

REFERENCES

Binford, L.
  1965 Archaeological systematics and the study of cultural process. *American Antiquity* **31**:203–221.
Davis, J. T.
  1961 Trade routes and economic exchange among the Indians of California. *University of California Archaeological Survey, Report* **54**:1–71.
Ericson, J. E.
  1981 *Exchange and production systems in californian prehistory.* Oxford: British Archaeological Reports, International Series **110**:1–240.
Ericson, J. E. and B. A. Purdy (Editors)
  n.d. *Lithic quarry production* (forthcoming).
Frederickson, D. A.
  1969 Technological change, population movement, environment adaptation, and the emergence of trade: inferences on culture change suggested by midden constituent analysis. *University of California Archaeological Survey, Annual Report* **11**:105–125.
Heizer, R. F.
  1964 The Western Coast of North America. In *Prehistoric man in the new world*, edited by J. F. Jennings and E. Norbeck, pp. 117–148. Chicago: University of Chicago Press.
  1974 Studying the Windmiller culture. In *Archaeological researches in retrospect*, edited by G. R. Willey, pp. 177–204. Cambridge: Winthrop Publishing.
Heizer, R. F., and A. E. Treganza
  1944 Mines and quarries of the Indians of California. *Department State Mineralogist,* **40**, 291–359.

Jack, R. N.
  1976   Prehistoric obsidian in California, I: geochemical aspects. In *Advances in obsidian glass studies,* edited by R. E. Taylor, pp. 183–217. Park Ridge, N.J.: Noyes Press.
Jackson, T. L.
  1974   The Economics of obsidian in central California prehistory: applications of x-ray fluorescence spectrography in archaeology. Unpublished M.A. thesis, Department of Anthropology, San Francisco State University, San Francisco.
Kroeber, A. L.
  1925   Handbook of the Indians of California. *Bureau of American Ethnology, Bulletin* **78**.
Michels, J. W.
  1965   Lithic serial chronology through obsidian hydration dating. Unpublished Ph.D. dissertation, Department of Anthropology, University of California, Los Angeles.
Moratto, M. J.
  1972   A study of the Prehistory in the Southern Sierra Nevada Foothills. Unpublished Ph.D. dissertation. Department of Anthropology, University of Oregon, Eugene.
Ragir, S.
  1972   The early horizon in central California prehistory. *Contributions of the University of California Archaeological Research Facility,* **15**:1–329.
Rappaport, R. A.
  1968   *Pigs for the ancestors, ritual in the ecology of a New Guinea people.* New Haven: Yale University Press.
Renfrew, C. J., E. Dixon, and J. R. Cann
  1968   Further analysis of Near Eastern obsidians. *Proceedings of the Prehistoric Society* **34**:319–331.
Singer, C. A., and J. E. Ericson
  1977   Quarry analysis at Bodie Hills, Mono County, California. In *Exchange systems in prehistory,* edited by T. K. Earle and J. E. Ericson, pp. 171–188. New York: Academic Press.
Tourtellot, G., and J. A. Sabloff
  1972   Exchange systems among the ancient Maya, *American Antiquity.* 37:126–135.
Wright, G. A.
  1974   *Archaeology and Trade,* Addison-Wesley Module in Anthropology. 49:1–48.
Wright, H. T., and M. A. Zeder
  1977   The stimulation of a linear exchange system under equilibrium conditions. In *Exchange Systems in Prehistory,* edited by T. K. Earle and J. E. Ericson, pp. 233–253. New York: Academic Press.

7

Reduction Sequences and the Exchange of Obsidian in Neolithic Calabria

Albert J. Ammerman
William Andrefsky, Jr.

INTRODUCTION

One of the more promising parts of the Mediterranean for the study of prehistoric exchange systems is the region of Calabria in southern Italy. Prior to 1974, our knowledge of the prehistory of the region was extremely limited. It is only in the last few years that we have come to appreciate the role that Calabria played in the long-distance exchange of obsidian between the island of Lipari and peninuslar Italy during Neolithic times. In our own studies, particular attention has been paid to the early history of exchange in obsidian as seen at sites with impressed-ware Neolithic pottery that date for the most part to the fifth millennium B.C. The area of Calabria that has been studied most intensively is one located near the village of Acconia on the Tyrrhenian coast (Ammerman and Shaffer 1981).

The results of some of our previous work on obsidian exchange networks in Calabria have been presented in two reports (Ammerman, Matessi, and Cavalli-Sforza 1978; Ammerman 1979). The first deals with more theoretical aspects of so-called down-the-line exchange systems, and draws attention to the dynamic time behavior of such systems as they are reflected, for example, in the increasing percentage of obsidian at a site over time. This pattern is documented in the stratigraphic sequences at sites such as Franchthi Cave in Greece (Jacobsen 1976) and Cayonu in Turkey (Redman 1973). In both of these cases, the trend toward an increasing proportion of obsidian takes place over a substantial period of time, suggesting that the exchange system does not achieve equilibrium rapidly. The second report is more empirical, describing the obsidian found at Neolithic sites in different parts of Calabria. The patterns observed in this region do not seem to fit the distributional models previously proposed for the Mediterranean and the Near East (Renfrew, Dixon, and Cann 1968; Renfrew 1977). What is implied by the patterns observed in Calabria is the need to develop more complex models of exchange systems. Specifically, we need to turn to models where certain Neolithic sites in a given area participate more actively than others in the long-distance exchange of obsidian as an alternative to previous models of reciprocal exchange where all sites are treated as participating to the same extent.

There is a growing awareness in the study of prehistoric exchange that attention should be paid not just to questions of distribution but to the wider context of the production of a commodity and its use or consumption as well. The purpose of this chapter is to describe some recent work that is concerned with the technology of obsidian reduction, and specifically, the development of better ways of recognizing the different stages of reduction or production at a site. Lithic replication experiments offer a controlled means of studying the various products and by-products that are produced at different stages in a reduction sequence. The study of such controlled sets of material can lead to the development of diagnostic indices that, when applied in turn to sets of prehistoric material, can help in the recognition of those stages of reduction represented at a site. For example, one might expect to find the full range of stages present at sites that engage more actively in the reduction of obsidian—whereas a single stage may be observed at other sites. If we can identify successfully the reduction stages present at sites, we shall then be in a position to examine the spatial distributions of sites in terms of their varying degrees of involvement in the production of obsidian and, by extension, their varying degrees of participation in exchange networks.

OBSIDIAN EXCHANGE IN CALABRIA: THE BACKGROUND

It is worth reviewing in somewhat greater detail what is known about obsidian exchange systems in Calabria before turning to the more recent study of reduction sequences. In the western Mediterranean, there are four known sources of workable obsidian for peninsular Italy and Sicily (see Figure 7.1): the islands of Pantellaria, Lipari, Palmarola, and Sardegna (Hallam, Warren, and Renfrew 1976; Dixon 1976). Characterization studies based on neutron activation analysis have shown almost all of the obsidian found at Neolithic sites in Calabria to come from Lipari (Crummett and Warren n.d.). In a more recent series of samples analyzed, one piece from a late Neolithic context would appear to come from the island of Pantellaria, which is located between Sicily and North Africa (Warren, personal communication). The almost exclu-

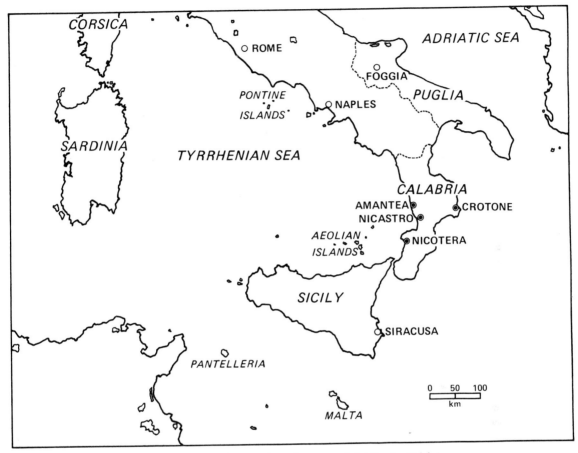

Figure 7.1. Map of southern Italy. The island of Lipari, the main source of obsidian for Calabria, is located in the center of the Aeolian Islands.

sive reliance on Lipari is not surprising in light of the proximity of the source and the abundance of obsidian on the island. The geographic distribution of Neolithic sites with obsidian from Lipari extends from the south coast of Sicily to the northern part of Puglia and beyond to central Italy (Bigazzi and Bonadonna 1973; Hallam, Warren, and Renfrew 1976). The percentage of obsidian in the lithic assemblages of sites in the region of Puglia seems to be quite low in general.

Since 1974, more than 200 sites with obsidian, which date from the Neolithic through the Bronze Age, have been located during survey work in Calabria (Ammerman 1979). The sites known at present comprise probably only a small fraction of the total number of sites with obsidian in the region. Obsidian is used in making chipped-stone tools: it thus represents a utilitarian commodity in terms of its consumption. The systematic collection of lithic material from the surface of sites in conjunction with the methodological control provided by the replicated collection of site surfaces (Ammerman and Feldman 1978) makes it possible to estimate the percentage of obsidian in lithic assemblages at Neolithic sites in various parts of the region. Obsidian commonly forms more than 90% of the lithic material recovered from impressed-ware Neolithic settlements on the west coast of Calabria. These same high values are also seen in the excavations at the site of Piana di Curinga in the Acconia area. The percentage of obsidian falls off rapidly, however, when we shift to impressed-ware Neolithic sites on the east coast of Calabria. The overall pattern of values does not conform to the one expected under the down-the-line models of exchange formulated by Renfrew and others (Renfrew, Dixon, and Cann 1968; Renfrew 1977). Nor does the pattern of high values all along the west coast support the interpretation that the movement of obsidian from Lipari to peninsular Italy is tied to a land-based route through northern Sicily (Hallam, Warren, and Renfrew 1976). Instead, it seems to be much more likely that the commodity moved in a radial pattern by boat from the island of Lipari to various points on the west coast of Calabria (Ammerman 1979).

It is worth commenting that there is evidence for occupation on the island of Lipari from impressed-ware Neolithic times onward (Brea and Cavalier 1960). In addition, a wide range of items that are not found or produced on the island—polished-stone axes, chert, and pottery, to mention only a few—reached Lipari by means of exchange with groups in Calabria and Sicily. It would seem to be reasonable to assume that those people then living on the island took an active part in the collection or quarrying of obsidian and in its initial processing. At the present time, it is uncertain who actually engaged in navigation on the Tyrrhenian—groups on Lipari, or groups from Calabria or Sicily, or possibly even some combination of the two—and the initial maritime step in the distribution of obsidian. Nevertheless, it is likely, if we consider the dependence of sites along the west coast of Calabria on chipped-stone tools made of obsidian and the overall size of the exchange networks in peninsular Italy and Sicily, that trips to and from Lipari were made on a regular, if seasonal, basis.

In examining the patterns of distribution of obsidian on a regional level, the percentage of obsidian at a site provides only a rough way of looking at an exchange system. A more promising approach would seem to be that of turning to the reduction technologies observed at sites and the weight of obsidian moving through an exchange network. The objective here is to study the various products and by-products of lithic reduction found at a site (e.g., blades, core-trim flakes, shatter, and cores) and the relative proportion of the overall weight of obsidian tied up in these respective classes. It is worth adding that the frequent recovery of cores and core-rejuvenation flakes at impressed-ware Neolithic sites in Calabria, Sicily, and Puglia indicates that the main form of movement of the material, at least insofar as long-distance exchange is concerned, is that of cores or semi-prepared cores, and not finished blades or flakes. In other words, obsidian was exchanged over long distances in a semi-processed form. The final preparation of a core and its reduction, or the actual making of tools, was carried out subsequently at various points throughout the exchange network.

As mentioned earlier, the working assumption in previous models of obsidian exchange systems for the Neolithic was usually that all sites participated in more or less the same way and to the same extent in exchange networks. If this were the case, we would expect to see essentially similar patterns of lithic reduction among those sites located at the same distance from a source. In the recent study of a group of sites in the Acconia area of Calabria, substantial differences were, however, observed between sites when their obsidian assemblages were examined in terms of size classes. It was found that concentration curves (see the discussion later in this chapter and Ammerman 1979 for a

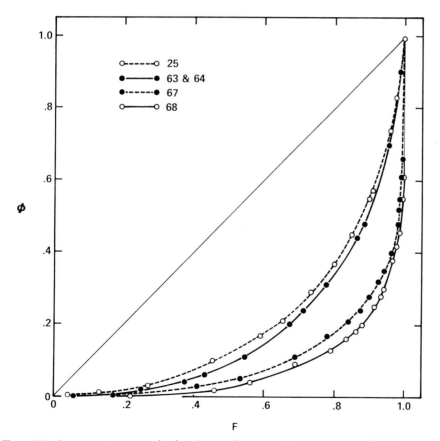

Figure 7.2. Concentration curves for four Stentinello sites in the Acconia area of Calabria (see Ammerman 1979:**Figure 8**).

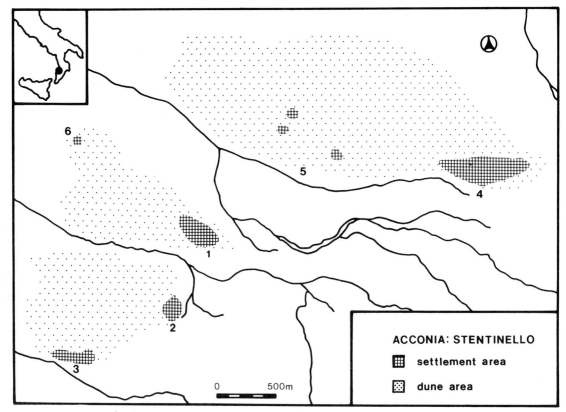

Figure 7.3. Distribution map of Stentinello or impressed-ware Neolithic settlements in the Acconia area of Calabria. The curves shown in Figure 7.2. relate to the settlement areas as follows: curve 25 is from 4; 63–64 from 2; and 67 and 68 from 3.

description of how the curves are constructed) provide a convenient way of comparing the assemblages from different sites. Such curves make it possible to display both the relative frequency of pieces belonging to a given size class and the proportion of overall weight within an assemblage tied up in each class at the same time (see Figure 7.2). At some sites, a high proportion of pieces is observed in the smaller-sized classes, and yet most of the weight of obsidian in an assemblage is tied up in classes of larger-size. The material at other sites falls predominantly in classes in the middle of the size range.

The inference was made that the differences observed are related to differences in the obsidian-reduction activities carried out at the respective sites. Those sites with low concentration curves (i.e., the first case described above) can be interpreted as having been more actively involved in the various stages of obsidian reduction. It is worth noting that larger quantities of obsidian are recovered from these same sites, and that they are situated nearest to the coast (see Figure 7.3). This raises the possibility that those sites that engaged more actively in obsidian production may also have taken a more active part in the long-distance exchange of obsidian, and that other sites in the Acconia area may have received at least part of their obsidian through local exchange with the major reduction sites.

OBSIDIAN-REDUCTION EXPERIMENT

It was with this research question in mind and with the aim of looking at production in a more refined way that the obsidian-reduction experiments were begun. If we can establish the steps in an obsidian-reduction sequence that are represented at a given site, we may be able to make clearer inferences about where that particular site was positioned in the exchange network. To do this, we need precise information on the flakes, blades, and other debitage that are produced at different points in the sequence of obsidian reduction. One way to gather this information is to perform experiments that replicate the reduction of obsidian. Starting with an unmodified chunk of obsidian, we can first work it into a core. Subsequently, the core can be progressively reduced by the removal of blades and trim flakes. During the process of reduction, we can stop at various points and weigh and measure the core and collect all of the products and by-products that have been removed. In this way, we can obtain a series of controlled sets of material reflecting the obsidian-working sequence from beginning to end. By examining the individual sets of material in detail, we can hopefully recognize patterns that are characteristic of different steps in the sequence and develop diagnostic indices that can be used to identify the respective steps present in sets of prehistoric material. In addition, reduction experiments can make a contribution along heuristic lines by forcing us to take systematically into account all of the steps involved in a reduction sequence as well as all of the products and by-products generated during obsidian reduction.

The basic stages in the reduction sequence are shown in Figure 7.4. The core-preparation stage begins with an obsidian chunk or precore, and the goal is to prepare the core for blade removal. In the core-reduction stage that follows, blades are removed from the core until no more blades can be produced. Various by-products, such as trim flakes and shatter, are generated during these first two stages. During the third or blade-requisition stage, only the final target products of reduction (e.g., blades and perhaps trim flakes offering good working edges), as well as some of the waste products associated with the secondary modification of blades, are seen.

The obsidian used in the experiment came from the Rocky Mountains of northern Idaho, and it is similar in structural terms (i.e., flaking properties) to the Liparian obsidian. The Idaho obsidian was recovered in cobble form and then worked down into large chunks, which can be categorized as precores. These resemble in shape and weight those pieces brought to Calabria from

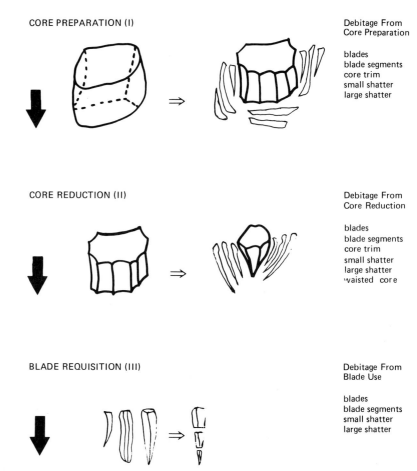

Figure 7.4. Idealized diagram of lithic-working sequence from core preparation through blade requisition.

Lipari. The actual working or reduction of the obsidian was done by Andrefsky. Ammerman acted as an evaluator of the pieces produced during the experiment. As each precore was made, it was inspected by Ammerman, who either rejected it or accepted it, depending upon its similarity to the precores recovered in Calabria.

Three precores that ranged in weight from 145 to 210 gm were ultimately chosen to be worked into cores. Percussion flaking (Crabtree 1972; Callahan 1974) with an antler billet was used to prepare each piece into a core. Occasionally, a hammerstone made of quartzite was used to peck and smooth down platforms before blade and flake detachment. Each piece was reduced separately so that comparisons could be made between the results of the three cases. As mentioned before, the reduction sequence was divided into two main stages: the core-preparation stage and the core-reduction stage (see Figure 7.4). During the first stage, an effort was made to be as economical as possible, with only as many flakes and blades being removed as was required to establish parallel flake scars so that the core was ready for the production of blades. Only after Andrefsky was satisfied that a core had enough parallel flake scars to insure adequate blade removal and Ammerman accepted it as an adequate replica of material from Calabria, was it then considered to be a prepared core. At this point, all of the debitage produced from the core-preparation stage was collected and set aside for classification.

The core was again weighed, and the actual removal of blades begun. During the core-reduction stage, the core had to be trimmed and rejuvenated at various points so that by-products other than blades were also produced. The core-reduction stage itself was also subdivided into two parts. When the weight of the prepared core was reduced by half, all of the blades and debitage produced up to that point were collected and set aside. The core was again weighed, and reduction was continued until the core could produce no more usable blades. This further division permitted us to have more control over possible changes in the character of debitage during the course of the core-reduction stage. When no more blades could be removed, reduction was stopped, and the wasted core weighed and stored. Again, this was done separately for each of the three cores so that comparisons could be made between the results of the three replicates.

ANALYSIS OF THE OBSIDIAN-REDUCTION EXPERIMENT

The first phase of the analysis of the material generated by the experiments involved the classification and weighing of the individual pieces. The system used in their classification derives from the technology of blade production and consists of three main classes: blades, core trim, and shatter. *Blades* are pieces characterized by parallel lateral edges, and they also have a slightly concave ventral surface. The dorsal surface has a single medial ridge or a pair of them. *Blades* are defined conventionally as pieces being at least twice as long as they are wide (Movius *et al.* 1968, e.g., Tixier 1974). While shatter can take various shapes, it consists of pieces weighing .1 gm or less. Core trim includes all those pieces not placed in the classes of blades, shatter, or wasted cores. It should be noted that each of these groups contains a range of morphological shapes that could be distinguished for purposes of more detailed studies of lithic technology. A more elaborate classification system is not required here, since our primary concern in this study is with the recognition of basic stages of reduction.

The analysis of the experimental data involves two issues of interest for the study of obsidian exchange. The first concerns the variability in the amount and weight of products and by-products generated during a given stage in the

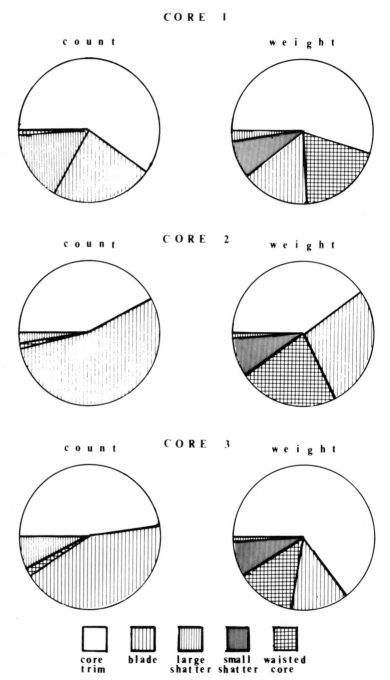

Figure 7.5. Relative proportions of experimentally derived products and by-products during the reduction process. Counts of small shatter are not included.

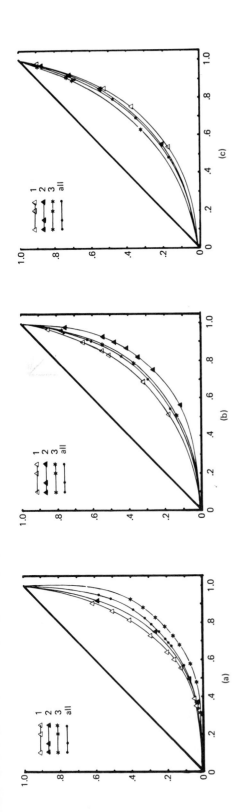

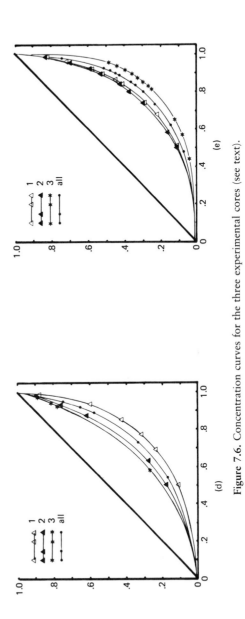

Figure 7.6. Concentration curves for the three experimental cores (see text).

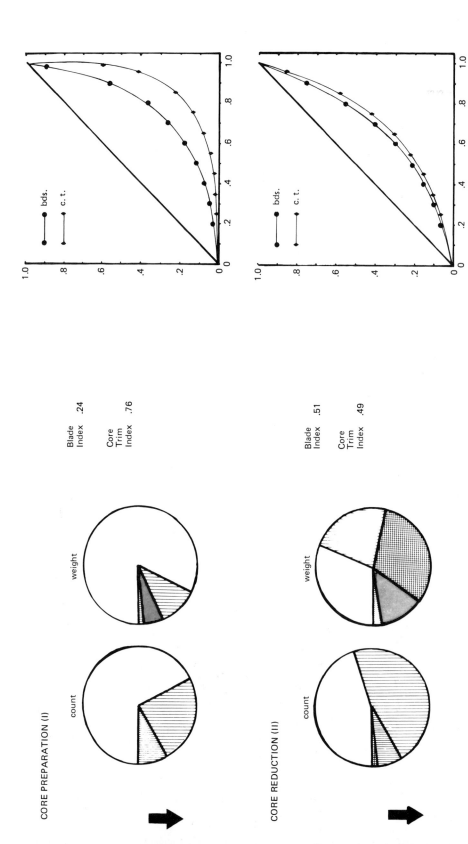

bds.

c. t.

Blade
Index   .24

Core
Trim
Index   .76

bds.

c. t.

Blade
Index   .51

Core
Trim
Index   .49

weight

count

CORE PREPARATION (I)

weight

count

CORE REDUCTION (II)

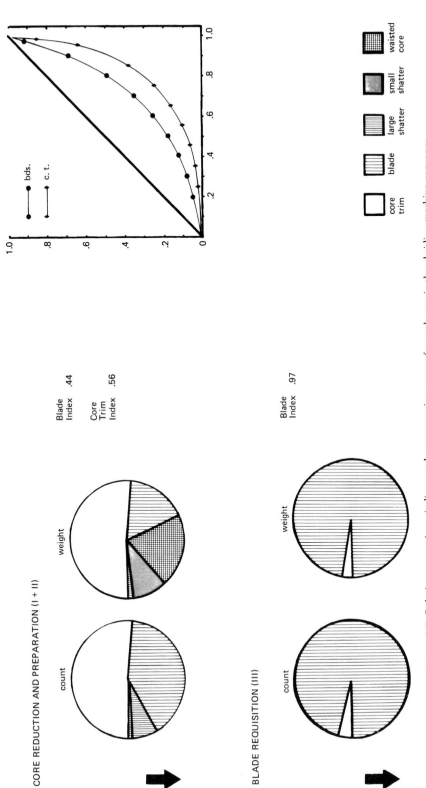

Figure 7.7. Relative proportions, indices, and concentration curves for each step in the obsidian-working sequence.

161

reduction process. Each stage in this process can be characterized by the sets of pieces produced during that particular stage. The second issue concerns the variability observed between the individual cores. When the products and by-products of reduction are tabulated for each core, we can observe a certain amount of variability in the counts and weights of material between the three cores. This variability is high in some respects and low in others. For instance, the proportion of blades obtained from a core can range from 25% to 55% of the pieces removed (with small shatter excluded from the counts). On the other hand, the weight of small shatter from a core ranges from 9% to 11%, or it is almost identical for the three cores. The amount of core trim can vary between 42% and 60%, but in all three cases the greatest amount of weight is always contained in the core-trim class. Figure 7.5 shows the relative proportions both by count and weight of the various classes of material for each core. It is useful to know that approximately 10% of the total obsidian weight takes the form of small shatter during the preparation and reduction process. This provides information on the amount of obsidian potentially "lost" to archaeological recovery, if we are interested in estimating the quantity of obsidian originally brought to a site. We also see that any obsidian-working activity that involves the production of large amounts of core trim will at the same time account for the major share of the overall weight of an obsidian assemblage. This has implications for identifying core-preparation activities that require high production levels of core trim. The point should be made that in the analysis of prehistoric assemblages, we usually deal with the remains of not a single core but of a number of cores. While each core may reveal some degree of individual variation, we are really concerned with developing a diagnostic key of the central tendencies or average trends of the experimental cores taken together.

The experimental results show differences between the reduction stages based on the counts and weights of material belonging to the respective classes. The use of concentration curves offers a means of displaying these differences. When the obsidian is being worked initially and prepared into cores, the curves for core trim run low in relationship to the horizontal axis. This type of concentration curve, in which a greater proportion of the weight is contained in the larger-sized classes, is shown in Figure 7.6a, where the curves are constructed for a given class of material rather than for the assemblage as a whole as in Ammerman's previous work (1979). It is worth noting the fair degree of variation for the core-trim class observed between the three cores for the core-preparation stage of reduction. Figures 7.6b and 7.6c diagram the core-reduction stage for the classes of core trim and blades, respectively. In both cases, the curves run closer to the diagonal line. As concentration curves approach the diagonal, the weight as well as the number of pieces in each size class tends to become more evenly distributed in the middle of the size range. When the pieces from the core-preparation and core-reduction stages are combined, as in Figures 7.6d and 7.6e, the concentration curves fall between those exclusively for core preparation (Stage I) and core reduction (Stage II), as we would expect.

Figure 7.7, which is organized in much the same way as Figure 7.4, models the products and by-products recovered from our experiments in the form of concentration curves and the relative proportions of material in the main reduction classes for each stage in the reduction sequence. In addition, two indices based on blade and core-trim counts are provided: (*a*) the ratio of blades to blades plus core trim; and (*b*) the ratio of core trim to blades plus core trim. The concentration curves in Figure 7.7 are derived from the three experimental cores taken together, and they permit a comparison of the patterns for core trim and blades. As mentioned previously, we can make inferences about an obsidian assemblage by examining the position of a given curve with respect to the diagonal. Of more consequence may be the relationship between one class and another (i.e., between blades and core trim) in terms of their relative amounts of concentration. For example, if we were to plot the curves for blades and core trim for an obsidian assemblage and the gap between the two curves was very small (see Figure 7.7, II), we would infer core-reduction activity at a site. If the gap between the two curves was large (see Figure 7.7 I + II), we would infer that both core preparation and core reduction were being carried out. If in the same case, the core-trim curve moved very close to the horizontal axis (Figure 7.7, I), then we would infer that core preparation was the predominant activity at a site as far as the working of obsidian is concerned.

By themselves, the concentration curves in some cases are not fully diagnostic of individual stages. It is only when they are used in conjunction with other indices, as shown in Figure 7.7, that definite identification can be made consistently. Thus, we may begin to speak in terms of a model for recognizing different stages in a reduction sequence. Drawing on the patterns seen in Figure 7.7, we have constructed a "reduction key" that can be used for the recognition of reduction activities. This diagnostic key will be applied to obsidian assemblages from Neolithic sites in the Acconia area in the following section.

Reduction Key

Core preparation. This stage (I) can be identified when core trim has a low concentration curve. Core trim will comprise about 80% of the weight of the assemblage as a whole. The core-trim index will be high.

Core reduction. This stage (II) can be identified when the concentration curves for both core trim and blades are basically the same and run near the diagonal. Blades and core trim will comprise roughly equal amounts of the assemblage by weight. The two indices will also have similar values.

Core preparation and core reduction combined. In this case where Stages I and II occur in combination, the concentration curve for core trim will be lower than the one for blades, and it will run fairly low in relationship to the horizontal axis. Core trim will comprise about 70% of the weight of the assemblages as a whole. The two indices will be roughly comparable in value.

Blade requisition. This stage (III), which has not been discussed in detail in the preceding paragraphs, can be identified by the predominance of blades in an assemblage. The blade index will be high. There will also be comparatively little in the way of waste debitage and shatter.

A TRIAL ANALYSIS OF FOUR NEOLITHIC ASSEMBLAGES

In order to see how well the diagnostic key works, four lithic assemblages from Neolithic settlements in the Acconia area were selected for an initial study. The aim was to choose sets of material from sites located both near the coast and in the interior of the area. From previous work, there was a suggestion of greater involvement in obsidian reduction at Settlement 3 (see Assemblages 67 and 68 in Ammerman [1979]), which is located near the coast (see Figure 7.3). The four assemblages all come from excavation quality contexts and derive respectively from the following settlements: A is from Settlement 3; B is from Settlement 1 (the site of Piana di Curinga); C is from Settlement 4 (see Ammerman, Diamond, and Aldridge 1978); and D is also from Settlement 4 (Site 435, which is located about 200 m east of Assemblage C at the same settlement).

In the analysis, the obsidian was first separated into blades and core trim. The pieces in each class were individually weighed, and concentration curves for blades and core trim were constructed for each assemblage (see Figure 7.8). In addition, the weight and count compositions for the assemblages as a whole were calculated and displayed. With the classification and the graphic display of the data completed, the next step was the comparison of the results with the patterns that were expected, according to the experimentally derived diagnostic key.

Figure 7.8 shows an interesting relationship between the distance of a site from the coast and the pattern of weight concentration among the pieces in an assemblage. As one moves from the coast toward the interior, we notice that the blade curves and core-trim curves both run closer to the diagonal line. For assemblages in the interior, the weight of pieces apparently becomes more evenly distributed in the middle of the range of size classes. The implication here is that the reduction activity is more refined at such sites. Our experimental work suggests that more refined working of obsidian is characteristic of later stages of obsidian reduction. The inference can be drawn that more core-preparation and initial-working-of-obsidian activities were carried out at Settlement 3 near the coast. The hypothesis of varying degrees of involvement in obsidian reduction among sites that we set out to examine is supported. It is worth commenting that when the concentration curves are constructed for specific reduction classes (i.e., blades and core trim) rather than for the assemblage as a whole as in previous work, we can characterize an assemblage in

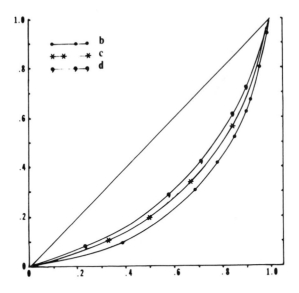

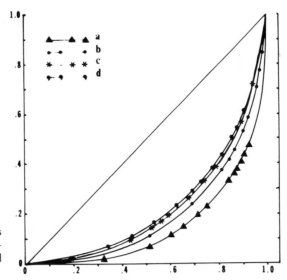

Figure 7.8. Concentration curves for four Neolithic sites in the Acconia area of Calabria: blades and core trim.

a more refined way. There is also a clearer idea of how these characterizations relate to obsidian reduction now that the experiments have been conducted.

When we turn to the composition diagrams for the main reduction classes (see Figure 7.9), we again see the difference between Settlement 3 and the sites in the interior. Over 90% of the weight of Assemblage A from the site near the coast consists of core trim. The weight for this same class at inland sites ranges

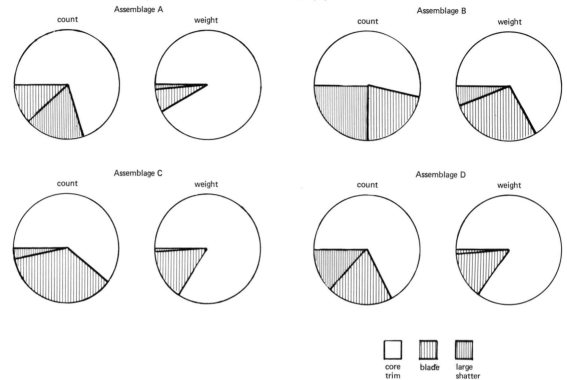

Figure 7.9. Relative proportion of products and by-products recovered from four Neolithic sites in the Acconia area.

from 60% to 80%. When these values are compared with those expected from our reduction key, it would appear that all four assemblages show reduced relative proportions of blades. Based on our experiments, the blades in terms of their counts should comprise about 50% of the material from a core-reduction site (with small shatter excluded). The three inland assemblages (B, C, and D), which we would identify as core-reduction sites on the basis of their concentration curves, contain blade counts of 19%, 22%, and 37%. The blade count for Assemblage A is 11% or roughly one half the size of the inland sites. This systematic shift to lower values for the blade class raises interesting questions about the basic reduction system in the Acconia area. One possibility is that the Neolithic knappers were much less efficient in extracting blades during the working of obsidian in comparison with our experimental work. The implication of this alternative would be that there was a fairly low level of efficiency in the overall production of blades in the Acconia area.

Another, more likely, possibility is that what we recover at sites are assemblages whose composition is modified by patterns of use and abandonment. There may be biases favoring the recovery within settlement areas of pieces of core trim and against the recovery of blades, which, as the target products of reduction, may have had a more prolonged use life (or lower dropping rate; see Ammerman and Feldman 1974) and were used and abandoned away from settlement areas. This is a fascinating question that needs to be explored in future work.

The point should be made in closing this section that the experimental work has revealed an unanticipated anomaly—one that would appear to have interesting implications along either of the two possible lines of explanation proposed here. If the latter turns out to be correct, this would provide all the more justification for basing the concentration curves on specific reduction classes. It would also mean that we have to shift or recalibrate the composition and index values that we use in our reduction key.

BEYOND OBSIDIAN

In the final section of this chapter, we would like to broaden the view on resource procurement and mention briefly some of the work that we have started in Calabria on inorganic resources other than the obsidian that are commonly observed at Neolithic sites in the Acconia area. It is in the wider context of these other resources that the exchange of obsidian operates. While the conceptual framework that we usually adopt sees reciprocal exchange as operating in terms of a number of different items (e.g., Wright and Zeder 1977), there has been a tendency in prehistoric studies to look at obsidian more or less in isolation. Among the main reasons for this are several practical considerations. It is relatively easy to recognize obsidian as a material during the course of archaeological fieldwork. In most parts of the world, there are comparatively few sources of obsidian. Methods such as neutron activation analysis are available for characterizing the source of an obsidian artifact. When it comes to other rocks and minerals, it is often less clear how to proceed. The geological mapping of source areas becomes a more difficult business, and much more work may be required in terms of the basic petrological identification of pieces of rock. It is understandable why the comprehensive study of resource procurement has remained underdeveloped and why obsidian has received the lion's share of attention.

Since 1977, a concerted effort has been made to extend the study of procurement and exchange to the wider range of inorganic materials utilized at Neolithic sites in the Acconia area. In comparison with organic remains, one of the advantages of dealing with rocks and minerals in procurement studies is that the remains are less subject to problems of preservation. Another attraction is that the natural distribution of a given resource can usually be mapped directly in the field. In the case of plant and animal remains, the spatial distributions of populations are usually obtained indirectly from ecological reconstructions. The work in the Acconia area of Calabria is facilitated by the fact that the impressed-ware Neolithic settlements are situated in dune areas of aeolian origin (see Figure 7.3). Such dune formations do not naturally contain sizeable pieces of rock, and fragments even as small as a centimeter in diameter can be treated as introduced into a site by human behavior.

We have found it useful to distinguish five basic functional groups of inorganic remains commonly observed at Neolithic settlements in the Acconia area.

1. Chipped stone	Obsidian	Long distance
	Chert	Long distance
2. Hand stones	Serpentine	Long distance
	Quartzite	Local
	Fine-grained gneiss	Local
	Pumice	Local
	Sandstone	Outside the area
	Amphibolite	Local
3. Structural rock	Gneiss	Local
	Amphibolite	Local
	Quartzite	Local
4. Pottery	Clay	Local
	Fine fluvial sand	Local
	Red ochre	Uncertain
5. Daub	Sandy-clay sediments	Local

The first group requires little further comment here except that chert suitable for the production of large blades, which are observed at the Neolithic sites, is rare in Calabria. While there is some evidence for the occasional use of low-quality pebble chert that may occur in the areas adjacent to Acconia in Calabria, the high-quality flint or chert comes from outside of the region, reaching the area via long-distance exchange. The second group includes a wide range of hand-held stones that are used for such things as pounding, knapping, and burnishing. The individual implements often take the form of pebbles and cobbles and, with the exception of serpentine used for polished-stone axes and sandstone used for grinding stones, all of the materials are of local origin. The third group consists of larger rocks—often cobbles and boulders—used in features such as hearths and roasting pits. There is also some evidence that fragments of rock are incorporated in the walls of wattle-and-daub structures. All of the rocks in this group are of local origin.

With regard to the fourth group, there are at least two good sources of clay suitable for pottery-making in the Acconia area itself. Studies are in progress on the characterization of geological and ceramic samples. Fine sand, which is apparently procured from local streams and not the sand dunes themselves, is used to temper the clay and red ocher for decorating the stamp-impressed bands of vessels. The fifth group involves the use of clayey sediments of various composition in wattle-and-daub structures. Several tons of such material had to be quarried from nearby alluvial terraces and transported onto the dunes for the construction of a single Neolithic building (Ammerman and Shaffer 1981). Detailed studies are being carried out by Shaffer on various aspects of the procurement and utilization of terrace sediments for Neolithic structures.

The point that should be made here is that the Neolithic inhabitants of the Acconia area exploited a wide range of inorganic materials for many different purposes. There is really nothing surprising in this, but it is important to document the specific array of resources either being procured locally or reaching the area by means of long-distance exchange. There are several resources that clearly come from outside the area, and we have no difficulty imagining obsidian cores, chert sickle blades, and serpentine axes moving through exchange networks. At the local level, we tend to think that all local resources are obtained through direct procurement. If we map the natural distributions of individual local resources in detail, however, we begin to see patterns that might suggest an alternative view. Based on the distributions that are mapped, estimates can be made of the distance that one would have to go from a given site to collect a particular resource. In Table 7.1, the minimum distance to each of four different sources of material for hand stones is given for the six impressed-ware Neolithic sites in the Acconia area (see Figure 7.10).

If we look at any one site, there are some resources that occur within its immediate vicinity, while others are found at a distance of 2 km or more away from the same site. Those resources that are distant from one site usually occur in the immediate vicinity of some other site. No one resource has consistently short distances for all of the sites. The overall pattern of the distances from sites to resources appears to be a complementary one. While even the longest distance could be covered on the ground in less than half a day and is no real obstacle to direct procurement, it is tempting to think that, rather than the

TABLE 7.1
Stentinello settlements in the Acconia area (see Figure 7.3): the nearest distance to a resource from a site measured in kilometers.

Site	Quartzite	Gneiss	Pumice	Amphibolite
1	.3	.3	1.5	3.0
2	.2	.8	1.4	3.5
3	.2	2.0	.6	4.5
4	2.0	.6	4.0	.7
5	.8	.7	2.5	2.0
6	1.0	.5	1.0	3.7

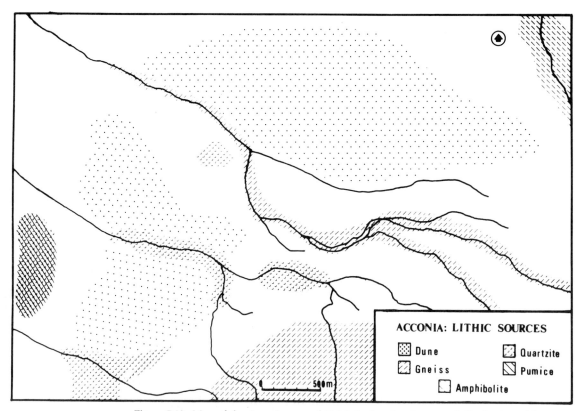

Figure 7.10. Map of the Acconia area of Calabria showing the natural distribution of four resources used for hand stones.

inhabitants of each settlement obtaining all of the items on the long list of local resources directly, some of the local resources moved between sites by means of local exchange. Patterns of procurement may have been more complementary in nature with those living closest to a given resource often doing much of its collection, and with the material subsequently circulating to those living at nearby sites. Such local exchange could take place at various times during social contacts between the inhabitants of the different settlements forming a community in the Acconia dune area. Such local exchange may even key in with the complementary patterns between sites that we observe with regard to obsidian reduction in this area. In order to evaluate the possibility of exchange in local materials, it will be necessary to make quantitative studies of the hand stones and structural rock found at the respective sites and to ascertain if distributional patterns reflect varying distance from a resource, which seems to be the case for structural rocks, or are essentially independent of distance. It is also worth attempting to see whether or not there is evidence for the production of hand stones at certain sites. Ideally, it would be useful to place the production of obsidian in the still wider context of the production of a whole range of things such as other tools, ceramic vessels, and wattle-and-daub structures.

In closing this chapter, we should recall that the study presented here has largely a methodological emphasis. We have not made an attempt to develop or describe more complex models of obsidian exchange as such in this chapter. One possibility that we may want to keep in mind when eventually formulating such models is that a commodity may have a dual nature: on the one hand, it may be "traded" between groups and yet at the same time it may circulate as a "gift" within a given group (Godelier 1977). We have turned to replication studies as one means of trying to follow up on the suggestion from previous work of differential involvement in obsidian production among sites in the Acconia area. The experiments presented here are only a start in this direction. Obviously, a much wider range of experiments could be performed. In terms of the analysis of Neolithic assemblages of obsidian, only a few have been examined as a means of trying out the reduction key derived from the experimental work. But even from this trial analysis, it would appear that we are on the right track. What remains to be done is a comprehensive study of the series of lithic assemblages recovered in association with individual structures during the excavations at the site of Piana di Curinga. The present study represents a major building block in the development and formulation of such an analysis that can provide the eventual basis for constructing more complex models of Neolithic exchange systems.

REFERENCES

Ammerman, A. J.
  1979 A study of obsidian exchange networks in Calabria. *World Archaeology* **11**:95–110.
Ammerman, A. J., and M. W. Feldman
  1974 On the "making" of an assemblage of stone tools. *American Antiquity* **39**:734–740.
Ammerman, A. J., and M. W. Feldman
  1978 Replicated collection of site surfaces. *American Antiquity* **43**:734–740.
Ammerman, A. J., G. P. Diamond, and D. Aldridge
  1978 Un insediamento neolitico presso Curinga (Catanzaro). *Rivista di Scienze Preistoriche* **33**:161–185.
Ammerman, A. J., and G. D. Shaffer
  1981 Neolithic settlement patterns in Calabria. *Current Anthropology* **22**:430–432.
Ammerman, A. J., C. Matessi, and L. L. Cavalli-Sforza
  1978 Some new approaches to the study of the obsidian trade in the Mediterranean and adjacent areas. In *The spatial organization of culture*, edited by I. Hodder, pp. 179–196. London: Duckworth.
Bigazzi, G., and F. Bonadonna
  1973 Fission track dating of the obsidian of Lipari Island (Italy). *Nature* **242**:322–323.
Brea, L. B., and M. Cavalier
  1960 *Meligunis–Lipara I.* Palermo: Flaccovio.
Callahan, E.
  1974 A guide for flintworkers: stages of manufacture. In *Experimental archaeology papers, No. 3*, edited by E. Callahan, pp. 185–192. Richmond: Virginia Commonwealth University Press.

Crabtree, D.
  1972 An introduction to flintworking. *Occasional Papers of the Idaho State University Museum* **28**.

Crummett, J. G., and S. E. Warren
  n.d. Analysis of Calabrian obsidian. In *Acconia monograph: neolithic settlement and the obsidian trade,* edited by A. J. Ammerman. London: Institute of Archaeology (forthcoming).

Dixon, J. E.
  1976 Obsidian characterization studies in the Mediterranean and Near East. In *Advances in obsidian glass studies,* edited by R. E. Taylor, pp. 288–333. Park Ridge, N.J.: Noyes Press.

Godelier, M.
  1977 "Salt money" and the circulation of commodities among the Baruya of New Guinea. In *Perspectives in Marxist Anthropology,* edited by M. Godelier, pp. 127–151. Cambridge: Cambridge University Press.

Hallam, B. R., S. E. Warren, and C. Renfrew
  1976 Obsidian in the western Mediterranean: characterisation by neutron activation analysis and optical emission spectroscopy. *Proceedings of the Prehistoric Society* **42**:85–110.

Jacobsen, T. W.
  1976 17,000 years of Greek prehistory. *Scientific American* **234**:76–87.

Kendall, M. G., and A. Stuart
  1969 *The advanced theory of statistics: vol. 1. distribution theory.* Third edition. London: Griffin.

Movius, H. L., N. C. David, H. M. Bricker, and R. B. Clay
  1968 The analysis of certain major classes of Upper Palaeolithic tools. *American School of Prehistoric Research Bulletin* **26**.

Pires-Ferreira, J. W., and K. V. Flannery
  1976 Ethnographic models for Formative exchange. In *The early mesoamerican village,* edited by K. V. Flannery, pp. 286–292. New York: Academic Press.

Redman, C. L.
  1973 Multivariate approach to understanding changes in an early farming community in southeast Anatolia. In *The explanation of culture change: models in prehistory,* edited by C. Renfrew, pp. 717–724. London: Duckworth.

Remmelzwaal, A.
  n.d. The geomorphology and soils of the Acconia area. In *Acconia monograph: neolithic settlement and the obsidian trade,* edited by A. J. Ammerman. London: Institute of Archaeology (forthcoming).

Renfrew, C.
  1977 Alternative models for exchange and spatial distribution. In *Exchange systems in prehistory,* edited by T. K. Earle and J. E. Ericson, pp. 71–90. New York: Academic Press.

Renfrew, C., J. E. Dixon, and J. R. Cann
  1968 Further analysis of Near Eastern obsidian. *Proceedings of the Prehistoric Society* **34**:319–331.

Tixier, J.
  1974 Glossary for the description of stone tools with special reference to the Epipaleolithic of the Maghreb. *Newsletter of Lithic Technology: Special Publication* **1**.

Wright, H., and M. Zeder
  1977 The simulation of a linear exchange system under equilibrium conditions. In *Exchange systems in prehistory,* edited by T. K. Earle and J. E. Ericson, pp. 233–252. New York: Academic Press.

The Social Context of Production and Exchange

Michael W. Spence

INTRODUCTION

Archaeological sequences in both Mesoamerica and northeastern North America reveal a shift in production and exchange patterns from a system of unspecialized artifact production with external trade by most adult men to one characterized by the semispecialized production of particular goods circulated through a network of elite individuals (cf. Pires-Ferreira 1975). This change may have been responsible in some instances for the development of hereditary ranking—a problem still not properly confronted by archaeologists (Flannery 1977:760). A combination of ethnographic and archaeological evidence allows some clarification of the processes involved in this shift and of its consequences for the participating societies. In the Teotihuacan Valley in Mexico, where specialists and elite did not become as closely associated as elsewhere, further developments culminated in an extensive and highly specialized industry that played an important role in Teotihuacan's domination of a large part of Mesoamerica in the Classic period.

Analysis will focus on the interrelationships among specialized production, distribution systems, and social organization (cf. Renfrew 1977:85–87). Some mechanisms for the movement of goods—like bridewealth—have been excluded from consideration, as have several factors that may well have played a role in the development of elite sets in some societies (warfare, argicultural intensification, etc.). Also, the analysis of production concentrates on craft

173

goods rather than on subsistence foods. These restrictions qualify the relevance of the findings to some degree, but they are necessary if the study is to achieve any depth.

OBSIDIAN PRODUCTION AND DISTRIBUTION IN MESOAMERICA

A number of significant changes occurred in the production and distribution of obsidian artifacts among the Formative-period societies of Mesoamerica (Pires-Ferreira 1975; Spence 1978). Although these changes generally centered on the Early-to-Middle-Formative transition, about 1100–900 B.C., their timing varied somewhat from region to region. They have been particularly well documented in certain archaeological sequences: the San Lorenzo site in Veracruz (Coe 1970; Cobean *et al.* 1971); Laguna Zope in the Isthmus of Tehuantepec (Zeitlin 1978; Zeitlin and Heimbuch 1978); the Valley of Oaxaca (Pires-Ferreira 1975; Winter and Pires-Ferreira 1976); Zohapilco and the Valley of Mexico (Niederberger 1976; Tolstoy *et al.* 1977; Boksenbaum 1980); and Chalcatzingo and related sites in Morelos (Grove 1974; Grove *et al.* 1976; Charlton, Grove, and Hopke 1978). These trends have been summarized and interpreted in several, more general studies (Grove 1974; Pires-Ferreira 1975; Charlton 1978; Spence 1978; Santley 1979).

The evidence comes largely from two sources: careful archaeological excavations of residential units and living floors (cf. Winter and Pires-Ferreira 1976) and trace element analyses of obsidian utilizing the neutron activation and X-ray fluorescence techniques. The earlier trace element studies were oriented toward the characterization of sources and the broad delineation of trade spheres (cf. Heizer, Williams, and Graham 1965; Weaver and Stross 1965). Recent work tends to have more tightly defined theoretical objectives and to place more emphasis on the internal structure of sites (cf. Pires-Ferreira 1975). Still, much can be done to improve the effectiveness of trace element analysis. Only a few Mesoamerican sources have been surveyed and collected thoroughly enough to ensure control over their internal variability. Furthermore, some previous studies were based on too limited a set of elements to differentiate the sources with confidence (Charlton, Grove, and Hopke 1978). In the future, more sources must be tested more widely—preferably with a carefully designed sampling program—and a larger series of elements must be used. The availability and use of standard source samples would help to ensure the comparability of results obtained from different analyses (Asaro *et al.* 1978). Samples from archaeological sites should include specimens from clearly defined contexts to aid in social interpretation (cf. Hodder and Lane, Chapter 10). These improvements, though, could make trace element analysis a rather expensive affair, and we may need to shift for preliminary analysis to less expensive chemical and petrographic techniques frequently used by geologists (P. D. Sheets, personal communication). Despite the drawbacks, trace element analyses have permitted the outlining of Formative-period changes in production and distribution systems.

In the Early Formative period, obsidian was circulated widely in Meso-america, largely in the form of nodules, chunks, and flakes. The principal sources were Guadalupe Victoria, El Chayal, Pico de Orizaba, Altotonga, Otumba, and Paredon. The careful excavations of residential compounds in Oaxacan sites have revealed that even among contemporaneous households within a single community there was considerable variation in the proportions of obsidian from particular sources. Probably each household developed its own procurement network based on individual trade partnerships (Pires-Fer-reira 1975).

With the Middle Formative period a number of changes occurred. Popula-tions were generally growing, and the per capita consumption of obsidian was increasing, as measured by a variety of indicators (ratios of obsidian to flint, sherds, or manos and metates). The obsidian was now frequently circulated in the form of prismatic cores and blades, which require some skill in manufac-ture. There was a concomitant shift toward those sources that produced obsi-dians with a physical structure more suitable for blade manufacture—sources like Cerro de las Navajas, Zinapecuaro, Zaragosa, Otumba, and the various Guatemalan deposits (Pires-Ferreira 1975:27, 31; Spence 1978). Middle For-mative obsidian workshops reflecting part-time specialization have been iden-tified at two major centers—Chalcatzingo and San Lorenzo—as well as in the Valley of Mexico (Coe 1970:28; Grove *et al.* 1976:1206; Tolstoy *et al.* 1977:102). In some areas, there were two distinct systems of obsidian work-ing—one based on cores and blades that were probably produced by a few specialists and circulated widely, and another that involved locally produced nodules and flakes (Boksenbaum 1980; Stanley 1980).

The Oaxacan excavations indicate that procurement had now shifted from individual household efforts to some form of elite "pooling" (Pires-Ferreira 1975). Sources were represented in each household in roughly equivalent pro-portions, suggesting that obsidian entered the site through a single channel and was then passed on to the rest of the community. The distribution of the material was not necessarily equal across the social spectrum. Blades—appar-ently a principal item in these networks—made up over 80% of the obsidian recovered from an area with elite associations at the San José Mogote site, but was only about 25% in a contemporaneous nonelite sector of the site and in a smaller subordinate community in the area (Pires-Ferreira 1975:31–32, Table 8; Drennan 1976:Appendix VI).

Robert Santley's excavations at Loma Torremote—an early Late Formative community in the Valley of Mexico—provide a tightly focused view of the shift from general household to elite procurement (Santley 1977, 1980; Sanders, Parsons, and Santley 1979:305–334). In the earlier levels of the site, obsidian was found in roughly equal proportions in the various households. Visually distinguished subvarieties of the dominant gray obsidian were irregularly distributed, suggesting that each household had developed its own trading network. In the later occupation levels, all households continued to show evidence of obsidian working and use, but the gray subvarieties were evenly distributed among them, suggesting some form of pooling. A single elite household is associated with the production of prismatic cores and blades, often of the fine Cerro de las Navajas green obsidian. Apparently then, the procurement of obsidian came under the control of the elite members of the community, who monopolized production of the more valued cores and blades but passed on the finished blades (though not the cores) and the rougher chunks and nodules of gray obsidian to the other residents of the site.

The Loma Torremote evidence reveals that elite control over the processing and movement of obsidian developed somewhat later in some parts of the Valley of Mexico than in others. In the Teotihuacan subvalley a strong association between the regional elite and the obsidian industry may not have evolved until the Classic period. The only evidence of Late Formative specialized production there is a small Cuanalan-phase (650–300 B.C.) workshop oriented toward the production of cores and blades from the local gray obsidian (Sanders, West, and Marino 1975:49, 82, Appendix A; Santley 1977). The associated residential structure does not appear to have been elite, although the possibility that it was the house of a local lineage or community leader cannot be eliminated.

During the Terminal Formative period, obsidian working in the Teotihuacan area underwent a marked change (Spence 1979). The craft expanded rapidly and was oriented primarily toward the supply of utilitarian items (bifacials, scrapers, and blades) to a burgeoning local population. Throughout its development, it remained distinct from the emerging urban elite. In the Patlachique phase (150 B.C.–A.D. 1), Teotihuacan had a population of about 30,000 to 40,000 souls (Cowgill 1979:55). Nine sites (residential loci) at the west edge of the community, covering a total area of some 6 ha, were apparently obsidian workshops. The quantities of obsidian on the site surfaces are greater than usual, with high proportions of waste and some unfinished or reject specimens. These criteria can be illustrated with data from some Classic-period workshop sites that, although later, are comparable in several respects (Table 8.1). Surface collections were not based on a rigid sampling design, but were conducted carefully and consistently enough to offer an accurate reflection of site function. In nonworkshop collections, the ratio of obsidian to sherds is considerably lower than in workshop collections, where obsidian frequently matches or surpasses the sherd count (see Table 8.1). Also, the proportion of waste is much higher in workshop collections, and specimens of particular artifact categories may be more numerous than expected (note the core and bifacial counts in the bifacially specialized 26:N5W1 and core–blade specialized 8:N6W1 workshops in Table 8.1).

The surface density of the obsidian on the Patlachique workshop sites does

TABLE 8.1
Classic Period Teotihuacan Obsidian Workshop Criteria

	Nonworkshop sites			Workshop sites			
	26:N2W4	35:N1E3	37:N5W1	44:N4W2	38:W:N5W1	26:N5W1	8:N6W1
Total sherds	169	304	831	423	224	44	334
Total obsidian	34	78	185	745	863	415	460
Waste	9	27	69	364	462	314	168
Cores	5	7	9	15	24	0	89
Crest-ridge flakes	0	0	0	3	0	0	2
Blades	16	31	69	290	138	15	179
Total bifacials	2	7	33	61	217	81	15
Unfinished bifacials	0	2	9	10	29	16	3
Scrapers	2	5	5	12	22	5	7

not approach that observed on some later workshops, where special surface collections of all the obsidian in a restricted area may produce counts of over 500 pieces per m². This suggests that the Patlachique-phase craftsmen were only part-time specialists. However, if one calculates a population density of roughly 40 people per ha (G. L. Cowgill, personal communication), there would have been about 240 people, or 50 craftsmen, involved in the obsidian industry at this time—considerably more than in the elite-sponsored workshops of Middle Formative societies.

The spatial clustering of the workshop sites suggests that the craftsmen may have been members of a single social group, while the generally equitable distribution of raw materials and of particular artifact types among the sites indicates that procurement and distribution were corporate activities, conducted by the craft group as a whole rather than separately by each specialist or family. The distance of 3 km between the workshop area and the zone where the principal public structures were presumably located reflects the institutional separation between the community elite and the obsidian industry.

In the succeeding Tzacualli phase (A.D. 1–150), Teotihuacan became a city with a population of about 80,000 (Cowgill 1979:55). The obsidian industry expanded rapidly to include 48 workshop sites and over 200 craftsmen, a number of whom were apparently full-time specialists. Most of the sites were clustered together in several workshop areas that, although internally homogeneous, were somewhat different from one another in terms of raw materials and products (see Table 8.2). Each such area probably represented a distinct social group that conducted its own procurement and distribution. The green obsidian—identified by trace element analysis as coming from the Cerro de las Navajas source some 50 km to the northeast—is particularly well suited structurally to the production of prismatic cores and blades. Its irregular distribu-

TABLE 8.2
Raw-material Proportions in Some Teotihuacan Workshop Areas

	Area #1	Area #2	Area #4	Area #6	Area #7
Tzacualli phase workshop areas:					
Percentage Navajas obsidian in blades	31.9	48.7	56.6	61.9	81.2
Percentage block material in gray obsidian	95.5	47.6	63.5	24.3	10.0

	San Juan	Santa Maria	Moon	Ciudadela	San Martin
Classic period workshop areas:					
Percentage Navajas obsidian in blades	89.2	89.2	86.0	93.3	90.7
Percentage block material in gray obsidian	8.3	6.4	79.1	5.6	81.9

tion among the various workshop areas, where it forms anywhere from 31.9% to 81.2% of the blades, indicates that each workshop group developed its own procurement network (Table 8.2). The gray obsidian, more useful for the manufacture of scrapers and bifacials, occurs naturally in the Otumba region 16 km east of Teotihuacan. It appears there in block form, but rivers passing by the deposits carry the obsidian to Teotihuacan in the form of water-rolled nodules. Although they were more accessible, the smaller size of the nodules limited the range of artifacts that could be produced from them. The varying proportions of nodular and block surfaces in gray obsidian waste again suggest that each workshop group developed its own set of raw-material procurement strategies (see Table 8.2). The majority of the Tzacualli-phase workshop areas were probably oriented toward the manufacture of artifacts for local consumption, although the most intensive areas produced bifacial blanks and end scrapers intended also for broader regional distribution in the Basin of Mexico.

The Teotihuacan state still played only a limited role in the industry. It was not responsible for raw-material procurement, and only a few small workshops were associated with the major civic–ceremonial structures in the center of the city. One of these workshops may have housed a few specialists supported by the state, while another was probably a special area where craftsmen came periodically from the workshop areas to work under state supervision, producing material as a form of "levy." Their output consisted of the same sorts of blanks that were produced in the regionally oriented workshops, indicating that the burden of this levy fell primarily on that sector of the industry involved in regional—rather than simply local—exchange. This is not surprising, since state agents and networks may have been important in the regional circulation of goods, and the state's political control of the region was a major element in its transformation into a market for workshop output. Still, though, the workshop areas were basically independent of the state; they were situated outside the central zone, procuring their own raw materials and probably handling much of the distribution of their output.

In the Miccaotli-to-Metepec phase span (A.D. 150–750), the city reached its peak size of 150,000, and extended its political control over much of Classic-period central Mexico. The number of workshops grew to about 100, with most of the increase falling in the regional sector of the industry. A number of these were subspecialized in the production of cores and blades or of bifacial artifacts. The collection from the workshop site labeled 26:N5W1, for example, included quantities of bifacials but few blades or scrapers and no cores, while workshop 8:N6W1 was obviously core–blade specialized (see Table 8.1). The lower proportion of waste in 8:N6W1 is probably due to the preliminary formation of cores at the quarries, leaving only limited refinement to be done in the Teotihuacan workshops.

Cores and blades, in fact, became major workshop items in the Classic period, their production being stimulated by the large quantities of superior Cerro de las Navajas obsidian now entering the city. The proportion of this obsidian in blade collections from Classic period workshop areas is considerably higher and covers a much narrower range (86.0–93.3%) than was the case in the Tzacualli phase (see Table 8.2). Clearly, Navajas material was now entering Teotihuacan through a highly efficient system and was being distributed equitably among the various workshop areas. The procurement system must have been markedly different from the individual workshop area networks of the Tzacualli phase craftsmen. To investigate this situation further, a detailed neutron activation analysis was conducted on 56 green obsidian cores from six Classic-period workshop areas. Twenty-one elements were measured. The results were processed with stepwise discriminant analysis and cluster analysis, leading to the identification of four distinguishable subgroups (Spence, Kimberlin, and Harbottle 1979). Since obsidian sources often display significant internal geochemical variation (cf. Bowman, Asaro, and Perlman 1973), each subgroup probably represents a separate locus of exploitation within the source region—perhaps on the order of what Hurtado de Mendoza and Jester (1978) term *localities* or *locality complexes*. Of particular interest is the fact that materials from the four exploitation loci were thoroughly intermingled in the six workshop areas, indicating that at some point the Navajas obsidian had been funneled together into a single system. The most plausible explanation for this—as it is for the large quantities entering Teotihuacan and their stringently fair distribution within the city—is a state-controlled procurement system.

The state exploitation of Navajas obsidian and the expansion of the market region for workshop products must have led to increasing reliance by the workshops on the support of state institutions. This developing interdependence is reflected in the location of some major workshop areas near the principal public structures in the city. Despite this, the workshops were not reduced to mere appendages of the state. Production was still conducted through the medium of well-defined social groups, and the varying proportions of nodular and block materials suggest that procurement of the gray obsidian used in bifacial and scraper production was generally still managed independently by each craft group, rather than by the state (see Table 8.2). Craftsmen from the regional workshops evidently repaid their obligations to the state by producing artifacts for it in special workshops located within the precincts of two of the major public structures (Spence 1981).

In the Tlamimilolpa phase (A.D. 200–450), the movement of Teotihuacan obsidian into the Maya region began. A number of artifacts clearly produced in Teotihuacan appear at sites like Altun Ha, Tikal, Mirador, Solano, and Kaminaljuyu (Kidder, Jennings, and Shook 1946; Agrinier 1970; Pendergast 1971; Moholy-Nagy 1975; Brown 1977). Most of the items are eccentrics, ornaments, fine prismatic blades, and well-worked bifacials, apparently designed for nonutilitarian functions. They generally occur in high-status burials and offerings, often with other evidence of Teotihuacan influence. Their appearance in the Maya region is a reflection of activities associated with the Teotihuacan state (e.g., gift exchanges with the Mayan elite, offerings for resident Teotihuacan officials, etc.). Although in some sites these artifacts constitute as much as 8% of the chipped-stone assemblage (Brown 1977:241–242), they generally are rare, and in Teotihuacan formed only a small proportion of the workshop output. In contrast to the Middle Formative situation, the ritual and exchange obligations of the Teotihuacan elite played only a minor role in defining the structure of the obsidian industry.

The unusual course of craft specialization in Teotihuacan was influenced by a variety of factors. One important factor was the lack of association between the craftsmen and the elite. It may be that the marginal position of the Teotihuacan subvalley through most of the Formative period did not encourage the close affiliation between specialist and elite groups that had developed in other areas. It is also possible, however, that the ruling element in Teotihuacan did not evolve from earlier, more localized elite groups, but rather developed from some other segment of the society. The foundation of political power may have shifted with the introduction of irrigation. In any event, craftsmen were oriented toward the production of quantities of utilitarian items for consumption by local populations, rather than toward production in support of the political goals and external relationships of the elite segment of the society.

As the number of consumers increased—through urban growth and the expansion of Teotihuacan's control in the region—access to them by craft specialists was probably facilitated by the development of a regional market system centered in Teotihuacan. Craftsmen were able to specialize and be assured of a wide set of consumers, rather than being dependent on the more limited needs of the elite (cf. Earle 1981). This increasing demand was accommodated by the expansion of producing units along established social lines—not by the creation of special craft groups organized and supported by the state (as might have occurred if the elite had sponsored isolated craftsmen in the earlier phases). Although the Teotihuacan administration eventually played a larger role in the industry, particularly in the regional sector, the well-developed social identities of the craft groups and their history of self-sufficiency protected them from being absorbed or replaced by the state.

ARCHAIC AND WOODLAND SOCIETIES IN ONTARIO

Several Ontario cemetery sites offer some insight into the widespread Late Archaic and Early Woodland burial complexes of the Great Lakes region. The societies represented in these cemeteries appear to have been relatively egalitarian. Most adult male burials were accompanied by some trade goods. Variations in the nature and extent of the grave offerings have been noted, but these seem to reflect differences in age, sex, or ability rather than in ascribed rank.

It has been noted that grave goods alone provide insufficient evidence of a system of hereditary rank. A burial offering, particularly one accompanying an infant or child, may really be an expression of the social identity of the donor rather than that of the deceased (Saxe 1970). In order to claim differences in rank, as opposed to achieved status, variations in mortuary offerings should be correlated with variations in mortuary treatment or location (King 1978:231–232; Tainter 1978:120–122). Braun (1979), in fact, has suggested even more stringent criteria, although I doubt that such formal requirements are really appropriate for the sort of simple ranking, tempered by achievement, that probably characterized most Middle Woodland societies.

The Late Archaic Glacial Kame complex is known largely from burial components (Cunningham 1948), in part because the exotic grave offerings have attracted archaeological attention. This has unfortunately made it difficult to associate cemeteries with habitation sites. The Hind site—a Glacial Kame burial area in southwestern Ontario (Figure 8.1)—has been radiocarbon dated to about 1000 B.C. At that time, the Great Lakes region was probably occupied by small, seasonally coalescing bands that subsisted by hunting, gathering, and fishing (cf. Fitting 1970:70–78, 82). Burial took place in special cemetery areas, perhaps at spring–summer macroband camps, and often included deposits of trade, ritual, and utilitarian items. Most of the grave goods at the Hind site were with adults—the males receiving the richest offerings and the bulk of the marine shell and ritual artifacts (Pfeiffer 1977:35–40; Wortner 1978). At the Picton site—a Glacial Kame cemetery on the north shore of Lake Ontario (see Figure 8.1)—the grave goods included a number of trade articles: galena, beads and gorgets of marine shell, and beads, awls, adzes, and celts of

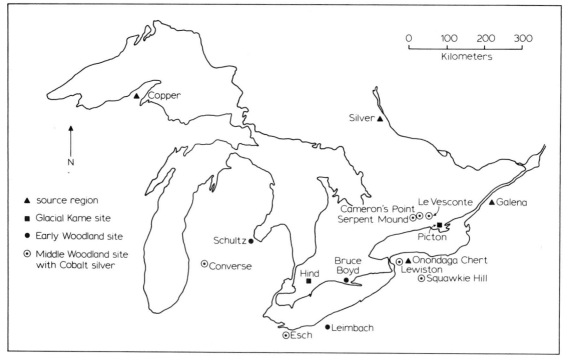

Figure 8.1. Raw-material sources and archaeological sites of the Great Lakes region.

native copper (Ritchie 1949; Pfeiffer 1977:33–34). Most burials had offerings, with no discernible differences noted between children and adults. Access to trade goods was not noticeably restricted; all adult burials included some. These ranged from a single copper bead in one grave to an offering, associated with an extended male, of two celts, one adze, four awls, and two beads of copper as well as several beads and three gorgets of marine shell. The Glacial Kame pattern suggests a social system comparable to those of Early Formative Mesoamerica, with most of the adult men involved in external trade.

Early Woodland occupations in the Great Lakes region (circa 900–450 B.C.) seem primarily to have been extensions of the Late Archaic system, with the addition of cord-marked ceramics and, particularly in Ontario and New York, the distinctive Meadowood lithic complex (Ritchie 1955). Finds of squash at the Schultz site in Michigan and the Leimbach site in northern Ohio (see Figure 8.1) indicate that horticulture played a minor role in some Early Woodland subsistence economies, but as yet there is no evidence of cultigens at this time in Ontario or New York. The Meadowood complex in western New York includes a number of bands that came together in larger groups for mortuary activities and exchange in the fall or spring (Granger 1978). Cemeteries were generally at some distance from the base camps. In southwestern Ontario, however, the Early Woodland settlement system may have been somewhat different. What little evidence we have suggests a pattern of winter dispersal inland in microbands and spring–summer coalescence in macrobands on the north shore of Lake Erie, at points where fish and migratory waterfowl were available (W. Fox and D. Poulton, personal communication). Burial took place in the spring at cemeteries located near the macroband camps. One such cemetery—the Bruce Boyd site (Figure 8.1)—has been dated to 520 B.C. (Spence, Williamson, and Dawkins 1978; Spence and Fox 1979). The grave goods include galena, a variety of chert items (including the distinctive Meadowood cache blades and side-notched points of Onondaga chert), ground-stone pendants and gorgets, and copper beads, awls, axes, and bracelets (see Table 8.3). Optical emission spectroscopy analysis of one bead indicates that the copper came from the Lake Superior area (S. Goad, personal communication). The galena of both the Bruce Boyd and Hind sites, tested by isotopic analysis at the University of Toronto, is from a source in northern New York state (see Figure 8.1; R. M. Farqhuar, personal communication).

Although most of the burials date to the Early Woodland component, circa 500 B.C., the Bruce Boyd site was also used for interment by a Late Woodland (circa A.D. 1100) group. Before the Early Woodland burial pattern could be properly interpreted, these later burials had to be isolated and excluded from the analysis. Unfortunately, Late Woodland burials were not generally provided with grave offerings; thus some other method of identification was required. Recent microchemical refinements allow measurement of the fluorine content of bone with far more precision than the techniques used to make the very broad discriminations adequate for Pleistocene materials (Singer and Armstrong 1968). When applied to the Bruce Boyd series, the new method permitted the assignment of several dubious burials to either the Early or Late Woodland component (Spence, Wall, and King 1981). Now, some 24 individuals and 19 features can be securely identified as Early Woodland (Table 8.3).

There are no artifact concentrations and burial clusters in the cemetery to suggest rank differentiation within the society. What variations exist are consonant with simple age–sex–achievement distinctions. Most of the burials received some grave goods (Table 8.3). Of the two adult males without goods, one (Burial E) had been severely crippled for some years before his death and so had probably been unable to participate in the activities that would have ensured him an offering. Trade, then, was apparently not monopolized by just one or a few individuals within the Bruce Boyd society. Furthermore, one of the burials suggests that a man's trade wealth and his status may have been independent of one another. The only artifact with the elderly male of Burial F1 was a single copper bead, but the remains of several fish and mammals, including four deer, indicate a considerable procurement effort on his behalf by the other members of the band.

In the Middle Woodland period, several changes took place in southern Ontario. There is some evidence to suggest a rise in population (J. Wright

TABLE 8.3
Early Woodland Burials of the Bruce Boyd Site

Burial	Individuals	Grave goods
A	2 adult females	1 copper bead, 1 bifacial (both with one female)
C	1 adult of unknown sex	1 copper awl, 1 bifacial, 1 adze, 1 gorget, 1 abrading stone
D	1 adult male	None
E	1 adult male	None
F	1 adult male, 1 child	1 copper bead, large faunal offering
H	2 adults (1 male, 1 female)	6 copper beads, 1 pendant
I	1 adult male	4 bifacials
J	1 adult of unknown sex, 1 child	Iron pyrites
K	1 child	None
L	1 adult of unknown sex	1 bifacial
M	1 adult of unknown sex	Disturbed (copper present)
N	1 child	40 copper beads, 5 bifacials, iron pyrites, 1 clam shell
P	1 adult male	Disturbed
Q	1 adult of unknown sex	5 copper beads, 1 copper awl, 53 bifacials, iron pyrites, 1 beaver incisor
R	1 adult of unknown sex	1 ceramic vessel, 3 bifacials, 1 celt, 2 small stones, 1 gorget, iron pyrites
S	1 child or adult	16 copper beads, 5 bifacials, 1 clam shell
T	1 child or adult	8 bifacials
U	1 child or adult	Disturbed (several copper beads, beaver incisor, probably other goods)
V	1 adult of unknown sex	Feature not fully excavated

1972:39; Noble 1975:107), although agriculture was still not practiced, and the external trade contacts of societies expanded as they were drawn into the Hopewellian interaction sphere (Johnston 1968a; Spence, Finlayson, and Pihl 1979). A dual-rank system developed in the Rice Lake region of southeastern Ontario, which is exemplified particularly in the Serpent and the Cameron's Point mounds (Johnston 1968b; Spence and Harper 1968). At the latter site, burials fall into two distinct categories: a small subfloor set, often partially or completely articulated, placed in pits beneath the mound floor; and a larger fill set of incomplete and disarticulated bodies buried during the erection of the mound. Grave goods were placed exclusively with the subfloor set and included such trade items as a silver panpipe band, a marine-shell pendant, and beads of copper, silver, and marine shell. There is thus a sharp social division in the mound, with burial offerings and access to trade goods combining with separate burial treatment and location to distinguish an elite set within the society. This group evidently controlled external trade and was probably based partially on descent. However, an argument for hereditary rank cannot be convincingly sustained with the evidence of burial treatment alone, despite the emphasis that it has received in the literature (cf. Saxe 1970; King 1978; Tainter 1978). The osteological characteristics of the cemetery population provide an important additional source of information. Age and sex, of course, have not been neglected, but a thorough analysis of the skeletal material can also produce invaluable data on the genetic and social structure of the group (cf. Lane and Sublett 1972; Spence 1974). A system of hereditary rank may be reflected in a skewed distribution of genetically based osteological features among the archaeologically defined units of the cemetery. Five of the Serpent Mound crania, for example, have a partial or full Os Inca—a surprisingly high incidence for this rare trait. Only three of the crania can be assigned a specific provenience within the mound, but all of these were from subfloor pits with burial offerings. This suggests close genetic (and presumably social) relationships among the elite, reinforcing the archaeological evidence for the existence of a hereditary rank system in the Middle Woodland societies of the area (Molto 1979).

The external links controlled by the elite involved exotic and ritual objects and materials, many of them associated with the Hopewellian interaction sphere, but they also included more mundane goods. Quantities of chert from the Onondaga deposits in western New York state were imported to be used in the daily activities of the Rice Lake people (see Figure 8.1). Both forms of trade were probably conducted through the elite set, with some goods then being widely distributed within the society, while others—the exotics—were restricted to the elite. In comparable situations it has been suggested that the function of the trade of exotics was to regulate an associated and more vital exchange of staple commodities (Rappaport 1968:106–107; Wright and Zeder 1977; but see Hughes 1973:123–125). The rapidly consumed exotics were supposedly in continuous demand, and thus they maintained an exchange system that also included the less perishable but more essential staples.

The concept, however, does not fit the Hopewell situation well. The exotic goods—copper, silver, marine shell—are not highly perishable, nor were they removed frequently from circulation. Mound burial in Ontario occurred only once or twice per generation in a band, and the quantities of exotics deposited with the dead were not large. The demand for exotics would have been neither large nor constant, so it is unlikely that their exchange regulated the system. More probably the exchange of the staple commodities, which were in wider demand and which would have been consumed more rapidly, required no real reinforcement (Spence, Finlayson, and Pihl 1979:119–120).

One of the principal exotic commodities moving through this network was native silver. Brian Fryer of the Memorial University of Newfoundland and I have been analyzing this material to determine its sources and the channels through which it was distributed. The first level of analysis was conducted with the Spark Source Mass Spectrometer at the University of Western Ontario. Relative abundances were obtained for a wide range of elements, some 40 in all, expressed as ratios of one another rather than as absolute abundances. This, however, allowed us to select a smaller set of elements (Co, Zn, Bi, Hg, Pb, Cu, Ni, Cd) that appeared to be sensitive in the discrimination of sources. These were then examined by atomic absorption, which not only provided absolute abundances for these elements but also allowed us to convert the mass spectrometer readings for the other elements into semiquantitative analyses. The preliminary assessment of our results indicates that most of the silver in Hopewellian sites is from the Cobalt source in Ontario, some 350 km north of Rice Lake (see Figure 8.1). Cobalt silver has been identified from the Cameron's Point, Serpent, and Le Vesconte mounds of the Rice Lake area of southeastern Ontario; Lewiston and Squawkie Hill sites in New York; Esch, North Benton, Marietta, Seip, and Harness sites in Ohio; Converse site in Michigan; Knight site in Illinois; and Tunacunnhee and Mandeville sites in Georgia (see Figure 8.1).

The silver with a Le Vesconte burial was in the form of ore, nuggets, hammered pieces, and finished panpipe bands. Evidently it was brought in from the Cobalt area as unprocessed ore to be reduced at Le Vesconte to thin sheets that could be worked easily into a variety of items or molded to a copper or wood base. In sheet or artifact form it was then passed to other sites in southeastern Ontario and to New York, Ohio, and beyond. However, the Converse site in western Michigan (see Figure 8.1) was apparently another center for the dispersal of sheet silver (Fitting 1971). The mound produced two large nuggets of Cobalt silver—one 7¾ lb and one 5 lb—a panpipe band, and a piece of sheet silver not yet shaped as an artifact. It is not clear which sites in the Hopewellian network received their silver through Le Vesconte and which through Converse.

Both the Converse and Le Vesconte silver was found as offerings in single graves, suggesting that control over the procurement and working of silver in these societies was vested in one individual. The large size of the Converse nuggets even raises the possibility that some of the silver circulating in the Hopewellian network entered it through only a few large-scale procurement efforts or transactions, as has been suggested for Hopewellian obsidian and galena (Griffin 1965:146–147; Walthall 1981:41). Once in the network, silver generally moved between major regional centers of Hopewellian ceremonialism, and did not "trickle down" to the minor sites. The distances covered by trade links indicate that the transactions were controlled by regional elites (Renfrew 1975:50–51; Goad 1979:244–246).

To sum up, the Late Archaic and Early Woodland societies of southern Ontario were relatively egalitarian, with most of the adult men in each band engaged in external trade to some degree. Although there were variations in grave offerings even among men of the same band, these seem to reflect differences in health, experience, or other personal factors, rather than a formal set of rules about which social categories could or could not participate in trade. As Hopewellian contacts developed, this egalitarian system evolved, at least in the Rice Lake area, into one based more on hereditary rank. New trade commodities were introduced, and access to them was under the control of an emerging elite. Low-level specialization in silver working is indicated by the Le Vesconte Mound, while in southern Ohio part-time specialists were attached to some of the major centers (Struever and Houart 1972:55, 69–72). There are several parallels here with the changes observed in Formative period Meso-america. In the earlier stage, many or all of the adult men were able to carry on trade for a variety of exotic and utilitarian goods. These exchange links were roughly equivalent to one another, with variations in their effectiveness reflect-ing differences in individual skills and life histories rather than formal re-strictions expressed in terms of office or rank. This system evolved into one in which at least some of the externally procured material entered the society through only one or a few high-ranking individuals, who then distributed some of it within the community. This shift was apparently triggered by the intro-duction of new commodities, accompanied by the incorporation of new and more distant societies into the exchange network.

THE TRADE PARTNERSHIP

Some insight into the processes involved in these changes can be gained by an examination of the trade partnership—the institution underlying much of the exchange conducted in simple societies (Malinowski 1920; Harding 1967; Ford 1972; Sahlins 1972:298–299). It is often viewed as a sort of kin relation-ship, linking individuals, families, and even kindreds in a lifelong tie that may be further reinforced by marriage. Other individuals are prohibited from in-truding upon a partnership or from attempting to steal one's trade partner, and the relationship is not lightly altered or abrogated by either of the participants. Like other personal resources, it is frequently inherited. Partnerships have been recorded among the Tewa, for example, that extended over three generations (Ford 1972:33). Even when they are not assigned to an individual by custom or law, a man may take over his father's trade partnerships simply because he has the inside track on them. Among the Telefolmin of New Guinea, a boy is taken along on trading trips by his father, and thus becomes familiar with his father's partners and their kin. When the time comes for him to develop his own network, it inevitably includes some of these people (D. Jorgensen, per-sonal communication). Of particular relevance to the present discussion are the exclusiveness and hereditary transmission of the relationship. Although these are not features of trade partnerships in all societies (cf. Brunton 1975:549), where they do occur they can have a strong effect on the society's response to new developments in external trade.

In the Mesoamerican and Northeastern situations described in this chapter there are several common factors: a change from egalitarian to ranked struc-ture, the entry of new and valued goods into the network, the restriction of some aspects of exchange to a few select individuals, the expansion of the network to include a wider area, and the appearance of craft specialization at some central points. All of these factors áre related, but the changes seem to have been set in motion by the introduction of new trade commodities. In order to actually transform the system, these commodities must be highly valued in either social or utilitarian terms, and access to them must be restricted geographically or socially. If they were widely available, the same egalitarian trade network would continue to function adequately, albeit with some change in personnel (cf. Strathern 1971:133–134). Freidel (1979:31), for example, suggests that a major change took place in early Maya society only when the items used to symbolize status shifted to materials that were not locally available. In the same vein, access to *kula* valuables in the northern Trobriand Islands was restricted to those individuals able to develop marriage ties with the people of the area from which the valuables came (Brunton 1975).

When the new goods play an important role but are of restricted availability, they do not become mere additions to the existing network. Rather, they act as catalysts in its transformation. There is an increase in flow through some trade links while others atrophy, and patterns of internal distribution change accordingly. In the case of Mesoamerica, the introduction of prismatic cores and blades increased the utility of obsidian and caused a shift to those obsidians best suited for blade production. Only some of the previously existing partnerships would have been effective in obtaining these materials. In the Early Formative household labeled LTL-1 at the Tierras Largas site in Oaxaca, for example, 84% of the obsidian was from the relatively poor Guadalupe Victoria source, while in the contemporaneous LTL-3 household 70% was of the finer Otumba variety (Winter and Pires-Ferreira 1976:Table 10.4). As the emphasis on cores and blades grew, the trade network of the LTL-3 occupants would have remained effective and may even have increased its flow, while the LTL-1 people would have been at a relative disadvantage.

In the face of a growing demand for the new goods, then, only those trade partnerships that can provide access to the goods and increase their volume will flourish. Others will become relatively ineffective, either because they are unable to obtain the goods, or because they cannot increase their flow to satisfy the growing demand. Too great a distance may intervene between source and consumer, or there may be too many intermediate links in the chain for the ultimate recipients to significantly alter the quantity or kind of goods reaching them. Trade partnerships are notoriously slow to respond to changes in the needs of the participants (Harding 1967:243; Rappaport 1968:106–107; Hughes 1973:123–124). This is not to say that these partnerships will necessarily die. They will simply remain less effective—unable to provide the materials that the participants need to manipulate their wider social environment. On the other hand, those with partnerships that do bring in the desired goods and that can increase volume will be able to broaden their influence, perhaps drawing others into subordinate relationships (for example, as sponsored craftsmen) that can then be tapped to underwrite still further expansion (cf. Santley 1980). Those without access to the goods may thus come into the social orbit of their more fortunate or skilled contemporaries. As an alternative, they may attempt to develop new and more effective partnerships. This, however, would run the risk of intruding upon established partnerships or of involving more numerous and indirect links, thereby impeding the flow of goods. Demand for the new commodities thus would be met in most cases by an increase in flow through those partnerships that could bear it, and by the concomitant development of supplementary mechanisms for the local dissemination of the goods.

In a system where the further distribution of the material was conducted under a strictly egalitarian ethic—through mechanisms that removed control from the hands of the importer (various leveling mechanisms, for example)—the gap between the importer and the other members of the community would remain relatively small. Among the historic period Huron, for example, an emphasis upon generosity prohibited the accumulation of wealth or its use in any obvious attempt to build personal power. A man was under considerable pressure to distribute his wealth widely at public occasions such as curing ceremonies and feasts, risking attack by a witch or accusations of witchcraft if he failed to do so (Trigger 1976:50–51, 66–67). Even the introduction of highly valued European trade goods was not enough to overcome the basic egalitarian principles of Huron society (Ramsden 1981). However, in some situations the disequilibrium created in the external trade network by the new goods could be expected to cause some compensating changes in the internal distribution system, quite possibly leading to the introduction of new mechanisms that would allow the importer much more control over the disposal of his wealth (parton–client relationships, bridewealth sponsorship, etc.). In that event, the importer's position might become more sharply differentiated from the rest of the population. This trend would be accelerated in situations where access to subsistence foods or staple goods was tied to the exchange of more exotic commodities (Brose 1979:7–8).

CONCLUSIONS

A variety of conditions may temper the effect that imported goods have on a society. In most of the Trobriand Islands, for example, a leader had only limited power. He differed from the other members of the society not so much through exclusive access to trade goods as through the greater number of his contacts (Malinowski 1920). Similarly, a New Guinea "Big-Man" may assemble a variety of contributors, partially through polygynous marriages, but he will be unable to shut out competitors for more than a limited period. All men in the society may develop their own trade networks, and since many materials enter through more than one point, monopolization is difficult (Strathern 1971:133–134, 225; Hughes 1973:124). Furthermore, trade partnerships there tend to be somewhat ephemeral unless reinforced by marriage, and they are not generally inherited (Strathern 1971:196, 204–213). Accumulated wealth is widely disseminated in the large distribution feasts like the *moka*, which force a "Big-Man" to fund his rivals instead of removing his wealth from the competition through burial or destruction (Rathje 1978:171).

In those societies where trade partnerships are inviolable and hereditary, the transmission of the partnership will generally mean the concomitant transmission of the status based upon it. This status will vary with the degree to which the importer controls the further distribution of the goods. The imbalance in the system caused by the appearance of new goods may allow the development of internal distribution mechanisms more favorable to the importer. The egalitarian ethic of the society need not be explicitly violated, nor are the traditional distribution mechanisms necessarily dismantled. It is simply that the new goods—entering through a new set of contacts and perhaps pertaining to a different sphere of community life—might fall outside the dominion of the traditional mechanisms, which may in any case be inadequate under the new conditions. Although supplementary to the older mechanisms, the new techniques might allow the importer more latitude to manipulate his wealth to his own advantage, while still submitting to the community will by distributing it rather than hoarding it. As the advantages of the position are exploited and its influence expanded, it may evolve into a more formal and widely recognized hereditary office in the society, perhaps eventually even becoming detached from the trade monopoly upon which it had originally been based. This shift from a trade partnership transmitted hereditarily to a formally defined and inherited office in the society may be a case in point of the general evolutionary mechanism that Flannery (1972:412–413) has termed *promotion*—the development of a new institution with a broader mandate from a more specific and limited predecessor.

There is also a possibility that the power and prestige derived from control over an exchange relationship will not accrue directly to the individual who developed the link. Trigger (1976:65) says that among the historic Huron, control over a particularly valuable trade route may have been transferred from the individual who had opened it to the head of his kin group. Framing a trade partnership in a kinship idiom probably makes it more durable and protects it from external intrusion by widening its field of reference, but it may also render the partnership more vulnerable to internal encroachment by kin-group superiors. It could come to be viewed as a resource of the larger group, whose leader could then appropriate its products to build his own status. This implies that some degree of differential status may have been established already in such societies on the basis of other considerations, the trade materials then being used largely to express and reinforce these distinctions (Flannery 1968; Santley 1980).

A system of elite exchanges would have several advantages over an egalitarian network of trade partnerships. The flow of material into the society would probably be more regular, and it might include goods from a wider area since more societies would be involved in the network and each trade link would cover a larger distance (Renfrew 1975:50–51; Goad 1979:244–246). The production and delivery of goods could be enforced more easily by an elite (Rappaport 1968:108; Pires-Ferreira and Flannery 1976:291). Furthermore, the quality of the goods would be superior in some cases because of the involvement of craft specialists. On the other hand, the elite network would be more vulnerable in certain respects. A major and widespread dislocation would be required to interfere seriously with the flow of goods through a number of independent and redundant trade partnerships, but with the funneling of this flow through a few elite positions political disruptions would have more immediate and wider consequences (cf. Wright 1977:391). Something of this nature may have been involved in the "collapse" of the Hopewell and Olmec spheres (cf. Zeitlin 1978:196–197; Charlton 1978).

The elaborate elite-based exchange networks of Middle Formative Mesoamerica were also limited by the fact that control over both production and exchange was not generally situated in the same center (Charlton 1978). The supply of goods could not be effectively coordinated with the perceived demand. Even where artifact production and exchange were conducted through a single center—as at Chalcatzingo and San Lorenzo—the obsidian sources were still too distant for the flow of raw material to be regulated.

With the development of Teotihuacan, production and exchange came together in a single center that was located near a major source (Charlton 1978). Rates of procurement and artifact production could be articulated directly with demand, which was rising rapidly with the growing regional population. The independence of the obsidian workers from the emerging urban elite allowed them to orient production toward the everyday needs of this burgeoning set of consumers, rather than toward the more narrowly focused needs of the elite. This is not to say that the industry was totally independent of the Teotihuacan administration. As early as the Tzacualli phase, the state supported the craftsmen by stopping the flow of unprocessed raw material to communities beyond Teotihuacan and by preventing the development of rival industries in other parts of the region. However, the industry was born and its basic pattern largely set before the state came to play a major role in it. The later contributions of the state apparatus—like the procurement of Cerro de las Navajas obsidian—brought state and industry into a symbiotic relationship but were insufficient to overcome fully the initial independence of the craft groups.

ACKNOWLEDGMENTS

Excavation of the Bruce Boyd site was supported financially by the University of Western Ontario and the Ontario Heritage Foundation, while the analysis of Hopewell silver was done with a Wenner-Gren Foundation research grant. The Bruce Boyd fluorine analysis was conducted by Dr. S. Wall of the University of Winnipeg and financed by a Royal Ontario Museum grant. The Teotihuacan analysis was supported by Canada Council, the University of Western Ontario, and the Richard Ivey Foundation. I would like to express my gratitude to these agencies for their support, and to Bruce Trigger and Dan Jorgensen for their comments on an earlier draft of this chapter.

REFERENCES

Agrinier, P.
 1970   Mound 20, Mirador, Chiapas, Mexico. *New World Archaeological Foundation Paper* **28**.
Asaro, F., H. V. Michel, R. Sidrys, and F. Stross
 1978   High-precision chemical characterization of major obsidian sources in Guatemala. *American Antiquity* **43**:436–443.
Boksenbaum, M.
 1980   Basic Mesoamerican stone working: nodule smashing? *Lithic Technology* **9**:12–26.
Bowman, H. R., F. Asaro, and I. Perlman
 1973   Composition variations in obsidian sources and the archaeological implications. *Archaeometry* **15**:123–127.
Braun, D. P.
 1979   Illinois Hopewell burial practices and social organization: a re-examination of the Klunk–Gibson mound group. In *Hopewell archaeology: the Chillicothe Conference,* edited by D. Brose and N. Greber, pp. 66–79. Kent: Kent State University Press.
Brose, D. S.
 1979   A speculative model of the role of exchange in the prehistory of the eastern woodlands. In *Hopewell archaeology: the Chillicothe Conference,* edited by D. Brose and N. Greber, pp. 3–8. Kent: Kent State University Press.
Brown, K. L.
 1977   The valley of Guatemala: a highland port of trade. In *Teotihuacan and Kaminaljuyu: a study in prehistoric culture contact,* edited by W. T. Sanders and J. W. Michels, pp. 205–395. University Park, Penn.: Pennsylvania State University Press.
Brunton, R.
 1975   Why do the Trobriands have chiefs? *Man* **10**:544–558.
Charlton, T. H.
 1978   Production and exchange: variables in the evolution of a civilization. Ms. on file, Department of Anthropology, University of Iowa.
Charlton, T. H., D. C. Grove, and P. K. Hopke
 1978   The Paredon, Mexico, obsidian source and Early Formative exchange. *Science* **201**:807–809.
Cobean, R., M. Coe, E. Perry, K. Turekian, and D. Kharkar
 1971   Obsidian trade at San Lorenzo Tenochtitlan, Mexico. *Science* **174**:666–671.
Coe, M.
 1970   The archaeological sequence at San Lorenzo Tenochtitlan, Veracruz, Mexico. *Contributions of the University of California Archaeological Research Facility* **8**:21–34.
Cowgill, G. L.
 1979   Teotihuacan: internal militaristic competition and the fall of the Classic Maya. In *Maya archaeology and ethnohistory,* edited by N. Hammond and G. R. Willey, pp. 51–62. Austin: University of Texas Press.

Cunningham, W. M.
 1948   A study of the Glacial Kame culture in Michigan, Ohio and Indiana. *University of Michigan Museum of Anthropology Occasional Contribution* **12**.

Drennan, R. D.
 1976   Fábrica San José and Middle Formative society in the Valley of Oaxaca. *University of Michigan Museum of Anthropology Memoir* **8**.

Earle, T.
 1981   Comment on P. Rice, "Evolution of specialized pottery production: a trial model." *Current Anthropology* **22**:230–231.

Fitting, J. E.
 1970   *The archaeology of Michigan*. Bloomfield Hills: Cranbrook Institute of Science.
 1971   Rediscovering Michigan archaeology: notes on the 1885 Converse Mound collection. *The Michigan Archaeologist* **17**:33–39.

Flannery, K. V.
 1968   The Olmecs and the Valley of Oaxaca: a model for interregional interaction in Formative times. In *Dumbarton Oaks Conference on the Olmec*, edited by E. P. Benson, pp. 79–110. Washington, D.C.: Dumbarton Oaks Research Library and Collection.
 1972   The cultural evolution of civilizations. *Annual Review of Ecology and Systematics* **3**:399–426.
 1977   Review of *The Valley of Mexico. Science* **196**:759–761.

Ford, R. I.
 1972   Barter, gift or violence: an analysis of Tewa intertribal exchange. In *Social exchange and interaction*, edited by E. Wilmsen, pp. 21–45. *University of Michigan Museum of Anthropology Anthropological Paper* **46**.

Freidel, D. A.
 1979   Culture areas and interaction spheres: contrasting approaches to the emergence of civilization in the Maya lowlands. *American Antiquity* **44**:36–54.

Goad, S. L.
 1979   Middle Woodland exchange in the prehistoric southeastern United States. In *Hopewell archaeology: the Chillicothe Conference*, edited by D. Brose and N. Greber, pp. 239–246. Kent: Kent State University Press.

Granger, J. E.
 1978   Meadowood phase settlement pattern in the Niagara frontier region of western New York state. *University of Michigan Musuem of Anthropology Anthropological Paper* **65**.

Griffin, J. B.
 1965   Hopewell and the dark black glass. In *Papers in honor* of Emerson F. Greenman, edited by J. E. Fitting. *The Michigan Archaeologist* **11**:115–155.

Grove, D. C.
 1974   San Pablo, Nexpa, and the Early Formative archaeology of Morelos, Mexico. *Vanderbilt University Publications in Archaeology* **12**.

Grove, D. C., K. Hirth, D. Buge, and A. Cyphers
 1976   Settlement and cultural development at Chalcatzingo. *Science* **192**:1203–1210.

Harding, T. G.
 1967   *Voyagers of the Vitiaz Strait: a study of a New Guinea trade system*. Seattle: University of Washington Press.

Heizer, R. F., H. Williams, and J. A. Graham
 1965   Notes on Mesoamerican obsidians and their significance in archaeological studies. *Contributions of the University of California Archaeological Research Facility* **1**:94–103.

Hughes, I.
 1973   Stone Age trade in the New Guinea inland: historical geography without history. In *The Pacific in transition: geographical perspectives on adaptation and change*, edited by H. Brookfield, pp. 97–126. New York: St. Martin's Press.

Hurtado de Mendoza, L., and W. A. Jester
  1978   Obsidian sources in Guatemala: a regional approach. *American Antiquity* 43:424–435.
Johnston, R. B.
  1968a Archaeology of Rice Lake, Ontario. *National Museum of Canada Anthropology Papers* **19.**
  1968b The archaeology of the Serpent Mounds site. *Royal Ontario Museum Art and Archaeology Division Occasional Paper* **10.**
Kidder, A. V., J. D. Jennings, and E. M. Shook
  1946   Excavations at Kaminaljuyu, Guatemala. *Carnegie Institution of Washington Publication* **561.**
King, T. F.
  1978   Don't that beat the band? Nonegalitarian political organization in prehistoric central California. In *Social archaeology: beyond subsistence and dating,* edited by C. Redman, M. Berman, E. Curtin, W. Langhorne, N. Versaggi, and J. Wanser, pp. 225–248. New York: Academic Press.
Lane, R. A. and A. J. Sublett
  1972   Osteology of social organization: residence pattern. *American Antiquity* 37:186–201.
Malinowski, B.
  1920   Kula: the circulating exchange of valuables in the archipelagoes of eastern New Guinea. *Man* **51:**97–105.
Moholy-Nagy, H.
  1975   Obsidian at Tikal, Guatemala. *Actas del XLI Congreso Internacional de Americanistas* 1:511–518.
Molto, J. E.
  1979   Genes in prehistory. Paper presented at the 12th Annual Meeting, Canadian Archaeological Association, Vancouver.
Niederberger, C.
  1976   Zohapilco. *Instituto Nacional de Antropología e Historia, Colección Científica, Arqueología* **30.**
Noble, W. C.
  1975   Canadian prehistory: the lower Great Lakes—St. Lawrence region. *Canadian Archaeological Association Bulletin* 7:96–121.
Pendergast, D.
  1971   Evidence of early Teotihuacan–lowland Maya contact at Altun Ha. *American Antiquity* **36:**455–460.
Pfeiffer, S.
  1977   The skeletal biology of Archaic populations of the Great Lakes region. *Archaeological Survey of Canada Paper* **64.**
Pires-Ferreira, J. W.
  1975   Formative Mesoamerican exchange networks with special reference to the Valley of Oaxaca. *University of Michigan Museum of Anthropology Memoir* 7.
Pires-Ferreira, J. W. and K. V. Flannery
  1976   Ethnographic models for Formative exchange. In *The early Mesoamerican village,* edited by K. V. Flannery, pp. 286–292. New York: Academic Press.
Ramsden, P. G.
  1981   Rich man, poor man, dead man, thief: the dispersal of wealth in 17th century Huron society. *Ontario Archaeology* 35:35–40.
Rappaport, R. A.
  1968   *Pigs for the ancestors.* New Haven: Yale University Press.
Rathje, W. L.
  1978   Melanesian and Australian exchange systems: a view from Mesoamerica. In *Trade and*

exchange in Oceania and Australia, edited by J. Specht and J. P. White, pp. 165–174. *Mankind* **11**(3).

Renfrew, C.
1975 Trade as action at a distance: questions of integration and communication. In *Ancient civilization and trade,* edited by J. Sabloff and C. C. Lamberg-Karlovsky, pp. 3–59. Albuquerque: University of New Mexico Press.
1977 Alternative models for exchange and spatial distribution. In *Exchange systems in prehistory,* edited by T. K. Earle and J. E. Ericson, pp. 71–90. New York: Academic Press.

Ritchie, W. A.
1949 An archaeological survey of the Trent waterway in Ontario, Canada and its significance for New York state prehistory. *Rochester Museum of Arts and Sciences Research Records* **5**.
1955 Recent discoveries suggesting an Early Woodland burial cult in the Northeast. *New York State Museum and Science Service Circular* **40**.

Sahlins, M.
1972 *Stone Age economics.* New York: Aldine-Atherton Inc.

Sanders, W. T., J. R. Parsons, and R. S. Santley
1979 *The Basin of Mexico: ecological processes in the evolution of a civilization.* New York: Academic Press.

Sanders, W. T., M. West, C. Fletcher, and J. Marino
1975 The Teotihuacan Valley Project final report, volume 2: the Formative period occupation of the valley. *The Pennsylvania State University Department of Anthropology Occasional Papers in Antrhopology* **10**.

Santley, R. S.
1977 Intra-site settlement patterns at Loma Torremote and their relationship to Formative prehistory in the Cuautitlan region, State of Mexico. Unpublished Ph.D. dissertation, Department of Anthropology, Pennsylvania State University.
1979 Obsidian exchange, economic stratification, and the evolution of complex society in the Basin of Mexico. Ms. on file, Department of Anthropology, University of New Mexico.
1980 Specialized production and exchange within a Late Formative community in the Basin of Mexico: implications for the study of exchange systems in prehistory. Ms. on file, Department of Anthropology, University of New Mexico.

Saxe, A. A.
1970 Social dimensions of mortuary practices. Unpublished Ph.D. dissertation, Department of Anthropology, University of Michigan.

Singer, L., and W. D. Armstrong
1968 Determination of fluoride in bone with the fluoride electrode. *Analytical Chemistry* **40**:613–614.

Spence, M. W.
1974 Residential practices and the distribution of skeletal traits in Teotihuacan. *Man* **9**:262–273.
1978 The archaeological objectives of obsidian characterization studies in Mesoamerica. Paper presented at the symposium Obsidian Characterization and Exchange Systems in Prehistory, cosponsored by the National Bureau of Standards, U.S. Department of Commerce, and the Smithsonian Institution, Washington, D.C.
1979 Craft production and polity in early Teotihuacan. Ms. on file, Department of Anthropology, University of Western Ontario.
1981 Obsidian production and the state in Teotihuacan. *American Antiquity* **46**:769–788.

Spence, M. W., and J. R. Harper
1968 The Cameron's Point site. *Royal Ontario Museum Art and Archaeology Division Occasional Paper* **12**.

Spence, M. W., and W. A. Fox
    1979   The Bruce Boyd site and Early Woodland societies in Ontario. Paper presented at the
           12th Annual Meeting, Canadian Archaeological Association, Vancouver.
Spence, M. W., R. F. Williamson, and J. H. Dawkins
    1978   The Bruce Boyd site: an Early Woodland component in southwestern Ontario. *Ontario
           Archaeology* **29**:33–46.
Spence, M. W., W. D. Finlayson, and R. H. Pihl
    1979   Hopewellian influences on Middle Woodland cultures in southern Ontario. In *Hopewell
           Archaeology: the Chillicothe Conference,* edited by D. Brose and N. Greber, pp.
           115–121. Kent: Kent State University Press.
Spence, M. W., J. Kimberlin, and G. Harbottle
    1979   Obsidian procurement in Teotihuacan, Mexico. Paper presented at the 44th Annual
           Meeting, Society for American Archaeology, Vancouver, B.C.
Spence, M. W., S. G. Wall, and R. H. King
    1981   Fluorine dating in an Ontario burial site. *Canadian Journal of Archaeology* **5**:61–77.
Strathern, A.
    1971   The rope of Moka: Big-Men and ceremonial exchange in Mount Hagen, New Guinea.
           Cambridge Studies in Social Anthropology **4**.
Struever, S., and G. L. Houart
    1972   An analysis of the Hopewell interaction sphere. In *Social exchange and interaction,*
           edited by E. Wilmsen, pp. 47–79. *University of Michigan Museum of Anthropology
           Anthropological Paper* **46**.
Tainter, J. A.
    1978   Mortuary practices and the study of prehistoric social systems. In *Advances in archae-
           ological method and theory, volume I,* edited by M. Schiffer, pp. 105–141. New York:
           Academic Press.
Tolstoy, P., S. K. Fish, M. W. Boksenbaum, K. B. Vaughn, and C. E. Smith
    1977   Early sedentary communities of the Basin of Mexico. *Journal of Field Archaeology*
           4:91–106.
Trigger, B. G.
    1976   *The children of Aataentsic.* Montreal: McGill-Queen's University Press.
Walthall, J. A.
    1981   Galena and aboriginal trade in eastern North America. *Illinois State Museum Scientific
           Paper* **17**.
Weaver, J. R., and F. H. Stross
    1965   Analysis of X-ray fluorescence of some American obsidians. *Contributions of the Uni-
           versity of California Archaeological Research Facility* **1**:89–93.
Winter, M., and J. W. Pires-Ferreira
    1976   Distribution of obsidian among households in two Oaxacan villages. In *The early Meso-
           american village,* edited by K. V. Flannery, pp. 306–311. New York: Academic Press.
Wortner, S.
    1978   The Late Archaic Hind site. Paper presented to the Ontario Archaeological Society,
           London chapter, London.
Wright, H. T.
    1977   Recent research on the origin of the state. *Annual Review of Anthropology* **6**:379–397.
Wright, H. T., and M. Zeder
    1977   The simulation of a linear exchange system under equilibrium conditions. In *Exchange
           systems in prehistory,* edited by T. Earle and J. Ericson, pp. 233–253. New York:
           Academic Press.
Wright, J. V.
    1972   *Ontario prehistory: an eleven-thousand-year archaeological outline.* Ottawa: National
           Museum of Man.

Zeitlin, R. N.
  1978   Long-distance exchange and the growth of a regional center on the southern Isthmus of Tehuantepec, Mexico. In *Prehistoric coastal adaptations: the economy and ecology of maritime Middle America,* edited by B. Stark and B. Voorhies, pp. 183–210. New York: Academic Press.
Zeitlin, R. N., and R. G. Heimbuch
  1978   Trace element analysis and the archaeological study of obsidian procurement in pre-Columbian Mesoamerica. In *Lithics and subsistence: the analysis of stone tool use in prehistoric economies,* edited by D. Davis, pp. 117–159. *Vanderbilt University Publications in Anthropology* 20.

Consumption and Symbolic Contexts

9

Toward a Contextual Approach to Prehistoric Exchange

Ian Hodder

Much analysis and interpretation of prehistoric exchange mechanisms can be seen to have certain similarities to the substantivist and formalist schools in economic anthropology and can be seen to be subject to the same criticisms. Even alternative approaches that emphasize the use of exchange for social advantage or that place exchange within a context of production are inadequate because they fail to incorporate the symbolism of the artifacts exchanged. An exchange act involves an appropriate choice of gift within a social and ideological context. The thing exchanged is not arbitrary, and its associations and symbolism play an active part in the construction of social strategies. As archaeologists, we need to examine the symbolic and ideological dimensions of exchange. First, however, it is necessary to review existing approaches to exchange—substantivism, formalism, and social exchange—and their application in archaeology.

THE SUBSTANTIVIST APPROACH

For the substantivists (Polanyi 1957; Dalton 1969), the economy is embedded in social relations, so that it can only be studied contextually as part of a local or regional cultural system. Economic institutions are cultural traits, and analysis of them must be inductive. The focus is on relationships between people and on the different types of exchange mechanisms such as *reciprocity,*

199

redistribution, and *market* systems. These different types of exchanges act as integrating organizational priciples of land and labor allocation, work organization, and the movement of goods between people. Society appears—according to this school—as static and self-supporting, aiming to preserve equilibrium with the "environment" (Schneider 1974). The substantivist approach is thus functionalist in the sense that assumptions are made concerning systemic equilibrium, adaptation in order to maintain equilibrium, and organic interrelations.

Sahlins's (1965, 1968) definitions of *generalized, balanced,* and *negative reciprocities* provided additional concepts that could be applied to the substantivist mold. Sahlins also placed the various types of exchange systems into an evolutionary framework with, for example, reciprocity being linked to segmentary societies and redistribution to chiefdoms and states. This evolutionary scheme has been grasped by many archaeologists (e.g., Renfrew 1972, 1973a, 1973b; Pires-Ferreira and Flannery 1976; Hodder 1978) as a convenient way of relating exchange to social relations through time. Other substantivist concepts such as *port of trade* and *money* have been used in the interpretation of archaeological material (Hodder 1979a). More generally, the widespread use of ethnographic models for the study of prehistoric exchange processes (e.g., Clark 1965; Rowlands 1971; Hughes 1977; White and Modjeska 1978; McBryde 1978) are concerned with understanding exchange as a part of social process—functioning to provide essential resources, maintain alliances, or to establish prestige and status.

Three basic criticisms that can be leveled against the substantivist economists are applicable to the archaeological applications. (For general criticisms of functionalism, see Hodder [n.d.].) First, exchange is seen by Polanyi as a moral act following social obligations. Dalton (1969) describes clearly how the individual is subject to the rules and demands of reciprocity. Society is seen as being made up of preformed rules within which the individual must act. There is little room for individual construction of social strategies and manipulation of rules, and there is little intimation of conflicts and contradictions between interests.

Second, the substantivists have argued that the economy is embedded in social relations in primitive societies, in contrast to modern Western nations. But even in our own society, the economy is embedded within relations of production and within political and social strategies. Modern economic models can be applied in the present day and in "primitive" societies to the study of output and performance. But in neither the present nor past is such analysis adequate, because exchange must always be considered as a part of social relations. The distinction drawn by substantivists between primitive and advanced economies is at least partly misleading. The distinction between the two schools of economists (formalist and substantivist) really concerns two different types of analyses—one of output and performance, and the other of the social context of exchange.

Third, the evolutionary relationships between the types of exchanges and types of societies on which archaeologists have relied now appear—in some cases at least—to be lacking in empirical support. In a cross-cultural survey of the various correlates of different types of exchange mechanisms, Pryor (1977) identified some positive relationships. For example, reciprocal exchange systems and noncentric transfers are characteristic of societies at low levels of economic development. At high levels, market and centric exchanges are common (Pryor 1977:4). Reciprocal exchange of goods is more likely to be found, other things being equal, in hunting, fishing, and farming societies than in gathering and herding societies because of the relative uncertainty of the food supply in the former cases. However, other correlates were not supported by the data. Wittfogel's thesis that economies relying on irrigation agriculture require stronger governments and centric transfers (in money, goods, and labor) in order to function efficiently had to be rejected. Similarly, the notion that centric transfers are likely to increase in areas of climatic risk (arctic, subarctic, desert), as used for example by Chapman (1981), was also not supported by the modern data. Earle's (1977) work on Hawaiian chiefdoms demonstrates the minimal part that redistribution plays in commodity exchange in ranked societies (see Earle and D'Altroy, Chapter 12). Hughes's(1977) study of New Guinea exchange systems emphasizes that reciprocity and redistribution may operate as complementary structures within one social context. Polanyi, Dalton, and Sahlins were concerned with overall distinctions between general modes of exchange, and it may not be helpful to cite detailed instances where the correlation between social form and exchange mechanism breaks down. However, it is clear that one-to-one relationships do not exist, and that studies of the functioning of exchange within social contexts must involve careful and sensitive studies of how exchange is generated as a part of the social strategies of individuals.

THE FORMALIST APPROACH

Concurrent with the strong substantivist and evolutionary influence in archaeological studies of exchange, there has been a concern to find analytical techniques that would allow particular modes of distribution to be identified. It is perhaps surprising that the methods chosen should be close to those used by the formalist school of economic anthropologists, although they were introduced into archaeology by way of human geography rather than directly from formalist anthropology. The formal methods that have been applied most widely are regression analysis (Renfrew, Dixon, and Cann 1968; Hodder 1974; Renfrew 1977; Sidrys 1977; Clark 1979) and gravity models (Hodder 1974; Hallam, Warren, and Renfrew 1976). The amount of an exchanged item found at a site is described mathematically as a function of distance from the source of the material and as a function of the size of the interacting centers.

The analytical methods make assumptions concerning minimization of effort and maximization of advantage (by assuming travel to the nearest source or to the most "attractive" center). The mathematical models derive from studies of modern Western society, and are applied cross-culturally to all societies.

The various types of mathematical curve-fitting procedures that have been used in archaeology have characteristics similar to those of formalist economic anthropology. Members of the latter group assume that universal concepts of economic theory—*scarcity, maximization, surplus*—are applicable in economic anthropology (Dalton 1969). It was accepted that the economy was linked to social relations (Schneider 1974), but it was felt that the economy could be described in modern terms using cross-cultural methods. Thus, for example, the question to be debated was not whether people *desire* to maximize, but whether accurate predictions could be made by *assuming* that people desire to maximize utility. Formalist economic anthropology is a deductive, theoretical enterprise in which abstract variables are fitted to empirical reality. In archaeology, the falloff studies are concerned to apply abstract mathematical models that allow prediction of the amount of pottery, flint, and stone found at a site.

The first limitation of the mathematical formalist approach concerns the lack of equivalence between prediction and explanation. It is clear that the successful fitting of some falloff model may allow accurate prediction of the amount of exchanged material to be found at any one site. But to say that y amount of pottery is found at a site because it is x distance from the source and because the relationship between y and x fits a regression formula is hardly an adequate explanation of the exchange process. In the same vein, concepts from modern economic theory may be adequate for describing and "predicting" the past, but since we cannot be sure that scarcity, maximization, and surplus are relevant concepts for past societies, attempts at explaining why a particular formal pattern is found are liable to be of limited value. Within the formalist approach, the inquiry is focused on the description of observables in economist terminology. There is little attempt made to explore the social contexts and political strategies that lie behind the observed "facts"—the artifact distributions, trade centers, and so on.

The second limitation of the mathematical modeling of exchange processes derives from the first. If the main aim of the analysis is to describe adequately the observed data within a mathematical equation, little success can be expected in differentiating between the numerous social processes that may have produced the same visible pattern. Simulation studies of hypothetical exchange processes (Hodder and Orton 1976) have shown that very different exchange mechanisms, such as redistribution and reciprocal exchange, may result in identical falloff patterns. It is now clear that "supply zones" (Renfrew 1972) may be produced by "random walk" processes. Certain gross correlations between types of falloff curves (concave and convex) and types of artifacts and exchange processes (low value, close contact and high value, multiple step) have been identified (Hodder 1974), but even here, the relationships now appear more complex (Hodder 1979b). In general, different processes may lead to the same form, and there appear to be few reliable correlations between falloff patterns and exchange processes.

Attempts to differentiate between the processes that lead to falloff patterns can be made by examining additional information. For example, it might be expected that the typology of artifacts will vary with increasing distance from a source if reciprocal, down-the-line exchange occurred. Stone axes might become reduced and shorter in length with greater distance from source (Hodder and Lane, Chapter 10). Obsidian might become more highly valued, be made into smaller tools, and be more extensively curated with increasing distance from origin. Metal types may show more signs of wear, and the composition of the metal itself may become less distinctive as recycling increases at greater distances. The frequency of metal hoards may also vary at different distances from source. Both the typology and context of finds of artifacts (in settlements, rich or poor burials, hoards, on or off sites) at different distances from the sources may provide further information in distinguishing between different processes, although the experience described in Chapter 10 indicates that interpretations may still remain equivocal.

Many falloff studies of observed frequencies have been conducted on a very generous scale. Much of the work on obsidian and Neolithic axe exchange has involved the analysis of a few sites spread over many hundreds or thousands of kilometers. More recently, work by Ammerman (1979) has shown that detailed regional surveys of small areas may produce results that contradict the proposals resulting from the earlier large-scale studies (see Ammerman and Andrefsky, Chapter 7). Ammerman has identified local variations in obsidian production and use that were not predicted by Renfrew's general model. This variation indicates apparent settlement specialization within the obsidian exchange network. There is certainly a need for more of these detailed, problem-oriented regional studies.

However ingenious the archaeologist becomes, mathematical and distributional studies of observed frequencies of exchanged material will always be limited in their ability to explain the processes that lead to the archaeological distributions. In particular, the social context is not adequately considered, and the emphasis is on describing the exchange distributions in their own right rather than on examining the exchange mechanisms as part of a system of production and social relations.

SOCIAL EXCHANGE

Certain types of formalist analyses do, however, attempt to absorb some of the criticisms of both the substantivist and formalist positions, and they provide viable alternatives. Schneider (1974), for example, describes the notion that all social relations can be seen as social exchanges, and thus can be studied as a part of economic analyses. Within an exchange act, participants can be described as attempting to maximize status tokens and symbolic ties. The interaction between people is the exchange of material and nonmaterial goods. It involves transactions between people with interdependent needs. According to this social-exchange theory as described by Schneider, "economic man" produces wealth, not to obtain food, but to give gifts that will obligate others to him and increase his social power. The aim is to maximize his profit and utility by balancing material and social wealth.

According to this view, the flow of transactions between interdependent individuals produces apparent structures such as the "family." This apparent form is described by Barth (1967) as epiphenomenal. The empirical pattern is an epiphenomenon of allocational decisions and transactions. To Barth, all behavior is new in that it consists of allocations of time and resources made or renewed at the time of action. Thus households persist in any society because their forms are recreated by behavior each day—behavior based on allocations. Thus empirical status differentiation is not a given, socially dictated structure. Rather, the gift-giving transactions may involve an imbalance that raises the giver's status and lowers that of the receiver, thereby locating social stratification.

Schneider provides an example of the way in which individuals within a society might use transactions in order to obtain status—by manipulating the balance between social and material value. Among the Yir Yoront (Sharp 1952), the status of older men is related to their control of the exchange of stone axes. These axes are loaned out to women and younger men, and it is though their control of the axes that the men achieve control of labor, prestige, and position. The subordinate–superordinate relationship based on the control and loaning of axes is disrupted when steel axes become more widely available and can circulate outside the control of the older men. In prehistoric archaeology, it may be possible to suggest similar relationships. For example, in the Nitra Neolithic cemetery in eastern Europe (Sherratt 1976), widely traded axes and shells are found only in the graves of men over 30 to 40 years of age. It seems reasonable to suggest that the status of these older men depended on the transactions they were able to control. Many other archaeological studies (e.g., Bender 1978; Frankenstein and Rowlands 1978) have suggested that hierarchical status can be obtained through privileged access to valued exchange items and their dispersal within a society.

One further hypothesis that might be classified under the heading of social-exchange theory concerns the relationship between the distribution of valuables and foods. Sherratt (1976; see also Wright and Zeder 1977) has used a notion derived from Rappaport that the exchange of valuables may act as a "fly-wheel" for the exchange of subsistence goods between areas of variable productivity. Halstead (1981) has suggested that exchange may function as a form of social storage—ironing out local variations and uncertainties in subsistence production—and he has indicated that the use of valued, durable tokens may provide a mechanism for vital exchanges of food between a far-wider network of communities than can be maintained by direct, reciprocal relationships alone. While this model has certain clear functionalist characteristics, social exchange and social relationships are described as economic, and Schneider's "economic man" is close at hand. Individuals make social transactions that involve obligations to provide food in areas and in times of uncertain productivity. The exchange network of food and prestige goods maximizes productive utility. Unfortunately, in Pryor's (1977) cross-cultural analysis of types of exchanges, no close nor necessary relationship could be identified between reciprocal exchange of food and nonfood reciprocal exchange or ceremonial exchange. Rowlands (1980:46) notes that in a hierarchical society, the exchange of weapons, ornaments, and livestock, for example, may form one system of circulation that is kept separated from the exchange of foods. For political reasons, wealth from one sphere cannot easily be converted into prestige in the other. While the exchange of valuables may act as a pump to stimulate food production, the relationship between the two types of exchanges may not result in immediate convertibility.

An emphasis on "social exchange" as described in preceding paragraphs allows the application of cross-cultural empirical methodologies, and it involves the use of economic concepts such as *maximization* and *profit*. In these senses it is formalist. Yet the approach also involves discussion of social strategies and functional interrelationships. It allows exchange to be seen within the context of social strategies, the availability of subsistence resources, and control over production. For Clammer (1978), the "new economic anthropology" involves approaches to exchange in which the major questions concern the relationships between production, the control of production, and exchange transactions. In the Yir Yoront example, attention is directed toward the relationship between the movements of goods and valuables and the control of productive labor.

There are weaknesses in the "transactional" or "social-exchange" viewpoint common to those found in formalism and substantivism. First, the analysis involves the description of "economic" acts. While we may describe social strategies as maximizing profit in some general sense, it is less clear that such descriptions allow adequate explanations of the strategies themselves. Society is viewed as a series of transactions, but the forms that these transactions take are not the main focus of concern. The emphasis is on performance and results rather than on the construction of strategies. Second, the symbolism of the objects exchanged plays little part in the analysis. Individual social actors are described as balancing social and material wealth, but the symbolic principles manipulated in this process are rarely discussed.

In an article of great interest, Rowlands (1980) provides an analysis of

Bronze Age European society that resolves some of the criticisms noted previously, although an approach similar to that described by Schneider is followed. An individual is seen as making gifts that will obligate others to him and increase his social power. Rowlands describes a patrilineal kinship system in which limited marriage prohibitions are associated with an expansionist and opportunistic marriage system. Ties are maintained with previous marriage partners through common rituals and gift giving. Senior men as household heads are locked in competition to create dense networks of reciprocal obligations through gift giving, the control of women, and the use of ritual. Intergroup ranking depends on the ability to manipulate these various transactions, and it does not depend directly or solely on descent. Successful groups can increase their size, labor power, and productivity, and this provides a further basis for their dominance.

In response to the criticisms of social-exchange theory mentioned before, the following aspects of Rowlands's account can be detailed. First, exchange transactions are securely placed within a structured set of social and political relations, and the overall form of the transactions is clearly specified. Second, the symbolism of objects, as used in the negotiation, and legitimation of the authority and dominance of senior men is described. Certain pieces of armor and weapons in Homeric society, for example, were symbolic of honor and the epic traditions that underlay claims to status. In the latter respect, Rowlands is describing oral traditions. In his description of the archaeological data to which his model is applied, a very different view of material culture is employed.

The core of Rowlands's model is a patrilineal kinship system. But the archaeological identification of this reified system is, at least, problematic. Rowlands sets up one-to-one correlates between kinship and material residues. Settlement organization and the distributions of styles are seen to reflect social organization directly. In fact, archaeologists have no reliable methods for determining kinship systems (see, however, Ember 1973; Ericson 1981). In Rowlands's discussion of exchanged items, little attention is paid to the symbolism of the objects and to the appropriate choice of symbols within transactions and social strategies. The relationship between material culture and society is behavioral and mechanistic, and is identical to the functionalist notion of artifacts as "tools." Rowlands's model, interesting as it may be, remains overdetermined and untestable in relation to the archaeological data (see Gilman [1981] for an alternative interpretation of these data). The relationships between material culture and social form are more complex than Rowlands allows, partly because artifacts are manipulated ideologically according to sets of structuring principles. The symbolism of the object as an active component of social action needs to be examined. The abstract kinship system is not the "given" that Rowlands implies. It is negotiated partly through the appropriate choice of material symbols in exchange.

SYMBOLS AND IDEOLOGY IN EXCHANGE

Exchange must be studied within a social context and as part of a system of production. But the artifacts exchanged are not arbitrary. They are appropriate within a cultural, ideological, and historical context. Objects come to have meaning as members of categories opposed to other categories, and as nodes in networks of associations and evocations. Any adequate analysis of exchange systems must consider the way in which the symbolism of the artifact legitimates, supports, and provides the basis of power of interest groups. If we are to avoid the difficulties encountered by Rowlands, it is necessary to develop models of exchange systems in which the transfer of goods—whether prestige items or foods—has a relative cultural value. The involvement of exchange in the active construction of social strategies depends on the manipulation of the symbolism and contextual significance of artifacts.

In some contexts, status may depend on access to material wealth, and certain material symbols may be restricted to the elite. In other contexts, emulation and downward movement of material symbols may form the principles of social stratification. It has yet to be shown that such differences are related mechanistically to different kinship systems. Rather, the two exchange strategies represent different ways to legitimate power, and it is possible for the prehistoric archaeologist to distinguish between them. The process of emulation, for example, involves the rapid appearance and turnover of new valued goods to reinstate the status lost by the downward movement of earlier high-status artifacts. New status goods must be found to replace the devalued artifacts (Miller n.d.).

In Chapter 10 of this volume, the symbolic power of an artifact within a particular Neolithic context is assessed by examining the associations of that artifact type in ritual contexts. The ritual associations and evocations would result in that artifact type's being appropriate for a system in which dominance was obtained through exchange. The ritual associations would act to legitimate authority and privileged access to valued goods. There is an interlinked network of exchange relations, social strategies, and symbolism within each historical context.

Beyond this one example, it may be possible to outline some components of an appropriate methodology for the study of symbolism in prehistoric exchange. A major part of such analyses must involve general theories concerning ideologies and the social manipulation of ideas through symbols. Certain types of data may be relevant for testing propositions in the ideological and symbolic spheres. First, it is necessary to identify different associations of single artifact types in each regional or cultural context. Within any such unit, an artifact type might be present or absent in burials, and in burials of particular age, sex, and status groups. The type may or may not occur in settlements of different classes and sizes, in particular buildings within settlements, and in particular types of refuse contexts. It might be found in ritual contexts, hoards, or as single finds away from sites. From the various and contrasting associations of exchanged artifacts in these different contexts, some picture can be obtained of their cultural value. For example, a highly curated artifact may have had high value, and it may be possible to obtain some notion of where that value lay from the associations of the artifact, as in the Neolithic ritual contexts of the axes described previously or in burials of high-status individuals, or from evocations of the form of the artifact itself (see the third point that follows).

Second, the associations and contexts of exchanged artifacts can be examined between regional units and at different distances from sources. Each artifact type may have different values and meanings within each local context, and the exchange of objects between cultural units and the maintenance of boundaries between ethnic groups may be based upon, and may manipulate, such differences. There is a link to the within-unit contexts in that whether artifacts cross or do not cross between ethnic groups is related to their meanings within each unit. It is thus necessary to examine variations in symbolic associations over space. The association of Neolithic shells in eastern Europe with older men has already been mentioned. In western Europe (e.g., the Paris Basin), however, the same type of shell occurs only in the graves of women (Burkill, personal communication). Grand Pressigny flint is exchanged between several distinct cultural units in the Neolithic of western Europe, and analysis of its varying contexts would provide some notion of variation in the degree and nature of its value in the different units. In the European Bronze Age, metal artifacts sometimes occur in burials and in hoards in nearby cultural units. There is a need for more careful analysis and the development of models for such variation, but it is at least clear that concern with the forms of the transactions themselves is inadequate, since the social effects of exchange depend on the different symbolic meanings of the artifact types in each context. Exchange must be understood in relation to these differences of meaning.

Third, attention can be focused on the shape and form of the artifact itself and on the evocations of that shape. An object may be widely exchanged within a particular context, because its associated symbolism is appropriate for certain ideological functions. For example, in Iron Age Europe, exchanged items associated with elites often refer directly to classical equivalents. The imports from the Mediterranean and their local copies provided a symbolism that could be manipulated to encourage further links with the classical world and to legitimate dominance in local hierarchies. The payment of tribute in coins modeled on classical prototypes sets up a symbolic association between the local and the Mediterranean distribution of power. Social units in late Iron Age Britain that rejected this form of legitimation used different, local symbols on their coins. The functioning of exchange depends on the choice of an object within an ideological framework.

CONCLUSION

Formal mathematical approaches to the study of prehistoric exchange are of value in that they allow better description of functional relationships. But understanding exchange processes depends on an adequate description of the social context within which exchange occurs. The substantivist model has all the limitations of a functionalist and evolutionary focus in which society is analyzed as a synchronic set of roles and obligations striving to maintain comfortable equilibrium with the environment. In social-exchange or transactional theory, on the other hand, transfers of goods allow individuals to maximize their chances of achieving some socially defined goal. But the organization of all social transactions remains "economic" so that it is difficult, within this viewpoint, to understand the construction of social strategies within meaningful cultural contexts. There is more to exchange than *economic* advantage—even if social advantage is included in that term. Exchange involves the transfer of items that have symbolic and categorical associations. Within any strategy of legitimation, the symbolism of objects is manipulated in the construction of relations of dominance. The exchange of appropriate items *forms* social obligations, status, and power, but it also *legitimates* as it forms. A fully contextual approach to exchange must incorporate the symbolism of the objects exchanged.

REFERENCES

Ammerman, A.
  1979 A study of obsidian exchange networks in Calabria. *World Archaeology* **11**:95–110.
Barth, F.
  1967 Economic spheres in Darfur. In *Themes in economic anthropology,* edited by R. Firth, pp. 149–174. London: Tavistock.
Bender, B.
  1978 Gatherer–hunter to farmer: a social perspective. *World Archaeology* **10**:204–222.
Chapman, R.
  1981 Archaeological theory and communal burial in prehistoric Europe. In *Pattern of the Past,* edited by I. Hodder, G. Isaac, and N. Hammond, pp. 387–411. Cambridge: Cambridge University Press.
Clammer, J.
  1978 *The new economic anthropology.* London: Macmillan.
Clark, J. G. D.
  1965 Traffic in stone axes and adze blades. *Economic History Review* **18**:1–28.
Clark, J. R.
  1979 Measuring the flow of goods with archaeological data. *Economic Geography* **55**.
Dalton, G.
  1969 Theoretical issues in economic anthropology. *Current Anthropology* **10**:63–102.
Earle, T. K.
  1977 A reappraisal of redistribution: complex Hawaiian chiefdoms. In *Exchange systems in prehistory,* edited by T. K. Earle and J. E. Ericson, pp. 213–229. New York: Academic Press.

Ember, M.
  1973 An archaeological indicator of matrilocal versus patrilocal residence. *American Antiquity* **38**:177–182.
Ericson, J. E.
  1981 *Residence patterns by isotopic characterization.* Abstracts, Society for Archaeological Science, Third Annual Meeting, San Diego: California.
Frankenstein, S., and M. Rowlands
  1978 The internal structure and regional context of early Iron Age society in south-west Germany. *Bulletin of the Institute of Archaeology* **15**:73–112.
Gilman, A.
  1981 The development of social stratification in Bronze Age Europe. *Current Anthropology* **22**:1–23.
Hallam, B. R., S. E. Warren, and A. C. Renfrew
  1976 Obsidian in the western Mediterranean. *Proceedings of the Prehistoric Society* **42**:85–110.
Halstead, P.
  1981 From determinism to uncertainty: social storage and the rise of the Minoan palace. In *Economic archaeology,* edited by A. Sheridan and G. N. Bailey, pp. 187–213. Oxford: *British Archaeological Reports, International Series* **96**.
Hodder, I.
  1974 Regression analysis of some trade and marketing patterns. *World Archaeology* **6**:172–189.
  1978 *The spatial organization of culture.* London: Duckworth.
  1979a Pre-Roman and Romano–British tribal economies. In *Invasion and response,* edited by B. Burnham and H. Johnson, pp. 189–196. Oxford: *British Archaeological Reports, British Series* **73**.
  1979b Pottery distributions: service and tribal areas. In *Pottery and the archaeologist,* edited by M. Millett, pp. 7–23. London: Institute of Archaeology.
  1981 Towards a mature archaeology. In *Pattern of the past,* edited by I. Hodder, G. Isaac, and N. Hammond, pp. 1–13. Cambridge: Cambridge University Press.
  n.d. Theoretical archaeology: a reactionary viewpoint. In *Symbolic and structural archaeology,* edited by I. Hodder. Cambridge: Cambridge University Press (forthcoming).
Hodder, I., and C. Orton
  1976 *Spatial analysis in archaeology.* Cambridge: Cambridge University Press.
Hughes, I.
  1977 New Guinea Stone Age trade. *Terra Australis* **3**.
McBryde, I.
  1978 Wil-im-ee Moor-ring. Or where do axes come from? *Mankind* **11**:354–382.
Miller, D.
  n.d. Structures and strategies: an aspect of the relationship between social hierarchy and social exchange. In *Symbolic and structural archaeology,* edited by I. Hodder. Cambridge: Cambridge University Press (forthcoming).
Pires-Ferreira, J. W., and K. V. Flannery
  1976 Ethnographic models for Formative exchange. In *The early Mesoamerican village,* edited by K. V. Flannery, pp. 286–291. New York: Academic Press.
Polanyi, K.
  1957 The economy as instituted process. In *Trade and markets in the early empires,* edited by K. Polanyi, C. M. Arensberg, and H. W. Pearson, pp. 243–269. Glencoe: Free Press.
Pryor, F. L.
  1977 *The origins of the economy.* New York: Academic Press.
Renfrew, A. C.
  1972 *The emergence of civilization.* London: Methuen.

1973a Monuments, mobilization and social organization in Neolithic Wessex. In *The explanation of culture change: models in prehistory,* edited by A. C. Renfrew, pp. 539–558. London: Duckworth.

1973b *Before civilization: the radiocarbon revolution and prehistoric Europe.* London: Cape.

1977 Alternative models for exchange and spatial distribution. In *Exchange systems in prehistory,* edited by T. K. Earle and J. Ericson, pp. 71–90. New York: Academic Press.

Renfrew, A. C., J. E. Dixon, and J. R. Cann

1968 Further analysis of Near Eastern obsidians. *Proceedings of the Prehistoric Society* **34:**319–331.

Rowlands, M. J.

1971 The archaeological interpretation of prehistoric metal-working. *World Archaeology* **3:**210–224.

1980 Kinship, alliance and exchange in the European Bronze Age. In *The British later Bronze Age,* edited by J. Barrett and R. Bradley, pp. 15–56. *British Archaeological Reports, British Series* **83.**

Sahlins, M. D.

1965 On the sociology of primitive exchange. In *The relevance of models for social anthropology,* edited by M. Banton, pp. 139–227. *ASA Monograph* **1.** London: Tavistock.

1968 *Tribesmen.* Englewood Cliffs, N.J.: Prentice-Hall.

Schneider, J. K.

1974 *Economic man.* New York: Free Press.

Sharp, L.

1952 Steel axes for stone-age Australians. *Human organization* **11:**17–22.

Sherratt, A. G.

1976 Resources, technology and trade. In *Problems in economic and social archaeology,* edited by G. Sieveking, I. Longworth, and K. Wilson, pp. 557–581. London: Duckworth.

Sidrys, R.

1977 Mass-distance measures for the Maya obsidian trade. In *Exchange systems in prehistory,* edited by T. K. Earle and J. E. Ericson, pp. 91–108. New York: Academic Press.

White, J. P., and N. Modjeska

1978 Acquirers, users, finders, losers: the use of axe blades made by the Duna. *Mankind* **11:**276–287.

Wright, H. T., and M. A. Zeder

1977 The simulation of a linear exchange system under equilibrium conditions. In *Exchange systems in prehistory,* edited by T. K. Earle and J. E. Ericson, pp. 233–253. New York: Academic Press.

10

A Contextual Examination of Neolithic Axe Distribution in Britain

Ian Hodder
and
Paul Lane

Studies of British Neolithic ground-stone axes have been characterized by an interest in broad areal distributions, exchange spheres, and exchange processes (Cummins 1974; Elliott, Ellman, and Hodder 1978). Ethnographic models have been introduced to aid the understanding of exchange mechanisms (Clark 1965). In these respects, studies of British axes have remained in line with current work on prehistoric exchange in other parts of the world. Most recent studies of widely distributed artifacts have been content to examine the distributions—the "dots-on-maps" alone—and they have paid little attention to the typology and context of the artifacts themselves. As suggested by Hodder (Chapter 9), an examination of the artifact's form at different distances from source may give information on use, value, and ultimately on exchange processes. This chapter attempts to contribute to studies of exchange distributions by developing distributional models that incorporate information on the forms of the objects exchanged.

BRITISH NEOLITHIC AXES AND RESEARCH AIMS

Since work began in the 1930s on the petrological identification of Neolithic stone axes, a number of conflicting views have been published on the mode of axe distribution. In the early reports (Keiller, Piggott, and Wallis, 1941; Stone and Wallis 1947; Stone and Wallis 1951), "trade" was seen as the dominant

213

exchange mechanism—an unsurprising conclusion as anthropological theory had yet to influence axe studies. Since the publication of those early reports, over 3000 axes have been thin-sectioned, and 24 petrological groups have been identified. Synthetic studies are now possible. Cummins (1974, 1979) was the first to attempt any analyses of the overall distribution patterns of axes, and he concluded that the distribution patterns of the relative abundance of two petrological groups indicated considerable bulk trade, perhaps followed by distribution from local centers. On the other hand, Clark (1965)—drawing on ethnographic information from Australasia—has suggested that British stone axes could have been distributed from their respective sources by a process of gift exchange. Falloff studies (Hodder 1974) and computer simulations (Elliott, Ellman, and Hodder 1978) have been applied also to the overall distribution patterns, and the conclusion reached in the latter study suggests that it is very hard to identify different exchange systems from artifact distribution patterns alone.

Yet any approach that seeks to move away from studying "dots-on-maps" toward an examination of the contexts of finds is extremely difficult in the case of British axes because so little is known of their context—so many result from chance finds in ploughed fields and other disturbed localities. Archaeological evidence supporting any hypotheses is rare and is often open to many interpretations. Houlder (1976) has recently attempted a summary of the evidence from western Britain in support of an axe "trade" with "middlemen." Settlements, such as Merthyr Mawr Warren and Gwaenysgor, with implements from several sources, roughouts, and evidence for reworking were thought to be indicative of the permanent bases of "middlemen of the axe trade." For example, the occurrence of an unused axe and a preform in ritual contexts (at a henge and with a cremation) distant from the stone source has been used to suggest middleman trade (Houlder 1976). These data are, however, clearly open to alternative interpretations, since reflaking need not be a specialist activity, and the presence of axes from various sources could simply be an indication of contact. Manby then takes the view that reworked axes indicate settlement, and "axes in rough-out form and in primary form. . . represent the actual article traded" (1965:1). For his analysis of the distribution of the latter, Manby suggested that a number of trade routes can be recognized, although he fails to test his assumptions against the contextual evidence.

Even a chronological context is difficult to provide with precision. Smith (1979) has recently summarized the evidence, and it would appear on the basis of her summary that the groups studied were broadly contemporaneous (see Table 10.1). While Group VIII rock may have been exploited as early as the later Mesolithic, the main period of exploitation need not have begun until circa 3000 B.C., by which time the Great Langdale (Group VI) and possibly the Graig Lwyd (Group VII) factory sites were in operation. It is possible that Group I axes are a later product, though their association with Grooved Ware assemblages demonstrates that production was well under way by about 2000

TABLE 10.1
Stone Axe Chronology: Radiocarbon Dates

Site	Date (B.C.)	Lab. no.	Group
Llandegai Gwynedd (settlement)	3290 ± 150	NPL 223	VII
Coygan Camp, Dyfed	3050 ± 90	NPL 132	VIII
Carn Brea, Cornwall	3049 ± 64	BM 825	I
	2747 ± 60	BM 824	
Ebenside Tarn, Cumbria	3014 ± 300	C 492	VI
Fengate, Cambs.	3010 ± 64	GaK 4196	VI
	2445 ± 50	GaK 4197	
Upware, Cambs.	2980–2740 Average of 4 dates		VII
Llandegai (Hengel), Gwynedd	2790 ± 150	NPL 220	VI, VIII
	2530 ± 145	NPL 224	
Thunacar Knott, Cumbria	2730 ± 135	BM 281	VI
	2524 ± 52	BM 676	
Shapwick Heath, Somerset	2590 ± 130	Q 430	VII
Windmill Hill, Wilts.	2580 ± 150	BM 74	VI
Abingdon, Oxon.	2510 ± 140	BM 355	VI
Durrington Walls, Wilts.	2050 ± 90	BM 400	I
	2015 ± 90	BM 394	
	1977 ± 90	BM 398	
	2000 ± 90	BM 396	
	1950 ± 90	BM 395	
	1900 ± 90	BM 397	
Marden Wilts.	1988 ± 48	BM 557	I
Rams Hill	1050 ± 90	Har 231	XX
	740 ± 70	Har 230	

B.C.—a date that may also hold for Group XX products. Although production may have begun earlier at some localities, the main phase of axe dispersal appears to have begun around the middle of the third millennium B.C.

A further aspect of context concerns use—the utilitarian and nonutilitarian functions. While the ceremonial or prestige value of the axes has been emphasized everywhere in the literature on British axe exchange, there is considerable archaeological evidence of utilitarian uses. Flakes and fragments from axes, produced either by fracture during use or the reworking of damaged or blunt axes, have been found at a number of sites, including Cairnpapple Hill (Piggott 1948), Windmill Hill (Smith 1965), Hambledon Hill (Mercer, personal communication), Briar Hill (Bamford, personal communication), Moel Hirradug and Merthyr Mawr Warren (Houlder 1961), Hurst Fen (Clark *et al.* 1960), and Carnaby Top Sites 1 and 2 (Manby 1974). At Hurst Fen, three possible polishing slabs were found, that showed traces of polishing grooves, and polishing grooves were also located on some of the orthostats of West Kennet (Piggott 1962). Clough and Green (1972) have noted that a number of axes from East Anglia—especially those belonging to Group VI—had been reworked, and a similar situation existed in East Yorkshire (Manby 1965). Although other workers rarely mention reworked axes, a large number are known.

As previously described, the axes occur frequently as chance finds, although they also are found in settlement sites, causewayed enclosures, and rarely in burial contexts. But the very lack of site contexts for so many of the axes, while being largely a result of collection strategies and circumstances of recovery, also indicates a possibly real off-site occurrence, given the number of sites that have been excavated and surveyed. The very paucity of site finds may thus be an important aspect of context, with the axes being curated and lost or discarded frequently off sites. White and Modjeska's (1978a) ethnoarchaeological study of axe use and discard patterns has indicated that the categories of axes that enter the archaeological record through loss during use can be different from those categories of axes that are abandoned or destroyed accidentally. Implements leaving the system by way of the former process tended to be unrepresentative of the range of observed axe sizes. This was partially because of the differences in the behavior of axes lost in settlements and garden zones (on-site contexts) and those lost in forest zones (off-site contexts). The probability was high that on-site losses would be found and recycled. Since axes used in the forest zone were generally large, due to functional reasons, and were more frequently lost permanently, a sample bias would accrue. This offers one explanation for the observed correspondence between pollen evidence for forest areas during the Neolithic and the densest distributions of axes (Bradley 1972).

Curation and the amount of reuse partly depend on the availability of replacements and alternative axe materials, and partly on the symbolic "meaning" attached to an axe—its local value in terms of prestige, dignity, and so on. Highly valued axes may be taken out of the work-use context at a relatively early stage, and undergo less of the sequence of use, resharpening, and reuse. Stone axes in ethnographic accounts are frequently said to have multiple purposes, including both work uses and prestige values (e.g., Strathern 1965:185; White and Modjeska 1978b). The relative importance of these two uses will affect the amount of curation.

But the social and use values of an axe type cannot be expected to be the same throughout its area of distribution. In particular, changes in axe value and use might be expected to occur at different distances from the source, resulting in changes in the size and form of the axes. Thus, aspects of value in local contexts can be studied by examining the dimensions of the axes at different distances from the source. Such an analysis of local differences in meaning may allow a reconsideration of the nature of the exchange mechanisms involved.

Thus, while the type of data presented by the British Neolithic hinders any straightforward assessment of the find and use context of the axes and their associated symbolism, some insight into variation in the context of exchange may be gained by examining differences in the dimensions of the axes themselves rather than simply on their spatial location as "dots-on-maps."

FOUR MODELS OF AXE EXCHANGE

Four exchange models are examined in this section in relation to the different types of dimensional distributions that might be expected in the axe data.

1. According to this model, the larger axes had a higher nonutilitarian value as prestige items and were passed on over greater distances than the smaller, less-valued axes. From any one source, then, longer axes should be found at greater distances than shorter axes. Sherratt (1976:567), in noting variation in sizes of axes, suggests that the larger axe in northern Europe had a symbolic value since it is one of the few representational elements in "megalithic" art. He notes the long distances traveled by some large forms in England, and suggests it would be interesting to discover whether the larger forms generally moved further than the smaller working forms. According to this model, the smaller axes have less value, and would have been replaced at great distances from a source by other local stones.

2. This model has the opposite expectation to the first model: The axes decrease in size with distance from the source (Elliott, Ellman, and Hodder 1978). As the axes were passed on from person to person, they gradually decreased in size. In their study of the distribution of stone-axe blades in the Papuan New Guinea highlands, White and Modjeska (1978b:28–29) note that, as distance from source increases and as the number of hands through which the blades have passed increases, the morphology of the blades changes as the blades are used, broken, resharpened, and otherwise altered. In particular, the axe blades become smaller and less finely finished. This decrease in size with greater distance occurs not only because the blades have been used for a longer time, but also because in New Guinea the larger blades were thought to be the most suitable for display. The largest blades were more frequently retained and pulled out of the reduction system near the axe source. In New Guinea, large blades occurred less frequently at great distances from the source, both because the bigger blades were kept for display and because those blades that were passed on within the exchange and reduction system gradually became smaller.

3. The third model differs from the first two in that it expects no overall change in axe dimensions with increasing distance from source. Long-distance

exchange in bulk and movements of middlemen may have carried axes of all sizes and values throughout Britain. Shipment of large batches of axes to secondary distribution centers has been suggested by Cummins (1979) as a result of the concentrations of Groups I and VI axes far away from the source areas. A difficulty, however, with Cummins's interpretation is that his analyses are based on the relative percentages of one axe type among all identified stone axes in an area (spatial quadrat). These relative percentages are therefore necessarily highly interdependent, and can in no way relate to absolute frequencies. A *high relative* concentration of Group I Cornish axes in Essex could occur with a very *low absolute* frequency, if there was a relative lack of other stone axes there. (It would be interesting to see the relative distribution pattern if flint axes were included in the analyses.) Equally, high absolute frequencies of Group I axes nearer the source could result in low relative frequencies if many more stone axes were produced in the same area, as is in fact the case (e.g., Groups IV and XVI in the southwest). It does not seem possible to argue for major secondary centers of bulk distribution on the basis of relative frequencies, and in any case there is nothing in what we know of the nature of third-millennium B.C. society in Britain that would lead us to expect such large-scale bulk shipments.

Nevertheless, some less organized, smaller scale, direct contact with the source areas may have occurred at all distances within the axe distributions. According to Model C, direct contact would not result in the chain of axe reduction and retention becoming associated with a gradual decrease in size with distance. The chain of reduction would occur equally at all locations.

4. Direct contact with the source might, on the other hand, still be associated with a decrease in size with increasing distance, if at greater distances axes were a scarcer commodity and were reused and worked out more frequently than those near the source. Thus, at greater distances, axes may have been obtained directly from the source, but the greater effort involved in acquiring new axes resulted in greater reuse and reduction of the already-acquired axes so as to minimize the number of trips. Some conception of the difficulty of getting to the source thus distinguishes Model D from Model C, and indicates a social environment that is, in some sense, bounded so that movements of large numbers of axes over long distances cannot be made with ease.

Models B and D thus have the same expectation—a decrease in axe size and/ or length with increasing distance from the source. The two models concern different exchange mechanisms, but there are similarities in terms of the meanings associated with the axes. In both models, large and small axes occur nearer the source, with the larger having greater prestige. There is more of a separation of work axes from display and prestige axes. Farther from the source, however, utilitarian and nonutilitarian values are linked within the smaller range of axe dimensions. One would expect that, according to Models B and D, nearer a source, the larger axes would often be used as display items and might occur in status burials more frequently than small axes. Lack of burial associations makes testing of this aspect of the hypotheses difficult.

ANALYSIS OF NEOLITHIC AXES

The expectations of the four models just outlined can now be considered in terms of the Neolithic axe data. In order to distinguish between the different hypotheses, axes produced at a number of localities were measured and statistical tests were carried out to determine the correlation between these measurements and the distance an axe was found from its source. In view of the limited time available,[1] only axes found in England and Wales were considered. As it turned out, even this was too large an area, and consequently axes from the counties of Cumbria, Durham, Northumberland, Sussex, and Kent were not measured. The sample was further restricted to axes belonging to only five petrological groups, the selection of which was conditioned by two factors. If the distance from "find-spot" to rock source was to be a major variable, it was important that the locality of the respective rock sources had been provenienced with a fair degree of accuracy. It was also considered advantageous if the main period of axe production at each of these localities could be considered to be contemporaneous.

The following groups were chosen for study:

Group I (Figure 10.1) is described as an uralitised gabbro, epidiorite or greenstone (Keiller, Piggott, and Wallis 1941), the most likely source of which is in the Mounts Bay area of Cornwall, especially between Penzance and Mousehole (Stone and Wallis 1951). No evidence for the different stages of manufacture has been found to date, partly because of the nature of the rock that does not facilitate conchoidal fracture. The technique of production was probably pecking and grinding, the waste products of which are less conducive to archaeological survival. The typical features of Group I axes—an oval cross section and a rounded butt (Cummins and Moore 1973)—can be accounted for by the methods of production and the qualities of the rock. Material from this source has been found associated with Grooved Ware in Wessex at such sites as Woodhenge, Wiltshire, and Poundbury, Dorset (Evens *et al.* 1962; Evens *et al.* 1972); and in Essex, for example at Lion Point, Clacton-on-Sea (Longworth, Wainwright, and Wilson 1971). The radiocarbon dates from Carn Brea (Mercer 1975), Durrington Walls (Wainwright and Longworth 1971), and Marden (Wainwright 1971) give some indication of the main period of production and dispersal (Table 10.1).

Group VI (Figure 10.2) is an epidotized intermediate tuff (Keiler, Piggott,

[1]The analytical work for this chapter was carried out as part of Paul Lane's undergraduate dissertation in the Department of Archaeology, Cambridge University.

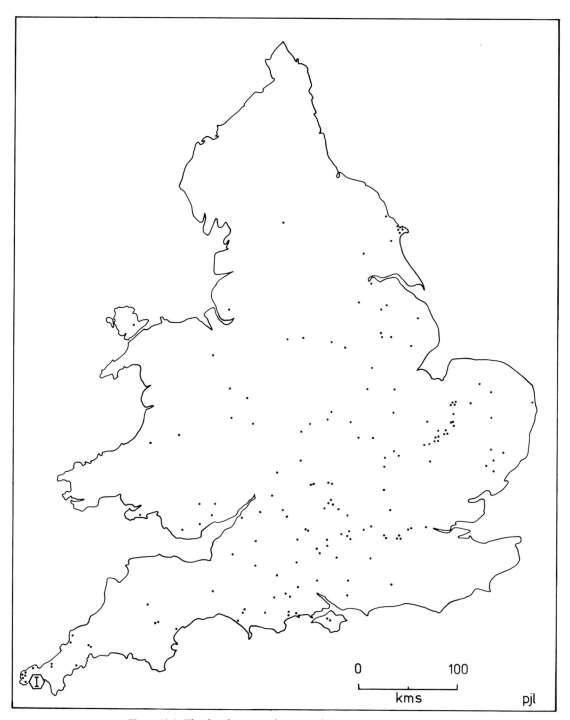

Figure 10.1. The distribution and source of Group I axes are shown.

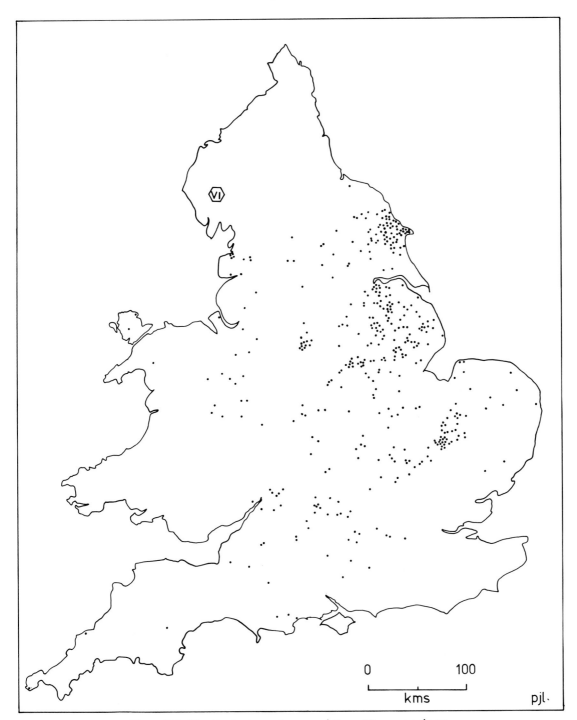

Figure 10.2. The distribution and source of Group VI axes are shown.

and Wallis 1941), the source of which lies in the Great Langdale area of Cumbria. This fine-grained rock can be flaked quite readily, and the waste products of axe manufacture have been found in many localities. The known distribution of chipping floors is concentrated on the fells at the head of Stake Pass and around Scafell Pike (Bunch and Fell 1949; Plint 1962). One of these chipping sites, lying 800 m north of the largest concentrations on Pike of Stickle at about 625 m O.D., has been excavated (Clough 1973). The material recovered consisted almost entirely of flakes and roughouts. There is a degree of standardization in the shape and size of Group VI axe roughouts, which is also present in the finished "Cumbrian" axes. These are thin-butted, long, and slender axes with an oval cross section with flattened side facets (Fell 1964). Two variant forms without the side facets have also been defined (Manby 1965). The radiocarbon dates from the chipping site on Thunacar Knott (Clough 1973), the Neolithic house at Fengate (Pryor 1974), the causewayed enclosures at Windmill Hill (Smith 1965), and Abingdon (Smith 1979) and the type A henge at Llandegai (Houlder 1968) support the hypothesis that exploitation and dispersal had begun by the first half of the third millennium B.C. (see Table 10.1).

Group VII (Figure 10.3) is an augite–granophyre (Keiller, Piggott, and Wallis 1941) outcropping in the Penmaenmawr and Graig Lwyd of Gwynedd. The location of chipping floors is more tightly determined by the nature of the rock that is more variable than, for instance, the rock that is found at Great Langdale. Easy flaking is possible only on the rock found at the margins of the main outcrop "where comparatively rapid cooling of the magma had made the rock more finely crystalline in texture than at the centre" (R.C.A.M. Wales 1956:xliii). Excavations have uncovered hearth and working floors with large numbers of flakes and roughouts (Warren 1921). On site axe production appears to have involved three stages: (*a*) rough flaking of material; (*b*) knapping into a more regular shape; and (*c*) final trimming to produce typically two types—long tapering forms from the quarried material and parallel-sided forms with angular corners from scree material (R.C.A.M. Wales 1956).

Graig Lwyd fragments have been found associated with Early Neolithic pottery at the site of King Charles's Bowling Green, Gwaenysgar, Clwyd (Glenn 1914). However, most of the other contextual finds indicate a predominately Grooved Ware date. For example, a Group VII axe was found in a sealed pit of Grooved Ware date near Woodhenge, Wiltshire (Stone and Young 1948), and fragments have been recovered in contexts assignable to the Late Neolithic at Windmill Hill (Smith 1965) and the West Kennet Avenue habitation site (Keiller and Piggott 1936). Another axe fragment has been found in a "Peterborough" habitation layer below a barrow at North Deighton, Yorkshire (Keen and Radley 1971), and one was discovered associated with pottery of a similar date in the henge on Cairnpapple Hill, West Lothian (Piggott 1948). At both these sites, Group VI axe fragments were found in the vicinity of the Graig Lwyd fragments.

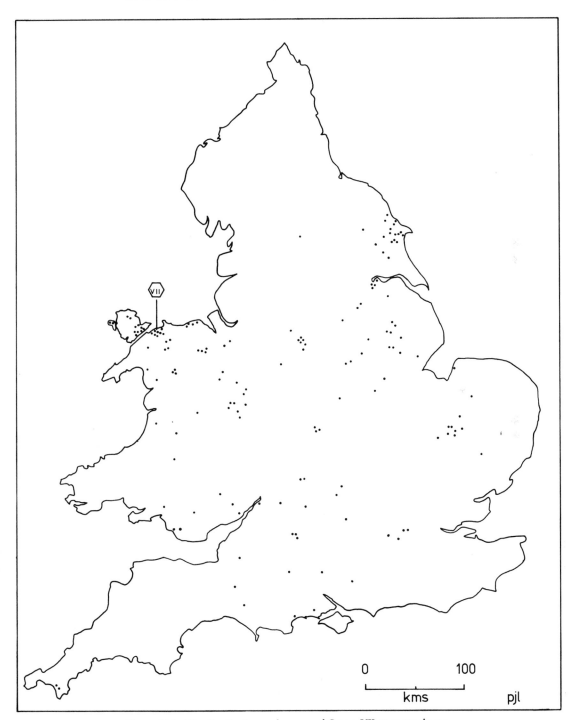

Figure 10.3. The distribution and source of Group VII axes are shown.

Figure 10.4. The distribution and sources of Groups VIII and XX axes are shown.

Group VIII (Figure 10.4) is a fine-grained silicified tuff or rhyolite (Keiller, Piggott, Wallis 1941), closely matching material from southwest Wales (especially the lower Ordovician System) that outcrops on Ramsey Island and on the mainland near Mountjoy, Pembrokeshire (Hope-Sanderson 1970). No chipping site has been found, although future fieldwork may reveal one. Of all the groups considered in this chapter, Group VIII may have been the first to be exploited. Flakes of this rock were found among Mesolithic flint implements at Trwyn Du, Aberffraw (Anglesey) (Ireland and Lynch 1973), while the axe fragment from Coygan Camp, Dyfed, was found close to a pit of an Early Neolithic date (Wainwright 1967). Associations comparable with those cited for the other groups are known—for instance, from the causewayed enclosure on Hambledon Hill, Dorset (R. Mercer, personal communication) and Henge A, Llandegai (Houlder 1968). An apparently unused Group VIII axe has also been found associated with Ebbsfleet and Fengate wares at Downton, Wiltshire (Evens *et al.* 1962).

Group XX (Figure 10.4) is an epidotized ashy grit, the source of which is probably in the Charnwood Forest area of Leicestershire (Shotton 1959). While the rock has the property of conchoidal fracture, no chipping site has been found to date. The number of associations are few: An axe of this rock was recovered from the upper fill in one of the ditches of Windmill Hill (Smith 1965); another was found at Rams Hill, Berkshire, and the associated charcoal has provided radiocarbon dates (see Table 10.1). The earlier estimation is more in keeping with the sequence in the rest of the site (Bradley and Ellison 1975).

The particular dimensions of the polished-stone axes that were selected for study were those that might be thought to be the most susceptible to modification through use and resharpening. Most of the data were collected from secondary sources (i.e., the Implement Petrology Card Indicies). In order to check the accuracy of the drawings on the Implement Petrology cards, relevant axes were measured at the British Museum and the museums at Cambridge University, Chester and Devizes. These measurements were compared with those obtained from drawings of the same axes, and the two groups were found to be almost identical—the average error of those obtained from cards being insufficient to have greatly affected the results. The number of measurements taken on each axe was limited to four: maximum length (mm); maximum thickness (mm); maximum breadth (mm); and angle of the cutting edge measured in degrees. The straight-line distance between axe find-spot and the respective locality of the parent rock was also recorded.

As an initial analysis of the five variables, a program was written to determine the average axe length and cutting-edge angle for every 30-km band (see Tables 10.2 and 10.3). Earlier inspection of the data had shown that long axes (>280 mm) are generally found within 200 km from their source. When the average values in Tables 10.2 and 10.3 are considered, two of the groups show some "tailing off." Of particular note is that Group VII axes appear to become

TABLE 10.2

Band number	Distance from source (km)	Average mm	Number of axes
Length by band for Group I			
1	0–30	165.67	12
2	31–60	160.00	3
3	61–90	167.00	2
4	91–120		no axes
5	121–150	146.00	3
6	151–180	109.00	7 1
7	181–210	141.00	3
8	211–240	118.00	7
9	241–270	139.62	13
10	271–300	122.29	7
11	301–330	125.21	14
12	331–360	127.12	17
13	361–390	148.38	8
14	391–420	139.87	15
15	421–450	128.38	8
16	451–480	131.21	14
17	481–510	123.84	19
18	511–540	136.19	16
19	541–570	125.50	2
20	571–600	122.00	7
Length by band for Group VI			
1	0–30		no axes
2	31–60	320.00	1
3	61–90	158.22	9
4	91–120	211.71	7
5	121–150	120.13	15
6	151–180	104.44	79
7	181–210	115.06	101
8	211–240	126.14	73
9	241–270	108.58	36
10	271–300	116.30	23
11	301–330	117.75	44
12	331–360	117.10	48
13	361–390	112.23	13
14	391–420	137.25	8
15	421–450	87.67	3
16	451–480	103.00	2
17	481–510	237.00	1
18	511–540	79.00	1
Length by band for Group VII			
1	0–30	176.91	23
2	31–60	169.83	18
3	61–90	190.00	2

(*continued*)

TABLE 10.2—*Continued*

Band number	Distance from source (km)	Average mm	Number of axes
4	91–120	174.00	10
5	121–150	141.56	9
6	151–180	150.33	3
7	181–210	154.06	16
8	211–240	146.14	21
9	241–270	114.58	24
10	271–300	137.00	4
11	301–330	135.29	14
12	331–360	108.00	1
13	361–390	106.50	2
Length by band for Group VIII			
1	0–30	114.67	3
2	31–60	133.33	6
3	61–90	201.50	4
4	91–120	210.50	2
5	211–150	133.56	9
6	151–180	133.50	2
7	181–210	85.50	2
8	211–240		no axes
9	241–270	112.50	2
10	271–300		no axes
11	301–330	142.00	2
12	331–360	103.00	1
13	361–390	198.00	1
14	391–420		no axes
15	421–450	133.00	1
16	451–480	187.00	1
Length by band for Group XX			
1	0–30		no axes
2	31–60	144.50	4
3	61–90	129.25	8
4	91–120	132.93	15
5	121–150	131.50	4
6	151–180	117.00	4
7	181–210	162.00	2

shorter as they get farther from their source—Graig Lwyd—and the Group I axes begin to display the same tendency. The remaining three groups do not clearly conform to this trend, and Group VI axes appear to fall within a constant length range. The results presented in Table 10.3 show the average cutting-edge angle for each 30-km band, but there are few clear trends that can be discerned in the angle variation.

These average values are liable to be insensitive to detailed interrelationships between the different variables studied, and therefore a multivariate procedure

TABLE 10.3

Band number	Distance from source (km)	Average degrees	Number of axes
Angle by band for Group I			
1	0–30	125.90	10
2	31–60	107.67	3
3	61–90	118.00	2
4	91–120		no axes
5	121–150	96.33	3
6	151–180	116.00	1
7	181–210	98.33	3
8	211–240	99.29	7
9	241–270	93.20	10
10	271–300	91.20	5
11	301–330	100.30	10
12	331–360	98.71	14
13	361–390	99.00	8
14	391–420	101.31	13
15	421–450	111.00	4
16	451–480	111.00	13
17	481–510	113.27	15
18	511–540	123.79	14
19	541–570	128.00	1
20	571–600	113.00	7
Angle by band for Group VI			
1	0–30		no axes
2	31–60	85.00	1
3	61–90	104.67	9
4	91–120	86.29	7
5	121–150	89.13	15
6	151–180	97.57	76
7	181–210	93.81	78
8	211–240	89.41	51
9	241–270	98.13	23
10	71–300	94.52	23
11	301–330	96.88	43
12	331–360	94.91	47
13	361–390	99.33	9
14	391–420	91.00	8
15	421–450	72.50	2
16	451–480	94.00	2
17	481–510	82.00	1
18	511–540	152.00	1
Angle by band for Group VII			
1	0–30	101.05	18
2	31–60	98.29	17
3	61–90	71.00	2
4	91–120	94.10	10

(continued)

TABLE 10.3—*Continued*

Band number	Distance from source (km)	Average degrees	Number of axes
5	121–150	97.80	5
6	151–180	107.00	3
7	181–210	99.87	15
8	211–240	100.93	15
9	241–270	107.83	23
10	271–300	99.00	4
11	301–330	98.91	11
12	331–360	96.00	1
13	361–390	82.00	2
Angle by band for Group VIII			
1	0–30	87.00	3
2	31–60	104.20	5
3	61–90	101.50	4
4	91–120	91.00	2
5	121–150	90.78	9
6	151–180	86.00	2
7	181–210		no axes
8	211–240		no axes
9	241–270	107.00	2
10	271–300		no axes
11	301–330	90.00	2
12	331–360	73.00	1
13	361–390	105.00	1
14	391–420		no axes
15	421–450	92.00	1
16	451–480	102.00	1
17	481–510		no axes
Angle by band for Group XX			
1	0–30		no axes
2	31–60	116.00	4
3	61–90	108.80	5
4	91–120	102.43	14
5	121–150	105.00	2
6	151–180	105.00	4
7	181–210	78.00	1

was applied. Principal components analysis was carried out for the axes from each group using the five variables—including distance from source. The results from all the analyses were similar in general outline. The first component accounted for 50–60% of the total variation in each data set, and the second for 15–20%. The contribution of the variables to each component indicated high values (all positive) for length, thickness, and breadth on Component 1, and high values for angle and distance on Component 2. Some covariation of angle and distance is suggested, but in view of the low percentage of the total variation that is accounted for by the second component, little weight can be given to the relationship. To the extent that there is a relationship between angle and distance, the principal components analyses and Table 10.3 show that the trend is in certain cases contrary to what might be expected. Groups VII and XX appear to get sharper as one moves away from their respective sources; however, these trends in the angle variation are very slight and are difficult to distinguish.

In an attempt to obtain more detailed information on spatial patterning of the four dimensional variables at different distances from source, two series of spatial autocorrelation analyses were conducted. In the first analyses (Table 10.4), the *I* coefficient (Hodder and Orton 1976) was assessed for axes within the first 200 kms from a source. Pairs of axes were given a weight of 1 if they both occurred in this distance band, and 0 if they did not. At this stage, the analysis thus assesses whether axes near the sources are more similar to each other than more widely distributed axes. The autocorrelation was then assessed between axes in the first band and those in the adjacent 100-km bands (201–300, 301–400 km from source, etc.) in order to find out whether axes were less autocorrelated at increasing distances from source. Because of the paucity of data collected for axes near the Group VI source and because of the restricted distribution of Group XX axes, these two types were omitted from the analyses. The results (Table 10.4) indicate several significant values for axes near the source. Groups I and VII demonstrate positive spatial autocorrelation in the 1–200-km distance band. Axes here are more similar to each other than to axes at greater distances from the source. Up to 400 km, the axes become negatively correlated with the axes in the 200-km band near the source as the dimensions change. In the wider zones beyond 400 km, there is no evidence of any spatial dependency in relation to the axes near the source.

These encouraging results were followed up by a second series of spatial autocorrelation analyses based on the axes in 100-km bands around each source. The null hypothesis was that axes within a band around a source are

TABLE 10.4

Spatial autocorrelation (*I*) values for the cutting-edge angles and lengths of the Neolithic axes at different distances from source. Values significant at $p = .05$ are italicized.

Group	Expected value of *I*	Km from source			
		1–200	201–300	301–400	401–500
I Angle	−.01	*.18*	*−.20*	*−.11*	.00
Length	−.01	*.32*	*−.12*	−.06	.04
VII Angle	−.01	.02	−.03	.02	—
Length	−.01	*.16*	*−.16*	*−.21*	—
VIII Angle	−.03	.00	−.02	.00	.01
Length	−.03	.02	−.02	.01	.02

TABLE 10.5
Spatial autocorrelation (*I*) values for the cutting-edge angles and lengths of the Neolithic axis. Values significant at *p* = *.05 are italicized.*

Group	Expected value of *I*	Km from source				
		1–100	101–200	201–300	301–400	401–500
I Angle	−.01	*.42*	.07	*.48*	.07	.03
Length	−.01	*.36*	.00	.03	.00	.02
VII Angle	−.01	.01	.03	.07	.04	—
Length	−.01	*.21*	.09	*.16*	*.29*	—
VIII Angle	−.03	.05	.11	*.75*	.13	.02
Length	−.03	.06	.06	*.48*	.00	.09
XX Angle	−.03	.00	.00	—	—	—
Length	−.03	*.11*	.04	—	—	—

not more similar to each other than they are to axes outside that band. The aim of the analyses was to identify whether spatial dependency varied at different distances from sources. The results in Table 10.5 indicate that the null hypotheses can in certain cases be rejected. Groups I and VII demonstrate some organization in the axe dimensions within bands up to 300 km from the source, although there is no regular falloff in *I* values.

The two sets of spatial autocorrelation analyses suggest that as one moves away from the major sources, axes do change significantly in length and cutting-edge angle. Beyond 300–400 km, however, the areas covered by the bands are very large, and there is little covariation with axes near the source.

CONCLUSION

The analyses have provided evidence that axes change in dimensions with increasing distance from the sources and that, in particular, the axes often decrease in length. Therefore, Models A and C have to be discarded in favor of Models B and D. As already described, Models B and D allow rather different types of exchange mechanisms, but they place similar values on the axes in different contexts, at different distances from the sources. Nearer to the sources, certain larger axes are less frequently used, perhaps because of a nonutilitarian, prestige symbolism. But at greater distances, all axes become broken down and reused so that work uses and symbolism become more mixed. It might, therefore, be expected that the sizes of axes in burial or ceremonial contexts would change with distance from source. But such expectations must await more controlled data collection and more evidence of find contexts before they can be tested.

However, some limited evidence can be provided about the special symbolic importance attached to axes within Neolithic British society. As already mentioned, axes occur in ritual sites such as the henges at Llandegai and Cairnpapple Hill, West Lothian, and in causewayed camps such as Windmill Hill and Hambledon Hill. Complete and fragmentary flint and stone axes occur associated with some burial mounds (e.g., Julliberries Grave, Kent; Seamer Moor, Yorkshire; Rodmarton; and several of the Severn-Cotswold and Clyde-Carlingford tombs). But perhaps of greater significance in determining the symbolic meaning of the axes are the two examples made of chalk in a form resembling polished-stone axes at Woodhenge. A fragment of a chalk axe has also been found at Stonehenge. The chalk is much too soft for any possible use, and the axes appear to have been intentionally buried. In Brittany, miniature polished-stone axes were found buried at the foot of a menhir. In the same area, the axe is the only artifact type or representational depiction to be repeated in several megalithic tombs. There seems little doubt that the appearance of axes in a wide range of ritual contexts indicates a special symbolic significance. In each exchange act, the axe would evoke these symbolic associations. Ownership of a polished-stone axe would confer status and prestige because of the symbolic associations in the major ritual centers of the object form. If it could be shown that the transfer of axes was controlled by a certain section of society (e.g., senior males or lineage heads), then the axes and the associated symbolism would not only provide prestige, but they would also legitimate through the links to the ritual context. The widespread axe exchange could thus be seen as much a part of the construction and legitimation of social position as a provision of tools to clear forests. For the moment, it is necessary to await the collection of further data on the relationship between axes and particular sections of the community before this aspect of the hypothesis concerned with the control of axe exchange can be tested.

That the results of the analyses presented in this chapter do not indicate a clear falloff in size with distance from source may result from a number of factors, two of which deserve particular mention. First, it is possible that the processes of exchange leading to the axe distributions were numerous. Aspects of Models A and C may also be relevant to the exchange process. Yet, since their archaeological expectations differ from Models B and D, the end result is a blurred pattern. Second, the archaeologist is immediately confronted in his data with the results of use and loss processes. Exchange processes are at some steps removed from his observations. In the earlier part of this chapter it was noted that use and discard behavior could affect and alter size and frequency distributions that might be expected from a consideration of exchange processes alone. Until better data can be obtained on the find contexts of the British axes, it is difficult to assess the play of depositional factors in the axe distributions (although such work is now underway at Cambridge).[2] In this

---

[2]The results of this work have recently been published and they tend to support the conclusions reached here (McVicar 1982).

chapter a move away from the statistical analyses of "dots-on-maps" of the British Neolithic has been initiated by paying greater attention to the axes themselves. But a full analysis of context remains a long way off.

REFERENCES

Bradley, R.
    1972   Prehistorians and pastoralists in Neolithic and Bronze Age England. *World Archaeology* **4**:192–204.
Bradley, R., and A. Ellison
    1975   Rams Hill—a Bronze Age defended enclosure and its landscape. Oxford: *British Archaeological Reports* **19**.
Bunch, B., and C. Fell
    1949   A stone axe factory at Pike of Stickle, Great Langdale, Westmorland. *Proceedings of the Prehistoric Society* **15**:1–20.
Clark, J. G. D.
    1965   Traffic in stone axes and adze blades. *Economic History Review* **18**:1–28.
Clark, J. G. D., E. S. Higgs, and I. H. Longworth
    1960   Excavations at the Neolithic site at Hurst Fen, Mildenhall, Suffolk, 1954, 1957 and 1958. *Proceedings of the Prehistoric Society* **26**:202–245.
Clough, T. H. McK.
    1973   Excavations on a Langdale axe chipping site in 1969 and 1970. *Transactions of the Cumberland and Westmorland Antiquarian and Archaeological Society* **73**:25–46.
Clough, T. H. McK., and B. Green
    1972   The petrological identification of stone implements from East Anglia. *Proceedings of the Prehistoric Society* **38**:108–155.
Cummins, W. A.
    1974   The Neolithic stone axe trade in Britain. *Antiquity* **48**:201–205.
    1979   Neolithic stone axes: distribution and trade in England and Wales. In *Stone axe studies,* edited by T. H. McK. Clough and W. A. Cummins, pp. 5–12. C.B.A. *Research Report* **23**.
Cummins, W. A., and C. N. Moore
    1973   The petrological identification of stone axes from Lincolnshire, Nottinghamshire and Rutland. *Proceedings of the Prehistoric Society* **39**:219–255.
Elliott, K., D. Ellman, and I. Hodder
    1978   The simulation of Neolithic axe dispersal in Britain. In *Simulation studies in archaeology,* edited by I. Hodder, pp. 79–81. Cambridge: Cambridge University Press.
Evens, E. D., L. V. Grinsell, S. Piggott, and F. S. Wallis
    1962   Fourth report of the sub-committee of the South-Western Group of Museums and Art Galleries on the petrological identification of stone axes. *Proceedings of the Prehistoric Society* **28**:209–267.
Evens, E. D., I. Smith, and F. S. Wallis
    1972   The petrological identification of stone implements from south-western England. Fifth report of the South-Western Federation of Museums and Art Galleries. *Proceedings of the Prehistoric Society* **38**:235–275.
Fell, C. I.
    1964   The Cumbrian type of polished stone axe and its distribution in Britain. *Proceedings of the Prehistoric Society* **30**:39–56.

Glenn, T. A.
1914   Exploration of Neolithic stations near Gwaenysgor, Flintshire. *Archaeologia Cambriensis* **14**:247–270.

Hodder, I.
1974   A regression analysis of some trade and marketing patterns. *World Archaeology* **6**:172–189.

Hodder, I., and C. Orton
1976   *Spatial analysis in archaeology.* Cambridge: Cambridge University Press.

Hope-Sanderson, H. A.
1970   A petrographical review of some thin sections of stone axes. *Bulletin Geographical Survey of Great Britain* **33**:85–100.

Houlder, C. H.
1961   The excavation of a Neolithic stone implement factory on Mynydd Rhiw in Caernarvonshire. *Proceedings of the Prehistoric Society* **27**:108–143.
1968   The henge monuments at Llandegai. *Antiquity* **42**:216–221.
1976   Stone axes and henge-monuments. In *Welsh antiquity: essays mainly on prehistoric topics presented to H. N. Savory,* edited by G. C. Boon and J. M. Lewis, pp. 55–62. Cardiff: National Museum of Wales.

Hughes, I. L.
1977   New Guinea Stone Age trade: the geography and ecology of traffic in the interior. *Terra Australis* **3**:1–197.

Ireland, J., and F. Lynch
1973   More Mesolithic flints from Trwyn Du, Aberffraw. *Transactions of the Anglesey Antiquaries Society* **41**:170–175.

Keen, L., and J. Radley
1971   Report on the petrological identification of stone axes from Yorkshire. *Proceedings of the Prehistoric Society* **37**:16–37.

Keiller, A., and S. Piggott
1936   The West Kennet Avenue, Avebury: excavations 1934–5. *Antiquity* **10**:417–427.

Keiller, A., S. Piggott, and F. S. Wallis
1941   First report on the sub-committee of the South-Western Group of Museums and Art Galleries on the petrological identification of stone axes. *Proceedings of the Prehistoric Society* **7**:50–72.

Longworth, I. H., G. J. Wainwright, and K. E. Wilson
1971   The Grooved Ware site at Lion Point, Clacton. In *Prehistoric and roman studies,* edited by G. de G. Sieveking, pp. 93–124. London: British Musueum.

Manby, T. G.
1965   The distribution of rough-out "Cumbrian" and related stone axes of Lake District origin in northern England. *Transactions of the Cumbrian and Westmorland Antiquarian and Archaeological Society* **65**:1–37.
1974   Grooved Ware sites in the north of England. Oxford: *British Archaeological Reports* **9**.

McVicar
1982   The spatial analysis of axe size and the Scottish axe distribution. *Archaeological Reviews from Cambridge.* **1**:2 pp. 30–45.

Mercer, R.
1975   Carn Brae. *Current Archaeology* **47**:360–365.

Piggott, S.
1948   The excavations at Cairnpapple Hill, West Lothian. *Proceedings of the Society of Antiquaries of Scotland* **82**:68–123.
1962   The West Kennet Long Barrow excavations 1955–56. *Ministry of Works Archaeological Report* **4**.

Plint, R. G.
   1962   Stone axe factory sites in the Cumbrian fells. *Transactions of the Cumberland and Westmorland Antiquarian and Archaeological Society* **62**:1–26.
Pryor, F.
   1974   *Excavations at Fengate, Peterborough, England: the first report*. Toronto: Monographs of the Royal Ontario Museum, *Archaeology*, **3**.
R.C.A.M. Wales
   1956   *Caernarvonshire I*. Cardiff: H.M.S.O.
Sherratt, A. G.
   1976   Resources, technology and trade: an essay in early European metallurgy. In *Problems in economic and social archaeology*, edited by G. de G. Sieveking, I. H. Longworth, and K. E. Wilson, pp. 557–582. London: Duckworth.
Shotton, F. W.
   1959   New petrological groups based on axes from the West Midlands. *Proceedings of the Prehistoric Society* **25**:135–143.
Smith, I. F.
   1965   *Windmill Hill and Avebury*. Oxford: Oxford University Press.
   1979   The chronology of British stone implements. *C.B.A. Research Report* **23**:13–22.
Stone, J. F. S., and F. S. Wallis
   1947   Second report of the sub-committee of the South-Western Group of Museums and Art Galleries on the petrological identification of stone axes. *Proceedings of the Prehistoric Society* **13**:47–55.
Stone, J. F. S., and W. E. V. Young
   1948   Two pits of Grooved Ware date near Woodhenge. *Wiltshire Archaeological Magazine* **52**:287–306.
Stone, J. F. S., and F. S. Wallis
   1951   Third report of the sub-committee of the South-Western Group of Museums and Art Galleries on the petrological identification of stone axes. *Proceedings of the Prehistoric Society* **17**:99–158.
Strathern, A. M.
   1965   Axe types and quarries: a note on the classification of stone axe blades from the Hagen area, New Guinea. *Journal of Polynesian Society* **74**:182–191.
Wainwright, G. J.
   1967   *Coygan Camp*. Cardiff: The Cambrian Archaeological Association.
   1971   The excavation of a late Neolithic enclosure at Marden, Wiltshire. *Antiquarian Journal* **51**:177–239.
Wainwright, G. J., and I. H. Longworth
   1971   *Durrington Walls: excavations 1966–1968*. London: Society of Antiquaries Research Report **29**.
Warren, S. H.
   1921   Excavations at the stone-axe factory of Graig-Lwyd, Penmaenmawr. *Journal of the Royal Anthropological Institute* **51**:165–199.
White, J. P., and N. Modjeska
   1978a Acquirers, users, finders, losers: the use axe blades make of the Duna. *Mankind* **11**:276–287.
   1978b Where do all the stone tools go? Some examples and problems in their social and spatial distribution in the Papua New Guinea highlands. In *The spatial organization of culture*, edited by I. Hodder, pp. 25–38. London: Duckworth.

11

The Relationship of Stylistic Similarity to Patterns of Material Exchange

Jeffrey L. Hantman
and
Stephen Plog

INTRODUCTION

Considerable attention has been given in recent years to prehistoric exchange. Unfortunately, indirect evidence has often been used to identify exchange items, particularly in studies of ceramics. The nestability and form of ceramic vessels (Colton 1941:317; McGregor 1965:101–102; Wilson 1969:311–312; Whittlesey 1974), the presence of decoration on pottery (McGregor 1965: 101–102), and the relative frequency of certain materials at sites are examples of such indirect indices. These methods require assumptions to be made—such as postulating that undecorated utilitarian vessels or large ceramic jars are not likely to be traded—in order to infer that certain goods were not locally made.

The indirect evidence that has been used most commonly is the analysis of style. Artifacts are often considered to be imports because they are stylistically similar to artifacts that are known to occur commonly in a second area. We can cite several examples of such studies within our primary research area— the American Southwest. In a recent analysis of trade between the Flagstaff, Gila, and Salt River areas of Arizona, McGuire and Downum (1980) included ceramic types that they assumed had been made to the northeast of their study area. The inference that the ceramics were manufactured in northeastern Arizona was based to a large extent on the stylistic similarities between pottery of that area and pottery found within the study area. Similarly, Graves (1978) has

CONTEXTS FOR PREHISTORIC EXCHANGE

analyzed the frequency of different styles of White Mountain Redware in parts of east-central Arizona and west-central New Mexico, and has made inferences concerning the extent to which ceramics were handled by redistribution. The analysis is based on the assumption that White Mountain Redwares with certain design characteristics were manufactured only in the areas where those design characteristics were most abundant. The occurrence of the design characteristics on pottery found outside the inferred area of manufacture is assumed to have been a result of exchange. Other examples of the often implicit use of stylistic similarities to infer the exchange of goods in the American Southwest can be found in the studies of Colton (1944), Wilson (1969), Schaefer (1969), Brunson (1979), and Cordell and Plog (1979:420). Numerous studies of this type have also been conducted in other areas.

While we do not deny the value of examining stylistic attributes as a means of identifying exchange goods, stylistic characteristics should be examined in conjunction with mineralogical, chemical, and geological analyses (Shepard 1971). The spatial distributions of stylistic characteristics that have been assumed in some studies to be caused by exchange also can be produced by a number of other processes. In the remainder of this chapter, we will first discuss some of those processes and their effects on the distribution of stylistic characteristics. We will then illustrate problems with the inference of exchange and exchange mechanisms through the analysis of style by discussing some of our own research in two regions of the American Southwest.

MODELS OF SOCIAL DISTANCE AND SOCIAL INTERACTION

The reliance on exchange to explain patterns in the distribution of specific styles is, in part, a reaction to the lack of recognition of this phenomenon in many of the classic stylistic studies of the 1960s (e.g., Deetz 1965; Leone 1968; Whallon 1968; Longacre 1970; Hill 1970). These studies have been reviewed, reanalyzed, and criticized in the literature (Stanislawski 1973; Lischka 1975; Dumond 1977; Watson 1977; Plog 1980a), and this chapter need not repeat these discussions. These analyses were characteristically based on a social learning–enculturation model of the factors underlying stylistic behavior. In this formulation, artifactual style was viewed as a passive epiphenomenon reflecting the intensity of social interaction between spatially defined social units. *Interaction* in these studies was a poorly defined term, although it most often referred to reconstructed patterns of kinship and residential descent systems, the heuristic value of which has been questioned (Allen and Richardson 1971). Style, particularly on pottery vessels, was viewed as learned behavior (mother–daughter transmission) that was largely unintegrated with other aspects of prehistoric social systems, except for the marriages and residential patterns of women.

An alternative model to explain stylistic distributions is that recently proposed by Wobst (1977), who considers style as functioning to maintain social systems. Herein, style is also an indicator of social interaction, but it is no longer restricted by the concept that style is solely a learned behavior that is passed along the paths created by marriage and kinship ties. In Wobst's functional model, style is interpreted as a dynamic variable, serving specifically in the processes of information exchange and boundary maintenance. The information-exchange model posits that zones of interacting individuals can be defined by an analysis of stylistic distributions (Wilmsen 1973:24), and that the recognition of variation in the size and stability of these zones reflects directly on patterns of change in regional social organization. It can be extrapolated further that population growth, with its impact on the size of mate and information exchange networks (Wobst 1974, 1976), would have a dramatic effect on the spatial distribution of stylistic attributes through time (Issac 1972:186; Hassan 1979:149–150). Conversely, where population size and density remain low and there is a fluid movement of people and information over large regions, stylistic distributions will remain spatially and temporally homogeneous (Yellen and Harpending 1972; Issac 1972:186).

The functional information-exchange model has been adopted by many archaeologists and has been postulated to explain stylistic distributions in such geographically (and temporally) distinct areas as Upper Paleolithic Spain (Conkey 1978, 1980), the Middle and Late Woodland periods in the Midwest in the United States (Braun 1977), and the Pueblo period in the American Southwest (Lightfoot 1978; Brunson 1979; Kintigh 1979; Plog 1980a). While this functional conception of style as information exchange may help to explain the distribution of styles, a serious difficulty is that the information-exchange model can too easily become a post hoc explanation for any and all prehistoric stylistic patterns. Without knowing other parameters of social and spatial organization, it is not possible to assume information exchange and boundary maintenance as the only mechanisms affecting style.

In fact, the communication of information does not always flow freely, and there are many socioeconomic factors that can affect the regional pattern of information flow. Population size and density, which we have already mentioned, are two such factors. In addition, variation in settlement patterns and the degree of population aggregation or dispersal will affect the costs of information exchange, and therefore affect the spatial distribution of that information (Moore 1977). Finally, and perhaps most importantly, the degree of social differentiation within a region will affect the distribution of information greatly. Many recent archaeological models that utilize the information-exchange theory of stylistic distributions assume that stylistic information will be distributed evenly across a region, except, of course, where it is impeded by social-network boundaries. However, in a socially and/or spatially differentiated society, information should be expected to be processed in a hierarchical fashion rather than spreading out contagiously across a region. There are many aspects of social differentiation that may affect the distribution of styles, including social status, political affiliations, entrepreneurial behavior, and economic specialization in production. These factors serve to accelerate information sharing between some subsets of the population, while deterring this process in others. In some instances, socially determined barriers (e.g., elite exchange, religious constraints) may completely bar some segment of the population from participating in exchanges of information.

In the next section of this chapter we will attempt to expand on the Wobst model of style as information exchange by incorporating some of the factors that can produce differential patterns of information exchange across space.

INFORMATION EXCHANGE AND THE IMPACT OF SOCIAL DIFFERENTIATION

In much of our previous work (Hantman and Lightfoot 1978; Hantman and Plog 1978; Plog and Hantman 1979; Plog 1980a), we have typically defined *ceramic style* in a non-value-laden manner, preferring to define it simply as a "correlated cluster of attributes" (cf. Spaulding 1953; Clarke 1978). Given this foundation, it may be argued that systematic change in combinations of those attributes may be treated as stylistic *innovations*, according to the classic definition of innovation offered by Homer Barnett:

> Any thought, behavior, or thing that is new because it is qualitatively different from existing forms [1953:7].

> Innovation does not result from the addition or subtraction of parts. It takes place only when there is a recombination of them [1953:9].

Working within this context allows us to approach stylistic distributions as a function, in part, of the mechanisms associated with the communication and adoption of innovations. This is in accord with the anthropological information-exchange theory of stylistic behavior developed by Wobst (1977), but it will also allow us to extend the model to socially and spatially differentiated societies. We propose that analyzing the distributional patterns of ceramic styles as regional forms of the communication and adoption of innovations can provide a satisfactory framework to understand distributions not explained by commodity exchange alone.

In a study of the adoption of innovations, Rogers (1962) and Rogers and Shoemaker (1971), have demonstrated that, cross-culturally, the rate of adoption takes the form of an S-shaped curve representing cumulative growth (cf. Hamblin, Jacobsen, and Miller 1973). The authors suggest a typology of five categories of *adopter types,* that reflects primarily the time lag in adoption between *initial innovators* and *laggards*. In a previous study, one of the authors (Hantman 1978) applied this concept to archaeological patterns of migration and colonization, attempting to place them in a spatial context. Although

Hodder (1978) has also summarized the work of Rogers with respect to the explanation of patterns of material culture distribution, most archaeological studies of the adoption of innovation have not recognized the way in which social factors influence the spatial communication of innovations.

There are two fundamental models that social scientists use to describe information diffusion. These are (a) the contagious wave model, or the neighborhood effect model (Hagerstrand 1967); and (b) the hierarchical diffusion model (Hagerstrand 1966; Hudson 1969; Pedersen 1970; Berry 1972). The neighborhood effect model focuses primarily on household adoption of innovations. These are innovations that diffuse among private households or individuals and have the probability of being accepted by all members of a population that have "certain characteristics" (Pedersen 1970:205). J. C. Hudson describes the spatial characteristics of such a phenomenon:

> In its simplest form, it expands outward from a single center until it eventually covers the entire areal extent of the region under study. Barriers serve to channel the flow, but they do not destroy the topology [Hudson 1969:46].

Ammerman and Cavalli-Sforza (1979) have used this model, developed originally in epidemiology, to account for the spread of agriculture in prehistoric Europe. The major problem with uncritical use of it is that it fails to recognize the potential effects of social differentiation and complex political and economic systems on the spatial pattern of information communication. These aspects of social structure do manifest themselves spatially, and they must be considered in regional studies.

Hudson (1969) provides a model that does take into account socially and spatially differentiated societies. He argues that, rather than spreading out contagiously across a region, goods and ideas move downward through a central-place system with a rank-size hierarchical structure. This model focuses on entrepreneurial innovation—one that will affect people in a community other than just the adopter (Pedersen 1970:205). In innovation diffusion of this type, the innovation is likely to occur first in the settlement that has the greatest amount of intraregional and interregional interaction, usually the largest settlement or a political center. In addition, many innovations have a threshold population size below which the innovation will not be adopted. Pedersen argues:

> Many products can only be produced economically at a certain scale, many technological innovations can only be adopted by production units of a certain size, and many forms for organization require a certain minimum support to exist. This means that [some] innovations can only be adopted in cities or regions of a certain size [Pedersen 1970:210].

Hagerstrand's (1966) analysis of innovation diffusion in Sweden adds the necessary time depth to the wave model. His model combines hierarchical diffusion with the neighborhood effect to produce a comprehensive synthesis of how information is communicated throughout a regional system. This is accomplished in the following manner:

> A closer analysis shows that the spread along the initial frontier is led through the urban hierarchy. The point of introduction in a new country is its primate city; sometimes some other metropolis. Then centers next in rank follow. Soon, however, this order is broken up and replaced by one where the neighborhood effect dominates over pure size succession [Hagerstrand 1966:40].

This synthesis of the two models, we feel, best explains patterns of information exchange in socially differentiated societies as reflected in ceramic design style. Before testing these models using data collected in the American Southwest, in the next section we will review some of the socioeconomic factors that can create both nonhierarchical and hierarchical patterns of information diffusion.

SOME FACTORS UNDERLYING HIERARCHICAL PATTERNS OF INFORMATION EXCHANGE

Socioeconomic Status

One factor that can affect the distribution of ceramic styles is the division of social groups into varying status levels. Status and prestige are cognitive constructs that, though based on material economic advantage, are often signaled through aspects of art and other symbolic systems. For instance, Anderson (1971), Fraser and Cole (1972), and Hodder (1979) have discussed the items that symbolize leadership and status in African society, and Wyckoff and Baugh (1980) have reviewed historic documents describing the material culture of governing elites of the Hasinai Confederacy of eastern Texas. Such goods include elaborate stools, decorated swords and staffs, and headresses of various types. The question we are asking is whether ceramic style can function to signal status in a similar vein.

Research conducted in historic archaeology provides a situation where status differences can be ascertained with relative certainty from other documents and related to the spatial distributions of artifacts in archaeological contexts. Stone (1970), Miller and Stone (1970), South (1971), and Miller (1980) have all used the distribution of ceramic classes to recognize status differences in historic archaeology. Otto (1977) conducted a study of the distribution of ceramics associated with varied socioeconomic-status groups on an antebellum plantation in Georgia. On the basis of his analysis, he concluded that there was a statistical association between site areas occupied by a particular status group and certain ceramic types (Otto 1977:105). Interestingly, the differences noted were manifested primarily in terms of stylistic distinctions. Miller (1980) has reviewed historic documents and scaled nineteenth-century ceramics in terms of their cost of production, and he observes that the social-status value of a ceramic type is a function of the cost of the object, which in turn is a function of the decoration put on the vessel (Miller 1980:3). Finally, in a study of ceramic distributions in a historic Islamic town, Rubertone (1978) investigated the relationship between certain ceramic classes and site areas designated as *high status* and *low status*. She found that a significant difference existed in at least three pottery-ware classes (Rubertone 1978:126). With respect to ceramic style, she found a significant difference in jar decoration between high-status and low-status groups (Rubertone 1978:159).

Although these researchers usually suggested that differential commodity exchange accounts for these distributions, the point of the discussion presented here is to document the prevalence of the symboling of status and prestige through such an apparently mundane medium as ceramic containers. Whether the goods are obtained through exchange or are manufactured locally is not relevant at this point to establishing the concept of *ceramic style as symbol*.

Regional Political and Economic Alliance

The archaeological literature is rich in the documentation of regional political systems that are defined on the basis of certain characteristic stylistic elements. In these instances, stylistic similarity is not a result of the intensity of interaction, but rather it functions as a symbol of affiliation within a regional political system. Certain symbols may act regionally as both symbols of alliance and of status, as in the case of the Olmec (Flannery 1967) and the Mississippian Southern Cult (Brown 1976). In discussing regional political alliance, however, we will focus here on the relationship of production to distribution in regional political systems.

The information exchange model, as traditionally applied in nonstratified societies, relies on the concept of stylistic similarity as a function primarily of the size of territorial mate and material exchange systems. In more complex systems where production is impacted by political determinants, ceramics and the adoption of stylistic innovations will often play an increasingly political role. For instance, Irwin (1978) has demonstrated how the increasing domination of the production and distribution of ceramics by the New Guinea island of Mailu served to augment the political centrality of this island over several centuries. Feinman (1980) has also documented the dynamic political role that the control of ceramic production played throughout several stages of social evolution in the Valley of Oaxaca.

Where the production of ceramics is a function of regional political competition, the distribution of regional ceramic styles should be expected to vary primarily in accordance with change in the size of polities. While the intensity of interaction and exchange between polities may be substantial, we would not necessarily expect stylistic patterning to reflect that interaction. In these systems it should be expected also that alliances between political leaders would be signaled stylistically. Once again, therefore, the regional distribution of stylistic classes would be hierarchically patterned and subject to boundaries created primarily by political determinants.

Variation in the Mode of Ceramic Production

As we have just discussed, the mode of ceramic production dramatically affects the distribution of ceramic styles. Too often the extremes of household production or regional specialization are assumed to be the dominant modes of production in an area, although considerable variation exists between these extremes.

Balfet (1965) and van der Leeuw (1977) have provided useful typological frameworks within which the variation in modes of ceramic production may be conceptualized. These studies are cited specifically because they view pottery production, not in terms of the activity of the potter alone, but also in terms of the distribution of the ceramic products. As Rubertone (1978) has argued, in order to infer interaction from the material record, a need exists to focus on patterns of consumption as well as on patterns of production.

In her ethnographic summary of North African pottery manufacture, Balfet (1965) suggests three different forms of production: (*a*) feminine domestic production with household consumption; (*b*) elementary specialized production, with local community consumption; and (*c*) corporations of workers, with regional or market consumption. Van der Leeuw's (1977) cross-cultural synthesis offers a more sophisticated six-class typology of ceramic production systems based on 12 economic variables, including the number of people involved in production and the size of the market area. A partial summary of this typology is presented in Table 11.1.

TABLE 11.1

A Cross-Culturally Derived Synthesis of Variation in the Economics of Pottery Production and Distribution

System of pottery manufacture	Number of individuals involved	Economic variables[a]	
		Time involved	Market
(1) Household production	one	occasional	own use
(2) Household industry	several	part-time	group use
(3) Individual industry	one	full-time	regional
(4) Workshop industry	several	full-time	village/town
(5) Village industry	several	part-time/full-time	region (wide)
(6) Large-scale industry	many	full-time	regional and export

[a]These are a sub-set of twelve variables presented by van der Leeuw (1977).

We present these typologies to offer evidence of the range of production–distribution systems that are known in the economics of pottery-making and to illustrate the association between the organization of production and the organization of distribution. The distribution of styles produced within these varied levels of productive modes should be expected to vary accordingly. For instance, where production is specialized and distribution widespread—and in the absence of market competition—a pattern of regional homogeneity may be expected in ceramic style. Conversely, household production and local distribution may produce patterns of extreme stylistic diversity. While other social factors may ultimately affect the distribution of styles, identifying the level of the organization of production and distribution should help establish a baseline from which to evaluate those factors.

ANALYZING STYLE DISTRIBUTIONS IN THE AMERICAN SOUTHWEST

In the final section of this chapter we show how the models developed in the preceding sections help to explain changing patterns of stylistic distributions through time and space in the prehistoric Southwest. We first discuss problems that exist with respect to the size of an area usually considered in stylistic analyses. Next, weaknesses in existing methods of obtaining stylistic information are discussed, and an alternative method is presented. Finally, using data obtained with this method we examine the factors that account for changes through time in spatial patterns of stylistic distributions in the Southwest.

Scale of Analysis

A significant problem with most existing stylistic analyses conducted in the Southwest has been the emphasis on intrasite or intraregional comparisons. As long as the prevailing assumption under which southwestern archaeologists worked was the perception of individual communities as economically autonomous and self-contained units, this approach was a viable one. Recent analyses, however, have questioned the validity of this assumption (Cordell and Plog 1979; Lightfoot 1979; Plog 1980a, 1980b; Toll, Windes, and McKenna 1980; Upham 1980), and the degree and intensity of interregional economic and social interaction and interdependence is now perceived as having been substantial. Given this conclusion, it can no longer be assumed that only local factors affect stylistic variation. In addition, regional and interregional factors that may account for stylistic distributions must be investigated.

Style Classification

Along with changes in the spatial scale considered in stylistic analyses, we must obtain better information on stylistic variation. Most previous studies have been conducted using information extracted from the ceramic-type system used in most areas of the Southwest. While type descriptions abound in the literature (Hawley 1936; Colton and Hargrave 1937; Colton 1955; Cibola White Ware Conference 1958), these normative typological designations often have obscured evidence of regional interaction. This has resulted from assigning different geographic type names to what, in many cases, are stylistically and technologically identical artifacts. This problem is hardly unique to the American Southwest (see Willey, Culbert, and Adams 1967; Demarest and Sharer n.d.). However, in that region, the assumption of community autonomy and household ceramic production exacerbated the problem and encouraged the differentiation of ceramic nomenclature based on geographic separation alone. The profusion of type names created a situation where type definition is not consistent or replicable from researcher to researcher (Fish 1978). This has resulted in a situation where interregional comparisons based on traditional typological classification is rendered difficult—if not impossible.

Nevertheless, our review of the published typological descriptions reveals that an interregional similarity in ceramic style can be isolated that crosscuts distinctions made on the basis of technology and assumed data of production (see also Wasley 1959; Sullivan 1978; Hantman *et al.* 1978). In conjunction with other researchers who have worked on the Chevelon Archaeological Research Project, we have defined a system of style designations—based on specific associations of a limited number of metric and nonmetric stylistic attributes—which uses most of the traditional style names originally developed

TABLE 11.2
Ceramic-design Styles as Defined by Systems of Attributes[a]

Style name	Attribute systems	Approximate date of occurrence
(1) Lino-Kana'a	Absence of hatched forms; secondary form present; uniformity of line width; primary lines of ca. 1mm	A.D. 650–950
(2) Black Mesa	Absence of hatched forms; secondary forms present; uniformity of line width; primary lines of ca. 3mm	A.D. 850–950
(3) Sosi	Absence of hatched forms; uniformity of line width; primary lines of greater than 5mm	A.D. 950–1200
(4) Dogoszhi	Hatched forms only	A.D. 950–1200
(5) Reserve-Tularosa	Hatched forms opposed to solid lines; absence of secondary forms	A.D. 950–1200
(6) Flagstaff	Absence of hatched forms; secondary forms present; heterogeneity of line width	A.D. 1000–1250
(7) Kayenta	Presence of hatched forms; presence of secondary hatched forms	A.D. 1100–1350

[a]After Hantman, Lightfoot *et al.* 1978.

by Colton (1953). This system is outlined in Table 11.2 along with the approximate dates for the styles. In the absence of detailed information of design-attribute frequencies, analyzing style in this manner should allow for interregional comparisons that are necessary for interpreting stylistic change in the Southwest.

Looking at the dates associated with the styles listed in Table 11.2, as well as a review of the limited research that has attempted stylistic comparison between regions, suggests that a broad synthesis of the evolution of ceramic styles may be generated. Researchers who have attempted interregional comparisons agree that in the earliest stages of ceramic production (circa A.D. 300 to A.D. 950), the stylistic patterning reveals a remarkable homogeneous distribution over a broad, nearly pan-southwestern area (Roberts 1931:133,134; Colton 1939:59; Beals, Brainerd, and Smith 1945:98–99; Danson 1957:92; Wasley 1959:292). Subsequent development (A.D. 950 to A.D. 1100) sees this regional stylistic homogeneity rapidly replaced by much stylistic diversity and localized distributions. Finally, in the post-A.D. 1100 period, there is a return to increased regional homogeneity in style, although on a smaller spatial scale than observed in the pre-A.D. 950 period. In this latest stage there are several styles that coexist in the Southwest, with each style largely corresponding to particular areas of assumed manufacture and/or exchange (Carlson 1970; Graves 1978; Upham 1980).

EVALUATING THE INFORMATION-EXCHANGE AND MATERIAL-EXCHANGE HYPOTHESES

In order to evaluate which factors account for these changing patterns of stylistic distributions, we will focus on two regions of the Southwest from which we control sufficient data to evaluate critically the competing hypotheses. These regions are (*a*) Northern Black Mesa in northeastern Arizona that has been studied by the Black Mesa Archaeological Project; and (*b*) the Chevelon Archaeological Project's sample survey of the Apache-Sitgreaves National Forest in east-central Arizona (see Figure 11.1). In both areas, systematic regional surveys were undertaken, and surface collections were made using statistical sampling procedures. In addition, a sample of ceramics from both regions was submitted for petrographic analysis to Elizabeth Garrett of the Department of Geology at Western Michigan University. Petrographic data from the two regions has therefore been analyzed in a consistent and replicable manner, allowing for reliable comparison between regions.

In the introduction to this chapter, we discussed the recent trend to posit exchange as the primary social mechanism underlying stylistic distributions. To evaluate the role of exchange in accounting for stylistic similarities and differences between ceramic collections from our two study areas, 135 black-on-white sherds were thin-sectioned and analyzed by E. Garrett (1979, n.d.).

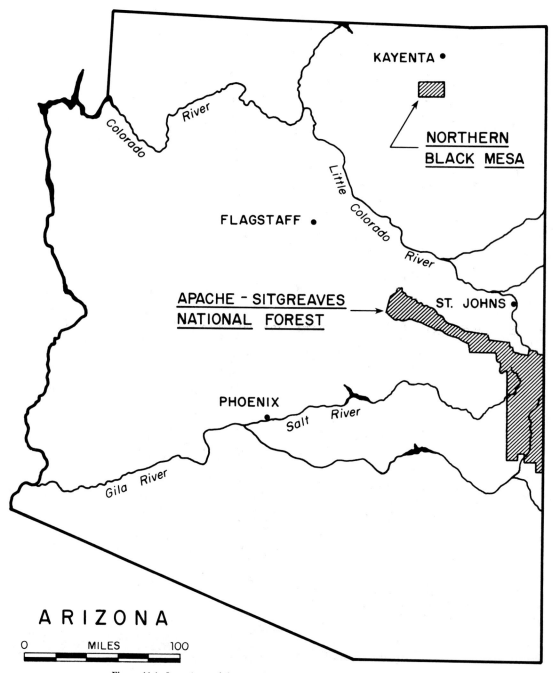

Figure 11.1. Locations of the Apache-Sitgreaves and Black Mesa study areas discussed in the text.

Eleven mineralogical elements were recorded by means of the point-counting method; 300 recordings were made per thin section. The use of point-count data is significant for our analyses because it allows for quantitative statistical analyses to be computed between samples.

In comparing the two collections, we avoided complex multivariate statistical analyses and instead used simple univariate statistics in order to be able to assess independently the significance of differences in the frequency of each element measured. With the student's t distribution (Thomas 1976:227–260), we determined whether or not, for each element recorded, the samples were drawn from the same or different populations. Table 11.3 presents the results of the t-test comparing all sherds from both the Black Mesa and the Apache-Sitgreaves areas. From this table, when all sherds are grouped together, the amount of exchange between the two regions appears to have been minimal. Of the 11 constituent elements recorded, 10 (91%) show statistically significant differences ($p < .05$) based on the point-count data. Of these 10 constituent elements, 5 are either completely present or absent in one of the two areas, suggesting different sources of manufacture for each region. At this point, we cannot offer any suggestions as to the locus or mode of production for either region. Our point simply is that the ceramics are clearly not being systematically or intensively exchanged between the two regions for all time periods under consideration.

If we restrict our analysis, however, to those sherds that we have defined as Lino-Kana'a style (see Table 11.2), a slightly different pattern emerges. This style is characteristic of the earliest stage of black-on-white production in the

TABLE 11.3
T test Comparing Sherds from Black Mesa and Apache-Sitgreaves Regions

Variable	Apache-Sitgreaves (N = 99)		Black Mesa (N = 36)		T value	Probability
	X	S.D.	X	S.D.		
Igneous	.25	.43	0.0	0.0	5.75	.001
Monoxyline quartz	15.59	7.80	23.83	8.90	−4.87	.001
Polyxyline quartz	1.18	1.75	3.72	3.00	−6.07	.001[a]
Chert	1.26	2.19	2.02	1.36	−1.96	.052[a]
Untwinned feldspar	1.76	2.35	2.28	1.86	−1.31	.195
Twinned feldspar	.24	.75	.75	1.07	−3.05	.003[a]
Microcline	.71	1.62	2.75	1.84	−5.84	.001
Rock fragments	.51	1.58	3.83	4.45	−6.43	.001[a]
Sherd	15.68	13.0	0.0	0.0	12.00	.000
Ferro-magnesium	.19	.50	0.0	0.0	3.75	.000
Opaques	.16	.50	0.0	0.0	3.04	.003

[a]Pooled variance estimate used due to unequal variance between samples (after Thomas 1976:257).

Southwest, and it has a homogeneous distribution throughout the region. On both the Black Mesa and Apache-Sitgreaves sites that date to pre-A.D. 950, this style completely dominates ceramic assemblages, and we observe no other styles unique to either area.

Petrographic analysis comparing sherds within this style from both Black Mesa and Apache-Sitgreaves suggests that some of the sherds may have come from a similar area of manufacture, although there are still several marked differences between samples. Although limited, due to the small sample size of sherds available, the results of the statistical tests are presented in Table 11.4. For 3 of the 11 elements recorded, statistically significant differences are noted, and the uniformity in style is at best only partly a result of ceramic exchange. Some early black-on-white ceramics are clearly being produced in distinct areas, as is indicated by the extreme differences in untwined feldspar and sherd fragments. Given these probable regional differences in manufacture, what then are the factors that cause stylistic homogeneity between regions?

We suggest that this homogeneity results from unbounded, nonhierarchical information exchange, which is characteristic of low-density, mobile populations. For this early time period, population density in the Southwest was low, ranging from .01 to .5 people per km^2 (Hantman n.d.), and populations in some areas of the Southwest, such as Black Mesa, were more mobile prior to A.D. 950 than during later time periods (Powell 1980; Plog 1980a). Under these conditions, it is unlikely that discrete networks with clear-cut social boundaries would develop. Such low-density networks would be so large that

TABLE 11.4

T test Comparing Lino-Kana'a Sherds from Black Mesa and Apache-Sitgreaves Regions

Variable	Apache-Sitgreaves (N = 99)		Black Mesa (N = 36)		T value	Probability
	X	S.D.	X	S.D.		
Igneous	.13	.35	0.0	0.0	1.47	.164
Monoxyline quartz	21.86	5.80	20.28	5.82	.59	.560
Polyxyline quartz	2.80	2.60	4.00	3.91	−0.73	.480
Chert	1.80	1.90	1.80	1.60	−0.07	.945
Untwinned feldspar	3.66	2.38	1.28	1.38	2.95	.008
Twinned feldspar	.46	.74	1.00	1.82	−0.99	.334[a]
Microcline	2.40	3.04	2.28	1.49	.12	.907
Rock fragments	.93	2.63	2.28	2.43	−1.18	.258
Sherd	3.66	5.94	0.0	0.0	2.39	.032
Ferro-magnesium	.13	.35	0.0	0.0	1.47	.164
Opaques	.06	.25	0.0	0.0	1.00	.334

[a]Pooled variance estimate used due to unequal variance between samples (after Thomas 1976:257).

groups on the periphery would be so distant from other parts of the same network that travel effort would be high, and efficient communication would be hindered (Wobst 1976:53). Under low-density conditions, therefore, it would be expected that each individual group simply would maintain ties with surrounding populations. Thus, a series of overlapping networks would be necessary, and distinct social boundaries would not develop. Dyson-Hudson and Smith (1978) have suggested also that resource unpredictability requires a group to maintain open territories and widespread information sharing. Neighboring groups are one critical source of information about food or other resources. Low population density and high group mobility increase the unpredictability of exchanging such information, necessitating widespread social ties and promoting the lack of discrete networks and clear social boundaries.

Owen (1965) and Isaac (1972) have both argued that the relationship between population density and network formation has an effect not only on information exchange but also on the probability of culture change. Isaac states that,

> It is conceivable that a widespread low density network lacking in mechanisms for preventing the equalization of information content between neighboring nodes would have great inertia to fundamental change (cf. Owen 1965), while a more tightly knit network involving culturally determined differentials in the rate of information exchange might engender localized partial isolates, which, on occasions, might be more prone to the acceptance and exploitation of innovations. This process may have the same kind of importance for cultural change as isolating mechanisms have in genetic evolution [Isaac 1972:186].

This argument is similar to the thesis of Pedersen (1970) cited previously, which suggests a strong correlation between population size and the propensity to adopt innovations. Ultimately, in the pre-A.D. 950 Southwest, the long-term stability and homogeneity in distribution of the Lino-Kana'a styles can be seen to be more a function of those factors affecting information exchange and regional patterns of stylistic-innovation adoption, than a result of widespread material exchange.

The period between approximately A.D. 950 to A.D. 1100 shows a markedly different pattern. During this time, a rapid increase in the number and diversity of styles occurred in the Southwest. Comparing Black Mesa and the Apache-Sitgreaves data, we see that some styles are shared between the two areas, but others are not. Specifically, the Sosi style of design occurs in high frequencies in both areas; however, the Dogoszhi style is found only on Black Mesa, and the Reserve-Tularosa style occurs only on the Apache-Sitgreaves sites.

In terms of the ceramic-exchange hypothesis, we compared Sosi-style ceramics from the two regions under study to determine if they were sufficiently alike to suggest a common locus of manufacture. The results of this analysis are presented in Table 11.5. Eight of the 11 elements recorded show marked differences in frequency of occurrence. Thus it appears that ceramic exchange

TABLE 11.5

T test Comparing Sosi-style Sherds from Black Mesa and Apache-Sitgreaves Regions

Variable	Apache-Sitgreaves (N = 99)		Black Mesa (N = 36)		*T* value	Probability
	X	S.D.	X	S.D.		
Igneous	.16	.37	0.0	0.0	2.14	.043
Monoxyline quartz	12.96	5.69	25.00	11.00	−4.67	.001
Polyxyline quartz	1.40	1.40	3.84	3.23	−3.35	.002[a]
Chert	1.30	2.10	2.26	1.48	−1.67	.102
Untwinned feldspar	1.48	2.80	2.63	2.00	−1.58	.121
Twinned feldspar	.44	1.15	.42	.69	.06	.950
Microcline	.24	.59	3.00	1.56	−8.11	.000[a]
Rock fragments	.20	.40	4.80	5.15	−4.50	.000[a]
Sherd	18.64	11.34	0.0	0.0	8.20	.001
Ferro-magnesium	.40	.70	0.0	0.0	2.83	.009
Opaques	.24	.59	0.0	0.0	2.01	.050

[a]Pooled variance estimate used due to unequal variance between samples (after Thomas 1976:257).

cannot be the primary factor accounting for the occurrence of Sosi-style ceramics in the two regions.

On an intraregional level, Garrett (1979) has suggested that Sosi-style and Dogoszhi-style ceramics on Black Mesa were being produced in separate areas of Black Mesa and exchanged locally (see also Deutchman 1980). On the Apache-Sitgreaves sites, a similar pattern occurs with Sosi-style and Reserve–Tularosa-style ceramics being produced in the region but in separate locales. In both cases, these local distinctions were made on the basis of the size of quartz grains in the temper, a factor that Garrett (1979) has argued indicates different sources of temper material.

Again we find that while exchange is clearly operating on the local level, the similarities in style between the two regions cannot be accounted for by exchange. During this stage we argue instead that increased population growth (Swedlund and Sessions 1976; Layhe 1977), sedentism (Powell 1980), and the use of alternative risk-minimization strategies (Braun and Plog 1980) helped form relatively closed social networks; hence the adoption of numerous stylistic innovations that are unique to individual regions. Rather than buffer environmental variation solely through spatial averaging mechanisms (Isbell 1978)—such as mobility—there was probably a greater emphasis on temporal averaging mechanisms—such as storage. Given such a change, the widespread social ties that are necessary for high mobility and that are maintained through the exchange of goods (Yengoyan 1972) would no longer be as necessary

(Wiessner 1977). The distance over which goods were exchanged thus would be expected to decrease, and such a change does appear to have taken place. For example, Fernstrom (1980) examined the frequency on Black Mesa sites of lithic raw materials from different sources, and she showed that the abundance of materials from the most distant sources decreased through time, while the frequency of materials from the closest sources increased.

Analysis of different types of red-ware ceramics from Black Mesa has suggested a similar pattern. Chemical, mineralogical, and stylistic analyses have demonstrated statistically significant differences between two such wares—San Juan Red Ware and Tsegi Orange Ware—in the frequencies of trace elements, mineral inclusions, and design attributes (Hardy, Plante, and Plog 1980). The stylistic and mineralogical analyses also have shown statistically significant differences between these red wares and black-on-white ceramics that are abundant on Black Mesa sites and that we assume were primarily (although not exclusively [Deutchman 1980]) manufactured locally. In addition, San Juan Red Ware is tempered with andesite, the nearest deposits of which are approximately 110 km from Black Mesa in the region of southeastern Utah and southwestern Colorado. San Juan Red Ware occurs in high relative frequencies on sites in the latter area. The presence of andesite temper in San Juan Red Ware, the mineralogical, chemical, and stylistic differences between San Juan Red Ware and Tsegi Orange Ware and black-on-white ceramics, and the high relative frequencies of San Jan Red Ware on sites in southeastern Utah and southwestern Colorado—all suggest that San Juan Red Ware was made in the latter area and distributed to Black Mesa populations through exchange networks. In addition, the mineralogical and stylistic differences between Tsegi Orange Ware and the black-on-white ceramics suggest that the former ware also may not have been manufactured on Black Mesa. Tsegi Orange Ware is abundant primarily in the northeastern Arizona area in which Black Mesa is located, indicating that San Juan Red wares were exchanged over longer distances than the Tsegi Orange wares. If the relative abundance through time of each ware out of all ceramics is plotted, a relationship similar to the lithic raw-material exchange is revealed, as is shown in Figure 11.2. San Juan Red Ware was highest in abundance between A.D. 800 and A.D. 950, and then decreased in frequency through time while Tsegi Orange Ware increased. Thus, both the lithic raw-material data and the ceramic-exchange information support the hypothesis that the distance over which exchange was occurring was decreasing between A.D. 950 and A.D. 1150 as a result of changes in methods of risk minimization (Braun and Plog 1980).

Finally, the number of ceramic production loci also increased as these more localized networks produced goods for their own consumption. While networks became more localized and boundaries between networks became more well defined, populations still needed some mechanism to crosscut these

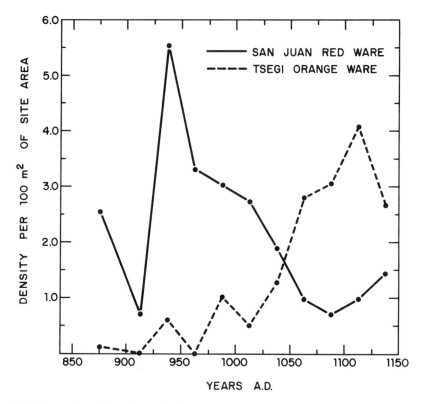

Figure 11.2. Comparison of the relative abundance through time of San Juan Red Ware and Tsegi Orange Ware on Black Mesa.

boundaries to insure economic stability during the periods of environmental fluctuations that characterize the Southwest (Barth 1969). That is, some type of spatial averaging mechanism was still needed to help counter temporal variation in resource availability in a given area. We suggest that the similarities in Sosi style between the Black Mesa and the Apache-Sitgreaves sites may be indicative of just such a mechanism.

Recent studies of the post-A.D. 1100 Southwest indicate that social differentiation and political complexity intensified markedly at about this time (Cordell and Plog 1979; Upham, Lightfoot, and Feinman 1981). While the onset of social stratification and leadership development is observed prior to this period (Lightfoot and Feinman 1982) and the Chacoan phenomenon occurs earlier, it is at this time that marked social differentiation appears to be characteristic of most areas of the Southwest. Concurrently, there is an increase in regional homogeneity of ceramic style, although not on the pan-southwestern level recorded in the pre-A.D. 950 period. We suggest that this pattern is, in part, a function of the changes in the distribution of information and goods associated with the development of complex political organizations. As northern Black Mesa is no longer occupied by A.D. 1130, we cannot present comparative data on its relationship with the Apache-Sitgreaves region. However, a recent analysis of southwestern data by Feinman, Upham, and Lightfoot (1981) provides information that bears directly on this phase of prehistory in the Southwest.

Feinman, Upham, and Lightfoot (1981) developed an index, termed the *production step measure,* which assesses the "relative cost and labor input involved in the manufacture of various categories of pottery." As with Miller's (1980) study of historic ceramics mentioned previously, most factors determining manufacturing cost involve ceramic design. The authors tested the hypothesis that more costly ceramics (e.g., polychromes) would be associated with large, centralized sites, which they argue are the loci of high-status individuals involved in regional political systems. They investigated two areas—the Pinedale region of east-central Arizona and the Chavez Pass locality in north-central Arizona. In both instances, a statistically significant association between the more labor-intensive and costly polychrome ceramics and the larger settlements was found. While it is possible that this pattern results from the presence of ceramic specialists at these sites, a subsequent distributional study suggests that these status-related products were being exchanged between regional centers (Upham, Lightfoot, and Feinman 1981). In addition, in an analysis of the burials at the large central site of Chavez Pass, they observe that these highly decorated ceramics are associated exclusively with those burials that contain nonlocal trade items such as turquoise, shell figurines, and exotic minerals (Feinman, Upham, and Lightfoot 1981; see also Upham 1980). Based on these analyses they conclude that,

> The localization of highly decorated, labor intensive pottery at the largest sites . . . in some areas of the Plateau Southwest suggest that access to these commodities was restricted. This . . . suggests that status differentials were important in structuring the distributional patterning observed in at least some parts of the Plateau Southwest [Feinman, Upham, and Lightfoot 1981:881].

The patterns identified by Feinman, Upham, and Lightfoot therefore reflect what we have argued represents the spatial and temporal patterning one would expect in the regional adoption of a status-related, stylistic innovation. The polychrome ceramics appear initially at several large regional centers, and they do not occur in the settlement systems associated with these centers during the initial stage of adoption. Only after a time delay are polychrome ceramics found in the smaller sites in the settlement systems. Whether this pattern is the result of differential commodity exchange or the hierarchical communication of stylistic innovations is central to our concern in this chapter.

Petrographic and distributional studies conducted by Upham (1980) suggest that these polychrome ceramics were the specialized products of a few regional centers. The uneven distribution of most of these ceramics is then seen as the result of elite-commodity exchange (Upham 1980:219). For the ceramic wares analyzed (Homolovi Polychrome, Jeddito Polychrome), the petrographic homogeneity within wares suggests that the ceramic distributions result from specialized production and elite exchange. Therefore, in these cases there is a strong association between stylistic similarity and material exchange.

A consideration of two additional polychrome ceramic classes of this time period, however, suggests a different mechanism underlying the occurrence of interregional stylistic similarity. Gila Polychrome and St. John's Polychrome are ceramic types defined primarily on the basis of style that have widespread distributions. Gila Polychrome has been analyzed petrographically by several researchers and determined to be—most often—locally produced (Danson and Wallace 1956; Rogers 1974; Robinson 1980) in several different areas. Upham (1980) has analyzed White Mountain Redware ceramics, of which St. John's Polychrome is a part, and has shown them to be technologically variable, suggesting several areas of manufacture (see also Martin, Rinaldo, and Longacre 1961:128–133). In these cases, we see examples of ceramic types that are stylistically identical from region to region and are also associated with large central sites (Upham, Lightfoot, and Feinman 1981), but that appear to have been produced in several locations and were not necessarily traded widely between regions.

In this final stage of the southwestern prehistoric record, both material and information exchange existed between regions. Considerable stylistic similarity is a function of material exchange, but some stylistic similarity instead reflects hierarchical communication and adoption of status-related stylistic innovations between regional centers. While the intensity and kind of social interaction suggested by these two mechanisms can sometimes be quite different, an analysis solely of stylistic patterns would not reflect these differences, and the assumption of stylistic similarity equating to material exchange cannot be made uncritically.

SUMMARY

In this chapter we have illustrated the problems associated with inferring exchange on the basis of stylistic similarity. Through an analysis of stylistic and technological attributes of southwestern ceramics, we have shown that a simple correlation does not exist between stylistic distributions and patterns of material exchange, as some researchers have assumed. The functional, information-exchange model (Wobst 1977) provides a partial framework for explaining style distributions that are not explained by commodity exchange alone. However, the sharing of information is a complex social mechanism that is closely interrelated with several other aspects of regional demographic, social, and political organization. By analyzing ceramic style through time in the American Southwest we have attempted to explain the changing patterns of regional stylistic distributions long observed by southwestern archaeologists, as well as demonstrate the complexity of factors that can create and affect those distributions.

ACKNOWLEDGMENTS

We would like to thank Gary Feinman, Kent Lightfoot, and Timothy Earle for their helpful comments on an earlier draft of this chapter. We also would like to express our appreciation to Fred Plog who, through his own research as well as many conversations over the years, has stimulated us to develop some of the ideas expressed in this chapter. Funding for a portion of the collection and analysis of ceramics discussed here was provided by the Black Mesa Archaeological Project and Peabody Coal Company for the Black Mesa area, and by the United States Forest Service for the Apache-Sitgreaves area. This support is gratefully acknowledged.

REFERENCES

Allen, W. L., and J. B. Richardson
  1971   The reconstruction of kinship from archaeological data: the concepts, methods and the feasibility. *American Antiquity* 36:41–53.
Altschul, J. J.
  1978   The development of the Chacoan interaction sphere. *Journal of Anthropological Research* 34:109–146.
Ammerman, A. J., and L. L. Cavalli-Sforza
  1979   The wave of advance model for the spread of agriculture in Europe. In *Transformations: mathematical approaches to culture change*, edited by C. Renfrew and L. L. Cooke, pp. 275–293. New York: Academic Press.
Anderson, R. L.
  1971   *Art in primitive societies*. Englewood Cliffs, N.J.: Prentice-Hall.
Balfet, H.
  1965   Ethnographic observations in North Africa and archaeological interpretations: the pottery of Maghreb. In *Ceramics and man,* edited by F. R. Matson, pp. 161–177. Chicago: Aldine.
Barnett, H. G.
  1953   *Innovation: the basis of cultural change*. Boston: Little, Brown.
Barth, F. (Editor)
  1969   *Ethnic groups and boundaries*. Boston: Little, Brown.
Beals, R. L., G. W. Brainerd, and W. Smith
  1945   Archaeological studies in northeast Arizona. *University of California Publications in American Archaeology and Ethnology,* **44.**

Berry, B. J. L.
    1972 Hierarchical diffusion: the basis of developmental filtering and spread in a system of growth centers. In *Growth centers in regional economic development,* edited by N. Hanson, pp. 108–138. New York: Free Press.
Braun, D. P.
    1977 Middle Woodland–early Late Woodland social change in the prehistoric central midwestern U.S. Unpublished Ph.D. dissertation, Department of Anthropology, University of Michigan.
Braun, D. P., and S. Plog
    1980 Tribalization in prehistoric North America. Paper presented at the 79th Annual Meeting of the American Anthropological Association, Washington, D.C.
Brown, J. A.
    1976 The Southern Cult reconsidered. *Mid-Continental Journal of Archaeology* 1:115–136.
Brunson, J.
    1979 Corrugated ceramics as indicators of interaction spheres. Unpublished M.A. thesis, Department of Anthropology, Arizona State University.
Carlson, R.
    1979 White Mountain Redware, a pottery tradition of east-central Arizona and western New Mexico. *Anthropological Papers of the University of Arizona* 19.
Cibola White Ware Conference I
    1958 First Southwestern Ceramic Seminar. Unpublished Ms., Museum of Northern Arizona, Flagstaff.
Clarke, D. L.
    1978 *Analytical archaeology,* 2d edition, revised by Bob Chapman. New York: Columbia University Press.
Colton, H. S.
    1939 Prehistoric culture units and their relationships in northern Arizona. *Museum of Northern Arizona Bulletin* 17.
    1941 Prehistoric trade in the Southwest. *Scientific Monthly* 52:308–319.
    1953 *Potsherds.* Flagstaff: The Northern Arizona Society of Science and Art.
    1955 Pottery types of the Southwest. *Museum of Northern Arizona Ceramic Series* 3.
Colton, H. S., and L. Hargrave
    1937 Handbook of northern Arizona pottery wares. *Museum of Northern Arizona Bulletin* 11.
Conkey, M. W.
    1978 Style and information in cultural evolution: toward a predictive model for the paleolithic. In *Social archaeology: beyond subsistence and dating,* edited by Charles L. Redman *et al.,* pp. 62–86. New York: Academic Press.
    1980 The identification of prehistoric hunter–gatherer aggregation sites: the case of Altamira. *Current Anthropology* 21:609–630.
Cordell, L., and F. Plog
    1979 Escaping the confines of normative thought: a reevaluation of Puebloan prehistory. *American Antiquity* 44:405–429.
Danson, E. B.
    1957 An archaeological survey of west-central New Mexico and east-central Arizona. *Papers of the Peabody Museum of Archaeology and Ethnology* 44.
Danson, E. B., and R. M. Wallace
    1956 A petrographic study of Gila Polychrome. *American Antiquity* 22:180–183.
Deetz, J.
    1965 The dynamics of stylistic change in Arikara ceramics. *Illinois Studies in Anthropology* 4.
Demarest, A., and R. J. Sharer
    n.d.   Inter-regional patterns in the Late Preclassic of southeastern Mesoamerica: a definition of highland ceramic spheres. Ms., Department of Anthropology, Harvard University.

Deutchman, H. L.
   1980   Chemical evidence of ceramic exchange on Black Mesa. In *Models and methods in regional exchange,* edited by R. E. Fry, pp. 119–133. *Soceity for American Archaeology Papers* **1**.
Dumond, D. E.
   1977   Science in archaeology: the saints go marching in. *American Antiquity* **42**:330–349.
Dyson-Hudson, R., and E. Smith
   1978   Human territoriality: an ecological reassessment. *American Anthropologist* **80**:21–41.
Feinman, G.
   1980   The relationship between administrative organization and ceramic production in the Valley of Oaxaca, Mexico. Unpublished Ph.D. dissertation, Department of Anthropology, City University of New York.
Feinman, G. M., S. Upham, and K. G. Lightfoot
   1981   The production step measure: an ordinal index of labor input in ceramic manufacture. *American Antiquity* **46**:871–884.
Fernstrom, K. W.
   1980   The effect of ecological fluctuations on exchange networks, Black Mesa, Arizona. Unpublished M.A. thesis, Department of Anthropology, Southern Illinois University, Carbondale.
Fish, P.
   1978   Consistency in archaeological measurement and classification: a pilot study. *American Antiquity* **43**:8–89.
Flannery, K. V.
   1967   The Olmec and the Valley of Oaxaca: a model for interregional interaction in Formative times. In *Dumbarton Oaks Conference on the Olmec,* edited by E. P. Benson, pp. 79–110. Washington, D.C.: Dumbarton Oaks Research Library and Collection.
Fraser, D., and H. M. Cole (Editors)
   1972   *African art and leadership.* Madison: University of Wisconsin Press.
Garrett, E.
   1979   A petrographic analysis of Black Mesa ceramics. Ms., Department of Geology, Western Michigan University, Kalamazoo, Michigan.
   n.d.   Petrographic analysis of ceramics from the Apache/Sitgreaves National Forest. Data on file, Arizona State University, Department of Anthropology.
Graves, M.
   1978   White Mountain Redware design variability. Paper presented at the 77th Annual Meeting of the American Anthropological Association, Los Angeles.
Green, M.
   1978   Variation in chipped stone raw material use on Black Mesa. Paper presented at the 43rd Annual Meeting of the Society for American Archaeology, Tucson.
   n.d.   The distribution of chipped stone raw materials at functionally non-equivalent sites. Ms., Department of Anthropology, Arizona State University.
Hamblin, R. L., R. B. Jacobsen, and J. L. L. Miller
   1973   *A mathematical theory of social change.* New York: Wiley.
Hagerstrand, T.
   1966   Aspects of the spatial structure of social communication and the diffusion of information. *Papers of the Regional Science Association* **16**. (Cracow Congress 1965.)
   1967   *Innovation diffusion as a spatial process,* translated by A. R. Pred. Chicago: University of Chicago Press.
Hantman, J.
   1978   Models for the explanation of changing settlement on the Little Colorado Planning Unit. In *An analytical approach to cultural resource management: the Little Colorado Planning Unit,* edited by F. Plog, pp. 169–187. *Anthropological Research Papers* **19**. Department of Anthropology, Arizona State University.

n.d.   A socioeconomic interpretation of ceramic style distributions in the prehistoric Southwest. Unpublished Ph.D. dissertation, in preparation, Department of Anthropology, Arizona State University.

Hantman, J. L., and K. G. Lightfoot
1978   The analysis of ceramic design: a new method for chronological seriation. In *An analytical approach to cultural resource management: the Little Colorado Planning Unit*, edited by F. Plog, pp. 38–63. *Anthropological Research Papers* 19. Department of Anthropology, Arizona State University.

Hantman, J. L., and S. Plog
1978   Predicting occupation dates of prehistoric Black Mesa sites: a comparison of methods. Paper presented at the 43rd Annual Meeting of the Society for American Archaeology, Tucson.

Hantman, J. L., K. G. Lightfoot, S. Upham, F. Plog, S. Plog, and B. Donaldson
1978   Cibola White Wares: a regional perspective. Paper presented at the 1978 Cibola White Ware Conference, Museum of Northern Arizona, Flagstaff.

Hardy, K. D., P. R. Plante, and S. Plog
1980   The structure of prehistoric southwestern U.S. ceramic exchange systems: a Black Mesa case study. Paper presented at the 45th Annual Meeting of the Society for American Archaeology, Philadelphia.

Hassan, F.
1979   Demography and archaeology. *Annual Review of Anthropology* 8:137–160.

Hawley, F. M.
1936   Field manual of prehistoric southwestern pottery types. *University of New Mexico Bulletin* 1.

Hill, J. N.
1970   Broken K Pueblo: prehistoric social organization in the American Southwest. *Anthropological Paper* 18. University of Arizona, Tucson.

Hodder, I.
1978   Social organization and human interaction: the development of some tentative hypotheses in terms of material culture. *In Spatial organization of culture*, edited by I. Hodder, pp. 199–269. Pittsburgh: University of Pittsburgh Press.
1979   Economic and social stress and material culture patterning. *American Antiquity* 44:446–454.

Hudson, J. C.
1969   Diffusion in a central place system. *Geographical Analysis* 1:45–58.

Irwin, G.
1978   Pots and entrepots: a study of settlement, trade and the development of economic specialization in Papuan prehistory. *World Archaeology* 9:299–319.

Isbell, W. H.
1978   Environmental perturbations and the origin of the Andean state. In *Social archaeology: beyond subsistence and dating.*, edited by C. L. Redman *et al.*, pp. 303–313. New York: Academic Press.

Issac, G.
1972   Early phases of human behavior: models in Lower Paleolithic archaeology. In *Models in Archaeology*, edited by D. L. Clarke, pp. 167–199. London: Metheun.

Kintigh, K.
1979   Social structure, the structure of style and stylistic patterns in Cibola pottery. Unpublished preliminary paper, Department of Anthropology, University of Michigan, Ann Arbor.

Layhe, R.
1977   A multivariate approach for estimating prehistoric population change, Black Mesa, northeastern Arizona. Unpublished M.A. thesis, Department of Anthropology, Southern Illinois University, Carbondale.

Leone, M. P.
1968   Neolithic autonomy and social distance. *Science* **162**:1150–1151.
Lightfoot, K. G.
1978   Multi-site communities in the prehistoric Southwest: an example from Pinedale, Arizona. Unpublished Ms., Department of Anthropology, Arizona State University.
1979   Food redistribution among prehistoric Pueblo groups. *The Kiva* **44**:319–340.
Lightfoot, K. G., and G. Feinman
1982   Social differentiation and leadership development in early pithouse villages in the Mogollon region of the American Southwest. *American Antiquity* **47**:64–86.
Lischka, J. K.
1975   Broken K revisited: a short discussion of factor analysis. *American Antiquity* **40**:220–227.
Longacre, W.
1970   Archaeology as anthropology: a case study. *Anthropological Papers* **17**. University of Arizona, University of Arizona Press, Tucson.
Martin, P. S., J. B. Rinaldo, and W. A. Longacre
1961   Mineral Creek site and Hooper Ranch Pueblo, eastern Arizona. *Fieldiana: Anthropology* **52**.
McGregor, J. C.
1965   *Southwestern archaeology.* Urbana: University of Illinois Press.
McGuire, R. H., and C. E. Downum
1980   A preliminary consideration of desert–mountain trade relations. Paper presented at the Mogollon Conference, Las Cruces, New Mexico.
Miller, G. L.
1980   Classification and economic scaling of 19th century ceramics. *Historical Archaeology* **14**:1–41.
Miller, J. J., and L. Stone
1970   *Eighteenth-century ceramics from Fort Michilimackinac.* Washington, D.C.: Smithsonian Institution Press.
Moore, J. A.
1977   The effects of information networks in hunter–gatherer societies. Paper presented at the Annual Meeting of the American Anthropological Association, Los Angeles.
Otto, J.
1977   Artifacts and status differences—a comparison of ceramics from planter, overseer, and slave sites on an antebellum plantation. In: *Research strategies in historical archaeology*, edited by S. South, pp. 91–118. New York: Academic Press.
Owen, R. C.
1965   Patrilocal band—a linguistically and culturally hybrid social unit. *American Anthropologist* **67**:675–690.
Pedersen, P.
1970   Innovation diffusion within and between national urban systems. *Geographical Analysis* **2**:203–254.
Plog, S.
1980a   *Stylistic variation in prehistoric ceramics: design analysis in the American Southwest.* Cambridge: Cambridge University Press.
1980b   Village autonomy in the American Southwest: an evaluation of the evidence. In *Models and methods in regional exchange*, edited by R. E. Fry, pp. 135–146. *Society for American Archaeology Papers* **1**.
Plog, S., and J. L. Hantman
1979   Measuring ceramic variation: the Black Mesa classification system. In *Excavation on Black Mesa, 1978*, edited by A. L. Klesert and S. Powell, pp. 217–220. *Center for Archaeological Investigations Research Paper* **8**. Southern Illinois University, Carbondale.

Powell, S.
1980   Material culture and behavior: a prehistoric example for the American Southwest. Unpublished Ph.D. dissertation, Department of Anthropology, Arizona State University.
Roberts, F. H. H.
1931   Ruins at Kiatuthlanna, eastern Arizona. *Bureau of American Ethnology Bulletin* 100.
Robinson, D. G.
1980   Ceramic technology and later Pine Lawn/Reserve branch exchange systems. Paper presented at the 45th Annual Meeting of the Society for American Archaeology, Philadelphia.
Rogers, E.
1962   *Diffusion of innovations.* New York: Free Press.
Rogers, E., and F. Shoemaker
1971   *Communication of innovations: a cross-cultural approach.* New York: Free Press.
Rogers, R. N.
1974   Gila polychrome analysis. In *Casas Grandes,* Vol. 8, edited by C. DiPeso, J. B. Rinaldo, and G. Fenner, pp. 148–150. Flagstaff: Northland Press.
Rubertone, P.
1978   Social organization in an Islamic town: a behavioral explanation of ceramic variability. Unpublished Ph.D. dissertation, Department of Anthropology, State University of New York at Binghamton.
Schaefer, P. D.
1969   Prehistoric trade in the Southwest and the distribution of Pueblo IV Hopi Jeddito black-on-yellow. *Kroeber Anthropological Papers* 41:54–77.
Shepard, A. O.
1971   Ceramics for the archaeologist. *Carnegie Institute of Washington, Publication* 609.
South, S.
1971   Evolution and horizon as revealed in ceramic analysis in historical archaeology. *The Conference on Historic Site Archaeology Papers, 1971,* 6:71–106.
Spaulding, A.
1953   Statistical techniques for the discovery of artifact types. *American Antiquity* 18:305–313.
Stanislawski, M. B.
1973   Review of archaeology as anthropology: a case study. *American Antiquity* 38:117–121.
Stone, G. W.
1970   Ceramics in Suffold County, Massachusetts Inventories 1680–1775. *The Conference on Historic Site Archaeology Papers, 1968* 3:73–90.
Sullivan, A.
1978   Styles of decoration and Cibola Whiteware taxonomy: examples from the Grasshopper area, east-central Arizona. Paper presented at the 1978 Cibola White Ware Conference, Museum of Northern Arizona, Flagstaff.
Swedlund, A., and S. Sessions
1976   A developmental model of prehistoric growth on Black Mesa, northeastern Arizona. In *Papers on the archaeology of Black Mesa, Arizona,* edited by G. Gumerman and R. C. Euler, pp. 136–148. Carbondale: Southern Illinois University Press.
Thomas, D. H.
1976   *Figuring anthropology.* New York: Holt, Rinehart & Winston.
Toll, H. W., T. C. Windes, and P. J. McKenna
1980   Late ceramic patterns in Chaco Canyon: the pragmatics of modeling ceramic exchange. In *Models and methods in regional exchange,* edited by R. E. Fry, pp. 95–118. *Society for American Archaeology Papers* 1.
Upham, S.
1980   Political continuity and change in the Plateau Southwest. Unpublished Ph.D. dissertation, Department of Anthropology, Arizona State University.

Upham, S., K. G. Lightfoot, and G. M. Feinman
n.d.   Explaining socially determined ceramic distributions in the prehistoric Plateau Southwest. *American Antiquity* (in press).

van der Leeuw, S.
1977   Towards a study of the economics of pottery making. *Ex Horreo*. Cingvla IV. Albert Egges van Giffen Institute of Prehistory, University of Amsterdam.

Wasley, W. W.
1959   Cultural implications of style trends in southwestern prehistoric pottery: Basketmaker III to Pueblo II in west-central New Mexico. Unpublished Ph.D. dissertation, Department of Anthropology, University of Arizona.

Watson, P. J.
1977   Design analysis of painted pottery. *American Antiquity* 42:381–393.

Whallon, R. E.
1968   Investigations of late prehistoric social organization in New York State. In *New perspectives in archaeology,* edited by S. Binford and L. Binford, pp. 223–244. Chicago: Aldine.

Whittlesey, S. M.
1974   Identification of imported ceramics through functional analysis of attributes. *The Kiva* 40:101–112.

Wiessner, P. W.
1977   Hxaro: a regional system of reciprocity for reducing risk among the ! Kung San. Ph.D. dissertation, Department of Anthropology, University of Michigan.

Willey, G. R., T. P. Culbert, and R. E. W. Adams
1967   Maya Lowland ceramics: a report from the 1965 Guatemala City conference. *American Antiquity* 32:289–316.

Wilmsen, E. N.
1973   *Lindenmeir: A Pleistocene hunting society*. Harper and Row, New York.

Wilson, J. P.
1969   The Sinagua and their neighbors. Ph.D. dissertation, Department of Anthropology, Harvard University.

Windes, T.
1977   Typology and technology of Anasazi ceramics. In *Settlement and subsistence along the lower Chaco River,* edited by C. A. Reher, pp. 279–370. University of New Mexico Press, Albuquerque.

Wobst, H. M.
1974   Boundary conditions for Paleolithic social systems: a simulation approach. *American Antiquity* 39:147–178.
1976   Locational relationships in Paleolithic society. In *The demographic evolution of human populations,* edited by R. H. Ward and K. M. Weiss, pp. 49–58. Academic Press, New York.
1977   Stylistic behavior and information exchange. *Michigan Anthropological Papers* 61:317–342.

Wyckoff, D. G., and T. G. Baugh
1980   Early historic Hasinai elites: a model for the material culture of governing elites. *Mid Continental Journal of Archaeology* 5(2):226–288.

Yellen, J., and H. Harpending
1972   Hunter-gatherer populations and archaeological inference. *World Archaeology* 4:244–252.

Yengoyan, A.
1972   Ritual and exchange in aboriginal Australia: an adaptive interpretation of male initiation rites. In Social exchange and interaction, edited by E. N. Wilmsen, pp. 5–9, *Anthropological Papers of the Museum of Anthropology,* University of Michigan, No. 46.

Additional Approaches to Exchange

12

Storage Facilities and State Finance in the Upper Mantaro Valley, Peru

Timothy K. Earle
and
Terence N. D'Altroy

INTRODUCTION

Storage provides vivid evidence of redistribution and the central finance of complex prehistoric societies, as our research on the Inca domination of the Mantaro Valley in Peru shows. Upon entering the broad Upper Mantaro Valley in the central highlands, one is struck by the sight of numerous storage sites standing prominently on the naked hills. Storage structures cover the knolls just above the Inca administrative center of Hatun Xauxa, and many more dot the hill slopes and crests extending south along the valley. Nothing demonstrates the Inca domination as clearly as these Mantaro storage sites, and this chapter analyzes their distribution to delimit the economic integration of this strategic central valley into the vast Inca empire.

The chapter begins with an overview and reassessment of redistribution as a traditional institution of exchange critical to the finance of complex societies. Difficulties encountered studying redistribution archaeologically are noted, and the importance of using facilities as auxiliary evidence of prehistoric exchange is stressed. The use of storage facilities to describe the operation of prehistoric redistribution is then illustrated with the research on storage conducted by the Upper Mantaro Archaeological Research Project (UMARP).

REDISTRIBUTION AS STAPLE FINANCE

Studies of redistribution have been chronically plagued by problems of understanding its form and functions. In his seminal article, Polanyi (1957) described three forms of economic integration—reciprocity, redistribution, and market exchange. In the subsequent use of this typology, researchers have accepted these categories as alternative ways to distribute locally produced goods in societies of different evolutionary complexity. Reciprocity and market exchange can be viewed as contrasting exchange mechanisms with differences in the social context of exchange and in the relative importance of supply and demand for establishing exchange rates (cf. Sahlins 1965). Redistributional exchange, however, appears as a fundamentally different economic system.

What is redistribution? In initial attempts to adapt Polanyi's ideas to an evolutionary framework, redistribution was seen as a functional alternative to reciprocity or market exchange found in ranked and early stratified societies. Service (1962), for example, argued that redistribution and chiefdoms evolved where environmental diversity and sedentism resulted in specialized local production and regional exchange. Redistribution was seen by Service as an administered exchange system coordinating locally specialized economies. Recent empirical studies, however, provide little evidence that redistribution has acted on any regular basis to coordinate exchange in specialized products (Morris 1967; Earle 1977).

Redistribution is rather a system of finance used to mobilize goods from subsistence producers either as a fraction of their production or as the produce from reserved lands worked by the commoners. Goods collected in this way are then used to pay for the full range of elite and governmental activities. In essence, the development of this rudimentary tax–tribute system underwrites the development of the chiefdom and early state superstructure.

This necessary support is typically accomplished by what Polanyi (1968:186–187, 324) has called *staple finance*—a finance in kind with defined accounting units. The staples, typically grains and livestock, are collected by the central government, stored, and paid out in return for state services. Polanyi (1968:321) calls staple finance a "submonetary device" that is associated with standardized values for key staples. A producer therefore gives to the state, either directly or indirectly, measured amounts of the main staples. These staples are then used to pay individuals working for the state.

For mobilization, the primary goods paid to the government are a region's dominant staples. As might have been predicted, therefore, Morris's (1967) excavations in Inca-state storage units in highland Peru recovered local agricultural products—highland tubers and maize. No evidence existed either in the historical documents or from the excavations for large-scale movement of specialized products between ecological zones. Apparently the Inca state used locally available goods as its financial units and was not involved in coordinating exchange in subsistence goods among specialized local economies.

In retrospect, this is not surprising. Once the state or chiefdom imposes a regional peace in an area, a strong constraint on exchange (i.e., hostile relations) has been removed. Reciprocal exchange within communities whose boundaries encompass several ecological zones, or market exchange among specialized communities apparently would be sufficient to coordinate local specialization. Little evidence exists that governmental interference was necessary or extensive, a point that is clarified later for the Andean case.

Two economic institutions frequently tied closely to a central finance system are specialized production of valuables and long-distance external exchange. While these elements are not necessary to redistribution, they are frequently linked to it in important ways. Valuables are symbolically important items exchanged ceremonially to mark the granting of political office and the formation of alliances. The central elites often control production of such valuables through the control of redistribution. Staples collected in the mobilization are used to support craft specialists attached to the elites, and key raw materials for the manufacture of the valuables are collected as part of the more general mobilization. In Hawaii, for example, part of a community's annual obligation was to provide bird feathers that were made by attached specialists into the elaborate capes used in key political prestations (Earle 1978:183–184).

Long-distance trade, although analytically distinct from redistribution (Dalton 1975:100), is often closely tied to it. Craft goods produced by attached specialists and special agricultural crops grown on governmental lands are traded externally for foreign goods. In most instances, these foreign products are valuables used in elite exchanges such as political gifts to establish alliances, to validate offices, and to mark ties of dependence (cf. Tourtellot and Sabloff 1972). It is possible, however, that foreign goods could also serve as payment by the state. Providing foreign goods to local populations thus may be important in some "redistributional" systems, but even in those systems it seems likely that the foreign goods would represent only part of the total goods used in payment.

To summarize, redistribution is geared to amassing local staples for payment uses by central authorities. Although secondary functions such as collection of key raw materials and distribution of foreign goods may be related to it, redistribution is primarily a mechanism of finance and not of commodity exchange.

With this revised understanding of redistribution, two problems remain. First, it may be difficult to distinguish redistribution from market exchange, on the basis of the regional distribution of exchanged products (Renfrew 1975; Hodder and Orton 1976). The highly centralized organization of both may result in a similar pattern—a falloff in the frequency of exchanged goods with distance from a center (see, however, Alden, Chapter 4). Second, the exchange of locally produced craft and agricultural products—typical of both market exchange and redistribution—involves products that are perishable or difficult to source precisely within the region. In other words, the artifacts themselves often provide poor evidence for redistribution (but see Pires-Ferreira and Flannery 1976), and it becomes necessary to investigate other evidence for the organizational context of the exchange.

Redistribution may best be identified and described through the technologies and facilities related directly to the financial institution. Where preserved, record-keeping devices, such as the Linear B tablets from Pylos, can give a vivid description of the system's operation. More frequently preserved archaeologically are the massive storage complexes associated with the staple finance. These elaborate and distinctive facilities are the central focus of the present study.

STORAGE FACILITIES AND EXCHANGE

As discussed elsewhere (Earle, Chapter 1), although the primary evidence for prehistoric exchange has been the spatial distribution of sourced materials, this evidence alone is often ambiguous and should be used with other data to establish the organization of prehistoric exchange. Particularly useful data may be recovered by studying the facilities directly associated with an exchange institution (cf. Sabloff and Freidel 1975). Facilities are the physical structures used by an institution, and it seems plausible that different exchange systems should require distinctive facilities.

Storage is a common facility integral to many exchange systems, wherever the flow of goods into and out of an exchange node is not equal at any point in time. It is our belief that the kind of storage used can be shown to be characteristic of the institutional form of the exchange. To illustrate this point, we consider the form and distribution of storage in several economic contexts, including household subsistence, reciprocal exchange, market exchange, long-distance exchange, and redistribution.

Perhaps the most common use of storage is within the household to even out seasonal availability of subsistence foods. In most environments, food products in particular are available unevenly through the year so that goods, harvested in periods of abundance, are stored and then consumed later. Storage in these situations is small scale, dispersed, and associated with individual household units.

For commodity exchange, the nature of storage is related to several characteristics of the exchange system. Down-the-line exchange is typically decentralized with many independent traders and a relatively low volume. Storage can be expected therefore to be small scale, dispersed, and associated with the households of traders. In contrast, market exchange is more centralized and has a higher volume. The critical characteristics are probably the volume handled by a single vendor and the periodicity of markets. Logically, a vendor would not tend to store greatly in excess of his volume in a single market, although factors of unpredictable supply will increase storage needs. In most market situations in traditional societies, vendors deal with small volumes, and storage should be small scale and dispersed among the vendors' retail locations and households (cf. Millon 1964).

Centralized and relatively large-scale storage would be expected in traditional society in two basic situations, the first being in association with high-volume, long-distance exchange. In long-distance exchange, goods are collected together, shipped, and then dispersed. The bulking and debulking of goods—related to changing transport modes—are associated with storage at specific transshipment locations. Examples from the literature include the specialized storage at the Roman port of Ostia (Vitelli 1980), at Casas Grandes on the Mesoamerican fringe (DiPeso 1974), and at the Postclassic port-of-trade of Cozumel in Yucatan (Sabloff and Freidel 1975). Such storage facilities are easily recognized by the highly localized and specific nature of their distribution.

Second, centralized, large-scale storage would be expected in association with staple finance in redistribution (cf. Polanyi 1968:153, 186). The degree to which storage is centralized reflects directly the degree of political centrality. It should be noted, however, that storage need not necessarily be associated with redistribution. In areas where staple production is not seasonal, as in the irrigated root-crop agriculture of Hawaii, mobilization can take place directly as needed (Earle 1978). In most cases, however, staple production is seasonal, and storage is a key element of central finance. As we now show for the Inca case, the distribution of state storage is highly patterned and may be used to determine the basic organization of the state finance.

THE ECONOMY OF THE INCA EMPIRE

The economy of Tawantinsuyu—the Inca empire—has been portrayed carefully in the ethnohistorical work of John Murra (1956, 1975). Here we sketch our understanding of the Inca economy, based largely on Murra's insights but departing from his reconstruction at certain points (cf. also La Lone, Chapter 13). The economy of the Inca period (A.D. 1440–1532) was composed of two distinct but interlocking components—the subsistence economy of the local community and the state economy of the empire.

The *subsistence economy* of a local, highland Andean community was generalized and organized to incorporate as wide a range of economic activities as possible. Community boundaries were laid out to crosscut ecologically diverse zones and, in certain circumstances, were extended by colonization to more distant, economically significant zones (Murra 1975:58–115). The apparent ideal was to integrate the vertically distinctive economic zones of the Andes within a single community to provide access to localized products through autonomous reciprocal exchange among community members. Where feasible, this circumvented the need for an intercommunity market exchange and for state-administered regional exchange (see La Lone, Chapter 13). In essence, the subsistence economy of these Andean communities was largely self-contained and required no direct state intervention to organize specialized production and exchange.

The ease of effecting this self-sufficient community economy was of course dependent on the spatial compactness of the ecological diversity. In areas such as the steeply sloping eastern flanks of the Andes, many zones from the high grasslands to the tropical forest may be found within 20 km of each other, and the generalized community economy continues in operation to this day (Brush 1976). In other areas, such as the intermontane valley of the Rio Mantaro, the low-elevation zones are at a greater distance, and the problem of control is more difficult. For example, the tropical-forest villages known by ethnohistoric documents to have been subservient to the Mantaro Valley communities were 50–150 km from the central valley (LeVine 1979:69). As LeVine (1979) has demonstrated for the Mantaro and as Murra (1975) has argued more generally for the Andes, the vertically integrated community was characteristic of the Inca period. Can this model of community economic organization be extended unmodified to earlier periods? We are skeptical that it can be.

During periods when a regional state organization did not exist to control peace among communities, the highly extended community would appear to have been risky and unstable. Rather, a simple intercommunity reciprocal exchange system, which is found quite generally in stateless societies, would seem a more feasible solution. While the vertical community economy most probably existed in areas of high ecological diversity, the development of the more extended community economy was likely to be dependent on the regional peace imposed by the Inca empire. The Inca may have granted and guaranteed a community's (or more likely the community leader's) rights to the more distant lands (see Cobo 1956 [1653]:111). The key point is that, during the Inca period, community-based exchange acted, and may have been encouraged, to handle most community needs *without* direct state involvement with distribution.

The *state economy* was distinct from the community economy in form and function. The state mobilized staples, and to a lesser degree valuables, from the local community to finance the operation of the empire. As Murra (1956) has described, this was accomplished by an elaborate labor tax. The Inca empire asserted ownership over all lands and herds, and a community's access to subsistence resources derived from the state in return for community labor on state projects. The household—as the elemental unit of assessment—provided labor for state and church lands, for public-works projects, and for special duties such as weaving. The products of this labor were then collected by the state; the staples were stored locally and the special products, such as fine textiles, were mainly shipped to the capital of Cuzco. Specialists recorded on the *khipu* (mnemonic knotted-string sets) all transactions of goods going into and out of the storehouses.

For this chapter, local storage and the use of the staples are of primary concern. These goods, produced by community labor on state lands or on state materials, were held in the massive state warehouses and were used to pay for state services. Murra (1956:204–208) provides an extended description of the payment uses for these staples. Most directly, stores were used to support the military and state functionaries associated with state operations. Additionally, all community personnel working on state projects were fed from these stores.

Other possible uses of the storage facilities are more problematic. Murra (1956:229) originally proposed that the goods mobilized by the state may have been exchanged regionally. However, this commodity-exchange function has now been largely dismissed following the archaeological work on storage by Morris (1967). Prior to Murra's detailed analysis of the historical sources, it was also believed that the central storage mechanism of the Incas had important welfare functions—supporting destitute individuals and communities. Murra (1956:222–228), however, found little support for this function, and he argued that security was largely the responsibility of the local community. State storage would have been used to support a local community only in times of severe disaster when community security mechanisms proved inadequate.

Based on historical records, the state warehouses were also used to hold military supplies and luxury goods, such as precious metals and fine textiles. The military supplies were held at the administrative centers throughout the empire where they could be used to sustain the state army when it was billeted locally. The luxury goods, essentially items of wealth, were held in storage at the administrative centers for two reasons: (*a*) They were collected from local craftsmen prior to shipment to Cuzco; (*b*) They were used as prestige gifts to local leaders as validation of political office.

In sum, storage as part of the Inca state economy served first and foremost as capital to finance the state in its many local operations. The bulk of goods that were held apparently consisted of local staples; however, military supplies and prestige goods were also held on a more limited basis. Possible additional uses of redistribution for commodity exchange and for local security appear to be of lesser importance.

THE MANTARO VALLEY IN LATE PREHISTORY

The Mantaro Valley is a high intermontane valley in the central highlands of Peru. Our research area in the Mantaro has concentrated on the region around the modern town of Jauja (Earle *et al.* 1980). This region includes the broad main Mantaro Valley, several tributary and isolated valleys, and the surrounding uplands. Three dominant economic zones characterize the Jauja region: (*a*)

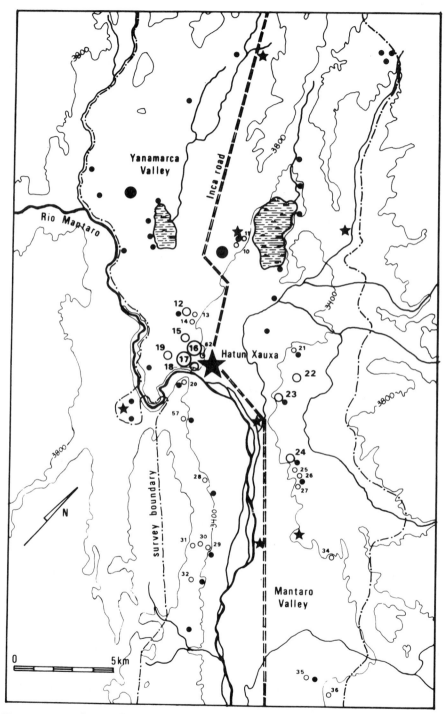

Figure 12.1. Distribution of Late Horizon storage sites in the UMARP research area. Storage sites are shown as open circles (small size less than 50 storage units; medium, 50–120 units; large, greater than 300 units) and are numbered. Inca administrative sites are shown as stars (small size, less than 30 ha; large size, greater than 30 ha). Local habitation sites are shown as black dots (small size, less than 30 ha; large, greater than 30 ha). Elevations are in meters.

the alluvial bottomlands of the main and side valleys (3300–3400 m), that were farmed intensively for cereal crops including maize, quinoa, and the introduced wheat; (*b*) the rolling upland soils (3400–3800 m) that ring the lower valleys, that were farmed extensively for potatoes and various cereals; and (*c*) the high upland grasslands of the surrounding ridges and plateaus (3800–4400 m), that were used extensively for grazing of camelids and introduced sheep. These environmental zones with their distinctive production strategies are closely juxtaposed, and most prehistoric communities would have had access to lands in all three zones. As mentioned earlier, however, an additional lower agricultural zone important for several crops (e.g., coca, ají, lucuma) was more distant (>50 km)—over the Cordillera Oriental and down the eastern mountain flank.

UMARP has concentrated its investigations on the Late Intermediate period (A.D. 1000–1460) and the Late Horizon (A.D. 1460–1532)—periods in which major social and political changes took place within the region (Earle *et al.* 1980). During the Late Intermediate period, population grew rapidly, and settlements shifted from scattered small sites on the valley floor and low ridges to a few large sites (up to 130 ha) and smaller, apparently dependent sites. During the latter part of the Late Intermediate period, internal warfare was prevalent; sites were fortified and were located on defensible hilltops (LeBlanc 1981). Then, during the Late Horizon, the Mantaro Valley was conquered by the rapidly expanding Inca empire and was incorporated into the state administrative system. The Incas constructed a major administrative center at Hatun Xauxa (near the modern town of Jauja), several smaller state sites, the valley's extensive storage complexes, and the main road running through the valley from Cuzco to Ecuador (D'Altroy 1981). Most defensive local settlements were abandoned at this time, and new, smaller, and unfortified settlements were located in more dispersed locations.

Storage during the Late Intermediate period and Late Horizon shows strongly contrasting patterns. During the Late Intermediate period, storage was decentralized and has been found thus far only in household contexts. While it seems likely that some larger storage areas were connected with the households of community leaders (cf. Morris 1967:20), there are no separate, recognizable village or regional storage complexes. During the Late Horizon, more than 2000 storehouses were constructed in many special complexes through the valley. These storage sites—strung out along the hills flanking the valley—provide the primary data on the redistributional economy of the provincial Inca in the Mantaro Valley (see Figure 12.1).

The description of these Late Horizon storage complexes in the Jauja region was made by UMARP teams, working from an intensive survey conducted by Jeffrey Parsons (Parsons and Matos 1978; Matos and Parsons 1979). The data were collected primarily under the direction of Terence D'Altroy, in whose dissertation the data are presented and analyzed (D'Altroy 1981).

The storage complexes consist of lines of individual storage units that follow the contours at the crests and are located along slopes of the valley's bordering hills. The arrangement and architecture of the storage units are distinct from local habitation and other state sites. The individual units are arranged in neat lines that curve gently to follow the topography. Storage units have two possible floor plans—circular and rectangular—and typically, structures of one plan are grouped as a separate line or as a segment of a line. Within a site line, structural design and construction are highly ordered: Units replicate a modular size; separation between units is uniform; and construction details such as facing of entrances are standardized (see Figure 12.2).

Both ethnohistoric documents and previous archaeological studies have been used to identify storage facilities. Chroniclers frequently recorded the systematic association of storage facilities with provincial centers (e.g., Cobo 1956 [1653], II:114), some mentioning Hatun Xauxa specifically (e.g., Sancho de la Hoz 1917 [1532–1533]:141; Polo de Ondegardo 1917 [1571]:77). As Morris (1967) has shown, certain features of storage sites can be used to differentiate them archaeologically from other types of sites. In particular, the linear layout and modular structure size distinguish storehouses from local villages, which contain variably sized buildings in patio groups. Inca habitation sites can be distinguished from storage facilities primarily by their layout around plazas and by the larger size of their structures. Storage sites also

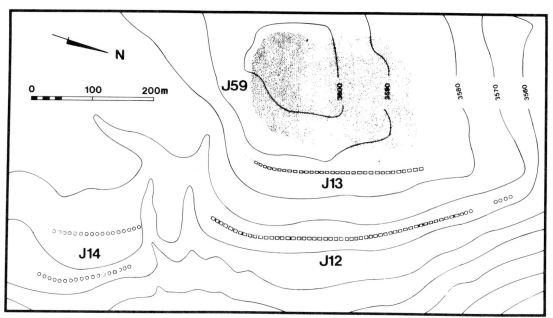

Figure 12.2. State storage sites J12, J13, and J14, in association with local habitation site, J59. Individual circular or rectangular structures are shown; mottling indicates areas of destroyed structures. Elevations are in meters.

typically lack surface ceramics and other habitation debris. Brief test excavations described below (see also D'Altroy 1981) showed storehouses to be designed to control humidity through use of drain floors (cf. Morris 1967). They gave no evidence of habitation. Rather, the ceramics recovered appear to be almost exclusively from large storage vessels, and remains of staple crops were abundant.

A problem that has plagued us is dating these sites, because pottery is often rare or absent on the ground surface. We have concluded on the basis of four lines of evidence, however, that all units date to the Late Horizon. (Browman [1970] has argued that many Mantaro complexes were constructed first in the Late Intermediate period.) First, ceramic collections, when present, typically contained Late Horizon styles—provincial Inca and composite Huanca–Inca. Second, the architectural canons and site designs were uniform across storage sites and closely resembled Inca storage complexes described from other highland sites (Morris 1967). Small elevated entrances, systematically located on either the uphill or downhill side of lines of structures, are characteristic of Inca storehouses, as are drainage floors, stone tenons, and modular unit sizes. Third, the area of highest Late Intermediate period occupation density—the Yanamarca Valley, just to the northwest of Hatun Xauxa—was devoid of such storage complexes. Fourth, the storage complexes were constructed in physical isolation and without defensive protection. This pattern would seem appropriate for the Late Horizon when the empire imposed a regional peace, but it would be highly inappropriate for the Late Intermediate period when internal warfare was endemic.

The individual storage units are easily described because of the regional uniformity. The circular units are like small silos. They appear as truncated cones, broad at the base and somewhat narrower toward the top. Average diameter is about 5.5 m, but sites near the administrative center of Hatun Xauxa have somewhat larger dimensions than those that are more distant (D'Altroy 1981). Most structures are poorly preserved, but walls often stand over 3 m in height. The walls are made of double-faced *pirka* masonry, composed of local fieldstone set in a mud mortar.

Entrances are typically small (.40–.70 m × .55–1.60 m), and are placed about a meter off the ground. At one site (J29), these entrances were purposefully blocked with unmortared rock walling, and it seems plausible that this was the way to seal a unit during storage. The entrance was probably closed, the unit was filled from the top, and it was opened later from below.

The rectangular units are generally similar except in several structural details. The average dimensions of a structure are about 7 m × 5 m. Like the circular structures, wall construction is of *pirka* masonry, but corners are usually squared off. It has been suggested that specific types of goods were stored within structures of each shape, with maize being kept in circular structures and highland crops (e.g., tubers) in rectangular ones (Morris 1967). It seems probable that the use of different shapes was in part an accounting device, but the specific organization of the system remains to be defined clearly for the Mantaro region.

STORAGE IN THE MANTARO VALLEY

The regional distribution of storage sites in the Mantaro Valley may be used to study the Inca state's financial system in the area. Initially, storage can be described for three regional components: (*a*) the central core, within 1 km of the administrative center, Hatun Xauxa; (*b*) the peripheral core, between 1 km and 2 km from the center; and (*c*) the countryside, more than 3 km from the center.

Within the central core are five storage sites (J15–J18, J62) with an estimated total of 1069 individual storage units and 64,618 m³ of storage space (Table 12.1; Figure 12.1). This represents 53.1% of the total capacity described in the surveyed area. (Additional sites, south of our survey area, probably reduce the proportion within the central core to less than half the region's storage capacity.) The core storage facilities stand alone on the hillslopes directly above the administrative center and are not associated with other sites.

The largest of the storage complexes, J17, contains an estimated 479 structures (27,075 m³) in at least seven distinct lines that curve gently around a knoll. On the hill just north of J17 are the sites of J15–J16, which contain 452 storage units (28,629 m³) between them, also in multiple parallel lines. A few structures at both sites are displaced from the main lines and may not have served for storage (Earle *et al.* 1980:Figure 9). J17 contains 86.6% circular units, in contrast to the 67.5% rectangular storehouses found at J15–J16. Below these two groups are J18 (118 structures) and J62 (20 structures), both of which have only rectangular buildings.

Within the peripheral core (1–2 km from the center) are five storage sites (J12–J14, J19, J20) with an estimated 244 structures and a capacity of about 16,871 m³ (Table 12.1). J13 and J19 contain only rectangular buildings, while J14 and J20 have only circular structures; J13 has 51 rectangular and 9 circular storehouses. Only J14, with two parallel rows, has more than a single line of buildings (see Figure 12.2). These five sites are distinct from the core facilities not just in their smaller sizes and simpler layouts, but also in their proximity to contemporaneous local villages.

In the countryside, 18 storage sites (J10, J11, J21–J32, J34–J36, J57) collectively contain 639 structures with an estimated storage capacity of 40,284 m³. The largest three of these sites (J22–J24) contain 63 to 75 units, and all other sites have fewer than 50 units. Fifteen sites contain only a single line of structures, and 11 have only a single structural shape, either circular or rectangular (cf. Earle *et al.* 1980:Figure 8; D'Altroy 1981:Appendix I). These storage sites are scattered along the hills bordering the Mantaro Valley mainly south of

TABLE 12.1
Distribution of State Storage Facilities in the Upper Mantaro Valley

Distance from Hatun Xauxa	Sites	Number of structures	Volume	Cumulative total of structures	Cumulative total of volume
			m³	No./%	m³/%
0–1 km	J15	93	5,231		
	J16	359	23,398		
	J17	479	27,075		
	J18	118	7,164		
	J62	20	1,730		
		1069	64,618	1,069/54.8	64,618/53.1
1–2 km	J12	60	4,048		
	J13	35	2,758		
	J14	32	2,112		
	J19	99	7,269		
	J20	18	684		
		244	16,871	1,313/67.3	81,489/66.9
3–4 km	J23	66	5,610		
	J57	37	1,838		
		103	7,448	1,416/72.5	88,937/73.0
4–5 km	J21	39	3,272		
	J22	75	6,278		
		114	9,550	1,530/78.4	98,487/80.9
5–6 km	J10	29	1,760		
	J11	24	1,286		
	J28	21	901		
		74	3,947	1,604/82.2	102,434/84.1
6–7 km	J24	63	5,079	1,667/85.4	107,513/88.3
7–8 km	J25	23	1,286		
	J26	15	838		
	J27	43	3,616		
		81	5,740	1,748/89.5	113,253/93.0
8–9 km	J29	15	490		
	J30	8	313		
	J31	41	2,207		
		64	3,010	1,812/92.8	116,263/95.5
9–10 km	J34	17	689	1,829/93.7	116,952/96.0
10–11 km	J32	46	2,078	1,875/96.1	119,030/97.7
16–17 km	J35	39	1,517		
	J36	38	1,226		
		77	2,743	1,952/100.0	121,773/100.0

Hatun Xauxa. This pattern appears to continue south past our survey area where Browman (1970:Map 14) records the locations for an additional 23 storage sites. This extensive spread of storage facilities away from the administrative center is, as we discuss in the next section, linked mainly to the distribution of the local population.

This brief overview makes clear two important points. First, the Inca-related storage system in the Mantaro Valley was massive. In the study area, the storage volume approaches 122,000 m³, which is equivalent to almost 3,500,000 bu, primarily maize, potatoes, and quinoa. Second, the bulk of this storage volume is found closely attached to the main administrative center of Hatun Xauxa, but a large number of storage sites are found removed from the administrative center. We will now analyze the organization and function of storage in the Mantaro region by first examining the regional control and use of storage and then the mobilization and distribution of stored products.

THE REGIONAL USE AND CONTROL OF STORAGE

In this section, we investigate how the distinctive storage complexes in the Mantaro Valley were used and controlled. This functional and political issue is first addressed by studying the association of the storage sites with contemporaneous nonstorage sites. In this analysis, we assume that, other considerations held constant, a storage facility should be located near the place it is to be used in order to minimize costs of transportation and maintenance. We thus suggest the use and, more tenuously, the control of the storage units, based on the kinds of sites most closely associated with them. Then we address the more general issue of regional trends in storage as evidence of state-controlled activities, based on the assumption that most storage in special complexes was used either directly or indirectly for state corvée labor.

To evaluate the association of storage sites with nonstorage sites, we continue to use the three-component division outlined before. The basic information on these associations is presented in the regional map that shows the distribution of Late Horizon sites within the study region (Figure 12.1). Within the central core (less than 1 km from Hatun Xauxa), the five storage sites (J15–J18, J62) are all closer to the administrative center than to any other contemporaneous nonstorage site. The close association with the center and the combined massive size of these sites strongly suggest that they were used primarily to finance state activities performed at the center. Based on ethnohistorical evidence (especially Cieza de Leon 1862 [1553]:432), these activities included administration, military billeting, craft manufacture of fine textiles and precious metals, and perhaps government projects with labor being recruited from the hinterland.

Within the peripheral core (1–2 km from the center), the five storage sites (J12–J14, J19, J20) are all located within 200 m of contemporary local habitation sites (see Figure 12.2). These storage sites have greater capacities than those associated with local habitations in the countryside. We tentatively suggest that these local habitation sites close to the center were involved differentially in special state activities such as craft production or services for the center.

In the countryside (more than 3 km from the administrative center) are the 18 storage sites in our study area (J10, J11, J21–J32, J34–J36, J57) and the additional 23 storage sites farther south in the valley. The critical issue that must be resolved is the use and control of these extensive storage facilities. Specifically, we need to know the kinds of activities supported by the storage units and the degree of state control over them.

Perhaps most surprising is the lack of association of the storage sites with the special state sites located away from Hatun Xauxa. Several small sites, on the basis of high-density Inca ceramics and some Inca architecture, have been identified as special sites that were probably involved in local state administration and traffic control along the roads (D'Altroy 1981). Only one such site, which is apparently a ceremonial place (LeBlanc 1981), however, is close to a storage complex, and it must be assumed that goods used to support the other sites were stored within them or were received regularly from other state warehouses.

Most storage sites in the outlying areas are closer to local habitation sites than to other sites (Figure 12.1). Several storage sites are closely associated with Late Horizon settlements, although the storage components themselves are architecturally distinctive and are spatially demarcated from the local habitations. The clearest association occurs when a local village is paired with a separate storage site located within 100 m of it (see Figure 12.1:J10, J11, J20, J35). For example, J35 is a single line of 39 circular structures at the crest of a low ridge projecting into the Mantaro floodplain; a Late Horizon settlement covers the ridge immediately adjacent to the storage site. Many of the associations, however, are not as close. Along the western side of the Mantaro Valley, Late Horizon residential sites almost form a strip settlement on the lower slopes adjacent to the alluvial flatland. On the slopes and crest lines above these residential sites are scattered storage lines (Figure 12.1:J28–32, J57). Along the eastern side, extended lines of storage units (Figure 12.1:J21, J23–J27) "string out" down the valley. Directly in back of these lines on the rolling uplands are extensive scatters of local ceramics and rubble that indicate low-density local habitation.

The strong implication is that many of the storage units located in the countryside were used to support activities taking place in the local settlements. Murra (1956) has argued that the Inca state economy was based on a type of reciprocity, whereby individuals working for the state received staples

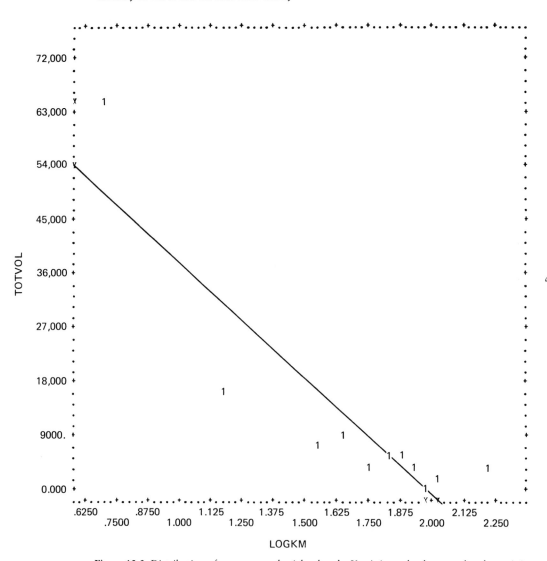

Figure 12.3. Distribution of state storage by 1-km bands. Y axis is total volume per band; x axis is the log of the distance from Hatun Xauxa in kilometers; (*a*) all bands; and (*b*) excluding the central core.

in compensation. The locally stored goods could therefore have been used to pay for state activities that might include work on state agricultural land, work on local projects such as road maintenance, and craft manufacture. We believe that the special storage complexes described in this chapter were used primarily for state finance rather than for strictly local activities. This conclusion is based on three points:

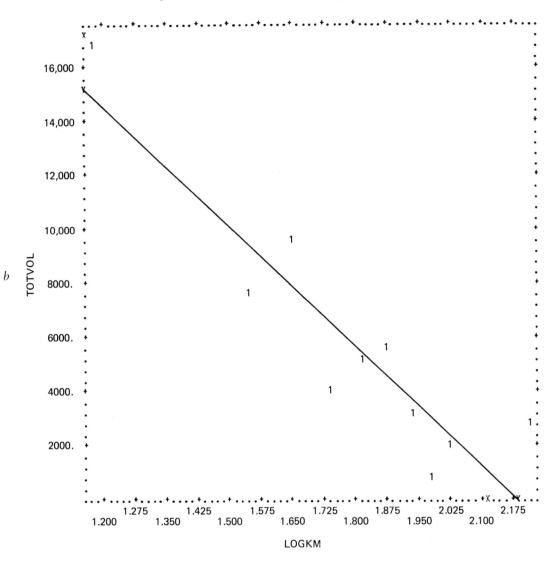

b

1. Distinct village-level storage was *not* found in pre-Inca sites and therefore was probably imposed by the state.
2. The storage complexes were all apparently constructed according to uniform canons of form and size (Earle *et al.* 1980; D'Altroy 1981).
3. As we now discuss, the storage mechanism was apparently not under direct community control.

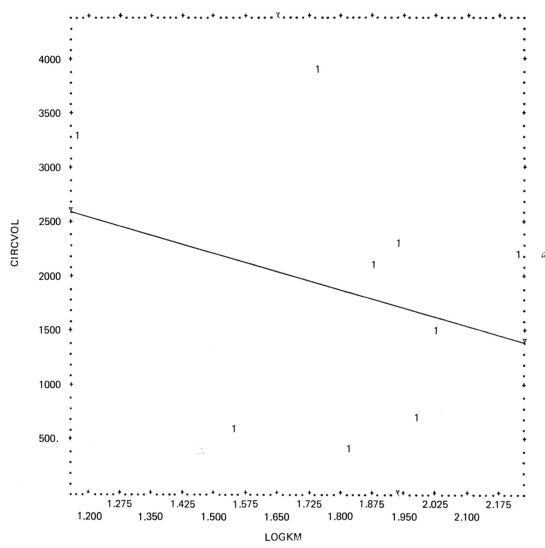

Figure 12.4. Distribution of state storage by 1 km bands, excluding the central core (*a*)

The lack of absolute control over the storage exercised by the local population is shown by the spatial segregation of the storage units from the local habitations. As seen in Figure 12.2, the storage areas form distinct zones not interspersed with habitation sites. The separate and highly visible location of the storage lines would have made it possible for state personnel to monitor the use of the storage units from a considerable distance.

In addition to the storage sites near local communities, several storage complexes (Figure 12.1:J22, J34, J36) appear to be isolated—not close to any

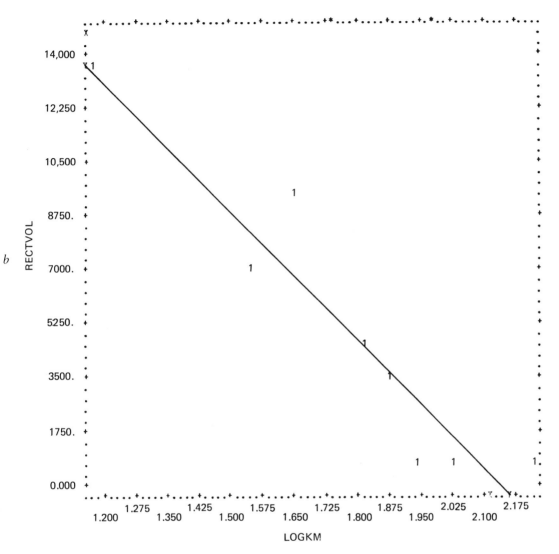

b

rectangular structures; (*b*) circular structures. Y axis and *x* axis are shown in Figure 12.3.

contemporaneous site. The most impressive of these is Site J22, located on a high rounded hill across the valley from Hatun Xauxa. The site consists of 75 rectangular storage units arranged as an ellipse around the summit (D'Altroy 1981). In the center on the hill's crest are an earth-and-rubble mound (18 m × 21 m, 2 m high) and a low rectangular arrangement of stones (23 m × 27 m). Without excavation, the function of this site remains in doubt. The unique arrangement, distinct central features, isolation, and imposing location indicate a distinctive use, however, and this site may have housed storage units for the state religion, which is said by some chroniclers to have been spatially segregated from state administrative storage facilities (cf. Polo de Ondegardo 1917 [1571]:59; Cobo 1956 [1653]:114).

We now turn our attention to a strong regional trend in the distribution of storage that supports several of the preliminary conclusions just made. The trend shows that with increasing distance from the administrative center of Hatun Xauxa, the volume of storage added for a 1-km-wide band decreases markedly (Table 12.1). This can be represented graphically in a number of ways. Figure 12.3a shows the volume of storage found in a 1 km band on the y axis and the log of distance from the center on the x axis. As might be expected from the high concentration in the central core, the correlation between volume and log distance is highly negative ($r = -.8875$) and significant ($p = .00327$). When storage in the central core is removed, the trend remains strong. Figure 12.3b shows the volume of storage in a band (excluding the 1-km band) on the y axis and the log of distance on the x axis. The correlation between volume and log distance remains highly negative ($r = -.9371$) and significant ($p = .00184$). Virtually all of the systematic decrease in storage volume outside the central core can be attributed to variability in the distribution of *rectangular* storehouses. Figure 12.4 shows how the volume of rectangular storehouses decreases sharply with the log of distance ($r = -.9639$; $p = .00047$). In contrast, the volume of circular storehouses shows no clear trend ($r = -.2218$; $p = .63264$).

What do these regional trends in storage volume mean? We must first make two assumptions: (*a*) The storage was used primarily to finance state activities. This seems reasonable based on our earlier discussions of storage use. (*b*) Population is uniformly distributed by 1-km bands. This can be supported preliminarily by site survey. Given these assumptions, the decrease in storage most probably reflects a decrease in state-related activities at greater distances from the center. As suggested in our discussion of the peripheral core, state-related activities may have been most commonly performed at the local settlements closest to the center. It should also be noted that some areas, such as the Yanamarca Valley to the northwest of Hatun Xauxa, had major local habitation, but no special storage facilities. Although further work is required on this important issue, the regional distribution of storage strongly suggests that parts of the region were differently integrated economically into the Inca system, and that these differences are partly a function of distance from the administrative center and of other political concerns.

THE MOBILIZATION AND DISTRIBUTION OF STORED GOODS

Another issue needing resolution is how goods were mobilized from the local communities and how they were distributed to storage locations. Three principal alternatives are the following:

1. In Case 1, goods deriving from community labor were divided into two parts, with one portion stored locally for community-level activities and the other sent to the central warehouses at Hatun Xauxa.
2. In Case 2, all goods mobilized from the region were sent first to the center where a portion was stored, and the remainder was allocated to the local communities.
3. In Case 3, apart from goods sent to support the center, stored goods were kept locally and were augmented with some critical goods, such as the religiously significant maize, which was distributed by the state more or less homogeneously throughout the region.

Case 1 is the simplest system of staple finance; Case 2 is more complex and could have served a commodity-exchange function; Case 3 is intermediary, being based primarily on simple staple finance, but also serving to distribute a limited range of key goods.

To evaluate which mechanism best fits the Inca state economy in the Mantaro Valley requires an analysis of the materials found in the storehouses and an assessment of their sources. Based on existing ethnographic evidence (C. Hastorf, personal communication; Mayer 1979), the considerable subregional variation in agricultural crops in the Mantaro Valley reflects differences in soil, rainfall, and temperature; this variation probably existed prehistorically. Given these conditions, contrasting patterns at the local settlements would be as follows for the three alternatives:

1. Case 1—Local storage should include local products, and local storage from subregion to subregion should contrast markedly according to local agricultural productivity.
2. Case 2—Local storage should include nonlocal products, and local storage within the region should be more homogeneous than in Case 1.
3. Case 3—Bulk goods at local storehouses should vary subregionally as in Case 1, but a discrete class of goods should be roughly homogeneous throughout the region.

At present, available evidence for storage contents is limited, but it is still suggestive of central planning. During 1979, six storage units were excavated in sites J16 and J17 within the central core above Hatun Xauxa, and macrobotanical remains were recovered systematically by water flotation. Based on preliminary analysis, plant remains were from locally grown crops—especially maize and quinoa. Historical documents that enumerate local *khipu* records (Espinoza 1971:Documents 1–3, analyzed in Murra 1975:243–254; LeVine 1979; Earle *et al.* 1980; D'Altroy 1981) list large quantities of local food staples (especially maize, potatoes, and quinoa); some craft products (blankets, sandals, and ceramics); and some special valuables (*cumbi* cloth and precious metals). With the exception of some metals, all goods were available within the valley.

While this evidence largely allows us to discount the possibility of interregional distribution associated with storage, it does not eliminate the possibility of local distributions of goods as suggested in Cases 2 and 3. To resolve this, we will need to sample storage units of local storage from different subregions in the valley.

The shapes of the individual storage units found at different sites provide one source of information on the economic differentiation and the organization of storage. Assuming that different forms—circular and rectangular—reflect differences in the kinds of goods stored (cf. Morris 1967), variations in regional storage can be assessed primarily by an analysis of structural composition. At the smaller storage sites characteristically associated with local habitation sites, the composition of structures varies from all "circulars" to all "rectangulars," with many storage sites containing both forms. This pattern suggests strong economic differentiation in storage that corresponds best with our expectations from Case 1 (local storage of local staples).

This local differentiation in storage appears clearly in the contrasting distribution of structural forms in the countryside on the eastern side of the valley and on the western side (Table 12.2). On the east side, the 418 storage units contain 118 circular and 300 rectangular buildings (ratio $C/R = .39$). On the west side, the 221 storage units contain 186 circular and 35 rectangular buildings (ratio $C/R = 5.31$). A chi-square testing for this difference is strongly significant with a $p < .001$. The most simple conclusion is that a contrast in agricultural production between east and west is mirrored in the local storage forms.

Case 1 also suggests that local surplus staple production should be divided between the local state storehouses and the central storehouses at Hatun Xauxa. This is the pattern documented ethnohistorically for Quito in Ecuador (Salomon 1978:241–242), and based on the evidence of the structural forms from the Xauxa region, this pattern appears to hold for the Mantaro Valley.

TABLE 12.2

Chi square test for the distribution of state storage by floor plan in the countryside (>3 km from Hatun Xauxa) of the Upper Mantaro Valley.

	Circular	Rectangular	Total
East	118	300	418
	(198.9)	(219.1)	
West	186	35	221
	(105.1)	(115.9)	
Total	304	335	639

$$\chi^2 = \Sigma \frac{f_o^2}{f_e} - N$$
$$\chi^2 = 820.5180 - 639 = 181.5180$$
$$df = 1$$
$$p < .001$$

Within the central core, there are 562 circular and 507 rectangular buildings; in the countryside, there are 304 circular and 335 rectangular buildings. The pattern within the central core roughly approximated the pattern in the countryside, suggesting the two-step mobilization discussed in Case 1.

More problematical is that the balance of circular and rectangular structures in the central core closely approximates the balance found in the remaining complexes on the west side of the valley. The ratio C/R within the central core is 1.11 (562/507), and the C/R ratio outside the core is identically 1.11 (245/220). Apart from coincidence, the most likely explanation for this similarity is that the core and west-side facilities were drawing their support from comparable environmental zones, as was suggested in Case 1. It is also possible that the system used to mobilize goods at the center was also applied to the west side of the valley, but not to the east side. At present, we remain unconvinced that this precise similarity is a deliberate function of state planning. Perhaps more important is that the storage in the central core is highly patterned. We tentatively suggest that this reflects the regional system of mobilization, with goods from each part of the valley stored in a specific sector of the core facilities. This question requires further field research.

DISCUSSION OF RESULTS

At this point, it is important to summarize what is known and what must be investigated further. Perhaps what is most obvious is that while a preponderance of the storage volume is concentrated above Hatun Xauxa within the central core, much of the storage is distributed throughout the countryside and is associated with local settlements.

The dispersal of storage facilities in the Mantaro countryside and the proposed dispersal of state activities contrast sharply with the pattern suggested for the Inca administrative center of Huánuco Pampa (Morris 1967). Huánuco Pampa, located on the main Inca road north of Hatun Xauxa, is in the high grassland zone where no dense local population existed. Virtually all of the storage in the Huánuco region is concentrated at the administrative center, with a few small complexes associated with smaller Inca sites and one local village. Morris (1974) has argued that some of the central storage was used to support local populations that came into the center on a temporary basis to perform corvée labor. In the Mantaro Valley, however, where a sizable local population was living close to the center, state production may have been more dispersed and required labor may have been performed in the local communities. This contrast between Huánuco and the Mantaro Valley illustrates the flexibility of Inca administration under different economic and political conditions.

This flexibility is also seen within the Mantaro Valley. The amount of storage decreases with distance from the administrative center, and we interpret this to mean that state financed activities were performed at local settlements, but that these activities were concentrated at settlements closer to the administrative center. At present, this interpretation is taken as a working hypothesis that must be tested with future research.

To test this hypothesis, we will need to evaluate the distribution of state-dominated or state-directed production. The best evidence for this may be the manufacture of the ceramics that duplicate Inca stylistic canons both in form and painted decoration. From our surface collections at Hatun Xauxa, we know that Inca-style ceramics were used extensively at the administrative center, but at present we have recovered no evidence for ceramic production there. In contrast, it appears that at least one local community was involved in the manufacture of Inca-style ceramics: Wasters in this style have been recovered from surface collections (Earle *et al.* 1980:30,42; D'Altroy 1981). Based on our working hypothesis, we would predict a falloff in the frequency of Inca-style wasters with increasing distance from the administrative center.

We also know that the composition of structural forms within the storage sites of the Mantaro Valley is patterned regionally, and we believe that this patterning reflects the way surplus was mobilized. We suggest that a portion of the local staples was stored near local settlements for support of state-required activities, and that a portion of the staples was removed to the core storage facilities for support of the center. To test this hypothesis, we will want to excavate a sample of storehouses in the countryside and in the central core to recover botanical and ceramic materials that may be sourced to particular locales within the valley. For the botanical remains that include both cereals and tubers, we will compare the percentages of recovered materials with the percentages predicted from the agricultural possibilities within the settlement sites' catchment areas. For the ceramic remains, we will compare style, temper, and paste data from storage units with comparable material recovered from local settlements.

In this chapter, we have argued that redistribution is a system of finance, and that such financial institutions can often be studied effectively by a systematic analysis of their associated storage facilities. For the Mantaro Valley, the study of the regional distribution of storage facilities has helped us to understand the organization of state finance and has focused our attention on differences in economic integration within the Inca empire. Equally important, the regional study of storage facilities has helped to develop specific hypotheses on state administration that can be tested with future research.

ACKNOWLEDGMENTS

We wish to thank James Hill and Jonathon Ericson, who read an earlier version of this chapter and offered helpful suggestions. We also wish to thank the Friends of Archaeology and Academic Senate at the University of California at Los Angeles, who helped support the fieldwork for this study. Figure 12.1 was drafted by Eliza Earle, for which we are most grateful.

REFERENCES

Browman, D. L.
  1970   Early Peruvian peasants: the culture history of a central highlands valley. Unpublished
         Ph.D. dissertation, Department of Antrhopology, Harvard University.
Brush, S. B.
  1976   Man's use of an Andean ecosystem. *Human Ecology* 4:147–166.
Cieza de Leon, P. de
  1862   [1551] La crónica del Perú. Historiadores primitivos de Indias. *Biblioteca de Autores
         Españoles* 26.
Cobo, P. B.
  1956   [1653] *Historia del neuvo mundo,* II Biblioteca de Autores Españoles 92.
Dalton, G.
  1975   Karl Polanyi's analysis of long-distance trade and his wider paradigm. In *Ancient civi-
         lization and trade,* edited by J. Sabloff and C. C. Lamberg-Karlovsky, pp. 63–132.
         Albuquerque: University of New Mexico Press.
D'Altroy, T. N.
  1981   Empire growth and consolidation: the Xauxa region of Peru under the Incas. Un-
         published Ph.D. dissertation, Department of Anthropology, University of California.
         Ann Arbor: University Microfilms.
DiPeso, C. C.
  1975   *Fallen trading center of the grand Chichimeca,* Vols. 1–8. Flagstaff: Northland Press.
Earle, T. K.
  1977   A reappraisal of redistribution: complex Hawaiian chiefdoms. In *Exchange systems in
         prehistory,* edited by T. Earle and J. Ericson, pp. 213–229. New York: Academic Press.
  1978   Economic and social organization of a complex chiefdom: the Halelea district, Kaua'i,
         Hawaii. *University of Michigan Museum of Anthropology, Anthropological Paper* 63.
Earle, T. K., T. N. D'Altroy, C. J. LeBlanc, C. A. Hastorf, and T. Y. LeVine
  1980   Changing settlement patterns in the Upper Mantaro Valley, Peru. *Journal of New World
         Archaeology* 4(1):1–49.
Espinoza S., W.
  1971   Los Huancas, aliados de la conquista. Tres informaciones inéditas sobre la participación
         indígena en la conquista del Perú, 1558, 1560, 1561. *Anales Científicos* 1:3–407. Huan-
         cayo, Perú: Universidad Nacional del Centro del Perú.
Hodder, I., and C. Orton
  1976   *Spatial archaeology.* Cambridge: Cambridge University Press.
LeBlanc, C. J.
  1981   Late prehistoric Huanca settlement patterns in the Yanamarca valley, Peru. Unpublished
         Ph.D. dissertation, Department of Anthropology, University of California, Los Angeles.
         Ann Arbor: University Microfilm.
LeVine, T. Y.
  1979   Prehistoric political and economic change in highland Peru: an ethnohistorical study of
         the Mantaro Valley. Unpublished M.A. thesis, Archaeology Program, University of
         California, Los Angeles.
Mayer, E.
  1979   *Land use in the Andes: ecology and agriculture in the Mantaro Valley of Peru with
         special reference to potatoes.* Lima: Centro Internacional de la Papa.
Matos M., R., and J. R. Parsons
  1979   Poblamiento prehispánico en la cuenca del Mantaro. In *Arqueología peruana,* edited by
         R. Matos M., pp. 157–171. Lima: San Marcos.
Millon, R.
  1964   The Teotihuacan mapping project. *American Antiquity* 29:345–352.

Morris, E. C.
   1967   Storage in Tawantinsuyu. Unpublished Ph.D. dissertation, Department of Anthropology, University of Chicago.
   1974   Reconstructing patterns of non-agricultural production in the Inca economy. In *Reconstructing complex society,* edited by C. M. Moore. *Supplement to the Bulletin of the American Schools of Oriental Research* **20**:49–68.

Murra, J.
   1956   The economic organization of the Inca state. Unpublished Ph.D. dissertation, Department of Anthropology, University of Chicago.
   1975   *Formaciones económicas y políticas del mundo andino.* Lima: Instituto de Estudios Peruanos.

Parsons, J. R., and R. Matos M.
   1978   Asentamientos pre-hispánicos en el Mantaro, Perú: informe preliminar. In *El hombre y la cultura andina: III Congreso Peruano,* edited by R. Matos M., pp. 539–555. Lima: San Marcos.

Pires-Ferreira, J. W., and K. V. Flannery
   1976   Ethnographic models for Formative exchange. In *The early Mesoamerican village,* edited by K. V. Flannery, pp. 286–292. New York: Academic Press.

Polanyi, K.
   1957   The economy as instituted process. In *Trade and market in the early empires,* edited by K. Polanyi, C. Arensberg, and H. Pearson, pp. 243–270. Glencoe: Free Press.
   1968   *Primitive, archaic and modern economies: essays of Karl Polanyi,* edited by G. Dalton. Garden City, N.Y.: Doubleday.

Polo de Ondegardo, J.
   1917   [1571] *Fundamentos acerca del notable daño que resulta de no guardar a los Indios sus Fueros,* edited by H. Urteaga. Lima: Sanmartí.

Renfrew, C.
   1975   Trade as action at a distance: questions of integration and communication. In *Ancient civilization and trade,* edited by J. Sabloff and C. C. Lamberg-Karlovsky, pp. 3–59. Albuquerque: University of New Mexico Press.

Sabloff, J., and D. Freidel
   1975   A model of a pre-Columbian trading center. In *Ancient civilization and trade,* edited by J. Sabloff and C. C. Lamberg-Karlovsky, pp. 369–408. Albuquerque: University of New Mexico Press.

Sahlins, M.
   1965   On the sociology of primitive exchange. In *The relevance of models for social anthropology,* edited by M. Blanton, pp. 139–236. London: Tavistock.

Salomon, F. L.
   1978   *Ethnic lords of Quito in the age of the Incas.* Unpublished Ph.D. dissertation, Department of Anthropology, Cornell University. Ann Arbor: University Microfilms.

Sancho de la Hoz, P.
   1917   [1532–1533] Relación. In *Colección de libros y documentos referentes a la historia del Perú,* Vol. 5, edited by H. Urteaga, pp. 122–202. Lima: Sanmartí.

Service, E.
   1962   *Primitive social organization.* New York: Random House.

Tourtellot, G., and J. Sabloff
   1972   Exchange systems among the ancient Maya. *American Antiquity* **37**:126–134.

Vitelli, G.
   1980   Grain storage and urban growth in imperial Ostia: a quantitative study. *World Archaeology* **12**:54–68.

13

The Inca as a Nonmarket Economy: Supply on Command versus Supply and Demand

Darrell E. La Lone

Ever since Adam—Adam Smith, that is—we have only with some difficulty been able to separate the concepts of *economy* and *market*. Even when Karl Polanyi and his colleagues argued that to understand ancient and non-Western economies we must separate these concepts, their book carried the seemingly ironic title *Trade and Market in the Early Empires* (Polanyi, Arensberg, and Pearson 1957). As they argue, however, it is precisely this unreflective association of "economy," "trade," *and* "market" that may lead us to misinterpret ancient economies by applying concepts appropriate to modern market economies.

My concern in this chapter is to explore this problem in the context of the Inca empire. Specifically, I believe that the study of the Inca economy is not the study of a market economy. This is not to deny that Spanish colonial sources on the Inca empire do occasionally mention markets. However, when documents use the familiar terms *market* or *marketplace*, we cannot assume that what is called a "market" was in fact a market gathering. This chapter will present a close examination of a number of specific cases to illustrate the importance of careful source evaluation. I believe the evidence shows regional variation within the Inca empire, to the extent that we can see clear references to marketplaces on the periphery of the empire, but an almost complete absence of references for the core.

Documenting this pattern is a relatively specific problem. Explaining why regional variation occurs and how the Inca economy was organized as a nonmarket economy is a much larger issue. Given the limitations of space, this larger issue cannot be documented in the same detail as the narrow problem of rejecting the market hypothesis. However, I shall begin with the larger question, so that we may have some idea of what the forest looks like before we get lost among the trees. I shall then return to the specific problem of evaluating the evidence on markets. Finally, I shall suggest ways in which ethnohistorians and archaeologists may collaborate in the study of exchange systems in the Inca empire.

INCA ECONOMY: A NONMARKET MODEL

In a long historical debate on how best to characterize the Inca economy, scholars have termed it *feudal, slave, socialist* (here one may choose between socialist paradise or socialist tyranny); a system based on reciprocity and redistribution; a system with markets and commerce; or an Asiatic mode of production. These diverse characterizations, however passionately argued, share common ground. They follow what I might humbly propose as "La Lone's law": The sharpness of debate is inversely proportional to the sharpness of evidence. Specifically, many of the large issues in the debate over Inca economy and polity are obscured by the scarcity of appropriate historical data. It has been only in relatively recent years that we have begun to uncover the historical documentation that allows us to proceed from polemic toward consensus.

Without intent to slight others, I believe it is appropriate to credit John Murra for much of the direction in Andean ethnohistory. For example, in his landmark dissertation, now 25 years old, Murra argues that portrayals of the Inca realm as a welfare state were based on a misunderstanding: The Inca state was improperly credited for welfare services that were in fact the responsibility of local communities (Murra 1956:223). Whether one agrees with this simple observation is relatively unimportant in comparison to its great importance in directing our attention to the intellectual "fault line" in Andean ethnohistory and archaeology. As he (Murra 1978:926) recently phrased the issue: "Perspectives change according to whether one focuses attention from above (organization of the state) or from below (the ethnic groups and former political units)."

Without this perspective, we would be like the proverbial blind men: Some describe the llama after feeling only its head, while others give a quite different view from the other end. Research, especially in the past two decades, has begun to give us a more accurate view, and this now gives us opportunity to draw a far more plausible picture of the whole llama. In a sense, we are only just beginning to overcome the deeply rooted habits of the early Spanish chroniclers who persistently called llamas *sheep*. Just as llamas are not sheep, Andean social systems are not "just like" our familiar European models.

Our view has changed as Andean research has turned from broad generalizations toward studies of regional variation within Tawantinsuyu (the Inca empire), and how the state responded to this variation. Such studies explore the relations between state and community by asking what we mean by *community* in different Andean regions. How did Andean communities recognize, organize, and allocate resources? How were communities organized within the regional polities known as *etnías?* What were the forms of economic and political stratification in different *etnías?* What were the relationships between the various *etnías* and the Inca administration?

Our view has changed as we recognize that "Tawantinsuyu is much more a complicated and extensive network of relations than the apparently monolithic and flashy apparatus of power that the chroniclers portrayed in the sixteenth century" (Pease 1979:116). These new perspectives result, in part, from a broader use of historical documentation. We have turned from excessive reliance on the traditional historical sources of the sixteenth century, commonly called *crónicas,* toward greater use of documents that open insights into structure and process at regional and local levels. Documents allowing us the "view from below" illustrate the two-tiered structure of this network of relationships between the state and regional units.

Local Nonmarket Economy

Murra's interpretation of documents providing a regional perspective on Chucuito and Huanuco led him to argue that Andean communities have, since pre-Inca times, sought autonomy through control over a maximum number of "vertical ecological floors" (Murra 1972:429). Communities able to exercise direct control over a full gamut of environmental zones would not be subject to the risks of having to trade for basic resources. When communities required goods from more distant regions, "regional differences in production were, by preference, handled by means of colonization instead of through barter or trade" [Murra 1965:201]. The vertical ecology model has been extremely influential in Andean ethnohistory and ethnography. However, I think it should not be seen as a special case, since the important issue is not the "verticality" or "horizontality" of environmental zones, but rather the *diversity* of environmental zones. When we examine other environmentally diverse regions, we find parallels with the Andean case. For example, in Hawaii "even in the case where environmental diversity selected for economic specialization, the definition of the community territory and the internal organization of the community permitted a self-sufficient (generalized) community economy" [Earle 1977:223].

We find generalized community economies both in Hawaii and in the Andes in which community self-sufficiency is maintained through direct control over a variety of environmental zones, and through reciprocal exchanges within the community. Through these strategies communities may guarantee access to necessary staple goods without necessity for market exchange.

State Nonmarket Economy

Although Murra once suggested that "the major commodity exchange role was assigned to the state" (1956:229), one point on which Andeanists—including Murra—have achieved consensus is that the Inca state was not in the commodity-movement business. Craig Morris, taking the "view from above," studied the state storage system and concluded that

> There appear to have been no massive movements out to the villages, giving the villages access to goods that were not locally available. There is also little evidence for inter-regional transfers between one major storage center and another (Morris 1967:174).

More recently, María Rostworowski summarized her study of documents giving the "view from below" by concluding that "the state redistributive organization never reached the level of the commoner, who remained under the authority and obligation of his local lord" (Rostworowski 1977:265).

In short, the state economy did not function as a vast market system, regulating discrepancies in supply and demand. The major role of the state economy was to mobilize labor to finance state operations. Key state operations included support of the elite population and retainers, support of military and political organizations, and capital investment in such projects as agricultural intensification and the construction and maintenance of roads, administrative centers, and storehouses (Earle 1977:226 shows parallels in Hawaii). Given these goals, market exchange is irrelevant to the operation of the state economy. To understand how and why the state economy worked, we must explore *mobilization* (cf. Earle and D'Altroy, Chapter 12).

MOBILIZATION: THE RULE OF SUPPLY ON COMMAND

The drama of Inca civilization is underscored when we consider how rapidly one of the ancient world's largest empires rose and fell. Its time scale is not the millennia of Egypt or even the centuries of the Classic Maya. According to John Rowe's absolute chronology, the Inca state was, despite its spatial vastness, only a flicker in time. It is conceivable that a few residents of Cuzco—born before the Inca expanded beyond the valley—may have lived through the rise of the Inca empire, and may have continued to live after the Spanish Conquest not even a century later.

To be sure, the Inca state was built from ancient materials. Our problem is not simply to recognize the ancient components of the Inca state, but also to understand the qualitative and quantitative innovations in its scale of organization. The revolutionary transformation from a small polity to a vast empire was not the result of technological change or dramatic changes in the material base, but was rather the outcome of organizational changes.

This is not a retreat from cultural materialism, but rather a recognition that technology and organization are inextricably bound together as productive forces. Lewis Mumford's eloquent statement of this point is as appropriate for the Inca as it is for Egypt:

> For the earliest complex power machines were composed, not of wood or metal, but of perishable human parts, each having a specialized function in a larger mechanism under centralized human control. The vast army of priests, scientists, engineers, architects, foremen, and day laborers, some hundred thousand strong, who built the Great Pyramid, formed the first complex machine, invented when technology itself had produced only a few simple "machines" like the inclined plane and the sled, and had not yet invented wheeled vehicles [Mumford 1961:60].

This was precisely the same machinery that built the monumental stone structures of the Inca. The Inca state was a machine—a machine with an unparalleled capacity to mobilize and organize human labor. In the Inca realm, the position of elites in the stratification system was measured neither in gold nor land, but in capacity to mobilize labor. Carried to the logical extreme, as it sometimes appears to have been, a labor-mobilization system may appear to Western eyes like a scene from *Alice in Wonderland* when it solves the problem of allocation by moving people rather than goods.

Labor mobilization did not originate with the Inca. The Inca state was only the last of a succession of stratified societies and states dating back at least to Huari times. Apart from states encompassing vast areas of the Andes, we also find hundreds of the smaller polities known as *etnías*. The rulers of these polities faced, albeit on a smaller scale, problems similar to those of the Inca state. The relative success of these political leaders would be measured by their capacity to control a full gamut of Andean environmental zones. According to Murra, Andean societies "preferred" to handle regional differences in production through direct control or through colonization rather than through trade. I would stress, however, that the critical issue is not *preference,* but *control.* The autonomy of political elites is a function of their ability to control and command. To the extent that political elites are able to control and command resources, they are less dependent on the vagaries of trade.

Furthermore, as I have argued above, the most important resource to control was human labor itself. A ruler's strength is measured by his capacity to mobilize labor, and as we know, in Inca times political officials were ranked according to the number of households they were responsible for. We know also that the Inca measured the strength of enemies and allies in similar terms. For example, at Cajamarca the native lord who appeared to be second in splendor only to the Sapa Inca himself was the lord of Chincha. When Pizarro asked why this lord was so important, he was told that it was because the lord of Chincha was a friend of the Inca, and he had 100,000 seagoing rafts. The number of 100,000 cannot be taken literally in early Spanish accounts, but we can be certain that the Inca was impressed with the great force the lord of Chincha could mobilize.

As we explore Andean regional variation, we find that the pre-Inca *etnías* range from powerful polities like Chincha or the Lupaca to relatively small and weak local ones. We should not be surprised to find that leaders differed in power, that some were subordinated to others, and that some were paramount over many subordinates. However, our knowledge of this stratification has been obscured by the Spanish chroniclers' insistence on applying the terms *cacique* or *curaca* indiscriminately to native leaders from the level of minor local lords all the way up to the Sapa Inca. But now, by using once overlooked documents such as wills, lawsuits, claims to privileges, and even early Quechua dictionaries, scholars are able to look more closely into regional and local hierarchies. A theme that emerges repeatedly in studies of Andean stratification is the role of the political elites in resource control.

Of course, resource control and political control cannot be separated. An understanding of resource control leads us to the larger question of political philosophy: How do leaders gain and maintain control over their people? According to one influential viewpoint on this question, the key to success is for leaders to keep their followers from escaping (Carneiro 1970). Another persuasive argument is that followers follow leaders because of the benefits everyone gains from political leadership (Service 1975). Andean civilizations, however, exemplify strategies that show that we need not fabricate a false dichotomy between tyranny and welfare.

One of the enduring strategies in Andean civilization is, as Murra has demonstrated over the past two decades, the fundamental importance of reciprocity and redistribution in Andean economic organization. There is, of course, something more to reciprocity and redistribution than their "economic" functions in moving goods. In hierarchically organized societies, *ideologies* of reciprocity and redistribution are particularly useful political tools. As ideology, they permit political elites to make what appears—in material terms—to be extremely asymmetrical exchanges with subordinates, and to portray such exchanges as *generosity*. A laborer whose years of toil are rewarded by dinner at a king's table may well feel honored, but a bowl of soup and a dollop of honor cost the king little. On the other hand, the systemic advantages of centralization and specialization may allow king and commoner alike to share real benefits. In any event, there is great advantage to leaders who are able to portray their resource-control strategies as *reciprocity, redistribution,* and *generosity*. Noncentralized resource-control strategies are, by definition, not "control" strategies. Specifically, market exchange is much less amenable to elites' attempts at control, so that it allows less opportunity for leaders either to demonstrate or to proclaim their usefulness.

Another critical achievement, with crucial evolutionary implications, is the ability of Andean societies to increase productive output and to protect their populations from potentially disastrous environmental fluctuations. This is an achievement we find in other complex societies such as ancient Polynesia where "the chiefs who could promote production through terrace irrigation were the most successful" (Goldman 1970:486). Agricultural intensification, control over a diversity of environmental zones, and storage are all techniques found in Andean polities that both increase production and provide protection from disastrous environmental fluctuations. These techniques then permit polities to support much higher populations than would otherwise be possible.

Population expansion in the Andes, as elsewhere, is correlated with territorial expansion and with warfare. We should not, however, assume that the cause behind these correlations is population pressure. In fact, we may find that it is the weaker polities that seek more land because they have too many people, while the stronger polities seek more territory to increase the population available for labor mobilization. Irving Goldman comments that in Polynesia it was poor chiefs whose "ambitions were fierce but small" who sought more land, while for rich chiefs "it was not territory alone they set out to seize but jurisdiction" (1970:489). Warfare, especially conquest warfare, is not a simple response to population expansion, but rather a form of "capital investment." In Hawaii, for example, we find that

> Agricultural intensification, through the expansion of irrigation, was therefore an outcome of political competition and *not* of population pressure. In fact, agricultural intensification was a strategy to increase local population as a means to increase surplus production. . . . Warfare should consequently be viewed as a form of capital investment. Warfare is never a spontaneous action, but requires both planning and finance [Earle 1978:183–184].

The rapid expansion of the Inca state becomes comprehensible when we recognize it as precisely this form of "capital investment." The lords of Cuzco may well have begun as "poor chiefs" with fierce but small ambitions. But their early military victory and consolidation of power in the Valley of Cuzco provided the foundation for them to "enter the game of reciprocity" in which the gains of conquest were given to reward loyal allies and followers (Rostworowski 1978:92). Leaders of subject populations also could be co-opted by sharing with them the gains of more distant conquests. Soon the lords of Cuzco had larger, if not fiercer, ambitions. They "sought perhaps not domination over lands and men in general, but rather over organized systems of resource production" (Pease 1972:42; cf. Llagostera 1976).

The captured labor was capital in the sense that it could be reinvested to promote further gains. Vast amounts of labor were invested in constructing the Inca administrative centers and roads, which in turn served as bases for further expansion of the state. Apart from their value in furthering military gains, the administrative centers were foci for production and storage in the state redistribution system. The large number of storehouses at Huanuco Pampa, the even larger number of storehouses in the Mantaro Valley, and the 2400 storehouses at Cotapachi (in the department of Cochabamba, Bolivia) indicate the unprecedented expansion in production that resulted from state mobilization (see Earle and D'Altroy, Chapter 12).

Archaeological exploration of the state storage system is of utmost urgency for our understanding of how the central economy worked. Expansion of storage implies that agricultural production in the rural hinterland also increased. This, of course, is not a new revelation, since we know the Inca state promoted intensive cultivation of maize (Murra 1973; Earls 1976). In its centers the state controlled not only stockpiles of maize, but also concentrated production of cloth, pottery, and *chicha* (Morris 1972). According to Cieza de León, 30,000 people "served" the administrative center at Huanuco Pampa alone. The state storage system was critical to the state's ability to absorb and use the greatly increased output of such massive labor mobilization.

Labor mobilization on such a grand scale has important implications not only for production but also for distribution. Labor mobilization was an alternative to commercial exchange as a means of responding to supply fluctuations. If population exceeded agricultural productivity in a region, the tradition of labor mobilization made it perhaps more logical to move people than to move goods, since the "excess" labor might then be employed more productively elsewhere. More temporary fluctuations might have been handled by calling on storehouses as state "generosity" or by increasing labor drafts during which workers were fed from state storehouses.

Although responsive to central direction, such a production system could be equally responsive to local conditions. Thus, the Inca case shows that a non-market economy need not be a centrally planned "socialist" economy. Even under the best of conditions, centrally planned economies are inefficient in their response to local or regional perturbations—or, to put it in more familiar terms, supply-and-demand forces. In the Andes, where environmental diversity is kaleidoscopic, rigid central planning of production and distribution would seem out of the question. The genius of the Inca "central economy," however, was its ability to impose order without sacrificing the flexibility required to respond to local conditions.

This flexibility, as I have argued previously, was based on a network of relationships within a two-tiered structure. At the level of local regions, we find communities that seek relative autonomy through direct control of multiple environmental zones. This generalized local economy responds to local environmental conditions in an effort to meet the staple needs of the population. These goals could be met through intracommunity networks providing security of supply without markets and the accompanying risks of trade.

The Inca state found models for sociopolitical control in these traditional systems of resource control, so that

> Regions of interest for the state economy were incorporated when they already existed as organized environments, and if a newly-incorporated region lacked an organized ecology . . . the Incas reorganized the local system according to central Andean precepts" [Llagostera 1976:45].

The state, then, was concerned with organization and mobilization. The functions served by market exchange in other societies were not within the sphere of the state economy, and they were served through nonmarket organization in the local economy.

REJECTING THE MARKET HYPOTHESIS

Previously, I have argued the importance of the Inca for furthering our understanding of how state societies may function without a market economy. My intention is not in so short a space to document and demonstrate conclusively what the Inca economy *was* but rather to offer suggestions on how it could have worked as a nonmarket economy. I have offered these suggestions first, so that I may now proceed to the task of refuting the alternative hypothesis by showing what the Inca economy was *not*. I am, of course, aware that references to marketplaces occur in the documents on Inca history and that a number of scholars have found them convincing enough to lead them to the conclusion that the Inca economy had a substantial market component. (Hartmann [1968, 1971] is the strongest advocate of this position). In the remainder of this chapter I shall attempt to show why careful analysis of the relevant documents leads me to conclude that the market-economy hypothesis cannot be sustained for the core of the empire.

European Preconceptions

In 1562, the officials charged with conducting a *visita* to Huanuco were ordered to report on

> que géneros de personas eran los que pagaban los tales tributos si eran solos los labradores que llaman ellos machiguales y si tambien pagaban en ellos mercaderes o de otra manera de gente y si había exentos o hidalgos y que manera de gente era . . . [Ortiz de Zúñiga 1967 [1562]:17].

> [what kind of people they were who paid tribute, if they were only the workers that they call *macehuales* and if *merchants* or other sorts of people also paid and if there were those who were exempt or nobles and what kind of people they were (emphasis mine)].

Although the instruction seems an honest enough attempt to discover "what kind of people they were," it is a less than ideal instrument for eliciting native categories. The Spanish investigators came equipped with preconceptions and leading questions. Brought up themselves in a market economy and having seen markets in Mexico, they seem to have expected that commerce was part of the natural order of things. They expected to find not only *mercaderes* but also nobles, and they expected commoners who would call themselves by the Nahuatl term *macehual*. They also expected to find marketplaces, and when the inspectors asked about merchants and marketplaces in Huanuco, even local native leaders regularly are reported to have employed the Nahuatl term *tianguez* for marketplace (Ortiz de Zúñiga 1972 [1562]:29, 36, 58).

If the Spaniards had observed marketplaces, they would have been likely to take them for granted, unless they were extraordinary or at least offered goods Europeans were especially interested in. If the Spaniards did not observe marketplaces, they would have been unlikely to report anything unusual, since they would have assumed that they simply made their observations on the wrong day, or perhaps in the wrong decade. Surely there "used" to be markets! The result in either case should be a paucity of early references to marketplaces. As I have demonstrated elsewhere (La Lone 1978; La Lone and La Lone 1979), we do have very few references to marketplaces that we can be reasonably confident were pre-Hispanic. This then puts us in the awkward position of having to deal with largely negative evidence. Later I shall suggest a solution to the problem of negative evidence on Andean market exchange. First, however, I shall attempt to make sure that we are not as confused as were the Spaniards in our search for the role of market exchange in ancient economies.

What Do We Mean by "Market"?

We can avoid much confusion by making it clear from the outset that *marketplace* and *market economy* are not synonymous. My argument that the Inca economy was a nonmarket economy does not imply that exchange, including some degree of marketplace exchange, was entirely absent. We must distinguish between *market* and *marketplace*. In economics a market is not a place, but a situation in which a good is supplied by some ("sellers"), demanded by others ("buyers"), and the value ("price") of that good is determined by the decisions of all the buyers and sellers. When we speak of the market for downtown real estate, the market for pork bellies, or the market for archaeology books, we are not talking about a supermarket. When supply-and-demand crowds actually meet and mingle, we have a marketplace. Just as we have markets in which the supply-and-demand crowds do not actually meet, we can also have marketplaces in which market forces are peripheral. Furthermore, the existence of marketplaces does not imply the existence of a market system or a commercial economy. Market systems entail the linking of marketplaces in such a way that a rise in the price offered for a good in one marketplace will attract greater supplies of that good from other market communities, or a decline in price demanded for a good will attract more buyers of that product. A commercial economy is one in which people depend on the market for their livelihood. In a commercial economy we find that market prices affect production decisions, and for some people, production *is* the market: Their livelihood comes from full-time trade.

Traders play a critical role in marketplace systems. As long as traders do not move goods between marketplaces, the impact of exchanges remains purely local and might be characterized simply as multiple instances of reciprocity. A market system integrates an economy only to the extent that goods flow between marketplaces in accordance with the forces of supply and demand. When supply and demand are brought into equilibrium by the market principle—what Adam Smith called "the invisible hand"—we are dealing with an economy very different from one that is regulated by the heavier hands of state officials.

For this reason, the search for references to markets should not be limited to an effort to find key words like *mercado, tianguez,* or *catu* (a Quechua term for marketplace). We should look also for references to traders, especially for references to full-time traders. The key point in our method, though, is skepticism—it is not enough simply to collect references that include the magic words *market* or *trader*. As Philip Grierson argues in his discussion of European commerce in the Dark Ages:

> The whole approach, that of accumulating evidence for the existence of trade instead of trying to form an overall picture of how and to what extent material goods changed ownership, is in itself profoundly misleading and can only result in conclusions that are far from the truth [Grierson 1974:75].

Our success in forming such an overall picture depends, of course, on the quality of the documentation at our disposal. However, it depends even more on the way in which we treat the documents—there is no substitute for careful source evaluation. Anthropologists and archaeologists may feel intimidated by the extremely detailed textual criticism typical in the work of historians and bibliographers. We do not, however, need to duplicate these bibliographic efforts if we show the good sense to use the bibliographic aids our historian and bibliographer colleagues produce. In any event, the admitted difficulty of source criticism is no excuse, and much of what I am urging upon colleagues not trained in history is little more than insistence that they give as much care to historical sources as they would to the data in their own specialty. By way of example, I shall illustrate the point by examining several cases of source evaluation in the study of Andean marketplaces.

"From Tiny Maize Kernels Mighty Markets Grow"

One scholar who argues that marketplaces were held in all communities of ancient Peru finds support for this argument in the important sixteenth-century historian—Fernández de Oviedo. Oviedo's *Natural History of the Indies* is generally excellent, but he never visited Peru, and he based his account on interviews with those who had been there. The key passage our colleague takes from Oviedo is a general summary of an interview Oviedo conducted in Santo Domingo with Diego de Molina, who had been with Pizarro at Cajamarca. In this report, trade is mentioned in a single line, which comments simply that "they have plazas in which they hold their *tianguez* or market every day" (Oviedo 1959 [1549]:93). Unfortunately, the passage in question makes no further specification of who or even where "they" were. Such vagueness is not unusual. Another passage cited in support of the argument that marketplaces were widespread in the Andes is taken from José de Acosta (1954 [1590]:91). Although it does mention "huge and frequent markets," it does not refer specifically to the *Andes,* but rather vaguely to the Spanish *Indies.*

Oviedo's reference to an Andean *tianguez* is perhaps our earliest "report" on an Andean marketplace. The passage is not only vague, but apparently little more than an afterthought, since it is given no more emphasis than a following line that comments on the good quality of "their" carrots. I think it is trivial as evidence for the importance or generality of marketplace trade, quite apart from the larger issue of commerce. The passage from Acosta gives the impression of being more informative because it mentions markets, barter, and media of exchange other than money. For example, it tells us that in Peru *coca* served as a medium of exchange. Before we get overly enthusiastic about it, however, we should remember that the passage is a generalization about the Spanish Indies, and in fact, only the line about *coca* refers specifically to Peru.

By compiling strings of citations to such passages, it is possible to create the impression that we have an abundance of references about markets and trade. Nonetheless, what such passages lack in quality cannot be compensated for by quantity. If Acosta's reference counts as one citation, can we strengthen the case by counting a strikingly similar passage in Herrera (1952 [1601–1615]:249) as a second? I am not satisfied that we can, especially since comparison between the passages shows that Herrera either "borrowed" from Acosta, or that both took their passages from a common source I have not yet identified. Such borrowings were typical in the early sources, and even uncredited use of another's work was taken as a demonstration of erudition. Even the most casual effort to use the work of Andean bibliographers will help us to be aware of these correspondences between sources.

In short, it is not enough to accumulate strings of citations to passages without providing contexts for evaluation. It is incumbent upon the user of historical documents to demonstrate the relevance of the documents to the argument (La Lone and La Lone [1979] use the more satisfactory method of appending the relevant passages in full at the end of the paper.) If we hope to demonstrate that trade and markets were important in the Inca economy, we must look for something more than the mere appearance of the magic words we seek.

Ideally, we hope to find passages that meet two essential criteria (I am assuming that sources have first been checked for authenticity):

1. The passage must offer not merely the word *marketplace* or *trader,* but sufficient description to allow us to judge whether what was described was likely to have been exchange in a definite location.

2. The passage must give us some basis for judging whether the context is clearly pre-Hispanic.

One passage that does include mention of a marketplace (*mercado*) allows us to illustrate the importance of these criteria in critical source evaluation. This is the case of a large gathering at Xauxa witnessed in 1533 by Miguel de Estete, who accompanied Hernando Pizarro on his mission to gather gold for Atahuallpa's ransom and to reconnoiter the Inca armies. Pizarro's search for the Inca "general" Challcochima brought his party to Xauxa in the Mantaro Valley, where Challcochima was reported to have been encamped with a large force. Estete marveled over the beautiful streets and great population of Xauxa, and he claimed that

> se juntaban cada día en la plaza central cien mil personas, y estaban los mercados y calles del pueblo tan llenos de gentes, que parecía que no faltaba persona. [Estete 1947:341]

> [Each day 100,000 persons gathered in the main plaza, and the markets and streets of the town were so full of people that it seemed everyone was there.]

Although the term *mercado* is applied to this gathering, the next line comments that

> Había hombres que tenían cargo de contar toda esta gente para saber los que venían a servir a la gente de guerra.

> [There were men charged with counting all these people, so that they might know those who came to serve the warriors.]

I believe that a reasonable interpretation of these passages requires us to look beyond the mere appearance of words like *mercado* and to attempt to understand the historical *context* of the reference. In this case, the remainder of the passage is concerned with the military prowess of Challcochima, who had not met Pizarro's party in Xauxa in part because he was busy subduing rebellious *curacas*. Accounts written both by Estete and Pizarro emphasize the wary maneuvers as Spaniards and Incas assessed one another's strength and intentions.

How, given these circumstances, might we assess the meaning of the gathering of "one hundred thousand people" (actually the number of 100,000 appears rather frequently in the early *crónicas* and seems simply to indicate a very large number) in Xauxa? Was it a marketplace? Although Estete uses the term *market* in his description of Xauxa, Pizarro makes no mention of a market, though he comments that "one hundred thousand" people were in the plaza (H. Pizarro 1959:90). Was it a ceremonial feast? Estete noted that when Pizarro first went to the Xauxa plaza, he found that the people gathered there were "townspeople who had gathered to hold fiestas" (Estete 1947:341). Pizarro commented that during the five days he stayed there, the people massed in

Xauxa "did nothing but dance and sing and make great drunken celebrations" (H. Pizarro 1959:90).

Although we cannot exclude the possibility that such a gathering and subsequent feasting may have been associated with a marketplace, can we simply ignore the presence of the most formidable Inca military leader and his army? To focus attention on the mere word *market* and to ignore the military context of the event distracts attention from an obvious alternative interpretation: What the Spaniards came upon was not a marketplace, but rather the mobilization and provisioning of a military force. Challcochima was attempting to hold a region not yet fully subdued, and surely his presence in Xauxa had much to do with such a large gathering. Both Pizarro and Estete refer to these people as *indios de servicio,* and Estete speaks about men assigned to count "those who came to serve the warriors."

In short, the historical context of the encounter at Xauxa and the precise language of the accounts of it lend little support to the interpretation that this was a marketplace. Even Hartmann (1971), who argues that market exchange played a significant role in the Inca economy, also interprets the Xauxa events not as a marketplace, but as military mobilization. I believe this example illustrates that we cannot simply accept uncritically the appearance of words such as *markets* or *merchants* as unequivocal evidence for the corresponding institutions as we now understand them.

Regional Variation: Periphery versus Core

The Xauxa example shows us little, other than the word *market* in one account, that would allow us to be confident that what was observed was in fact market exchange. We do find, however, several references that do come closer to the criteria stated earlier. For example, one of our best references to a marketplace comes from a Spaniard who was making the first European contact in a northern Andean area. Captain Andrés Contero was sent in 1568 to pacify the Provincias de Esmeraldas in what is now Ecuador. In his report, Contero describes rich and populous provinces whose leaders warred against one another, and whose settlements were fortified with palisades. In what is clearly referring to a preconquest context, we find the following comments:

> Dicen que hay un pueblo grande que se llama *Ciscala* que tiene paz con todas las demás provincias, y aquel pueblo es seguro a todos, y allí se hacen ferias o mercado, y los *Tacamas* traen oro y esmeraldas a vender, y los *Campaces* y *Pidres* (?) llevan sal y pescado, y los *Beliquiamas* llevan ropa, algodón, y hacen allí sus mercados [Contero 1965 (1569):89].

> [They say there is a great pueblo called *Ciscala,* which is at peace with all the other provinces, and which is safe for everyone, where they have fairs or marketplaces, where the *Tacamas* take gold and emeralds to sell, and the *Campaces* and *Pidres* (?) bring fish, and the *Beliquiamas* bring clothing and cotton, and there they hold a marketplace.]

It is clear from the report, unfortunately, that Contero did not see Ciscala himself. However, his account is intriguing on two counts: His reference to the goods provided in the marketplace and their provenience indicated care in questioning informants, and his statement that Ciscala was a place at peace with its neighbors, where everyone could go safely, suggests a neutral trading ground amid these warring domains.

Similarly, a 1577 report from east of the Quito area on the "governing of the Quijos, Zumaco, and the Canela" refers to what appears to be a weekly market cycle. The time referred to is pre-Hispanic, and the document comments that in pre-Hispanic times the market included slave trade:

> es de ocho a ocho dias en ciertas partes tienen señaladas donde se juntan a un mercado que llaman ellos gato y alli venden lo que tienen asi rropa como joyas de oro comyda e otras cosas de la tierra trocando uno por otro e antes que los españoles poblasen esta tierra entre los yndios e indias tenyan yndios e yndias esclavos que los vendian e regataban por las cosas dichas [Ortegón 1958 (1577):235].

> [In certain areas every seven days places are designated where people gather in a market which they call *gato* and there they sell the things they have such as clothing, golden jewels, food, and other native products, trading one for another, and before the Spaniards settled this land among the Indians there were Indian slaves which they sold and traded for the mentioned items.]

A 1573 report on Quito and vicinity also refers to marketplaces in a clearly indigenous context:

> Entre los indios hacen sus mercados en sus pueblos, de manera que hoy se hace en un pueblo y mañana en otro más cercano, y ansí andan por su rueda. Entrellos no tienen peso ni medida, sino su contratación es trocar una cosa por otra, y esto es a ojo [Anonymous 1965 (1573):220].

> [The Indians hold their markets in their towns in such a way that today it is held in one town and tomorrow in another closer town, and so they proceed through their route. They use neither weights nor measures, but instead they deal by trading one thing for another, "by eye."]

For the Piura region—site of the first Spanish settlement in Peru—we find another passage that seems to be a reliable report on pre-Hispanic marketplace trade. A report on the city of Sant Miguel de Piura in the *Relaciones geográficas* tells us that the natives of the region had been organized into three "nations," each with its own language, so that they were unable to speak to one another without interpreters. However,

> como contrataban unos con otros, había muchos que se entendían [Salinas 1965 (ca. 1571):42].

> [since they traded with one another, there were many who understood one another.]

The same report also indicates pre-Hispanic marketplaces:

> Que en cada uno de los pueblos de indios tienen su orden de congregación para sus contrataciones en todos tiempos, trocando unas cosas por otras o con oro y plata, para lo cual tenían sus pesos y pesas y medidas, generalmente diferente de las nuestras, las cuales han dejado y usan ya de las nuestras de España [Salinas 1965 (ca. 1571):44].

> [In every Indian town they have their gatherings for trade all the time, trading some things for others or for gold and silver, for which they had their weights and measures, generally different from ours, which they have abandoned and now use our Spanish measures.]

Before I create an impression that we could continue at great length to produce specific references to marketplaces, I should warn that these passages are not typical, but are rather some of the best. However, even these passages present some difficulties. For example, Captain Contero is reporting hearsay, and the Piura report mentions that native weights and measures had already been abandoned for Spanish measures. This last point calls our attention to the first of what I believe to be the two most important problems in interpreting the documents—the problem of historic change.

One can, of course, find many clear references to trade and markets by failing to exclude passages that refer rather obviously to colonial rather than pre-Hispanic contexts. As I have demonstrated previously (La Lone 1978; La Lone and La Lone 1979), the debate is greatly confused by this common failure to distinguish between pre-Hispanic and colonial exchange systems. From the very beginning of the colonial era we find Spaniards founding markets. Frank Salomon makes the point most effectively:

> Fernando de Santillan, Presidente of the newly founded Audiencia de Quito, ordered the inauguration of "tiangueces" in practically every place where colonists lived, and as a result, when he stood *residencia* in 1568, the witnesses affirmed that "tiangueces" could be found far and wide but that one could not always tell which existed "por mandado de los dichos presidente e oidor" and which were "antigua cosa entre los yndios" [Salomon 1978:150].

If—even as early as 1568—witnesses are unsure whether markets were ordered by a Spanish official or were native, we must be extremely cautious today in our source evaluation. When we apply the criteria of descriptive specificity and control for pre-Hispanic context to the extensive compilation of passages collected in La Lone and La Lone (1979) or to all passages cited in Hartmann (1968, 1971), the result is remarkable. With the exception of several references to the marketplace in Cuzco's Cusipata Plaza, I believe that we do not have a *single* description of what may reasonably be considered a pre-Hispanic marketplace anywhere south of Tumbes. Even the references to Cusipata are inconsistent (cf. Betanzos 1924 [1551]:90–91; Poma de Ayala

1936:338; Morúa 1946 [1600?]:368–370; Cieza de León 1947 [1553]: cx,449; Garcilaso de la Vega 1966 [1609], Part I:429).

This brings us to the second critical issue in interpreting the documents—the problem of regional variation. All of the preceding passages with clear references to trade and marketplace come from regions from Tumbes northward into what is today Ecuador. We could group these clear references to trade and market in the northern periphery of the Inca region with the vague references from the Inca heartland. To do this, however, we would have to ignore the question of why the references from the north are different from the references from the heartland. If we do ask this question, two probable explanations suggest themselves. First, for reasons we have not yet determined, the apparent differences are artifacts of *differences in reporting and recording*. Or, second, the apparent differences are *empirical differences* that reflect regional variation within and at the periphery of Tawantinsuyu.

As should be apparent by now, my interpretation of the corpus of texts on Andean marketplaces leads me to conclude that exchange systems differed from periphery to heartland. Specifically, I believe that market trade and full-time traders were characteristic on the northern periphery of Tawantinsuyu, but peripheral at best in areas fully under Inca control. Frank Salomon's excellent dissertation, "Ethnic Lords of Quito in the Age of the Incas," supports this interpretation, since it shows a clear north–south gradient in political and economic institutions. For example, one of Salomon's more interesting findings is a relative abundance of references to traders in areas north of Quito, and a scarcity of reports of traders in regions south of that city (Salomon 1978:153).

For more southerly regions, references to traders are rare and vague. We do find isolated references to *mercader* or *mercaderes*, but the terms often refer simply to people who were present at a gathering in a plaza—people who were apparently assumed to be *mercaderes*. One of the few references to what might be full-time traders comes from Blas Valera (1950 [1590]:137). In a discussion of Inca astronomical beliefs, he tells us that the planet Mercury was special to "merchants, travelers, and messengers." The similarity between the beliefs he attributes to the Inca and those of Greco–Roman mythology strains our credulity when he tells us that the Inca saw Mars as the god of war and Saturn as the god of plague and hunger. Other references to traders can be extracted from our sources, though they are difficult to evaluate. For example, Cieza de León refers to spies disguised as traders in Topa's reign (1959 [1553]:244). Montesinos tells us that Inca Roca sent traders to spread rumors and confusion, and Sarmiento and Calancha recount legends of traders coming across the sea from the west (Murra 1956:246).

Seafaring traders perhaps may have been more than legendary. The lord of Chincha's "one-hundred-thousand" rafts on the sea may have been trade rafts linking the coastal valley of Chincha with the Ecuadorian trade centers. Sixteenth-century documents on Chincha are a striking exception to the general lack of description of traders south of Quito. María Rostworowski has published the relevant documents, and she argues convincingly that Chincha was the base for 6000 *mercaderes* who traded in Cuzco, in the Colla region, and in Ecuador (Rostworowski 1970, 1975). Unfortunately, we know nothing about the sponsorship and organization of these trading expeditions. Furthermore, I think it is significant that despite the extensive material Rostworowski has now presented on Chincha, she has not been able to connect these traders with marketplaces. Her failure to do so seriously undermines her assertion that this represents "commercial exchange" (Rostworowski 1976).

On the other hand, if we have a noncommercial economy, we should be surprised neither by "merchantless" marketplaces nor by "marketplaceless" merchants. In marketplaces without merchants, the exchanges between "buyers" and "sellers" are much like reciprocity, and local conditions of supply and demand are not articulated with conditions in other locations by "price" differences and transmission of price information. Traders, or merchants, may also be found even where marketplaces are nonexistent, as in administered trade (see discussion of administered trade in Polanyi, Arensberg, and Pearson 1957).

As I have argued before, as a minimum condition to identify an ancient commercial economy, we should expect to find *both* traders and marketplaces. Perhaps—as in the Chincha case—linking the traders to the markets only awaits further archival research. But even Rostworowski with her unparalleled knowledge of unpublished as well as published documentary sources seems forced to fall back on the argument that early Quechua and Aymara dictionaries document markets through their "ample" vocabulary on the topic (Rostworowski 1975). However, the dozen dictionary terms she finds hardly seem to constitute an ample vocabulary when contrasted to Jurgen Golte's seemingly endless list of words, extracted from the same sources, which refer to reciprocity and redistribution rather than market trade (Golte 1974).

In summary, the evidence I have presented in this section demonstrates the need to explore regional variations in exchange systems in the Andes. Documentary evidence indicates that marketplace exchange and traders were found on the northern periphery of the Inca realm. We may, as Rostworowski suggests, also find "commercial exchange" in coastal regions, but the evidence to date suggests administered trade. When we look to the highland core of the Inca empire, we find no clear evidence for pre-Hispanic marketplaces or traders.

In the core region it seems that the more carefully we focus our search for markets, the more they seem—like the Cheshire cat—to fade in and out of view. We may suffer from the same confusion as did Alice at being caught in dialogue with what we cannot see. However, my argument that markets are most probably not to be found in the empire's core is not founded on the solipsism that if we cannot see markets in the documents, they must not have existed. The solution I suggest to the lack of evidence, or negative evidence, is that we ask why there are *differences* in reporting marketplaces. Unless I am deluded by meaningless variations in the way reports were recorded, I believe that the differences are real, and that what we are seeing is regional variation in exchange systems. To state the argument in these terms makes at least two tangible contributions to further research. First, the argument can be negated by convincing evidence for marketplaces and traders in the core of the Inca empire. Second, we are forced to ask *why* regional variation in exchange systems took the form it apparently did. I shall conclude on this last point by offering some suggestions on how ethnohistorical and archaeological approaches may be used in collaboration in exploring Andean economy.

USES OF ETHNOHISTORY AND ARCHAEOLOGY IN THE STUDY OF ANDEAN ECONOMY

Ethnohistory and archaeology may collaborate most fruitfully in the study of patterns, processes, and change in exchange systems. Research strategies combining both approaches promise insights we may be less likely to achieve through either alone. Advances in archaeology, for example, are well suited to uncover patterns in exchange that may not be at all apparent in the documentary record. Ethnohistory, in turn, offers insight into underlying processes associated with these patterns, and the documentary record preserves what the archaeological record often does not. Together, archaeology and ethnohistory share a focus on the problem of change over time. When these powerful tools for comparative study of patterns, process, and change can be focused on common problems, we are engaged in what might truly be called *diachronic anthropology*—a term suggested by Plog (1973).

In the development of my argument on Inca economy, I note a pattern in the documents that refer to marketplaces. This leads to the hypothesis that exchange systems differed significantly between the Inca core region in the central Andes and the northern periphery of the Inca realm in the Ecuadorian Andes. I shall now turn to a brief discussion of how this hypothesis—derived from ethnohistorical materials—might be explored both archaeologically and ethnohistorically. Using this problem as an example, I hope to show the broader relevance of archaeology and ethnohistory to one another in the refinement of formal models, the study of ecological variation, and analysis of the relationship between politics and exchange.

Combined archaeological and ethnohistorical strategies allow us to refine our models of exchange and test their applicability in the Inca core-versus-periphery problem. For marketplace exchange, two of the key difficulties are to identify what a marketplace looks like archaeologically, and to trace the paths of archaeologically identifiable items exchanged. Earle and D'Altroy (Chapter 12) and Spence (Chapter 8), for example, offer suggestions on what production, storage, and display facilities might be correlated with marketplaces, and Alden (Chapter 4) traces the spatial falloff pattern of marketed products. Such strategies may be fruitfully applied and tested in further exploration of the hypothesis I have outlined. Use of historical documents and ethnohistorical synthesis (e.g., Salomon 1978) enables us to identify sites claimed to be centers of marketplace trade or of traders—what are known in Ecuador as *mindalaes*. Archaeological exploration of such sites should contribute to our understanding of the archaeology of markets. Furthermore, since the northern polities retained distinctive pottery traditions even into Spanish colonial times (Meyers 1976), we may also expect to be able to trace trade connections and falloff curves.

Patterns of trade, such as we see through falloff curves, are not in themselves sufficient to explain processes of trade. As one of the leaders in spatial analysis in archaeology comments: "It is now clear that very different exchange processes can produce the same fall-off curves" (Hodder 1980:152; see also Renfrew 1977). This should not lead to despair, but to further questions about the processes underlying the patterns. For this task, we may find that ethnohistorical (and ethnographic) data are essential. Our documents may offer insights into the organization and sponsorship of trade that may be extremely difficult to detect archaeologically. As I have argued before, market exchange and administered trade are different phenomena, even though both may occur in a marketplace. Documents may give us rather explicit evidence showing that what might appear to be market exchange might better be understood as resource-control strategies under the direct control of political elites (e.g., Salomon 1978:Chapter VII; Golte 1970). We should not expect administered trade and market exchange to produce the same falloff curves, but failure to distinguish between them might lead to the impression that the "same" exchange processes produce different falloff curves. Ethnohistorical analysis enables us to correct for the premature conclusion that the same processes produce different curves. Likewise, we may hope that ethnohistorical analysis may also help us to refine our assumptions so that we can show why "very different" exchange processes appear to produce similar falloff curves.

We cannot, of course, separate the study of pattern from the study of process. If we find different patterns of exchange in the core and the periphery, we must attempt to explain when and why these differences appeared. One of the first issues we would consider is the striking environmental differences between the core and northern periphery. In the north, for example, we find marked differences between the Ecuadorian *paramo* Andes and the *puna* Andes of the Inca core region. The basins of the *paramo* Andes are lower, have year-round precipitation, and are smaller than those of the *puna* Andes. Three of the identifying characteristics of central Andean civilization are practically absent in the north: (*a*) irrigation agriculture; (*b*) camelid herding; and (*c*) tubers as a dietary staple (Troll 1968; Salomon 1978:37). It would then seem reasonable to expect that resource-control strategies may have differed significantly between *paramo* Andes and *puna* Andes. If this was the case, we should expect to find differences in political and economic organization as we cross the line dividing the two Andean zones. This line runs approximately through Trujillo and Cajamarca (Salomon 1978:37; Troll 1968:34,Figure 15). And, as I have argued previously in this chapter, all our clear references to marketplaces come from north of this line.

Archaeologists and ethnohistorians alike may make significant contributions to ecological analysis of the core–periphery contrast. Ethnohistory can make an additional vital contribution. As I have argued throughout this chapter, to understand exchange systemically we must understand the role of elites in resource control. Details of political process relevant to exchange may be more clearly focused in documents than in archaeological sites. For example, the relationship between marketplace trade and warfare between rival polities appears quite clearly in documents from Ecuador. Such an association between warring groups and marketplaces is found also in other areas of the world where rivalrous groups meet at neutral trading places at their boundaries (Benet 1957; Berry 1967:101; Hodder and Orton 1976:76). Documentary references to warring polities in Ecuador can be verified by exploration of extensive pre-Hispanic fortifications (Meyers 1976). This knowledge may then lead us to explore the role of the *mindalaes* not so much as *merchants* in the modern sense of the term, but as political agents. According to Salomon:

> Thus what seems on surface examination to be an example of precolumbian commerce, on closer examination turns out to be a method for adapting the redistributive mode of politics to a situation of permeable and shifting political boundaries [Salomon 1978:304].

Ethnohistorical analysis thus aids significantly in our efforts to understand the processes underlying the patterns. It promises also to allow insight into processes of change. Study of the expansion of the Inca state beyond its core region allows us to see adjustments and rearrangements of resource control and exchange systems in response to local conditions. This is well documented in the comparison between the core and northern periphery, and similar work is now underway at the southern periphery beyond the Titicaca Basin. Such comparative studies promote a broader and deeper understanding both of regional variation within the Inca realm and of how the central economy articulated with diverse regions. Study of regional variations and of the central economy are inextricably linked—it is only as the views from above and the views from below converge that we begin to see the whole picture or, if you will, the whole llama.

SUMMARY

The objective of this chapter has been to demonstrate the uses of ethnohistory in the study of Inca economy. If the story has had any moral, it would be that things are not always what they seem. Specifically, we must reject the notion *a marketplace is a marketplace is a marketplace.* Three themes run through my discussion of the role of marketplaces in the Inca economy. First, careful source criticism shows that the appearance of terms such as *market* or *merchant* in documents is not sufficient justification to assume that what was described was in fact a market gathering. It is meaningless to discuss "ancient marketplaces" when we have insufficient evidence to believe that they were either *marketplaces* or *ancient.* Second, even when we have good evidence for the presence of ancient marketplaces, we still cannot assume that marketplace trade or market economies in ancient civilizations were similar in organization and function to markets in the capitalist world economy. Third, the best evidence for marketplace exchange comes from the northern periphery of the Inca empire, and we find little evidence for marketplace exchange at the core of the empire. This leads to the hypothesis that marketplace exchange was characteristic on the northern periphery of Tawantinsuyu and was unimportant in integrating the central Inca economy. Combined archaeological and ethnohistorical research may be directed toward validating or negating this hypothesis, and it should also attempt to explain why such different patterns would occur.

The title of this chapter succinctly expresses my premise that the Inca economy was *politically* integrated. Market exchange in ancient economies cannot simply be equated with the self-regulating price-making market model that contemporary market systems are based on. This is not a denial of the validity of concepts such as supply and demand, but instead a recognition that supply-and-demand forces in hierarchical societies require analytical models different from those appropriate in consumer societies. In short, command economies seriously distort supply-and-demand forces, and marketplace exchange in such politically integrated economies is very different from marketplace exchange elsewhere. Ancient Mexico, for example, would appear to be a place where market exchange clearly played a larger role than in the Andes, yet one leading scholar concludes that "the economic organization of ancient Mexico was politically integrated and that market organization played a subordinate role" (Carrasco 1980:468 see also Carrasco 1978; Parsons 1980).

My portrayal of the Inca as a politically integrated economy emphasizes a two-tiered organization. I argue that communities were provisioned through a generalized economy based on direct exploitation of a variety of environmental zones. The state economy, on the other hand, was directed largely toward financing state operations through labor mobilization. In addition to support of the political hierarchy, the state mobilization sector promoted increased production through agricultural intensification and an extensive state storage system (cf. Earle and D'Altroy, Chapter 12).

Finally, I offer some suggestions on the mutual relevance of ethnohistory and archaeology in the study of Andean exchange. I observe that these are complementary approaches to the discovery of patterns, processes, and change in exchange—or other—systems. When these strategies can be combined, the resulting synthesis promises to go beyond culture history and toward a genuinely diachronic anthropology.

REFERENCES

Acosta, J. de
1954 [1590] Historia natural y moral de las Indias. *Biblioteca de Autores Españoles* **73.**

Anonymous
1965 [1573] La cibdad de Sant Francisco del Quito. In *Relaciones geográficas de Indias,* Tomo III, edited by Don M. Jiménez de la Espada. *Biblioteca de Autores Españoles* **184.**

Benet, F.
1957 Explosive markets: the Berber highlands. In *Trade and market in the early empires,* edited by K. Polanyi, C. Arensberg, and H. Pearson, pp. 188–217. Glencoe: Free Press.

Berry, B. J. L.
1967 *The geography of market centers and retail distribution.* Englewood Cliffs, N.J.: Prentice-Hall.

Betanzos, J. de
1924 [1551] Suma y narración de los Incas. *Colección de Libros y Documentos Referentes a la Historia del Peru* **8.**

Carneiro, R. L.
1970 A theory of the origin of the state. *Science* **169:**733–738.

Carrasco, P.
1978 La economía del Mexico prehispánico. In *Economía política e ideología en el Mexico prehispánico,* edited by P. Carrasco and J. Broda, pp. 15–76. Mexico: Nueva Imagen.
1980 Comment on E. M. Brumfiel's "Specialization, market exchange, and the Aztec state: a view from Huexotla." *Current Anthropology* **21:**468.

Cieza de León, P.
1947 [1553] La crónica del Peru. *Biblioteca de Autores Españoles* **26.**
1959 [1553] *The Incas of Pedro Cieza de Leon,* translated by H. de Onís. Norman: University of Oklahoma Press.

Contero, A.
1965 [1569] Relación de las provincias de Esmeraldas. In *Relaciones geográficas de Indias,* Tomo III, edited by Don M. Jiménez de la Espada. *Biblioteca de Autores Españoles* **185.**

Earle, T. K.
1977 A reappraisal of redistribution: complex Hawaiian chiefdoms. In *Exchange systems in prehistory,* edited by T. K. Earle and J. E. Ericson, pp. 213–232. New York: Academic Press.
1978 Economic and social organization of a complex chiefdom: the Halelea district, Kaua'i Hawaii. *University of Michigan Museum of Anthropology Anthropological Paper* **63.**

Earls, J.
1976 Evolución de la administración ecológica Inca. *Revista del Museo Nacional* **42:**207–245.

Estete, M.
1947 In *Verdadera relación de la conquista del Peru y provincia del Cuzco* [1534], by F. Jerez. *Biblioteca de Autores Españoles* **26.**

Garcilaso de la Vega
1966 [1609] *Royal commentaries of the Incas and general history of Peru,* Parts I and II, translated by H. V. Livermore. Austin: University of Texas Press.

Goldman, I.
    1970   *Ancient Polynesian society.* Chicago: University of Chicago Press.
Golte, J.
    1970   Algunas consideraciones acerca de la producción y distribución de la coca en el estado
            Inca. *Proceedings of the 38th International Congress of Americanists* 2:471–478.
    1974   El trabajo y la distribución de bienes en el runa simi del siglo XVI. *Proceedings of the
            40th International Congress of Americanists* 2:489–505.
Grierson, P.
    1974   Commerce in the Dark Ages: a critique of the evidence. In *Studies in Economic An-
            thropology,* edited by G. Dalton, pp. 74–83. Washington, D.C.: American An-
            thropological Association.
Hartmann, R.
    1968   Maerkte im alten Peru. Unpublished Ph.D. dissertation, University of Bonn.
    1971   Mercados y ferias prehispánicos en el área andina. *Boletín de la Academía Nacional de
            Historia* 54(188):214–235.
Herrera, A. de
    1952   [1601–1615] *Historia general de los hechos de los Castellanos en las islas firme del mar
            oceano* Tomo X. Madrid: La Real Academía de la Historia.
Hodder, I.
    1980   Trade and exchange: definitions, identification and function. In *Models and methods in
            regional exchange,* edited by R. E. Fry, pp. 151–156. Washington, D.C.: Society for
            American Archaeology.
Hodder, I., and C. Orton
    1976   *Spatial analysis in archaeology.* Cambridge: Cambridge University Press.
La Lone, D. E.
    1978   Historical contexts of trade and markets in the Peruvian Andes. Unpublished Ph.D.
            dissertation, Department of Anthropology, University of Michigan.
La Lone, D. E., and M. B. La Lone
    1979   Trade and marketplace in the Inca realm. Paper read at the 43rd International Congress
            of Americanists, Vancouver B.C.
Llagostera, M., A.
    1976   El Tawantinsuyo y el control de las relaciones complementarias. *Proceedings of the 41st
            International Congress of Americanists* 4:39–50.
Meyers, A.
    1976   Die Inka in Ekuador. *Bonner Amerikanistische Studien* 6.
Morris, C.
    1967   Storage in Tawantinsuyu. Unpublished Ph.D. dissertation, Department of Anthropol-
            ogy, University of Chicago.
    1972   Reconstructing patterns of non-agricultural production in the Inca economy. In *Recon-
            structing complex societies,* edited by C. B. Moore, pp. 49–68. Chicago: American
            School of Oriental Research.
Morúa, M. de
    1946   [1600?] *Historia del origen y genealogía real de los reyes Incas del Peru.* Madrid:
            Bermejo.
Mumford, L.
    1961   *The city in history.* New York: Harcourt, Brace and World.
Murra, J. V.
    1956   The economic organization of the Inca state. Unpublished Ph.D. dissertation, Depart-
            ment of Anthropology, University of Chicago.
    1965   Herds and herders in the Inca state. In *Man, culture, and animals,* edited by A. Leeds and
            A. P. Vayda, pp. 185–215. Washington, D.C.: American Association for the Advance-
            ment of Science.

1972 El "Control Vertical" de un máximo de pisos ecológicos en la economía de las so-
ciedades andinas. In *Visita de la provincia de León de Huanuco en 1562,* Tomo II, edited
by J. V. Murra, pp. 429–476. Huanuco: Universidad Nacional Hermilio Valdizán.

1973 Rite and crop in the Inca state. In *Peoples and cultures of native South America,* edited
by D. R. Gross, pp. 377–389. Garden City, N.Y.: Doubleday/The Natural History Press.

1978 La guerre et les rébelions dans l'expansion de l'état Inka. *Annales* 33(5–6):926–935.

Ortegón, D. de
1958 [1577] Gobernación de los Quijos, Zumaco y la Canela. In *Diego de Ortegon's be-
schreibung der "Gobernacion de los Quijos . . . ,"* by Udo Oberem. *Zeitschrift fur
Ethnologie* 83(2):230–251.

Ortiz de Zúñiga, I.
1967 [1562] Visita de la provincia de León de Huanuco, Tomo I. In *Visita de la provincia de
León de Huanuco en 1562,* Tomo I, edited by J. V. Murra. Huanuco: Universidad
Nacional Hermilio Valdizán.

1972 [1562]Visita de la provincia de León de Huanuco, Tomo II. In *Visita de la provincia de
León de Huanuco en 1562,* Tomo II, edited by J. V. Murra. Huanuco: Universidad
Nacional Hermilio Valdizán.

Oviedo y Valdes, G. F. de
1959 [1549] Historia general y natural de las Indias. *Biblioteca de Autores Españoles* **121.**

Parsons, J. R.
1980 Comment on Elizabeth M. Brumfiel's "Specialization, market exchange, and the Aztec
state: a view from Huexotla." *Current Anthropology* 21:471.

Pease, G. Y., F.
1972 *Los últimos Incas del Cusco.* Lima: Villanueva.

1979 La formación del Tawantinsuyu: mecanismos de colonización y relación con los uni-
dades étnicas. *Histórica* 3(1):97–120.

Pizarro, H.
1959 In *Historia general y natural de las Indias* [1549], by Gonzalo Fernandez de Oviedo y
Valdes. *Biblioteca de Autores Españoles* **121.**

Plog, F. T.
1973 Diachronic anthropology. In *Research and theory in current anthropology,* edited by C.
L. Redman, pp. 181–198. New York: Wiley-Interscience.

Polanyi, K., C. M. Arensberg, and H. W. Pearson (Editors)
1957 *Trade and market in the early empires.* Glencoe: Free Press.

Poma de Ayala, F. G.
1936 *La nueva crónica y buen gobierno.* Paris: Institut d'Ethnologie.

Renfrew, C.
1977 Alternative models for exchange and spatial distribution. In *Exchange systems in prehistory,* edited by T. K. Earle and J. E. Ericson, pp. 71–90. New York: Academic Press.

Rostworowski de Diez Canseco, M.
1970 Mercaderes del valle de Chincha en la época prehispánico: un documento y unos comen-
tarios. *Revista Española de Antropología Americana* 5:135–177.

1975 Coastal fishermen, merchants, and artisans in pre-Hispanic Peru. In *The sea in the pre-
Columbian world,* edited by E. P. Benson, pp. 167–188. Washington, D.C.: Dumbarton
Oaks Research Library and Collections.

1976 Reflexiones sobre la reciprocidad andina. *Revista del Museo Nacional* 42:341–354.

1977 La estratificación social y el hatun curaca en el mundo andino. *Histórica* 1(2):249–285.

1978 Una hipótesis sobre el surgimiento del estado Inca. In *III Congreso Peruano, Actos y
Trabajos,* Tomo I, edited by R. Matos M., pp. 89–101. Lima: Universidad Nacional
Mayor de San Marcos.

Salinas, J. de
1965 [ca. 1571] Relación de la ciudad de Sant Miguel de Piura. In *Relaciones geográficas de*

Indias, Tomo II, edited by Don M. Jiménez de la Espada. *Biblioteca de Autores Españoles* **184.**

Salomon, F. L.
 1978   Ethnic lords of Quito in the age of the Incas. Unpublished Ph.D. dissertation, Department of Anthropology, Cornell University.

Service, E. R.
 1975   *Origins of the state and civilization.* New York: Norton.

Troll, C.
 1968   The cordilleras of the tropical Americas: aspects of climatic, phytogeographical, and agrarian ecology. In *Geo-ecology of the mountainous regions of the tropical Americas, Proceedings of the UNESCO Symposium (Mexico 1966),* edited by C. Troll, pp. 13–56. Bonn: Ferd. Dümmlers Verlag.

Valera, B.
 1950   [1590] Antiguas costumbres del Peru. In *Tres relaciones de antigüedades peruanos,* edited by Don M. Jiménez de la Espada. Buenos Aires: Editorial Guarania.

Subject Index

STUDIES IN ARCHAEOLOGY

Consulting Editor: Stuart Struever

Department of Anthropology
Northwestern University
Evanston, Illinois

Thomas F. King, Patricia Parker Hickman, and Gary Berg. **Anthropology in Historic Preservation: Caring for Culture's Clutter**

Richard E. Blanton. **Monte Albán: Settlement Patterns at the Ancient Zapotec Capital**

R. E. Taylor and Clement W. Meighan. **Chronologies in New World Archaeology**

Bruce D. Smith. **Prehistoric Patterns of Human Behavior: A Case Study in the Mississippi Valley**

Barbara L. Stark and Barbara Voorhies (Eds.). **Prehistoric Coastal Adaptations: The Economy and Ecology of Maritime Middle America**

Charles L. Redman, Mary Jane Berman, Edward V. Curtin, William T. Langhorne, Nina M. Versaggi, and Jeffery C. Wanser (Eds.). **Social Archeology: Beyond Subsistence and Dating**

Bruce D. Smith (Ed.). **Mississippian Settlement Patterns**

Lewis R. Binford. **Nunamiut Ethnoarchaeology**

J. Barto Arnold III and Robert Weddle. **The Nautical Archeology of Padre Island: The Spanish Shipwrecks of 1554**

Sarunas Milisauskas. **European Prehistory**

Brian Hayden (Ed.). **Lithic Use-Wear Analysis**

William T. Sanders, Jeffrey R. Parsons, and Robert S. Santley. **The Basin of Mexico: Ecological Processes in the Evolution of a Civilization**

David L. Clarke. **Analytical Archaeologist: Collected Papers of David L. Clarke. Edited and Introduced by His Colleagues**

Arthur E. Spiess. **Reindeer and Caribou Hunters: An Archaeological Study**

Elizabeth S. Wing and Antoinette B. Brown. **Paleonutrition: Method and Theory in Prehistoric Foodways.**

John W. Rick. **Prehistoric Hunters of the High Andes**

Timothy K. Earle and Andrew L. Christenson (Eds.). **Modeling Change in Prehistoric Economics**

Thomas F. Lynch (Ed.). **Guitarrero Cave: Early Man in the Andes**

Fred Wendorf and Romuald Schild. **Prehistory of the Eastern Sahara**

Henri Laville, Jean-Philippe Rigaud, and James Sackett. **Rock Shelters of the Perigord: Stratigraphy and Archaeological Succession**

Duane C. Anderson and Holmes A. Semken, Jr. (Eds.). **The Cherokee Excavations: Holocene Ecology and Human Adaptations in Northwestern Iowa**

Anna Curtenius Roosevelt. **Parmana: Prehistoric Maize and Manioc Subsistence along the Amazon and Orinoco**

Fekri A. Hassan. **Demographic Archaeology**

G. Barker. **Landscape and Society: Prehistoric Central Italy**